AGE OF DELIRIUM

AGE OF DELIRIUM

The Decline and Fall of the Soviet Union

DAVID SATTER

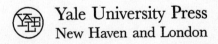
Yale University Press
New Haven and London

PAPERBACK EDITION FIRST PUBLISHED IN 2001
BY YALE UNIVERSITY PRESS.

Cloth edition published in 1996 in the United States by Alfred A. Knopf
and in Canada by Random House.

Designed by Robert C. Olsson.
Set in Baskerville types by Creative Graphics, Allentown, Pennsylvania.
Printed in the United States of America.

Library of Congress catalog card number: 00-107715

ISBN 0-300-08705-5 (pbk.)

A catalog record for this book is available
from the British Library.

10   9   8   7   6   5   4   3   2   1

To the Memory of My Parents

He found the Archimedean point, but he used it against himself; it seems that he was permitted to find it only under this condition.

—Franz Kafka

Contents

Preface

THIS BOOK IS INTENDED to be a collective chronicle of the last fifteen years of the Soviet Union, a period during which the Soviet system began to rot and finally collapsed.

The persons whose fates are related in these pages are, for the most part, people I met during nearly two decades of reporting and writing from Russia, but they also include individuals whose experiences were described to me by relatives or friends because they were unwilling, inaccessible, or in jail.

For the most part, my heroes were not "typical" Soviet citizens. But what was typical in Soviet life forms the inevitable backdrop against which the lives and histories of those who were not typical were played out to their often unhappy conclusions.

I arrived in the Soviet Union in June 1976 and spent six years there as the correspondent of the *Financial Times* of London. I continued to write about the Soviet Union in the 1980s and was able to live there again for long periods after 1990. In light of this experience, I, too, figure in these pages. In fact, what some of the dramatis personae have in common, and a contributing factor to their often tragic destinies, is the fact that, at one time or another, they agreed to meet with me.

Although the Soviet Union is now fading into the mists of history, the Soviet experiment in total domination still needs to be understood. The Soviet Union was the product of a purely modern form of megalomania, the notion that human affairs can be ordered without the help of transcendent rules. This book can be taken as a record of the consequences of the application of this notion, as well as a description of human experience under extreme social conditions.

In the latter respect, it has special relevance for people in the United States because, as their experiences demonstrate, Soviet people are not as far from us as we might hope.

Introduction

NOT LONG AGO, American scientists once again turned their attention to the case of Phineas P. Gage, whose strange fate raised the possibility that the brain contains a "moral center."

On September 13, 1848, Gage, a twenty-five-year-old construction foreman for the Rutland and Burlington Railroad, was at work in rural Vermont, supervising the detonation of rocks to level terrain for railroad tracks, when he became the victim of a bizarre accident. The blasting required drilling holes in the stone, partially filling the holes with explosive powder, covering the powder with sand, and using a fuse and a tamping iron to trigger an explosion into the rock. On the day of the accident, a distraction led Gage to begin tamping directly over the powder before his assistant had had a chance to cover it with sand. This caused a powerful explosion which sent the sharply pointed tamping iron shooting, rocketlike, through Gage's face, skull, and brain and into the sky. The iron landed many yards away.

The accident horrified onlookers, but Gage was only momentarily stunned; he quickly regained consciousness and soon was able to talk and even walk with the help of his men. In the weeks that followed, he remained able-bodied and showed no loss of either movement, memory, or speech. He seemed to be as intelligent as before the accident. It soon became obvious, however, that his personality had radically changed.

Gage had been liked and respected by those who knew him, but now his respect for social conventions vanished. He became foul-mouthed and rude. His failure to honor commitments soon caused his employers, who had once called him the "most efficient and capable" man in their employ, to let him go. John Harlow, the physician who treated him, said, "the equilibrium or balance, so to speak, between his intellectual faculty and his animal propensities" had been destroyed. In the words of his friends and acquaintances, "Gage was no longer Gage."

Gage began a life of wandering that ended twelve years later in San Francisco, where he died in the custody of his family. Although his accident made headlines, his death was barely noticed. Harlow only learned of it five years later, and he then asked Gage's family for permission to have his body exhumed so that the skull could be recovered and kept as a medical record. The request was granted and Gage's skull, along with the tamping iron, became part of the Warren Anatomical Medical Museum at Harvard University.

In 1994, a group of American neuroanatomists took the skull and, using modern techniques of image processing, reconstructed in three dimensions the brain it had once contained, to determine the exact points of entry and exit of the tamping iron and to establish with as much precision as possible which parts of that brain had been affected by the accident. They concluded that the tamping iron had affected the ventromedial region of both frontal lobes, while sparing structures involved in the cognition of space, objects, language, and arithmetic. Since the role of the frontal lobes is still not fully understood, the neuroanatomists concluded that Gage's accident illustrated the existence in man of a "moral center" that could be damaged, leading to the destruction of morality, but which, at least in theory, might be amenable to treatment, raising the possibility that immorality could be "cured."*

LEARNING OF THE RENEWED interest in Gage and the moral problem his unique fate posed, I wondered if the neuroanatomists involved in this work were aware of the history of the Soviet Union, which can actually be understood as an attempt to destroy the moral center of an entire nation. The Soviet leaders did not look for a physiological moral center but acted instead to cripple people psychologically by creating a hermetically sealed environment in which Marxism-Leninism was treated as a higher form of truth.

·   ·   ·

*See Hanna Damasio et al., "The Return of Phineas Gage: Clues About the Brain from the Skull of a Famous Patient," *Science*, vol. 264, May 20, 1994, pp. 1102–05.

THE SOVIET UNION was something new. It was the first state in history to be based explicitly on atheism, and it compensated for the missing absolute by endowing itself with the attributes of God. If previous governments recognized a power above themselves, however much they ignored it in practice, the Soviet regime deferred to no one, treating its every act as the realization of its ideology's ultimate truths.

The depiction of itself as the expression of the absolute had its advantages. It lent to the system that single-mindedness, amorality, and blind fanaticism that always result from the absolutization of political goals.

At the same time, however, the regime's dependence on Communist ideology left it deeply vulnerable. Marxism-Leninism claimed to be the science of history, and stated that its analysis of the past could be projected into the future. Religion looked for ultimate truth in a transcendent sphere. It therefore was Soviet ideology, not religion, which could be discredited by historical events that refuted its basic assumptions.

In the end, the nature of the state's domination was determined by this vulnerability of its core ideas. The Soviet ideology predicted that the victory of communism would lead to a perfect democracy, characterized by voluntary unanimity and unprecedented wealth. When, following the Communist seizure of power, this utopia did not materialize, intellectual failure threatened to have political consequences, and the authorities proceeded to remake reality by force.

THE DRIVE TO CREATE reality transformed Soviet life into a masquerade. What became important was not what was true but what could be made to appear to be true as the structure of factual reality was replaced with organized falsification so that real life might, if only after the fact, appear to conform to the Soviet ideology.

As the outside world looked on in stupefaction, the Soviet Union became the scene of a whole set of miragelike imitations of democratic institutions: trade unions that defended management, newspapers that contained no information, courts to which there was no recourse, and a parliament that always unanimously supported the government.

.   .   .

THE OBLIGATORY MENTAL UNIVERSE of the regime was imposed on Soviet citizens and it split their consciousness, leading to the phenomenon known as "dual consciousness"—what George Orwell called "doublethink." Dual consciousness separated the regime's ideological fabrications from each individual's normal patterns of perception and moral judgment, in that way making it possible for the individual to act out his ideological role automatically in required situations while, in other respects, perceiving reality accurately.

In many cases, the splitting of personalities led individuals to identify with their imposed roles. "After long acquaintance with his role," wrote Czeslaw Milosz, "a man grows into it so closely that he can no longer differentiate his true self from the self he simulates. . . . To identify oneself with the role one is obliged to play brings relief and permits a relaxation of one's vigilance. Proper reflexes at the proper moment become truly automatic."

There were also those, particularly among officials responsible for dealing with foreigners, who were cynical about the official version of reality and found in the need constantly to dissemble a source of inner satisfaction. "To say something is white when one thinks it black," wrote Milosz, "to smile inwardly when one is outwardly solemn, to hate when one manifests love, to know when one pretends not to know and thus to play one's adversary for a fool (even as he is playing you for one)—these actions lead one to prize one's own cunning above all else."

Often, Soviet citizens simply absolved themselves of responsibility for their public utterances and tried to preserve a space of intellectual freedom within their own heads. When Sergei Zamascikov, a Komsomol leader in Yermala, Latvia, looked in the mirror in the morning, he believed that he was looking at the one person in the world with whom he could safely communicate. In the course of the day, he looked at other faces—in the city Party Committee, in the Central Committee of the Latvian Komsomol, and in the Central Committee of the Latvian Communist Party—but those faces were little better than masks. He assumed that they concealed minds which were completely programmed, but there was no way to be sure. After all, when he was with his party colleagues, his face was a mask too.

WHATEVER THE ADAPTATION of individuals, a personality cannot be split without consequences for morality, which must be applied to all situations equally. The attempt, during the seventy-four-year history of the Soviet Union, to impose a substitute for empirical reality by force produced instances of courage and nobility, but, considered overall, it drove a martyred people to new depths of misery and degradation.

The state can abolish God, but the result of the attempt to substitute itself for the missing absolute can only be the remaking of human nature under conditions in which consciousness is split and universal lying comes as close as anything can to destroying an entire people's "moral center."

AGE OF DELIRIUM

Prologue

We are an exception among people. We belong to those who are not an integral part of humanity but exist only to teach the world some type of great lesson.
—*Pyotr Chaadaev*, First Philosophical Letter

OCTOBER 4, 1993, 7:30 A.M.

THE MACHINE-GUNNING CONTINUED.

In the Square of Free Russia there were bodies everywhere, including those of teenagers, as the Russian parliament building, known as the "White House," came under attack from troops loyal to President Boris Yeltsin, who, only two years before, had risked his life to defend it.

The ferocity of the bombardment surprised the present defenders of the White House, who included members of parliament. They had expected that the building would be cleared with the help of special commando units, but not shelled.

In the sixth-floor buffet, Nikolai Troitsky, a reporter for the *Megapolis Express*, stood watching with others as two men in the square beneath him dragged a body, its intestines spilling out, into an entryway. "Now they are going to shoot out the windows," one of Troitsky's neighbors explained. The row of windows facing the Square of Free Russia was then shattered by bullets. Troitsky and the other reporters left the buffet and hurriedly took cover in the office

3

of Konstantin Zlobin, the press secretary of Ruslan Khasbulatov, the chairman of the Supreme Soviet,* which faced an internal courtyard.

For a few hours, Zlobin's office provided relative safety, but by noon, as intense machine-gun fire ricocheted off the walls of the corridor outside, the security became increasingly dubious. Vakhtan Yakobidze, a correspondent for Georgian Television, left the office to get a better view and, as he stepped out into the hall, an incendiary bomb landed about a hundred feet in front of him, setting fire to the rug and sending up thick clouds of reddish-black smoke.

"We've got to get out of here," Yakobidze said. There were bullets flying in the corridor, but the group of reporters ran ten yards to a staircase deep in the center of the building. With the noise of breaking windows all around them, they proceeded down the steps to the hall of the Council of Nationalities, which had been designed as a bomb shelter and was the one place in the building that was considered to be safe.

THERE WAS AN ATMOSPHERE of controlled chaos in the hall. Veronika Kutsillo, who wrote for the newspaper *Kommersant*, noticed Khasbulatov surrounded by reporters.

"What will happen, Ruslan Imranovich?" she asked.

Khasbulatov, standing with one hand in a pocket of his raincoat and the other hand holding a pipe, shrugged his shoulders. "I've known Yeltsin for a long time," he said calmly, "but I would not have expected this from him. How is it possible to treat your own people like an enemy?"

Suddenly, the building was rocked by a withering series of blasts that seemed to tear holes in the building's facade, as well as in any hope of a last-minute compromise.

Kutsillo had lived through the August 1991 coup, during which Khasbulatov and Yeltsin had been allies, defending the White House against a threatened attack from the leaders of a pro-Communist coup. "I won't survive another putsch," she said, as the hall filled with the smell of powder.

Khasbulatov shook his head and, smiling slightly, said, "What makes you think you're going to survive this one?"

*The official name of the Russian parliament.

. . .

SOON, THERE WERE NEARLY a thousand people in the hall—deputies, reporters, cooks, police guards, washerwomen. With no electricity in the building and the light from an inner courtyard barely visible through a half-open door, their ghostly outlines were illuminated only by the wavering flames of occasional candles, giving the hall, which in normal times resembles a bunker, the atmosphere of a crypt.

In an adjacent corridor, armed fighters were carrying the bodies of the injured and dead on stretchers to a nearby medical point; a corpse lay face up and bloody on the floor, blocking the door of one of the elevators. Outside, the crackle of automatic weapons fire from the building's upper floors was being answered by machine-gun fire from the armored personnel carriers on the street.

Nonetheless, various anti-Yeltsin deputies, recognizable only by their voices in the gloomy hall, were making speeches from the podium demanding that the people in the hall hold out for final victory. Mikhail Chelnokov, one of the speakers, said, "To die for the motherland is not a bad thing. In any case, what kind of choice do we have now?"

BY NOON, troops loyal to Yeltsin had seized all of the buildings surrounding the White House, and as the bombardment continued, the return fire from the parliament building grew steadily weaker. Explosions wracked the thirteenth and fourteenth floors, sending orange flames shooting up the face of the building, and with each direct hit, the building shook from top to bottom like a house of cards.

Troitsky listened to the sound of tank treads and tried to guess the vehicles' exact location. They seemed nearby. He began to wonder what would happen if a stray shell or grenade landed in the packed hall. "Do you think they'll start firing in here?" he asked, turning to Valery Shuikov, a deputy who had just returned to Moscow from Abkhazia.

"I don't think they would do that," said Shuikov.

At that moment, the machine-gun fire unexpectedly ceased and there was a series of hammering explosions as tanks on the Kalinin Bridge blew out huge sections of the long-deserted upper floors.

"I'm not so sure," Troitsky said.

. . .

BY 2 P.M., everyone in the hall was waiting for capitulation. Buffet workers began distributing cooked chickens that had been donated before the attack by a farmer sympathetic to the parliament's cause. With the army clearly supporting Yeltsin, however, even extreme-nationalist deputies such as Sergei Baburin, Ilya Konstantinov, and Iona Andronova agreed that it was time to give up. The problem was that no one wanted to go out carrying a white flag, and no one was sure that it would be possible to leave safely in any other way.

The members of the crowd sang Russian folk songs, recited po-etry, and prayed. A little after 3 p.m., the internal White House radio reported that Valery Zorkin, the chairman of the Constitutional Court, was on his way to negotiate a truce. No sooner was the an-nouncement made, however, than the machine-gunning of the White House intensified, and there was a deafening crash and several explo-sions one right after the other. With no further news of the truce mis-sion, the crowd began to fear that the entry of armed units into the building was imminent.

Suddenly, at 4 p.m., two officers of the "Alpha" antiterrorist unit, wearing bulletproof vests and helmets with visors and goggles that made them resemble extraterrestials, appeared in the hall of the Council of Nationalities. One of them got up to address the crowd from the podium in the front of the hall in what was, in effect, the last session of the Russian Supreme Soviet. He said that the purpose of the Alpha group was to fight terrorism, not to kill the country's elected representatives, and that if the defenders of the White House would give up their arms, the Alpha unit would guarantee their safety.

The two officers then left to negotiate the surrender of the White House with Vice President Alexander Rutskoi. At that moment, the hall resounded with deafening automatic weapons fire that seemed to be coming from the internal courtyard. Panic broke out in the semi-darkness, but just as suddenly as the shooting began it ceased, and members of the Alpha unit reappeared and began to organize the evacuation.

At 4:45 p.m., the first group of evacuees, nearly three hundred persons, were led out of the side of the building facing the square with their hands behind their heads. They passed the bodies of de-fenders who had been cut down at the barricades at the beginning of the attack, many of them with parts of their heads blown away or missing limbs. They also got their first look at the White House from the outside, and saw how the windows of the lower floors were shot out and the venetian blinds tangled in contorted patterns while the upper part of the building was wreathed in orange flames and clouds of black smoke.

At 5:20 p.m., a second group, consisting mainly of administrative personnel, also left without incident. A short time later, a third group—which included Konstantinov; Oleg Rumyantsev, author of the parliament's proposed constitution; and many others among Yeltsin's most prominent parliamentary opponents—was led out to a veranda overlooking the Moscow River. As darkness fell, the Russian capital was shrouded with a reddish hue. Suddenly, shooting broke out from all sides. The evacuees hit the ground and, with their faces pressed hard against the mud, waited for another hour and a half before being escorted by members of the Alpha group to a nearby apartment block, where they were released to proceed on their own.

In this way, the Russian tradition of settling disputes by force was reaffirmed, and the crisis that was a result of two years of refusal by either side to share power, and provoked by Yeltsin's decision to abolish the Russian parliament, came to an end.

1

The Coup

Under the spreading chestnut tree, I sold you and you sold me.
—*George Orwell,* 1984

AUGUST 19, 1991

IN MOSCOW, a light rain washed the peeling facades and potholed streets. Russia's towering white parliament building, which had come to symbolize the democratic aspirations of an entire nation, was shrouded in mist, its gray shadow reflected in the dappled waters of the Moscow River. Except for bread trucks making early-morning deliveries and workers finishing the night shift at factories, the city slept.

This, however, was to be no ordinary day. In the Crimean resort of Foros, eight hundred miles to the south, where Mikhail Gorbachev had an opulent dacha, two heavy trucks, under cover of darkness, rode to the airstrip nearest the dacha and positioned themselves lengthwise across the runway. The approaches to the dacha from the sea were then quietly blocked by military ships, and KGB units sealed off the road to Gorbachev's residence, surrounding the compound and isolating Gorbachev, his family, and the thirty-two members of his personal guard inside.

At 6:06 a.m., a report began to be tapped out over the teletype at the headquarters of Tass, the Soviet news agency, on Herzen Street. Gorbachev, the Soviet president, had been removed from his post for reasons of health. His responsibilities were being assumed by Gennady Yanaev, his vice president. Authority would be exercised on a temporary basis by a Committee for the State of Emergency, whose members were Yanaev; Vladimir Kryuchkov, the head of the KGB; Dmitri Yazov, the defense minister; Boris Pugo, the minister of internal affairs; Vasily Starodubtsev, the chairman of the "farmers' union"; Alexander Tizyakov, an industrialist; Valentin Pavlov, the prime minister; and Oleg Baklanov, the vice president of the Defense Council. Almost all of the members of the committee had been appointed by Gorbachev and were considered to be his close colleagues or friends.

At the barracks of the Taman and Kantemirov divisions in the Moscow oblast, soldiers were roused from their beds and ordered to leave for Moscow. As daylight spread over the villages and fields of the Moscow oblast, long columns of tanks and armored vehicles were already filling the roads leading to the capital.

EMMA BRUK, a cardiologist in the Botkin Hospital, woke to a strange silence. For months, she had been awakened by the sound of drilling and hammering as workers repaired the nearby American embassy. On this occasion, however, everything was quiet. She went to the window and saw that all work on the embassy had stopped.

Emma turned on the television. Instead of the news, the station was playing classical music, and then an announcer began to read a prepared statement. "Six years ago," he said, "Gorbachev began perestroika." Emma was stunned by the reference to "Gorbachev" instead of "Comrade Gorbachev" or "Mikhail Sergeievich." She realized that no one would refer to him so disrespectfully if he were still in power. The announcer continued: "The reforms of Gorbachev have come to a dead end. The country has become unmanageable and extremist forces are bent on the liquidation of the Soviet Union." Accordingly, a Committee for the State of Emergency had been formed to save the country from collapse.

As the announcer's image melted into the next frame, Emma was overcome by a feeling of panic. Her thoughts went back to the years before perestroika, when she had lived in a state of constant fear. In those years, her principal consolation had come from books. Every Friday, she and a group of friends met in one of their apartments and discussed banned literature which one or the other of them had, with great difficulty, been able to obtain. When Gorbachev came to power, Emma did not expect any improvement in conditions. But her attitude began to change in early 1987, after the authorities started to release the Soviet Union's political prisoners. When, with the onset of glasnost, she began to be able to reread in official editions books she had read earlier in samizdat, she lost her fear entirely. But now, as she stared at the blank television screen, her first reaction was that the coup leaders were trying to drive her back into that corner of oppression and fear from which she seemed so recently to have emerged.

At 9 a.m., Emma left home to run errands. On the street there was nothing unusual, only the normal Monday traffic jam at the entrance to the tunnel under Kalinin Prospekt as four lanes of traffic tried to squeeze into two. When she entered a local grocery store in a building on Vostaniye Square, however, she witnessed a mob scene similar to what she recalled seeing as a seven-year-old girl, after the German attack on the Soviet Union in 1941. The store was choked with people who were pushing and shoving to get into the long queues to buy up whatever they could, only this time what they feared was not a foreign invasion but the start of civil war.

Emma fought her way through the crowd and joined a long queue for butter. All around her, there were violent arguments. Some people were saying, "It's about time," while others denounced the coup leaders as fascists. One old woman said, "Finally, there will be order."

"What kind of order are you talking about?" Emma said to the old woman. "You'll be behind barbed wire and they'll give you a bowl of soup. That will be your order."

As soon as she'd said this, however, Emma was seized by a wave of fear. It had once been dangerous to make antiregime remarks in the queues. If things were changing, she could not forget herself like that.

When she returned home, Emma received a call from her mother-in-law, who had been on her way to see her. She said that tanks were beginning to cross the Krimsky Bridge.

SERGEI LATISHEV, a veteran of the Afghan war who had been working in a veterans' organization in Moscow, was motoring down the Sadovoye Ring Road at 7:30 a.m. when, to his surprise, he saw several armored personnel carriers parked in front of the Paveletsky Station. He wondered what they were doing there, but did not trouble himself further about it. He continued on the Varshavsky Highway and, crossing the Moscow Ring Road, headed due south to Podolsk, where he was scheduled to receive some land set aside for cottages for invalids of the Afghan war. On arrival in Podolsk, he parked his car, got out, and began to walk to the city council building.

The sun had come out and Latishev was struck by the dust and dilapidation of this provincial town. At the entrance to the city council building, he was met by an official who seemed agitated.

"What do you think about what's happening?" the official asked.

"What do you mean?"

"Gorbachev has been overthrown."

"You're joking."

When the official assured him that he was serious, they returned to Latishev's car, turned on the engine, and began listening to the news on the car radio, which featured the mechanical repetition of the first proclamations of the coup committee. The committee was promising to reduce prices and to give land to city dwellers by 1992. Listening to the announcements, Latishev became enraged. He knew it was absurd to talk about reducing prices when there were no goods in the stores.

Latishev decided to return immediately to Moscow and contact other Afghan war veterans. He was sure that in the absence of resistance the Soviet Union would fall under the heel of a new totalitarianism.

As he drove back to Moscow, he thought back over the events of the last ten years. In the early 1980s, he was the deputy commander of a unit stationed near the city of Imam-sahib in the Kunduzska province of Afghanistan. He believed in the rightness of the Soviet cause in those years, but the cruelty of the war unhinged him. In his dreams, he relived the deaths of men and the slaughter of horses.

When he returned home, he felt an aggressiveness he could not explain. He couldn't sleep without the sound of gunfire and was plagued by a constant sense that something was missing. He later realized that this was his automatic weapon. One day, during a train trip between Moscow and Leningrad, he was sitting across from a father and a little girl. Suddenly, the girl began singing. Latishev

looked at her and, in spite of himself, began smiling. When he arrived in Leningrad, he felt he had become human again.

He had not doubted that all the blood that was spilled in Afghanistan was justified in the interests of protecting the Soviet Union's
southern border, but as he looked for work and a place to live in his
hometown of Nikopol in the Ukraine, he became aware of his right-
lessness in dealing with bureaucratic organizations. He saw that they
were completely independent of him, would not listen to him, and
that at the head of every bureaucratic organization was a member of
the Communist Party. He began to wonder if, when he fought in Afghanistan, he had been defending the Afghan people or only the
Afghan Communist Party.

At first, there was almost nothing in the newspapers about Afghanistan. When the war was mentioned at all, the impression was
given that all the fighting was being done by the Afghans. After a big
operation in the Panshir Gorge which cost the Soviet army many
lives, Soviet newspapers wrote that the gorge had been taken by the
Afghan army.

The silence about Afghanistan disturbed Latishev, as did the im-
mobility of Soviet life. He had left part of himself in Afghanistan and
he believed that he had fought for a worthy cause, but his sacrifice
seemed to melt away in the face of the inertia of a system run by the
few for the few, with little regard for anyone else. He began to be
overwhelmed with the feeling that nothing could ever change in the
Soviet Union. He thought that the sheer ordeal of daily life had
turned the people into a brainless herd.

When Gorbachev came to power, Latishev had the impression
that an honest person was finally in charge. In 1986, Gorbachev
made a speech in Khabarovsk in which he said that Communists
should not be afraid to criticize each other, and it seemed to Latishev
that maybe things could change.

In 1988, the newspapers began to acknowledge that the war in
Afghanistan was being fought primarily by Soviet troops, and that
losses had been heavy. They also began to write about atrocities in
Afghanistan, and about the popular support for the Afghan resistance. This greater frankness had a traumatic effect on many former
soldiers.

When Latishev moved to Moscow a short time later, he joined a
group of Afghan veterans and, for the first time, began to discuss the

possibility that he had participated in an immoral war. One day, Mikhail Shilnikov, a friend who had been blinded in Afghanistan, called Latishev and told him that he had heard on television that the war in Afghanistan had been unnecessary. "Is it possible," he asked Latishev, "that our soldiers died in vain?"

For Latishev, the final blow came in 1990, when articles appeared in the Soviet press admitting that Hafizullah Amin, the former leader of Afghanistan, had been overthrown by the KGB and not the Afghan army. This meant that the official justification for the war—that the Soviet Union had entered Afghanistan in response to a call for help from the legitimate government—was absurd.

In Moscow, Latishev went to the local veterans organization and began calling former soldiers to come to the headquarters. As he dialed the numbers of his comrades and friends, however, he realized that he was not emotionally prepared to fight the coup plotters. He had spilled enough blood in Afghanistan. He did not want to spill any more.

His hesitation was reinforced when he called other veterans and he sensed their fear of a bloody fight. The wife of one grabbed the phone and said, "What are you doing? In Afghanistan they didn't kill him, so you want to kill him here?"

AT 6:45 on the morning of August 19, Valentin Perfilyev, an adviser to Alexander Rutskoi, was awakened by the ringing of his telephone. It was a close friend calling: "Bad news, old man, the generals have taken over. I just heard it on the radio. Gorbachev has been arrested."

Perfilyev got dressed and ran to his desk, where he found the membership lists of Communists for Democracy, the organization he and Rutskoi had founded in opposition to the existing Communist Party. Saying goodbye to his wife and sons, he headed with the lists to the Krylatskaya metro station, looking around constantly to see if he was being followed.

Above all, Perfilyev wanted to get the lists to his office in the Russian parliament building before the KGB could seize them and use them to make arrests. Perfilyev rode to the Barrikadnaya metro station and arrived at the White House at about 9:15 a.m. Strangely, the building was relatively empty. He walked in through the main en-

trance, past a sleepy militiaman and a washerwoman who did not react to him, took the elevator to his office in the vice-presidential suite
on the fourth floor, and put the materials in his safe.

A GIFTED student from a poor family, Perfilyev enrolled in the
1970s in the Institute of World Economy and International Relations
(IMEMO), which was then the favored training ground for the children of the Soviet elite. Perfilyev was angered to see the effects of the
invisible class structure at the school. At first, as someone from a
poor family, he was shunned and snubbed by the other students, who
included the children of members of the Central Committee. With
time, however, he made a few friends and was astonished, when he
visited their homes, to see the difference between the way they lived
and the way of life of ordinary citizens.

Years later, when he witnessed the dictatorship of party functionaries over all aspects of Soviet life, Perfilyev often recalled his student
days. By then he was a member of the party himself, and the leader
of a small party organization in the international bank where he
worked as a juridical consultant. He saw the enormous gap between
the apparatus and ordinary party members, and the way in which the
party apparatus strove to regulate all aspects of its members' lives.

With the coming to power of Gorbachev, little changed in the
methods of the party hierarchy. Party functionaries continued to demand unconditional political loyalty, and any person in a managerial
post who deviated from the established line paid for it with his job.

One day in January 1990, while walking his dog, Perfilyev noticed a candidate for the Russian parliament addressing a group of
people with the help of a loudspeaker. The candidate was Rutskoi.
After Rutskoi finished his remarks, he and Perfilyev met and they became friends. Both were longtime Communists, and as they discussed
the situation in the country, they found that they agreed on the need
in the party for radical reform.

Rutskoi won election and a year later, on March 8, 1991, announced formation of the parliamentary faction Communists for Democracy. Perfilyev began to organize a supporting movement outside
the parliament whose program called for intraparty democratization,
stated that the doctrines of Marx and Lenin had outlived themselves,
and advocated a market economy with a social safety net for the
disadvantaged.

Communists for Democracy began to receive thousands of letters from ordinary party members. Entire party organizations wrote asking where they could sign up. In August, however, both Rutskoi and Perfilyev were expelled from the party. Other members of the movement were also purged, and exclusion was often followed by dismissal at work. Perfilyev became convinced that the party leadership was preparing a coup.

PERFILYEV WENT to see Rutskoi. It was still early and Rutskoi did not know if Gorbachev was alive or whether Yeltsin had been arrested. "This is imbecility," Rutskoi said, referring to the coup, "nothing will come of it." But then he added, "If these scoundrels come to power, they'll stop at nothing."

Perfilyev returned to his office and studied the traffic moving up and down Kutuzovsky Prospekt, the long avenue along which Napoleon's army had invaded Moscow. In the distance, he saw the first column of tanks.

Gradually, the White House was coming to life as Russian deputies and, finally, Yeltsin and other members of the Russian government arrived. Ordinary citizens and dissident army and KGB officers began calling deputies with information. Through the veil of confusion and disarray, Perfilyev could see that a confrontation was building.

IN ALL, an estimated ten thousand men and four hundred tanks poured into Moscow, taking up positions in the center of the city. The armor and troops also moved into two staging areas, the central army airfield on Leningradsky Prospekt and the Tushino airfield in northwest Moscow. At the same time KGB officers seized the press runs of independent newspapers, and independent Russian television was taken off the air. State-controlled central television continued to broadcast, however, and began to air a tape of the ballet *Swan Lake*, which was to be shown repeatedly throughout the day.

At the White House, typists began to reproduce an "appeal to the citizens of Russia" that Yeltsin, Khasbulatov, and Ivan Silaev, the Russian prime minister, had composed at Yeltsin's dacha in Arkhangelskoe and telephoned in at 9 a.m. before arriving at the parliament building. It denounced the seizure of power by the committee as a "right-wing, reactionary, anticonstitutional coup," and called for a general strike.

Soon, other members of the Russian government arrived. General Viktor Samoilov was astonished to see that the coup plotters had not turned off the building's water or electricity. Even more important, they had not cut off the building's communications, and by mid-morning, the phones were ringing in virtually every office as people called their deputies continually with updated reports on the movement of troops and armor in and around the city.

At 11 a.m., a meeting was held of thirty members of the Russian parliament's presidium. Yeltsin, who had taken charge, asked what means were available to the Russian government to resist the coup. Viktor Ivanenko, head of the newly formed Russian KGB, said he had thirty men under his command. Viktor Barannikov, the head of the Russian Interior Ministry, stated that he had a little over three hundred.

Despite these minimal forces, Yeltsin said that he would resist. At the close of the meeting, he and several aides stepped out onto a balcony overlooking the river and began throwing out copies of his "appeal." Returning inside, Yeltsin issued an edict ordering the KGB, the Internal Affairs Ministry, and the Defense Ministry to subordinate themselves to him. He then called on soldiers to resist the coup committee.

At 1 p.m., a long column of tanks moved down Kutuzovsky Prospekt, crossed the river, and split in two directions, surrounding the White House.

Flanked by guards, Yeltsin walked down the steps and approached the lead tank. "Did you come here to kill Yeltsin?" he asked the tank's officer.

"No, of course not," the officer answered.

Yeltsin then climbed up on tank No. 110 of the Taman Division. "Citizens of Russia," he said, as a crowd of people gathered around him, "the legally elected president of the country has been removed from power.... We are dealing with a right-wing, reactionary, anticonstitutional coup d'état.... Reaction will not be victorious. I have no doubt but that the army will refuse to go against the people.... The criminals will be brought to the bar of justice."

There would be no compromise with the coup plotters. Yeltsin and his government had made their choice.

· · ·

AT FIRST, Perfilyev was shaken by the situation. The corridors of the White House were being flooded with armed men, including some in stocking masks, and deputies repeated rumors of an imminent attack. Outside, part of the column of tanks that had crossed the Kalinin Bridge stood with their guns pointed toward the White House. By 2 p.m., however, Perfilyev started to receive encouraging reports. Members of the Alex cooperative, a private security firm that included many Afghan veterans, announced that they would help defend the White House, as did police cadets from the Tula-Orlovsky Academy of the Ministry of Internal Affairs and the OMON militia for the Moscow oblast. On Sakhalin Island, in the Far East, the entire military garrison announced that it would defend the Russian republic.

The news that units were rallying to the cause of the Russian republic gave Perfilyev hope that it would be possible to head off bloodshed. He had little doubt, however, that, if the coup leaders tried to take the White House by force, army units would begin fighting each other and the country would be plunged into civil war.

Meanwhile, a mood of resistance was gradually building on the streets. The crowd around the White House, which started to form around 11 a.m., was growing. Cranes were commandeered and barricades of concrete, pipe, bricks, and pieces of wooden fences and railroad ties began to be erected. In the Barrikadnaya metro station, the walls were plastered with calls for people to resist, and in the hall leading to the trains a woman stood shouting through a megaphone, "Everyone go to the White House." Valentin Poluektov, a leader of the fledgling Russian Democratic Party, noticed a woman in her seventies walking toward the White House and asked, "Where are you going? They're going to shoot."

"Let them shoot," the old woman said. "I don't want to listen to any more lies."

INSIDE THE WHITE HOUSE, General Konstantin Kobets, the Russian defense minister, and his staff spread out a huge map of the Moscow area on a table. On the basis of information being called in by citizens, they were able to pinpoint the location of the military units being deployed in Moscow. Among Kobets's informants were KGB agents who worked in military counterintelligence.

While this was going on, reconnaissance teams from the Alpha group were mixing with the crowd, taking videofilms of the various entrances and of the security precautions. At 2 p.m., Major General Viktor Karpukhin, the commander of the Alpha group, brought one of the videofilms to the Defense Ministry, and at a meeting attended by General Valentin Varennikov, the leader of the ground forces, and Pavel Grachev, the paratroop commander, the order was given to storm the White House. According to the plan, paratroopers under Major General Alexander Lebed and special internal Ministry detachments (OMON) were to storm the eighth entrance and clear a path for the Alpha group, which would then take the elevator to the fifth floor, where Yeltsin's headquarters was located. Troops on the ground were to shoot out the windows to create a distraction, and the Alpha group was then to strike the Yeltsin headquarters, destroying the guards and killing the Russian leaders. The attack was to take place at 3 a.m. on August 20.

When Karpukhin returned to the headquarters of the Alpha group, he called together his subordinates and gave them the order. To his surprise, however, two of his officers, Mikhail Golovatov and Sergei Goncharov, said that they would have to consult with their men—which suggested that they reserved the right to refuse.

As Karpukhin waited for an answer, his direct subordinates communicated with their men by radio in the various Alpha bases around the city. The Alpha group had studied the videos of the White House and had been given weapons and ammunition. No one doubted that the Russian leadership could be quickly destroyed. But the Alpha group did not want to fight the civilian population and as the minutes ticked away, each member wondered how he would get out of the White House after destroying Yeltsin and his associates. What if they had to shoot their way through an enraged crowd? They all had families in the city.

To the surprise of everyone present, the members of the Alpha group unanimously agreed not to carry out the order. It was the first time in the history of the group that they had refused a direct command.

At that point, Karpukhin became disoriented and left for KGB headquarters. There was no longer any possibility of an Alpha group attack.

• • •

AT THE WHITE HOUSE, tanks that had been positioned around the building began to withdraw.

Across the river, however, ten tanks under Major Yevdokimov of the Taman Division took up positions in front of the Hotel Ukraine. Sergei Yushenkov, a Russian deputy, was watching the maneuver from the window of his eleventh-floor office when he received a call from Sergei Bratchikov, a civilian who had talked with Major Yevdokimov and who said Yevdokimov was ready, in principle, to bring his tanks back across the river and defend the White House. Yushenkov recruited Viktor Aksuchits, another Russian deputy, and they walked across the Kalinin Bridge and were introduced to Yevdokimov.

"As I see it, you have two choices," Yushenkov said. "You can carry out the orders of a criminal band that has seized power, or carry out the orders of the elected president of the whole people." Yevdokimov went back to his unit accompanied by Yushenkov and informed the soldiers that they were crossing the bridge to defend the White House.

As the first tanks moved over the bridge and penetrated the barricade, the roar from the crowd drowned out the sound of the tanks, and the people surged around the first tank, forcing it to halt as hundreds tried to shake the hands of its crew. After the crowd placed the red, white, and blue Russian flag on each of the tanks, the vehicles formed a semicircle around the White House, their guns pointing outward.

The news that a tank unit had defected to the Russian side was reported by Western radio to the entire Soviet Union.

Yeltsin, working in a war room on the third floor of the White House, signed a decree creating a shadow government and sent twenty-three military and civilian leaders to a secret location thirty-five miles from Sverdlovsk. If the White House was captured, this group would begin operating in the name of the Russian government.

AT 9 P.M., during the evening news program, an announcer read a statement from the Committee for the State of Emergency justifying the coup as a means of defending the country from extremist forces. The program, however, also showed a segment of film of

Yeltsin on top of a tank and reported his call for a general strike. Next, there was footage of a press conference held earlier in the day by the members of the coup committee. The cameraman had noticed that Soviet vice president Yanaev's hands were trembling, and he focused on the hands for long periods, confirming for millions of viewers that the coup leaders were not sure of themselves. At the end of the news program, the authorities announced that there would be an 11 p.m. curfew, which inspired people to leave their homes for the White House. Soon, citizens were coming out of the Barrikadnaya metro station in streams. Many were carrying Thermoses, umbrellas, and blankets, preparing to spend the night. At the same time, a group of Russian deputies issued an appeal to the crowd outside the White House to remain where they were.

"Don't leave us here alone," the appeal said. Bella Kurkova, the hostess of "The Fifth Wheel," a popular television program, came over the loudspeakers to announce that Radio White House, broadcasting from the basement, was now in operation and would continue until the end of the crisis.

By the beginning of the second day, the coup leaders' hope that the mere appearance of tanks in the streets would be sufficient to intimidate the population had been disappointed. By 10:30 a.m. it was raining hard, but there was already a large crowd outside the White House, made up of those who had spent the night and fresh recruits.

Yeltsin emerged on the balcony and began to address the crowd from behind a bulletproof shield.

"This junta used no restraint in grabbing power and will not show any restraint in keeping it," he said. "Doesn't Yazov have his hands covered with blood from other republics? Hasn't Pugo bloodied his hands in the Baltics and the Caucasus? The [Russian] prosecutors and the Interior Ministry have their orders; whoever fulfills the commands of this illegal committee will be prosecuted! Democracy will win and we will stay here as long as it takes for this junta to be brought to justice!"

WHEN EMMA BRUK arrived at about noon, she was encouraged by the size of the crowd. The sight of thousands of people standing under umbrellas and plastic sheets in the rain convinced her that resistance was possible.

At noon, a series of speakers addressed the crowd from the balcony. They called on the crowd to defend the White House and asked people not to leave. Among the speakers were Rutskoi; Gennady Burbulis, an aide to Yeltsin; Yelena Bonner, the widow of Andrei Sakharov; Gleb Yakunin, a priest and former political prisoner who was now a member of the Russian Supreme Soviet; and Gennady Khazanov, a humorist who amused the crowd by saying it was impossible to carry out clean politics "with dirty, shaking hands."

A first-aid station had been set up under an awning at an entrance to the White House on the side of the river, and after the meeting, Emma went there to offer her help. A dozen persons with armbands with red crosses were standing behind tables on which were spread out antiseptics, alcohol, gauze, and bandages. A few nurses, exhausted after a long night without sleep, were lying down on a ledge under the windows of the building trying to get some rest.

There began to be announcements over the White House radio that the members of the crowd should keep wet handkerchiefs or gauze with them, and cover their mouths and noses in the event of a gas attack. Doctors and nurses at the station asked Emma to get bandages and equipment. Emma then left to go to her apartment and call her daughter in the United States. When she returned a few hours later, the first-aid station had been moved to a trolleybus that was being used as a protective barrier on the side of the building facing the park.

Doctors and nurses from hospitals all over Moscow who had converged on the White House with supplies and medical personnel now said that they did not need any more doctors, especially since there were so far no patients.

Emma then entered a second bus, where women were busy making sandwiches.

One of the women said, "What are you doing here? We're preparing food." Emma hesitated and began to leave.

"Well, what are you standing there for?" the woman said. "Come and help us."

Emma took a seat in the rear of the bus and began making sausage and cheese sandwiches and placing them in a large basket to be distributed to the crowd.

As Emma worked and the rain beat a steady rhythm on the roof of the bus, she listened to the other women talking about popular singers and movie stars, seemingly oblivious to the danger.

WHEN SERGEI LATISHEV showed up at the White House on the morning of the twentieth, he saw a table at the central entrance manned by several men under a sign: HEADQUARTERS— SELF-DEFENSE. He joined a queue of people waiting to sign up to defend the White House, but the process seemed to be very disorganized. Once a volunteer signed up at the table, he was led to a nearby group and then stood around doing nothing. The groups began to fraternize. In the meantime, the line got longer. Feeling that he could do more by acting independently, Latishev left the White House and returned to the headquarters of the Afghan veterans to discuss a plan of action with Vladimir Nikolaev, the director of the road-building concern attached to the group.

The concern, which earned money to support the Afghan veterans' activities, had dump trucks, rollers, bulldozers, and tractor trailers at its disposal. Latishev told Nikolaev that the defense of the White House was badly organized, and suggested using the vehicles to block traffic on the Altufinskoe and Dmitrovskoe Highways, thereby blocking the movement of armor into the city. Since there was still a considerable number of armored vehicles on the ring road surrounding Moscow, any move to cut off the center could have strategic significance.

The two men weighed the consequences of such a move. They knew they could create massive and probably impassable traffic jams, but they worried about the effect on ambulances and firefighters. Unsure what to do, Latishev decided to return to the White House to confer with the defenders.

By the time Latishev got back, a human chain was already in place around the building. There were large gaps, but at least some type of defense was being organized. A group of Afghan veterans were forming a chain in front of the twentieth entryway at the corner of the building nearest the American embassy, one of the few entryways still in use. They had knives and iron bars, and they agreed that, in the event of an attack, they would use them to try to disarm at least one of the attackers, and then use his automatic weapon on the others.

Latishev looked at the other defenders—the students and teachers, the housewives and fledgling businessmen—and thought to himself that they did not understand the horror that awaited them. Still, in time, the defenses became tighter. Gradually, the gaps in the chain were eliminated and first a second and then a third chain of defenders was added. It became much harder for unauthorized persons to approach the White House.

As he stood in the driving rain, Latishev heard constant reports of tanks moving toward the parliament building. The mood became tense and people gathered around anyone with a radio.

Latishev asked an official of the White House if he should give the signal to set up barricades with road-building equipment, but after a long delay he was told that there was no need. Some of the veterans were asked to investigate reports that there were snipers on the surrounding roofs.

As the demonstrators huddled together in the cold, the gray smoke from dozens of campfires in front of the White House rose into the sky. There was nothing to do but wait.

BY LATE AFTERNOON, there was a growing sense that the coup plotters had run into difficulty. A coup is supposed to take place instantaneously, but this one seemed to be working in slow motion, the plotters watching passively as Yeltsin proclaimed his defiance and resistance around the White House continued to build.

Encouraged by the indecisiveness of the coup leaders, Russian deputies and members of the Moscow City Council began traveling to military units in an attempt to persuade them to change sides.

GEORGY ZADONSKY, a Russian deputy, arrived at the barricade on the Kalinin Bridge after traveling all day from his dacha in the countryside. He asked a passerby what was going on. The latter replied, "On the left are our tanks, on the right are their tanks, and in the middle is the bridge."

Zadonsky showed his deputy's badge, climbed over the barricade, and walked to the parliament building, where he was assigned to a group of other deputies on their way to the Fili raion at the end of Kutuzovsky Prospekt to talk to the soldiers there. On arrival, Zadonsky asked to talk to the unit commander, but the officer refused to meet with him. The commander, however, did not try to prevent Zadonsky from talking with the soldiers, and Zadonsky and several of the deputies began handing out copies of Yeltsin's appeal to servicemen to refuse the orders of the Emergency Committee. Zadonsky and the other deputies then crossed a bridge and talked to the commander of a company.

"Part of the Taman Division has come over to our side," said Zadonsky. "Why don't you?"

"Whatever the army does," he said, "we're going to be blamed. If we go against the people, we're going to be blamed, but if we don't, we'll be blamed for disobeying orders."

Zadonsky returned to the White House and was immediately sent to talk to the soldiers manning the tanks near the Electrozavodskaya metro station on the Yauza River. When he and the other deputies arrived, however, they saw that the soldiers had been surrounded by local residents, who accused them of having come to "shoot your own people." Their commander complained that Yazov had put the army in an impossible situation. When Zadonsky asked him whether he would carry out an order to shoot the people, however, he did not reply.

Sergei Zasukhin, another deputy, was sent with a group of deputies to the Minsk Highway, where they came upon several military trucks carrying searchlights for illuminating the sky in the event of a parachute drop. Since there was fear of an attack on the White House from the air, Zasukhin and the other deputies decided to try to prevent the searchlights from being brought into the center of town. They stepped into the highway and flagged down two tractor-trailer trucks and asked them to park lengthwise across the road. They did this, blocking the path of the flatbed trucks. Zasukhin and the other deputies then began a conversation with the soldiers and their commanding officer.

"What is your mission?" Zasukhin asked.

"We don't know," said one of the soldiers. "They didn't tell us where we were going, all they said was the 'city of Moscow.' "

The deputies told the soldiers that if they did not turn around and leave Moscow, they would smash the searchlights. Instead of reacting angrily, the soldiers asked the deputies not to touch their trucks. "We are responsible for the trucks," one of the soldiers explained. "If you want to break something, break the lights—we're not responsible for those."

The commanding officer finally said that the unit would turn around and leave Moscow, and Zasukhin and the other deputies got in their cars and escorted the unit past the city limits.

Zasukhin went next to the Aeroport metro station, where ten light tanks were parked on Leningradsky Prospekt. He began to talk with the colonel in command. Zasukhin asked him the number of his unit, but the colonel declined to answer. He did say, however, that he had received an order to move toward the center into a populated area and had decided not to obey it.

The colonel's decision was one of many acts of insubordination that began to take place at all levels of the army.

A political officer with the unit, who was responsible for Communist indoctrination, tried to explain his personal position to the deputies. "I should be part of the crowd outside the White House," he said, "but I'm in uniform, and since I'm in uniform, if there is an order to go to the White House and shoot, I'll go to the White House and shoot."

Zasukhin became furious. "You're not a child," he said. "That helmet is on your head, and that head was given to you in order to think. If you have a wife and children, then think about what would be better for them." The conversation went on for three hours, during which time the deputies handed out leaflets and talked to the troops. By the time he left, Zasukhin was convinced that large sections of the army would refuse orders rather than open fire on the people.

PERFILYEV WONDERED what to do. Reports from around the country indicated that local governments and KGB and military units were beginning to rally to the side of the Russian government. The crowd outside the Russian parliament was growing, and world attention was now fixed on the confrontation taking place just outside his door. At the same time, he understood that all the coup plotters needed to end the resistance of the Russian government was one reliable unit. He decided that the defenders had to use every means available to contact high-ranking officers in the KGB, Ministry of Internal Affairs, and army and to persuade them not to take part in any attack.

At 4:30 p.m., Yeltsin emerged from his office and quietly shook hands with the people in the anteroom. Assembled there were people who had worked with him for many years. Yeltsin paused to chat briefly with each person. "Thank you for staying," he said. "We will stand firm no matter what it costs."

Yeltsin's manner was calm, but it was obvious from his eyes that he was worried and anxious. All sources were now indicating that the coup committee had resolved to storm the White House that night. Plans were being made to evacuate Yeltsin in the event of an attack. Nonetheless, his appearance boosted the morale of everyone in the room.

Contacts with the coup leaders were carried on by Yeltsin and Rutskoi. Rutskoi called Yazov, Yanaev, and Pugo and asked them what their intentions were. Each insisted that there would be no attack on the building, and that they only wanted to save the country from collapse.

Rutskoi also called Kryuchkov, but he refused to take the call. Perfilyev, using the government telephone, spoke to a general he knew and warned him that there were three hundred armed men in the building. The general seemed surprised by this information, and Perfilyev got the impression that there were elements in the army that did not want to see bloodshed.

In fact, as the day wore on, it became obvious that the military commanders were hesitating, and the members of the White House defense staff saw it as their job to do everything possible to increase their lack of confidence. Each member of the council who had friends in the Ministry of Defense, the KGB, or the Internal Affairs Ministry called them constantly. In every conversation, the message was the same: The army should not become involved in politics. The issue should be decided legally, according to the constitution.

Nikolai Stolyarov, a colonel who had earlier been chairman of the Revision Commission of the Russian Communist Party, called Yazov, Pugo, Yanaev, and Anatoly Lukyanov, the chairman of the Supreme Soviet, and urged them to pull back the troops. They replied that they did not want to use the troops but sought only to prevent disorders.

All day long tension heightened, yet at the same time nothing was done to disrupt the activity in the White House. The telephones continued to operate normally and there was no effort to turn off the water or the electricity. Rutskoi was puzzled by the behavior of the coup leaders. After one conversation with Yanaev, he said, "He is always justifying himself. All he says is that he doesn't want to see victims. He only wants to improve the economy."

Nonetheless, as the hours passed, there began to be signs that the coup leaders were preparing for military action. A KGB colonel defected to the side of the Russian White House and presented a plan for an attack by a squad of commandos. The armor, which before had moved back and forth in a seemingly haphazard manner, now started to take up positions in a broad circle around the building, and the defenders of the White House began to spot snipers on the surrounding rooftops.

In a meeting of the defense staff, Perfilyev and others of Rutskoi's advisers tried to decide how best to defend against an attack. Perfilyev suggested that a cordon of fifty meters be cleared around the White House, and that anyone crossing that zone be open to attack. This was agreed to, and Radio White House urged the members of the crowd to move back away from the building and to leave a fifty-meters-wide area free.

BY 11 P.M., the White House resembled a war zone. Searchlights lit the face of the building, the rain came down in slanting sheets, and there were many fires.

Despite the 11 p.m. curfew, waves of people were descending on the area from the Barrikadnaya metro station. The White House was surrounded by three rings of guards, with arms locked at the elbow, and even journalists were having trouble gaining entry to the building. The cloud cover was low, less than two hundred meters—bad weather for an air attack. Nonetheless, the red warning lights on the roof, which, in this situation, could serve as a guide for helicopters, were smashed and a shower of splinters fell on the crowd. Machine guns were mounted on the roof.

In the crowd, fear competed with hope as people sought any fragment of information no matter how dubious its reliability. There were constant reports of the movement of armor in the direction of the White House. At the same time, rumors spread that Yazov and Kryuchkov had resigned and that Pavlov had had a heart attack.

But outside the immediate area of the White House, life went on normally. When Valentina Linikova, a Russian deputy, entered the Hotel Rossiya, she was amazed to see that in the hotel restaurant, music was playing and people were dancing and enjoying themselves. A friend offered to buy her roses. "You're out of your mind," she told him. "I'm struggling on the barricades and you offer to buy me flowers."

AS IT GREW LATER, the tension outside the White House continued to increase.

Yeltsin, who would be the first target of any attack, was removed to the bomb shelter in the basement of the building.

A guard came into the bus where Emma Bruk was working and said that the volunteers would have to leave.

"We're making sandwiches," one of the women said.

"What kind of sandwiches," shouted one of the guards, "we're expecting an attack."

A short time later, Emma joined the crowd. As the warnings over Radio White House became more insistent and more ominous, she looked around at the other people and wondered what would happen to them. Strangers offered her cigarettes and food or a cup of tea that had been brewing over an open fire. People smiled and tried to cheer each other up, and the sense of brotherhood made her forget things like food shortages and the rudeness in the queues.

Deputies carrying automatic weapons emerged from the White House and began to walk in front of the defensive chain, now fifty meters away from the building, and to talk to members of the crowd and offer encouragement. Rutskoi spoke over Radio White House. "If the tanks move toward you, step aside and don't scream. Don't provoke them. Take no active steps against them. The resistance should not be armed resistance but spiritual resistance. So anyone with iron bars should throw them away. You protect us with your presence."

Radio White House then said there had been information that the attack was scheduled for after midnight, but there were new predictions about when it would take place.

Rutskoi then asked women and children to leave the square. "Friends," Rutskoi said, "if something tragic happens, you should not despair. Life won't stop with this. Life continues and you will continue the struggle."

When Emma heard these words, her heart froze. She looked at the young boys standing near her and thought of them being run over by tanks or crushed or shot. She wanted to offer them help, but she was as defenseless as they were. The movement of some women leaving the area rippled the crowd. Emma wondered for a moment whether she should leave, too, but the sight of these young boys made her decide to stay. In fact, she knew there was nothing she could do to defend them. But as she watched them standing in the rain, it seemed to her that they had a spiritual quality. They were ready to fight for their future and for their children's future.

Emma looked at the Russian federation flag flapping in the wind above the clocktower of the parliament building, and felt that the fate of the Russian people hung in the balance at that moment.

The crowd that now filled the square was tightly packed together, reaching to the rows of newly erected barricades that blocked access to the White House from Pavel Morozov Park in the rear. Emma did not believe the barricades would stop the tanks from crashing into the square, but she was certain that, in the event of a gas attack or general panic, they would make it almost impossible for the members of the crowd to get out.

As she stood expectantly in the crowd, Radio White House issued a stream of bulletins. At 12:20 a.m., a group of tanks began moving toward the White House from the direction of Taganskaya Square. At 12:45 a.m., armored personnel carriers smashed the barricades near the Barrikadnaya metro station. Shots were fired in the area of Teply Stan. Along Leningradsky Prospekt, ten tanks moved into the center of the city. Suddenly the crowd was electrified by the sound of shooting from the direction of the Sadovoye Ring Road. An announcement came over the loudspeaker, "All who know Tadjik, Uzbek, or the Caucasian languages should leave the chain and go to the Sadovoye Ring Road." At that, many of the Afghan veterans left the chain and began running toward the ring road to try to help communicate with non-Russian-speaking soldiers from the southern republics.

There were continued volleys in various locations, and signal rockets were launched in the sky.

At 2:30 a.m., Bella Kurkova announced over Radio White House, "Brothers and sisters, we're expecting an attack within the next ten minutes." The defenders began turning off the lights until the entire building was dark.

Burbulis made an appeal to all of those inside or near the building. He said that it was necessary to give way to the tanks, that this would be a sign not of fear but of the desire to avoid unnecessary casualties. Minutes later, Radio White House stopped broadcasting, and to the uncertainty of the situation was added an information blackout. More shots echoed through the night.

A BLOCK AWAY, a large crowd had formed on the Sadovoye Ring Road at the mouth of the tunnel under Kalinin Prospekt. A barricade of concrete blocks had been set up at the entrance to the tunnel, and a row of trolleybuses had been parked end to end at the other side to block the exit.

At about 2:15 a.m., a column of six light tanks and an armored car began heading for the tunnel from the direction of the American embassy. As the tanks approached, members of the crowd jumped down into the tunnel, forming a human chain in front of the first set of concrete barricades. The soldiers began firing in the air. As the crowd split, the tanks broke through the barriers and headed toward the row of parked trolleybuses blocking the tunnel at the other end.

The first tank in the column pushed its way through the row of trolleybuses, but after it had passed, the crowd ran into the tunnel and began pushing the trolleybuses back into place to close the breach.

The crowd shouted to the soldiers, "What are you doing, you should be on our side."

Once the trolleybus barrier was restored and all of the tanks had entered the tunnel, the crowd began to push the concrete barriers at the entrance to the tunnel back into place, leaving the military vehicles no avenue of escape.

As minutes passed, the tension increased. While the tanks waited, in the tunnel some members of the crowd threw a tarpaulin over the armored car, effectively blinding the soldiers. The soldiers removed the tarpaulin and got back into the car, but as they began moving again, Dmitri Usov, an Afghan veteran, climbed onto the back of the armored car and opened one of the hatches to try to talk to them. The soldiers opened fire and Usov was killed. He fell backwards, but his leg was caught in the hatch and his head and arms were dragged along the asphalt, leaving a bloody trail in the rain.

As the armored car began pulling Usov's body back and forth, pandemonium erupted in the tunnel. The crowd shouted, "Murderers!," "Scoundrels!," and cursed the soldiers. No one knew if Usov was alive or dead. In the collective panic, a young man tried to free the body and was shot in the shoulder. Two more young men ran to free the body, and first one and then the other was crushed under the wheels of the armored car. More and more people filled the tunnel until finally the armored car stopped and let the crowd remove the body.

Once the body was removed, the armored car tried to break through the barricade, and a Molotov cocktail flew through the air and exploded nearby. This was followed by a second Molotov cocktail. The armored car tried again to penetrate the barricades. A third Molotov cocktail was thrown, but it missed the armored car. Then four more bottles were launched, and the car began to burn. The soldiers got out and began to shoot, and another member of the crowd was wounded.

At this point, however, the soldiers from the burning armored car abandoned the vehicle and ran and hid in other tanks. People were afraid of an explosion and started to pour water on the armored car. The victims were removed in ambulances and police cars.

The soldiers stood holding their automatics to stave off the crowd. They were afraid of being lynched. Several Russian deputies went into the tunnel, calmed the crowd, and arranged for the military vehicles to leave on the condition that they drive away from the White House.

AS PERFILYEV WALKED back and forth in the vice president's suite of offices on the fourth floor, the defense staff received constant information about the movement of armor toward the White House. Yazov had delegated some of his authority to General Mikhail Moiseyev, the chief of the general staff. Perfilyev had a close friend call an assistant to Moiseyev and ask if he could call the general. The answer was positive and Perfilyev went in to see Rutskoi and told him that he could be in touch with Moiseyev. Rutskoi, however, waved his hand and said, "That's useless, he won't speak with me."

To everyone's surprise, however, Moiseyev called Rutskoi. The general tried to calm him, and said that the troops now moving in and around Moscow would not try to seize the White House. Rutskoi replied that if the troops did attack, there would be a bloodbath but that he, for his part, would do everything possible to avoid a battle.

Stolyarov joined Perfilyev in Rutskoi's office, and Rutskoi and

Perfilyev waited while Stolyarov called Yanaev. By this time, the noise of tanks on Kalinin Prospekt was already audible, and the three men began to hear shots. There were also reports of the landing of airborne troops at the Kubinka airfield outside of Moscow as well as the movement of the Kantemirov Division down Kutuzovsky Prospekt in the direction of the parliament building.

"You must stop the movement of troops," Stolyarov told Yanaev.

"There are no troop movements," Yanaev replied.

Perfilyev next tried to call the KGB. Kryuchkov did not answer and his deputy did not answer.

By 2 a.m., the reports had become so menacing that Perfilyev tried to speak again with Moiseyev. When he reached Moiseyev's assistant, the latter said that the chief of the general staff was relaxing at his dacha. Perfilyev asked for the dacha's number. "I'm under orders not to disturb Moiseyev and not to give anyone his telephone number," the assistant said. He then nonetheless gave him the number, and Stolyarov called Moiseyev.

"Tell him the tanks are already moving in," Perfilyev told Stolyarov. "Let him hear what's going on." Stolyarov then extended the cord as far as possible and placed the phone near the window. It was possible to hear howls and cries and shots because the window was slightly open.

"Do you hear that they are already killing people," Stolyarov said. "Stop the tanks immediately."

Moiseyev said, "Good," and then hung up.

There was a torturous pause. The defenders began to draw the venetian blinds and turn out the lights throughout the building. Rutskoi gave an order to the guards to open fire without warning if KGB officers in plainclothes entered the building. There was a report from the Defense Council that the KGB's 103rd Airborne Division had begun moving down Kalinin Prospekt in the direction of the White House and that three helicopters were being prepared in order to land paratroopers.

Perfilyev asked Rutskoi for a weapon. Rutskoi smiled.

"Your chief weapon is your head and your pen," he said. The two men then parted.

Rutskoi turned on a lamp which he had taken off his desk and put it on the floor. He then sat down alone at his desk and, with an automatic pistol in his hand and an ordinary pistol on the table, waited for the attack.

Perfilyev walked down the darkened corridors. He noticed that there were still an unusual number of lights on in the apartment buildings along the river.

At the entrance to the vice president's wing, the exhausted defenders had fallen asleep. They sat bent over with their automatic weapons cradled in their arms. Perfilyev walked past them and thought that in minutes there would be an attack. At the first sound of shots, he would wake them. All of Rutskoi's civilian aides were awake.

Perfilyev went to his office and called his mother-in-law. "We have twenty minutes to an attack," he told her. "It's doubtful that we'll all survive. In any case, take care of my family."

IN THE SQUARE OUTSIDE, there was a deathly calm. At about 2:40 a.m., Radio White House went off the air and was silent for the next twenty minutes. Shortly afterward, Eduard Shevardnadze, the former foreign minister, wearing a warm-up suit, appeared and waved to the people and shook hands before entering the White House. A short time later, Father Gleb Yakunin, a member of the Russian parliament, also appeared and told the defenders, "God is with us."

At 3 a.m., Emma fell into conversation with two elderly men. "This is not the end," she said, "the behavior of these fascists is unpredictable. They acted without a reserve option and they have everything to lose."

"They've already lost," said one of the men. "They were not decisive enough to attack the building right away. Now it's too late for them. But what's important is that we are here and for the right cause."

IN THE DEFENSE COUNCIL, attention narrowed to the behavior of two units: the KGB operations group in the Mir Hotel across the street from the White House, and the special KGB brigade that was based in the outlying region of Teply Stan.

Gennady Yankovich, who was in charge of intelligence-gathering, realized that with the apparent collapse of support for the coup among the leaders of the army, the coup leaders' only hope was to make use of the special KGB detachments that were still presumed to be loyal to the conspiracy. The KGB brigade at Teply Stan was more than sufficient to put an end to resistance at the White House; it was composed of experts in hand-to-hand combat, equipped with bulletproof vests, tear gas grenades, and other specialized equipment. What had focused the council's attention on the brigade was a call from two of the group's members to the White House earlier in the day, in which the two officers told the defenders that the KGB brigade had been ordered to launch an attack on the building at about 3 a.m.

When this information was received, a group of deputies was sent to Teply Stan to talk to the members of the unit to try to depropagandize them. To the surprise of the deputies, the commanding officers allowed them complete access to the members of the brigade. The deputies told the men that the coup was unconstitutional and directed against the people, and that the people were right to defend their elected representatives.

The Defense Council had no way of evaluating the deputies' success in influencing the members of the brigade.

Shortly before the time of the expected attack, the brigade left its basing area and began moving in the direction of the White House.

When the brigade arrived at Profsoyuznaya Street in southwest Moscow, however, it came to a stop. For more than an hour, Yankovich had no information. Finally, at about 4:30, as dawn began to break over Moscow, Yankovich received a call from friends of some of the men in the KGB brigade: The brigade was not going to attack the White House, the men were refusing to carry out the order to attack. Yankovich realized now that nothing was working for the coup leaders, and for the first time, he began to relax.

AT JUST ABOUT the same time, Emma Bruk left the area in front of the White House and walked up Devyatinsky Lane, past the new American embassy building. A passerby told her that Echo Moscow, the local radio station that had rebroadcast the transmissions of Radio White House, was back on the air.

Emma passed rows of American cars that had been left in the middle of the street as a tank barrier, and then turned onto the Sadovoye Ring Road and began walking in the direction of Vostaniye Square. Dawn was breaking, and Emma saw that it was another gray morning. In the distance, there was a mass of dark tanks on the square. Suddenly, a man approached and started shouting at her: "Leave the ring road. This isn't a game. There is a war. This is blood. You can die here."

Emma became frightened but, looking around, saw no sign of danger. Then she noticed that the tanks on Vostaniye Square had turned their lights on. They then began moving away from the White House in the direction of Mayakovsky Square.

As she watched the tanks leaving, Emma felt an inexplicable wave of relief. She went home at 5 a.m. and told her twelve-year-old stepdaughter, "I think it's over."

WHEN YELENA RAISKAYA arrived at the scene of the shooting on the ring road, there was terrible shouting. People were running into the tunnel in a state of near-hysteria. Soldiers were waving their automatic weapons to hold off the crowd, and several Russian deputies were shouting into megaphones, "Don't shoot, don't shoot." With the demonstrators ready to hurl rocks at the soldiers and the soldiers prepared to fire again on the crowd, the deputies shouted that they would remove the barricades so that the tanks could leave.

Moments later, dozens of men began to push away the concrete barriers, and the tanks and armored cars were given Russian flags so they would not be touched. As the tanks left, Yelena walked to the White House, which was now ringed with barricades. There was a mood of controlled panic as people repeated reports that the KGB Vitebsk Division, known as cutthroats, was on its way to the White House. It would require very little for them to seize the building.

Suddenly, Bella Kurkova came on Radio White House. "The attack is beginning," she said. "An enormous number of tanks are headed this way."

The announcement was followed by silence and then by the sound of shooting in the area of the American embassy. Yelena was certain that the attack had begun.

She then had an eerie experience. A group of people were listening to Echo Moscow, but the normally reliable radio station began giving false information. It broadcast that waves of tanks had attacked the White House, that the building had fallen and that many people had been killed. Yelena realized immediately that she was listening not to Echo Moscow but to a KGB imitation complete with announcers who mimicked the usual announcers' voices.

An hour or so later, the real Echo Moscow was back on the air and announcing that the Taman and Kantemirov divisions were withdrawing from Moscow. For the first time, it seemed to Yelena that the danger was receding.

At 6 a.m., Yelena left for home. She got in a cab with an older man who was also leaving the area.

"Is there any chance," she asked, "that we can win?"

"I think there is," said the man.

"I think there isn't," said the cabdriver.

Yelena returned home, still not sure what was happening. At 11 a.m., when Echo Moscow began broadcasting the proceedings of the Russian parliament, she was sure that it was over.

ON THE MORNING of August 21, Sergei Latishev was still not convinced that the crisis was past. It was pouring rain, and the crowd outside the White House was bigger than it had been the night before. Some fires were burning, others had been extinguished, and people talked constantly about the shooting at the tunnel on the Sadovoye Ring Road. How many had died? How many had been wounded? How had it happened?

The Afghan veterans who had stood guard at the building were exhausted after the long night but unwilling to count on success. Sergei tried to analyze the situation and came to the conclusion that the putschists had been afraid of the international consequences of an attack on the crowd. Yet with every passing hour, their indecisiveness led them to disaster.

The first sign that the crisis was really over was when the Russian parliament started holding its session. Sergei was still on guard at the twentieth entryway when the session began to be broadcast over White House radio, and, unable to hear, he left his post to walk closer to one of the loudspeakers. First, the deputies rescinded the acts of the coup committee. Khasbulatov made a speech and some of the deputies accused him of not properly formulating a phrase about the illegality of the committee. Other deputies began asking what difference it made.

As he stood in the rain, it seemed to Sergei that there was something comic yet also moving about what was going on in that hall, which he was now guarding with his fellow veterans. This is our legal parliament, he thought. Had we had such a parliament ten years ago, there might never have been an Afghan war.

In the middle of the afternoon, Khasbulatov announced that a plane with members of the Russian government, including Rutskoi, was on its way to the Crimea to meet with Gorbachev. He asked the defenders to remain at their posts until the next morning to help guard against provocations. Sergei and the other veterans decided to stay. All day the news got better. The last military units left Moscow and there were reports that the coup leaders were under arrest. At 5 p.m., the evening edition of *Izvestiya* went on sale with the banner headline, "Reaction Has Failed."

Finally the session of the parliament began to be broadcast on Russian television, which was back on the air.

With this, Sergei knew that the danger had passed. The debate in the parliament was being watched by the entire country. He was free to go home.

2

The Ideology

Marxism is omnipotent because it is true.
—*V. I. Lenin*, Collected Works

LIKE MANY OTHERS in our generation, I was brought up under socialism and without belief in God," wrote a young mother to *Pravda*, January 18, 1988. "One might say that socialism and its ideals were our God. . . . As a result of the policy of glasnost and unrestrained criticism, the idea of socialism has, to some extent, been discredited. I cannot speak for everyone, but my faith has been shaken."

An agricultural economist in Moscow first learned about the crimes of the Stalin era in the 1970s by reading Western sources during his frequent trips abroad. But he kept in mind that he was reading the writings of "enemies." After the history of the Stalin period began to appear in Soviet publications, however, he suddenly told his friend Anatoly Strelyani, "All our history, all our system is a disgrace. If I were younger, I'd turn in my party card. What kind of socialism, what ideals, can you talk about after this?"

"Everything in life that I believed in," wrote Sergei Chapaev, a Communist Party member for nineteen years, in a letter to *Pravda*, "has turned to dust. Nothing sacred has been left. Stalin, Molotov, Voroshilov . . . We sang songs for them. We believed in them more than in ourselves. And we taught others to believe. How can I look others in the eye? My whole life turns out to have been useless."

An Aeroflot stewardess in her thirties told her friend Alexander Lyakin, a religious dissident, "With all these publications, it is simply awful to live. I don't see after all this where is the way. There is only darkness and horror. When I see Bovin and Zorin [veteran Soviet propagandists] defending perestroika, I want to throw a brick through the television set."

"They destroyed in us belief and truth," said Tanya Zavyaskin, a party member and warden in the Sailor's Silence Prison. "Now we don't believe in anything and are convinced that there is no truth."

BY 1988, a crisis of faith began to seize the Soviet Union. The reason was the policy of glasnost, which, permitting for the first time an increasing flow of truthful information, undermined the core of the Soviet system, the Soviet ideology.

Mountains of books have been written about Marxism-Leninism, the Soviet ideology, many of them extolling its analysis of capitalism or its description of how to seize power. The essential characteristic of the ideology, however, is that it makes it possible for man to disregard that part of his nature which is irrational, and hence instinctual, by presenting a logical, self-contained view of the universe that systematically excludes the presence of God.

The attempt to eliminate God has its roots in the radically negative, demystifying intellectual tendencies of the Enlightenment. The effort was successful in Russia in part because organized religion had grown weak. "The churches," Carl Jung wrote, "stand for traditional and collective convictions, which in the case of many of their adherents are no longer based on their own inner experience but on unreflecting belief, which is notoriously apt to disappear as soon as one begins thinking about it. The content of belief then comes into collision with knowledge, and it often turns out that the irrationality of the former is no match for the ratiocinations of the latter."

The ontological core of Marxism is the theory of dialectical materialism, which holds that everything that exists is matter in motion. There is no spirit, no God, and no soul. Consciousness is an attribute of highly developed matter. Matter is characterized by the "unity of opposites," the contradictory aspects of an object that nonetheless presuppose each other.

The theory of dialectical materialism, which posits a purely mechanical universe in which everything is perpetually turning into its opposite, represented a radical rejection of the religious worldview, which assumed that earthly life derives its meaning from a transcendent source, and it eliminated the basis for human rights because it deprived the individual of any other worldly point of reference.

Against the background of this featureless universe, it was necessary to establish a source of meaning, and this was accomplished in the theory of historical materialism, the ideology's "revealed truth."

In the theory of historical materialism, Marx and Engels asserted that history is shaped through the material transformation of the economic conditions of production, which leads to a conflict between the forces and relations of production, inspiring a sharpening of the class struggle that is resolved at each stage with the victory of the most progressive class. Slave society was succeeded by feudal society, feudal society by capitalist society, and, with the victory of the working class, capitalist society is to be succeeded too—by a classless society in which private property will be abolished and there will be a perfect democracy, with complete unanimity and unprecedented wealth.

The contribution of Lenin was, maintaining the Marxist framework, to stress the role of a disciplined Communist Party as the vanguard of the working class. In this way, the party instead of the workers became the protagonist of history, and the aspiration of Communists to absolute power was linked to a universal theory making it possible for Communist regimes to claim for themselves the infallibility and inevitability of history itself.

Marxism opposed to a world created by God which held out the hope of paradise after death a universe without God which promised heaven on earth. Leninism attached to Marxism a technique for seizing power. Taken together, the combination of a new theory of reality and a technique for "realizing" that reality had a powerful psychological effect. It was an all-encompassing worldview. Claiming to be completely rational, Marxism-Leninism was a device for mobilizing all of a people's resources—spiritual, emotional, and political— toward the creation of a Communist regime, the establishment of which became the crowning achievement of a godless religious faith.

FOR DECADES, Marxism-Leninism held millions in its grip. Then, in the mid-1980s, a crisis of faith began in the Soviet Union because, with the introduction of the policy of glasnost, the vulnerability of Marxism-Leninism started to be obvious.

A religion that reserves paradise for the next world is never put to an empirical test, but a secular religion like Marxism-Leninism, which promises paradise in this world, is forced constantly to remake reality in order to confirm its own legitimacy.

The Soviet regime dealt with this problem by using overwhelming force to create illusions. With the beginning of glasnost, however, the plausibility of this world of illusions was seriously undermined. For the first time, Soviet citizens began to sense the outlines of the real world, and as faith in the utopia promised by Marxism-Leninism began to fade, the ideological universe of their imagination ceased to make sense.

IN FACT, in the years before Gorbachev, the Soviet ideology was supported by an "imaginary city"—a hall of mirrors created at every level of Soviet society.

The nature of this imaginary city was reflected in what was taught in the schools. In history classes, the creation of the Soviet Union was presented as the seminal event of world history, and all events since 1917 were taken to confirm the inevitability of a world-wide Communist victory. In literature classes, the great nineteenth-century authors were said to have been looking for a positive ideal, thereby anticipating the Bolshevik Revolution.

In biology, students were taught the theories of Academic Oparin, whose work on early forms of life was said to have "disproved" the idea that life was created by an external force. The evolution of man from the apes was explained on the basis of Engels's theory in *The Dialectics of Nature*, which said that apes became men after they started using tools to survive. It was therefore labor and not reason that distinguished man from the animals. In chemistry courses, the laws of dialectics were said to be verified by the arrangement of elements in the Periodic Table.

Most important, however, were the moral laws. In the Marxist-Leninist universe, there was no absolute truth, only the truth of a particular class, with the highest truth being that of the working class, which was defended by the Soviet regime. The "class morality" of Marxism-Leninism was described by Lenin in a speech to the Komsomol on October 2, 1920, in which he said that Communists reject any morality based on "extra-human" and "extra-class" concepts.

For Communists, morality was entirely subordinated to the class, struggle, and anything was good that destroyed the old, exploiting society and helped to build a "new communist society."

The picture of the world inculcated in the classroom was reinforced by the operation of the press, which also depicted the Soviet Union as being on the way to becoming an earthly paradise. The chronicling of events that were typical of life in the real world—accidents, crime, corruption, and struggles for power—was replaced in the media by the reporting of the only news that could issue from paradise—an unending succession of anniversaries, harvest results, and unanimous votes of approval in the Supreme Soviet, the Soviet parliament. Any problems mentioned in the Soviet media were described as "shortcomings."

One of the places where information for Soviet citizens was processed was the headquarters, in downtown Moscow, of the Soviet news agency Tass.

One day, shortly after Valery Fyodorov began to work at Tass, a UPI story from New York arrived on the foreign desk. The story said that an American company had developed a new, higher-quality tire and, to advertise its breakthrough, was ready to replace older tires from a certain year of issue free of charge.

The duty editor decided to kill the story. The fact that it dealt with technical improvements and an offer to replace a product free made it a poor illustration of the abuses of capitalism. The duty editor's boss, the editor for American news, however, said, "We can use this in the service." He took the dispatch away and returned with an edited story five minutes later. "Release this for publication," he said.

"In the crafty capitalist market," the story read, "firms frequently offer low-quality products, aware that the buyers can not always judge which product is better. This is why a well-known American tire firm was recently forced to replace tires it had produced, which were of inferior quality. . . ." The story was sent out under the title "Deception of Buyer."

Tass did not claim to be a news organization in the usual sense but rather an agency that conveyed the "correct depiction" of events. When the strikes began in Poland in the summer of 1980, Tass was silent until the confrontation reached its most critical point. It then reported in a dispatch from Warsaw that Poland had one of the highest rates of potato production in the world. The article pointed out that Poland had been cultivating potatoes for three hundred years.

Tass's attitude to reality was reflected in its terminology, which was standard in newspapers and television throughout the Soviet Union. The Western states were "imperialist." The Socialist countries were "democracies." In Asia, the leading democracies were North Korea and Vietnam.

Usually, when the journalists at Tass began arriving in the morning, they spoke about what they had heard on the foreign radio stations the night before, treating these stations as completely reliable sources of information. They never, however, discussed the contents of the Soviet press, including their own work, which, by implication, they treated as unimportant.

At first, Fyodorov did not write articles of his own, but only corrected the language in dispatches from Asian countries. His first story grew out of a news agency report about prison conditions in the Fiji islands that he was asked to edit. The story said that prisons in Fiji were so comfortable that people preferred to spend time there than to be at liberty.

Fyodorov knew the story was not usable in its original form, and at first was not certain what to do with it. Yet after having worked at Tass for only a short time, the mentality of the Tass newsroom had begun to have an effect on him. As he started writing, he found to his surprise that he knew what was required of him, and in a short time the article was completed. In its edited form, the report said that life in Fiji had become so unbearable that people preferred to live in prison, and it mentioned, as among the reasons, inflation and unemployment, although Fyodorov had no idea whether these phenomena really existed there.

Fyodorov gave the article to the duty editor, who read it and, without asking where Fyodorov had gotten the information about inflation in the Fiji islands, said, "Well done. That's exactly what we need." As he walked back to his desk, Fyodorov felt satisfaction that was quickly followed by a wave of panic. "If I don't get out of here," he said to himself, "I'm going to go out of my mind."

LIKE TASS, *Moskovskaya Pravda* tried to give a "correct" version of the news. The paper contained the texts of government communiqués and telegrams, editorials on ideological subjects that made no point, and stories about economic achievements under headlines such as "Higher and Higher" and "Justified Satisfaction," which could just as easily have been used to describe the act of love. The heart of the paper, however, was its reports on the mood of the masses. Once, after Leonid Brezhnev had received his second Hero of Socialist Labor award, the reporter at *Moskovskaya Pravda*, who regularly reported on the mood of the workers, called a garage and asked the director what the workers thought of it.

"The workers approve of the award," the director said, and then provided the reporter with the names of several of his leading "shock workers."

The reporter then wrote out several statements of approval and pledges to overfulfill the plan in light of the award to Comrade Brezhnev, attributing the statements to the workers.

Moskovskaya Pravda also published articles about specific abuses, which were described as "shortcomings." The paper once decided to investigate complaints that it was impossible to buy milk at certain times in some Moscow stores. A reporter was told by the Moscow Directorate of Trade that the stores were not receiving enough milk from the factory. At the milk factory, he was told that there were not enough trucks. In fact, there were enough trucks but half of them were idle because of a lack of spare parts. On a normal newspaper, the reporter would have written about the consequences for efficient milk deliveries of unusable trucks, but this would have reflected on the state of the economy as a whole. Instead, he decided to attribute the problem to slack in the schedule of deliveries. To gain his honorarium, however, he needed to offer a solution, and so he suggested increasing deliveries to three times a day even though it was quite impossible to fulfill the schedule that was already in force. In the end, the article was published. The workers at the truck depot passed a resolution thanking *Moskovskaya Pravda* for its criticism and promised to correct the problem. And with that, the matter was quickly forgotten.

THE PROPAGANDA of the regime was organized to depict the Soviet Union as an earthly paradise and the West as a living Hell, and it gave citizens a false view of their own lives, which was often more appealing than the reality that they saw around them. It was then reinforced with the help of the constant manufacture of mirages.

.   .   .

MOSCOW, DECEMBER 1981

The city spreads out for miles beneath the Lenin Hills, a metropolis of wide avenues and brownish-yellow apartment blocks, crisscrossed by bands of forest and parks and divided by a meandering river, along whose banks factories pour smoke into an already hazy sky. It is only down below, on crowded streets full of bare shops and hortatory slogans, that one senses its uniqueness not as a physical phenomenon but as a state of mind.

Outwardly, the city is often grim and uninspiring. But appearances are misleading. Moscow exists on two levels: the real city, and the imaginary city, which is the product of its citizens' collective imagination.

The first aspect of the imaginary city is a bewildering assortment of false facades.

Cleaving the center of Moscow is Kalinin Prospekt, the broad boulevard lined on both sides by twenty-five-story skyscrapers. On one side of the street is a steel-and-glass arcade. On the other, a cinema and large stores. In the valley between the skyscrapers, streams of traffic move in both directions and official black limousines speed down the center lane. On an outdoor screen, scenes are shown from the latest Soviet movies, the films' green and red images splashed in the windows of the arcade.

The boulevard is clearly intended to resemble, but has little in common with, a grand avenue in the West. The sidewalks are filled with thousands of people, but the crowds are absolutely orderly. There are no kiosks, no hawkers, no graffiti, and almost no advertisements. The uniformed and plainclothes police are almost superfluous because the crowd is completely regimented. In fact, there is so little variation in the crowd that it almost seems as if the flow of pedestrians is regulated by some celestial counterpart of the same traffic police who monitor the flow of vehicles.

IN A CROWDED grocery store, a long line forms at the meat counter. It is the peak of the rush hour, but the salesgirl leaves to go to the toilet. When she returns ten minutes later, she resumes working at a glacial pace.

"Hurry up. We work all day. We're tired," people in the line begin shouting. Many of them bear the marks of some inner distress. Grim and unsmiling, often with puffy faces and bloodshot eyes, they look less like the builders of the twenty-first century than the survivors of a civil war.

"There are so many of you and only one of me," the salesgirl says.

The people in the queue continue complaining.

Finally, the salesgirl says, "Do you want to work in my place?" and then, taking off her apron and holding it in front of her, she adds, "Here it is. Come and work in my place."

Suddenly, a fresh supply of meat is rolled into the store on a little carriage and pandemonium erupts as customers grab for the meat, which a salesman is throwing onto the counter. He is indifferent to their struggling and behaves as if he is feeding animals.

At another counter there is a wave of panic as an announcement comes over the loudspeaker: "Cheese is finishing. Cheese is finishing."

"No milk, no cheese," says a woman in the queue. "Soon things will be as bad as in America."

Meanwhile, a male shopper who has been waiting half an hour is becoming impatient.

"How long can these queues go on?" he asks. "What kind of existence is this?"

"Never mind," an old woman replies, "the whole world is afraid of us."

In another line, shoppers inspect a frozen block of fish, trying to guess if the fish is rotten. They know from bitter experience that fish is often allowed to unfreeze, and if it spoils, is then refrozen and sold.

Not far away, an old washerwoman has noticed Clara Yakir, whom she has correctly identified as Jewish.

"Sarah, Sarah, Sarah," she says, "these Sarahs are always throwing papers on the floor."

"Do you know what Sarah is?" Clara asks. "Sarah is beauty, you disfigured hag, so shut up, plague, and do your job."

.   .   .

AS DARKNESS FALLS, the streetlights go on, the metro disgorges large crowds, and the bus stops begin to fill with people on their way home from work. The lights in the skyscrapers become visible in slanting rows on the ceilings of each floor, and the sound of traffic is more audible in the cold night air.

A queue forms to get into a café that is lit with red and violet lights from behind gauze curtains. Dinner consists of cutlets, macaroni, and "compot," flavored water with discolored apple bits in a brown film. In the main hall, the clatter of tin knives and forks combines with the sound of loud slurping. Occasionally, a fight breaks out as one of the waitresses, anxious to minimize her workload, refuses to allow a group of patrons to sit at an empty table. Soon, the scene becomes even more depressing as, seated in even rows, the diners eat single-mindedly, their cheeks bulging, chewing visibly, their concentration broken only by occasional attempts at rudimentary conversation. Watching this scene, it is hard to avoid the impression that if labor created man out of an animal, it was the achievement of communism to have changed him back again.

At this hour, messages are flashed on the outdoor movie screen. The first urges passersby to insure their household goods. The next advises pedestrians to cross only at the traffic light. This is followed by a warning to drivers to obey the speed limit and a warning against fire hazards followed by a drawing of someone smoking in bed. The cycle is repeated throughout the evening.

As the crowds of people filling the sidewalks hurry to catch buses or do late shopping, they pass florist shops that sell only plastic flowers and lines of people waiting to get into restaurants where the tables are half empty upstairs. Overhead, a model supersonic airplane circles an illuminated globe advertising international air tickets that passersby cannot buy.

IN A NEARBY APARTMENT, Arkady Shapiro has fallen into conversation with his parents' cleaning woman, an old crone in her eighties from a village outside Moscow.

"What was life like in Russia before the Revolution?" Arkady asked.

"Oh, it was very good," she said, as she mopped up in the kitchen. "Everyone had their own farm and there was plenty to eat."

"Was there meat?"

"Yes, little son, lots of meat."

"Butter?"

"Oh, yes, lots of butter."

"And every farmer had his own plot of land?"

"Yes, little son, the land was good and every farmer worked his own land."

"Grandmother, do you think life was better then than it is now?"

The old lady stopped mopping the floor and looked at Arkady in a way he had never seen before.

"No, little son," she said, "it's better now."

"But if before the Revolution everyone had their own land and there was plenty of meat and butter, how can you say that life is better now?"

"Now, the Americans surround us with their bases," she said, looking at Arkady intently. The lines in her simple face did not change and there was no change in her tone of voice, but for the first time in all the years he had known her, Arkady thought he saw a cunning gleam in her eyes.

BESIDES FALSE FACADES like Kalinin Prospekt, Moscow contained fictitious institutions organized, like the facades, to give the impression that the Soviet Union had realized the ideology's promise of perfect democracy.

Of these institutions, the most pervasive were the organized political rituals—elections, *subbotniks*, and socialist competitions—which, although they served no practical purpose, were important because they forced Soviet citizens to participate in the creation of illusions.

THE ELECTIONS WERE ORGANIZED to demonstrate the Soviet people's civic consciousness. About six weeks before the election was to take place, "agitators," who were assigned to each precinct, canvassed the area to register changes since the last election—who had died or moved away, gone into the army or returned from a labor camp. In each apartment, the agitator asked if anyone in the household was ill, in case there was a need to bring the ballot box to an apartment.

On election day, the agitators were waiting at the polling place to check off each voter in their precinct. In the hall, there was usually a modest buffet and patriotic marches were played on a scratchy record player. At the end of the room was a bust of Lenin surrounded by red flags and two ballot boxes for voting. The ballots instructed the voter to leave only the name of the candidate for whom he was voting. They then listed only one name.

The elections, in which all voters approved a single candidate, were said to demonstrate "genuine" versus "formal" democracy. The "unanimity," however, was the product of compulsion.

ABOUT A WEEK before elections to the Supreme Soviet, an agitator visited Mikhail Baiserman, who had a record of refusing to vote, and asked cheerfully, "Well, will we vote or won't we?"

"My neighbors will but I won't," Baiserman said.

"Why?" the agitator asked.

"I haven't voted for years," Baiserman said.

"Maybe you're dissatisfied?"

"I'm completely satisfied, but I won't vote."

A short time later, Baiserman was called in by the boss at his factory. "The party secretary tells me that you are refusing to vote. You have a good record, you're a leading worker, you have a higher education, yet you refuse to vote. Is there something you don't understand?"

"I understand everything," Baiserman said, "but I still won't vote."

"I'm asking you man to man, not as a boss, why don't you want to vote?"

"Why should I? My vote won't change the outcome."

"You know," said Baiserman's boss, "I was hoping you would come up with something more original."

Baiserman smiled slightly.

"Let's speak frankly," his boss continued. "I was called in by the party secretary and told, 'Your worker is refusing to vote, take measures.' Now I have to give an accounting."

Baiserman understood his boss's dilemma. If he continued to refuse to vote, his boss would be blamed for poor educational work in the collective.

"All right," Baiserman said finally, "I agree. Tell the party secretary that I've thought it over and that I'll go and vote."

Baiserman's boss sighed with relief. Baiserman went to the

polling station and took a detachable coupon, an indication that he intended to vote in another place.

IRINA McCLELLAN, the wife of Woodford McClellan, an American professor, who had been denied an exit visa for nine years, was also in no mood to vote. Shortly before the 1980 elections, there was a knock on the door.

"Mrs. McClellan?" asked the agitator.

"That's me."

"Are you going to vote?"

"No, I won't vote," Irina said. She explained that she had been trying to emigrate to join her husband and that she had been continually refused permission without an explanation.

The agitator explained that the candidate for deputy from Irina's district was Brezhnev himself.

"My story has been connected with Brezhnev," she said. "I wrote him hundreds of letters and never got a reply."

"But how do you know that that was the fault of Brezhnev?"

"I'm waiting for a visa. If I get a visa before the elections, I'll come and vote for everyone, for Mr. Brezhnev and even for you."

Three weeks later the agitator called again and asked Irina if she had gotten her visa. "No," she said, "and I don't expect it before the election."

"So you won't vote?"

"No," she said, "I won't vote."

On election day, there was a knock on the door. "You won't go?" the agitator asked when Irina opened it.

"No," she replied, trying not to show annoyance, "I won't go."

BESIDES THE ELECTIONS, Soviet citizens took part in *subbotniks* and socialist competitions, in which they supposedly demonstrated their "enthusiasm." *Subbotniks* were days of "voluntary" work for the state, nominally a gift of labor from the workers, and they could be announced by the management of any Soviet workplace at any time. The Leninist *subbotnik*, on or about April 16, was held in every enterprise in the Soviet Union.

A technician at the research institute of the vegetable conservation industry asked the head of his laboratory if he could be excused from the all-Union Leninist *subbotnik.*

"You cannot be excused from the *subbotnik*," his boss said, "because your appearance there is strictly voluntary."

"You don't understand," the technician said, "it really is difficult for me to attend."

"That's your business," the head of the laboratory said.

The technician went next to the secretary of the Communist Party organization at the institute. "I am looking," he said, "for clarification of my social status in the event that I do not attend the *subbotnik.*"

The party secretary said that, of course, attendance at a *subbotnik* was voluntary. Then, with the help of winks and hints, he gave the technician to understand that if he did not attend, his record for social activism in the collective—less than brilliant to begin with—would be negatively affected.

SOVIET CITIZENS also participated in socialist competitions, in which they "voluntarily" "competed" with one another to increase production. At the beginning of the year, each citizen wrote out "socialist obligations" in his office or factory. The workers then "strove," individually and collectively, to be the first to fulfill these promises.

In the Moscow chemical factory where Sonia Isakova worked, the pledges were collected by the head of the factory trade union. "Girls," she said, "let's write our socialist obligations. I'll give you half an hour."

The women in the sulfuric acid shop each wrote roughly the following: "In connection with the 64th anniversary of Soviet power, I pledge to help produce five tons of sulfuric acid over the plan target by the end of the year, to raise my ideological level by attending lectures on the works of Lenin, and to maintain labor discipline." Similar pledges were organized in the other departments until every worker had signed a pledge.

Each worker was then matched with another worker, with whom she was said to be competing, and each department was matched with another department. Accounting competed with financial, engineering with the constructor's bureau. The shop that produced sulfuric acid competed with the shop that produced potash. As for the factory as a whole, it competed with a factory in Kazakhstan.

The results of the contests were tabulated by trade union representatives, who gave free rein to their imaginations, inventing production, ignoring absences, and crediting workers with efforts to improve their ideological level that never took place. For example, seven hundred employees of the chemical factory were signed up for courses in Marxism-Leninism. When a class was held, three attended. Nonetheless, the trade union representative reported that all the employees were present, creating problems for the factory in Kazakhstan, which had only five hundred employees.

FOR AS LONG AS IT LASTED, the hall of mirrors created by the regime had a mesmerizing effect. Everywhere the individual turned—in the newspapers, radio, and television; in parliament; at his place of work; and in public meeting halls and schools—he was confronted with false facades confirming the veracity of a single point of view. Free expression ceased to be regarded even as a human possibility, and ideas which could not be expressed were never formulated, as individuals, seeking shelter in conformity, fell back into stereotyped and self-protective patterns of thinking.

When glasnost was inaugurated in 1986, however, information began to become available which contradicted the official version of reality. Each piece of truthful information in the press, such as the true Soviet infant mortality rate, came as a shock against the background of years of official lying. The newspapers soon began to call the Brezhnev years the "period of stagnation."

By 1988, as the policy of glasnost gained force, all aspects of the false reality created by the regime started to come undone—its false version of history, its false depiction of contemporary reality, and the countless mirages created to give to both citizens and foreigners the impression that Soviet citizens were unanimous in support of the regime.

Almost overnight, Moscow seemed to become resigned to a reduced metaphysical status. Slogans disappeared from the sides of buildings. The portraits of Politburo members, including Gorbachev, became less visible on the streets. Buildings went unpainted; drunks and invalids who had long been sequestered by the police appeared once again in public, and refuse started to pile up in the yards. The fictitious utopia created by the regime was revealed in all its artificiality, and faith in the ideology collapsed.

3

Gorbachev and
the Party

"Who art thou, then?"
"Part of that power which eternally wills evil and eternally works good."

—*Goethe*, Faust

AUGUST 23, 1991. A rainy, overcast day. There was an atmosphere of growing panic in the headquarters of the Communist Party Central Committee on Old Square, once the epicenter of Soviet power. As top officials wandered the corridors in a daze, secretaries and messengers continued to work. Piles of documents stamped "top secret" and "absolutely secret" accumulated on desks. Outside, officials leaving the building were being forcibly searched, and an angry crowd carrying Russian flags was demanding a war crimes trial for the Communist Party.

In the international department on the sixth floor, a meeting was being held to decide whether to exclude Vice President Yanaev from the party for his role in the coup. One official said Yanaev should be removed because the coup was a blow to ordinary Communists who knew nothing about it. Another official, however, said, "We should leave Yanaev and the coup leaders in the party and exclude all of you, because they are the real Communists and you are betraying them." In the end, the meeting voted to bar Yanaev.

Suddenly, an announcement was broadcast over the public address system: "Everyone must vacate the building within ninety minutes. The Moscow City Council cannot guarantee the safety of anyone who remains in the building for more than ninety minutes. . . ."

The hall in the international department emptied immediately. Many of those who had been judging Yanaev returned to their offices and began searching through their files for anything that might incriminate them. Valentin Falin, head of the international department, issued an order to destroy all secret documents, but as officials brought armloads of files into the office of the secretariat, custodians warned that they could not be burned because the crowd in the square would attack the building if smoke started to appear over the roof.

Soon, officials were lined up at shredders, destroying documents indiscriminately. Shouting matches broke out in the queues as the metal file holders caught in the machines.

Falin finally succeeded in reaching Gorbachev by phone. He could hear the shouts of the crowd outside and the sound of breaking glass.

"Are you in agreement with this action?" he asked.

"Yes," Gorbachev replied.

"Are you aware that in the safes of the Central Committee there are documents which are extremely delicate and which affect you?"

"I know," Gorbachev said, and then, raising his voice, added, "Don't you understand the position I am in?"

Falin put down the phone and turned to a subordinate.

"He's cooperating with the democrats to save his own skin."

THE SCENE in the building on Old Square had been in preparation since April 1985, when Gorbachev gained power. Founded to realize one illusion, the party lost power, in the course of six years, because it fell victim to another one—that Communist rule could be preserved without force.

Reform had been discussed in the Soviet Union for almost thirty years, but the possible benefits of change had always been thought not to outweigh the anticipated risks. By the mid-1980s, however, three factors began to persuade Soviet leaders that reform would have to be attempted: changes in military technology, the ideas of Communist "liberals," and the failure of efforts at modernization.

Military technology. On October 27, 1982, Leonid Brezhnev made his last major speech before an audience of high-ranking military officers in the Kremlin. Months earlier, Israeli pilots, flying American F-15 and F-16 jets and taking advantage of the latest advances in micro-electronics and computer technology, had destroyed eighty-one Syrian MiG-21 and MiG-23 jets over the Bekaà Valley in Lebanon without losing a single plane. The shock of that defeat resonated in the Soviet Union.

"The Central Committee undertakes all measures in order to satisfy the demands of the armed forces," Brezhnev said, "and we expect you to be worthy of that concern. . . . American imperialism has begun a new phase of the political, ideological, and economic attack against socialism. To lag behind is unacceptable. The . . . battle readiness of the armed forces should be even higher. We must take into account the latest developments . . . in the area of military technology. . . ."

On March 23, 1983, President Ronald Reagan appeared on television in the United States and described the program for the Strategic Defense Initiative (SDI), which would make it possible to intercept Soviet ICBMs in space. The effect of this announcement was to convince many Soviet leaders that in order to compete with the West in military technology, Moscow would have to undertake major reforms.

The Communist liberals.   The ruling elite in the Soviet Union appeared to be monolithic, but in fact it contained a number of officials who held liberal views. The "liberals" were not anti-Communist, but they were anti-Stalinist. They took the view that Marxism-Leninism could be applied more humanely. They argued that Communists could dispense with both repression and censorship without losing power. Had the Soviet Union not begun to face a systemic crisis, it is unlikely that the liberals would ever have gained importance, but as the need to introduce reforms began to be accepted, their views received a hearing because they seemed to offer an ideological alternative within the party.

An early sign that the liberals would gain influence was the promotion in August 1985 of Alexander Yakovlev, the director of the Institute of World Economy and International Relations (IMEMO) and former ambassador to Canada, to the post of head of the department of propaganda in the Central Committee. Yakovlev illustrated the attitudes of Communist liberals during a speech at the Higher

Party School in October. He was asked, "What will we do if the West begins to direct television broadcasts to this country?"

He said: "We'll watch."

Failed attempts at modernization. When Gorbachev became the Soviet leader in 1985, he attempted to improve efficiency through traditional methods, including a drive for discipline, campaigns against alcoholism and illegal revenues, and a new system of state inspection. In May 1986, a new law made it possible to prosecute anyone who received unregistered income outside his official employment. In Volgograd, the authorities launched a "tomato war," smashing the backyard greenhouses that were kept by housewives and pensioners and had, until that time, supplied the city with a large part of its fresh vegetables. By the end of 1986, however, as its self-defeating character became evident, enforcement of the law was dropped.

Gorbachev also introduced a new system of state inspection that gave independent boards wide powers to reject inferior production. At first, *gospriemka* was praised for encouraging quality, but since workers were paid on a quota basis, the sharp increase in rejected production lowered workers' pay and created turmoil in the factories. The boards were soon corrupted and coopted by factory management and, under pressure from the ministries, quietly dropped.

Perhaps the most dramatic measure was the struggle against alcoholism. The supply of vodka and wine was cut, the hours of sale reduced, and the price of alcohol raised. At first, worker absenteeism and accidents declined. But in the course of a few months, during which time thousands of people poisoned themselves drinking eau de cologne, deodorant, aircraft fuel, and other alcohol surrogates, the population began producing liquor on its own. The proportion of legal to illegal vodka production, which had been two to one in favor of legal production, shifted to two to one in favor of illegal production, with no decline in consumption and an enormous loss in revenue for the state.

BY THE MID-1980s, the failure to improve economic performance coupled with the technological challenge from the West had created a deep sense of concern in the Soviet Union. In this situation, the ideas of Soviet "liberals" seemed to offer a new basis for policy. For the first time, reform was a historical possibility, and what was more important, Gorbachev himself accepted the need for reform.

THE CHANGES BEGAN SLOWLY. In May 1985, Gorbachev said in a speech in Leningrad that it would be necessary to "reconstruct [*perestroit*] society."

Less than a year later, he inaugurated the policy of glasnost ("publicity"), which was reflected in articles in the press on crime and economic inefficiency. Not everyone liked the idea of glasnost. Some reacted to articles about prostitution by saying, "Do you see where Gorbachev's democratization has led us? Now we have prostitution." Nonetheless, processes were beginning in society that were soon to have major importance.

ONE AFTERNOON IN MAY 1986, Victoria Moonblit was at her desk in the editorial office in Kishinev of *Molodezh Moldavia*, the youth newspaper, when a friend told her that a "lecturer from Moscow" had arrived and his talk would be starting in the nearby House of the Press in five minutes.

When Moonblit arrived in the assembly hall, she took a seat and listened as the lecturer described the political situation. "The American 'Star Wars' program," the lecturer said, "is intended not to attack us but to suffocate us economically. We can't keep up with it. This is a competition which we cannot win. If they want to beat us economically, they can do it because we are lagging behind. . . . "

At first, Moonblit did not believe what she was hearing. She looked around the hall and saw that other journalists were just as shocked as she was. The Soviet Union was always getting ready to "catch up and surpass." Moonblit had never heard the phrase "lagging behind" applied to the Soviet Union before.

"We have to change the image of the United States," the lecturer said. "Americans do not want to destroy the Soviet Union. The Americans are friendly as people to the Soviet Union. It is only isolated persons who want war with the Soviet Union and the arms race. We have always written that the United States is a degenerate country but, in fact, there are no fewer drug addicts in the Soviet Union than in the United States, and if the drug addiction in this country continues, soon the whole country will be addicts.

"The people should know that we are lagging behind. They should know that we are not only behind the West but also behind the advanced socialist countries like the GDR [German Democratic Republic]. Let's not hide the truth. The people should know the real situation."

Moonblit returned to her office badly shaken. She had an eerie feeling that this strange lecture signaled a change in the way the Soviet Union would be run that would have far-reaching consequences. In the weeks that followed, Moonblit learned that the same lecture had been given to other journalists as well as to teachers and members of the party apparatus. At the same time, instructions had come down to lower the tone of abuse in articles about Israel, and a set of conservative editors had been removed and replaced with people who were more liberal. There now could be no doubt that there had been a change in official policy.

AS PREPARATIONS were being made to expand the public's access to information, the leadership also began to consider releasing the country's approximately one thousand political prisoners, most of whom had been imprisoned for circulating information. To hold them while the regime itself was preparing to widen access to information made little sense and created problems for the nation's foreign policy. On December 16, 1986, Gorbachev called Andrei Sakharov, who was in exile in Gorky, and informed him that he would be allowed to return to Moscow. The release of Sakharov was followed by the freeing of hundreds of other political prisoners in 1987.

THE DISCUSSION OF REFORM, however, provoked a deep split in the party, many of whose leaders sensed that any liberalization would be dangerous. The depth of the antipathy was demonstrated after an unexpected speech by Boris Yeltsin at a Central Committee plenum on October 21, 1987.

The party leadership had split into two groups, referred to as "academics" and "practitioners." The practitioners, who were by far in the majority, argued that reform could lead to a loss of political control and end in catastrophe. The academics spoke about the need to liberate the economy from bureaucratic control and responded to warnings of catastrophe by saying that a catastrophe was looming in any case, and delay in introducing reforms would be fatal. The leader of the "practitioners," who included members of the Politburo with economic experience and party leaders in the provinces, was Yegor Ligachev, the boss of the secretariat. The "academics" were principally members of academic institutes and persons with experience of international affairs. Their leader became Yakovlev.

During 1987, Gorbachev introduced several new laws. These allowed enterprises to dispose of above-plan production at market prices, legalized cooperatively held businesses, and made it possible for collective farmers to rent land. Party officials reacted to these reforms by sabotaging them. The law on enterprises was neutralized by the introduction of "state orders," which accounted for nearly 100 percent of production. Cooperatives were discouraged by making it difficult for them to obtain supplies. In rural areas, collective farmers who tried to rent land were denied equipment by the chairmen of their collective farms. Faced with this resistance, Gorbachev saw that he had to find a way to compel party officials to do his bidding, and he decided to take the first step in ending the party's monopoly of power by expanding glasnost to include attacks on the party apparatus itself.

At the June 1987 plenum, Yakovlev was named a full member of the Politburo, which put him on an equal footing with Ligachev. With Yakovlev's encouragement, some newspapers turned their attention to cases of party corruption. Soviet citizens noted with astonishment that articles began to appear in the papers that, only months earlier, would have led to the author's arrest. At the same time, the Yakovlev-aligned press began to publicize the activities of newly formed "informal organizations," thereby encouraging them. As a result, to the traditional totalitarian landscape were added independent social organizations and a partially liberated press capable of putting pressure on the party apparatus.

The new policy set off a bitter and protracted struggle in the leadership between liberals and conservatives, the first episode of which took place at the October 1987 plenum.

Gorbachev opened the plenum with a report on plans for the celebration of the seventieth anniversary of the October Revolution. Yeltsin was then given the floor and to the surprise of those present, he made an attack on Ligachev.

Yeltsin said that although the June plenum had been a signal to all party organizations, beginning with the secretariat, to "reconstruct" their work, nothing had changed in the work of either the secretariat or of "Comrade Ligachev." Bullying reprimands were still used by party bosses. Two years had passed since the party congress at which the goals of reform were outlined, but now the people were being told that it was necessary to wait an additional two or three years. But "after [another] two years, we may well find that in the eyes of the people, the party's authority has fallen drastically." In light of the lack of support from "certain quarters"—especially Ligachev—Yeltsin offered to resign.

YELTSIN'S CHALLENGE was particularly disturbing for the members of the Central Committee, because they had already been shocked by the first mass protests in the country, particularly a demonstration in Estonia.

At 11:30 a.m., on August 23, 1987, Tunne Kelam, a member of the Estonian nationalist underground responsible for sending information about nationalist activities to the West, strolled toward the town hall square in Tallinn through the narrow streets of the Old City.

A historian by profession, Kelam had worked for years as a night watchman at a poultry farm after being blacklisted in the 1970s for dissident activities. Now, for the first time, Estonian nationalists had made plans to hold a public demonstration in the square to mark the anniversary of the signing of the Molotov-Ribbentrop Pact. Both the Voice of America and Radio Liberty had broadcast that the demonstration would take place in the square at noon, and thirty U.S. senators had written to Gorbachev urging him not to use force against the demonstrators. Yet Kelam was apprehensive. There were reports that special KGB units were being moved into the city to deal with the demonstration.

After two days of rain, the sun had come out and the side streets leading to the square were filled with people. Some were preparing to demonstrate but others hesitated, trying to decide whether to take part.

As the town hall clock struck twelve, groups of people began walking into the square; still, large numbers remained behind in the shadows. To Kelam's surprise, however, the crowd entering the square from the side streets continued to grow, until it numbered almost two thousand. Heiki Ahonen, a newly released political prisoner, addressed the demonstrators. He told them that he had been warned there could be no meeting in the square, so he asked the crowd to follow him to Hirve Park in the Upper City.

The demonstrators then marched in the direction of Hirve Park under the eyes of the police, who did nothing to interfere. As the long stream of demonstrators filled Harju, the narrow street leading from town hall square to the Upper City, the demonstrators began taking out banners and placards that they had hidden in their clothes. The banners read: "JUDGE STALINIST CRIMES," "PUBLISH THE MOLOTOV-RIBBENTROP PACT," AND "FREE POLITICAL PRISONERS."

Kelam was certain the police would seize the signs and banners, but they took no action. Provocateurs circulated in the crowd, suggesting that the demonstrators begin shouting "Russians, get out," but they were ignored.

Finally, the demonstrators began to ascend to the Upper City, the site of Toompea Castle, the traditional Estonian seat of government. As they climbed, the red-tiled roofs and patinaed copper church spires of the Old City spread out beneath them. In Hirve Park, the demonstrators gathered in a valley that formed a natural auditorium. Tiit Madisson, a worker from Pärnu and a newly released political prisoner, was the first speaker. He said that the fate of Estonia had been sealed in the Molotov-Ribbentrop Pact's secret protocols, and in the spirit of glasnost the Estonian people should now be told what they contained.

The meeting lasted for almost an hour. Some in the audience applauded while others wept to be witnessing a scene they had never expected to live to see. Members of the crowd began to circulate petitions calling for the erection of a monument to the victims of Stalin-era repression in Estonia. But the fear was still great enough to prevent members of the crowd from trying to sing the Estonian national anthem. The meeting dispersed peacefully, and several hours later, Kelam met Ahonen and Arvo Pesti, another of the organizers, in the Old City. They agreed that the demonstration had been a success and that in the future much larger actions would be possible.

News of the demonstration in Estonia, however, shocked party leaders, in whom it rekindled a latent fear of the popular masses.

Yeltsin was a representative of that wing of the party which was making events like the demonstration in Estonia possible. For that reason, his speech did not rally others but gave Central Committee members the chance, by defending Ligachev, to show their total opposition to reform.

AFTER YELTSIN FINISHED SPEAKING, S. I. Manyakin, chairman of the Committee of Popular Control, went to the rostrum and praised Ligachev. So did Sergei Shalayev, chairman of the Soviet trade unions, and five oblast party first secretaries.

The eighth speaker, Georgy Arbatov, director of the Institute of the U.S.A. and Canada, said that Yeltsin deserved credit for courage, but that he had done great damage to the cause of perestroika. "It's probably impossible to correct it because circles from his speech are spreading."

Arbatov was followed by Nikolai Ryzhkov, chairman of the Council of Ministers, who accused Yeltsin of "driving a wedge in the Politburo" and praised Ligachev for "pursuing a correct line and doing enormous work."

Ryzhkov was a close associate of Gorbachev's, and his speech was a signal that Gorbachev realized antireform forces had coalesced around Ligachev, and that it was too early to try to remove him. Under the circumstances, the other members of the Politburo also began to affirm their support for Ligachev.

"There are no disagreements," said Vitaly Vorotnikov. "[I]t is necessary for all to know clearly and precisely that we have complete unity."

After a brief break, Viktor Chebrikov, the head of the KGB, spoke. He described Yeltsin's statements about the work of the secretariat as "slander."

"Suddenly, we hear talk of a split in the leadership," he said. "What groups are we talking about? You see, we are all before you. What groups are we talking about?"

Finally, it came Yakovlev's turn to speak. As Ligachev's principal rival, Yakovlev probably would have been glad to back Yeltsin, but in view of the strong support for Ligachev, he had no choice but to condemn Yeltsin. He said that the speech was "politically mistaken" and "inconsistent."

After Yakovlev, it was the turn of Eduard Shevardnadze, Yakovlev's close ally. Noting the balance of forces, Shevardnadze also denounced Yeltsin and defended Ligachev. He accused Yeltsin of "treason" before the party. "Who in this hall doubts that Comrade Ligachev is a person of crystalline purity, of high moral principles, devoted body and soul to the business of perestroika?" he said.

This was the first and last time that Shevardnadze would offer such praise of Ligachev.

Finally, Yeltsin was given the last word. "This has been a severe school, of course, for me," he said. "For my whole life, I have worked in those posts where there was a question of the trust of the Central Committee of the party. . . ." Yeltsin's speech was then declared mistaken by a unanimous vote of the plenum, and the question of his resignation was referred to the Politburo and the Moscow city Party Committee "in light of the discussion in the plenum."

That night, rumors about what had happened at the October plenum swept Moscow, and within a few days had swept the country. The party leaders, however, were not finished with Yeltsin.

On November 11, 1987, at a meeting of the Moscow city Party Committee chaired by Gorbachev, Yeltsin was removed from his post as head of the committee. Gorbachev described Yeltsin's speech as "politically immature, extremely confused and contradictory." He said the speech "did not contain a single constructive suggestion," was "demagogic," and showed "complete theoretical and political incompetence." He was followed to the rostrum by a long line of city party officials who also denounced Yeltsin. V. A. Zharov, deputy chairman of the Moscow City Council, said that Yeltsin's speech "was a stake on a split. Tomorrow we'll undoubtedly hear . . . from [those] . . . who try to make out of Boris Nikolaevich a Jesus Christ who suffered for his . . . devotion to socialist renewal and democracy."

In all, almost fifty party officials spoke and all of them denounced Yeltsin. Finally, Yeltsin rose to speak. He said, "I am very guilty before the Moscow party organization, very guilty before the city Party Committee, before you, certainly, before the bureau, and certainly, I am very guilty before Mikhail Sergeievich Gorbachev, whose prestige in our organization, in our country, and in the whole world is so high."

AS THE MONTHS PASSED, it became clear that, despite growing grass-roots activism in the country, glasnost would not be enough to push the party in the direction of reform. Accordingly, Gorbachev decided to create a new political system, which was inaugurated on March 25, 1989, with the first session of the Congress of People's Deputies.

Seeing that he could not confront Ligachev in the Central Committee, Gorbachev turned to less direct maneuvers. At a meeting of the Politburo on January 7, which took place in Ligachev's absence, major questions of personnel and economic and foreign policy were removed from the secretariat on the grounds that they were already being considered in the Politburo. The change, presented as an effort to end duplication, effectively emasculated the secretariat.

In the meantime, conservative party leaders became the targets of exposés in the press, and Yakovlev, who met with editors regularly, began to discuss the exposure of Stalin, which was capable of totally discrediting the party.

Slowly, a wave of puzzlement spread through the party apparatus. Most officials agreed that there was a need for "reform," which they tended to identify with greater efficiency. For the first time, however, they began privately to express the view that the policies of the general secretary were directed against the party.

In April 1988, Ligachev endorsed the publication, in the newspaper *Sovetskaya Rossiya*, of a letter from an unknown Leningrad teacher, Nina Andreeva, which defended Stalin. The letter, however, was subsequently denounced in *Pravda*, and the press, with Yakovlev's encouragement, began an anti-Stalin campaign that was to contribute fundamentally to the eventual collapse of the Soviet Union.

SUDDENLY NEWSPAPERS, magazines, and television began to publish all that was previously hidden about the crimes of the Stalin period. From the Bykovnya forest outside Kiev to the Kuropaty woods in Belorussia and the Kalitnikovsky Cemetery and Novospassky Monastery, the press described the Stalin-era burial grounds and began printing survivors' stories as well as the testimony of some of the executioners.

For thirty-five years, anyone trying to tell the full truth about the Stalin period risked arrest, but now the details of the acts of genocide carried out by the Soviet leadership against their own people began to be discussed everywhere. The horror was presented as a betrayal of "Leninism," but amid descriptions of parents taken away in the night and bodies heaved into pits by drunken executioners, the ideological mystique of the Soviet system was thoroughly destroyed.*

The Soviet regime had been organized like a church. Its purpose was to realize an idea, the utopia described in Marxist-Leninist ideology. As absurd as Communist ideology appeared from the outside, it identified each Soviet citizen as a participant in a great historical enterprise and thereby made him feel that his life had meaning, fulfilling, albeit falsely, a basic spiritual need. It was in the service of this enterprise that citizens were ready to sacrifice their fundamental rights and freedom.

Soviet people endured because they believed, and they believed because, with the help of terror that created an entire fictional universe, they were systematically misled. When glasnost and the anti-Stalin campaign demonstrated that the Soviet enterprise, instead of being glorious, was a senseless, barbaric fabric of atrocities that morality could not envisage or reason comprehend, citizens were no longer willing to accept their rightless situation and began to reject the Soviet system as such.

THE DEFEAT OF LIGACHEV and the anti-Stalin campaign, however, did not change the strong opposition of the party apparatus to reform. To protect himself and secure the future of the reform process, Gorbachev called a special party conference in June to change the political system. The conference, which opened on May 23, approved the creation of a democratically elected Congress of People's Deputies, which would be the country's "supreme organ of power."

In July, massive cuts were made in the industrial departments of the Central Committee, for years the absolute rulers of the vast, centralized economy. Party officials who remained were instructed not to "interfere" in the operations of the economy.

The changes approved at the Nineteenth Party Conference prepared the way for the election of March 1989. Of the 2,250 members of the new Congress of People's Deputies, 750 were to be named by

---

*Glasnost also led to the publication of the secret protocols of the Molotov-Ribbentrop Pact, first in the Baltic republics and then in the central press. The protocols provided for the Baltic states and the eastern part of a divided Poland, which included the fervently nationalist Western Ukraine, to be annexed by the Soviet Union. Their publication catalyzed the national movements in the Baltic republics, whose example inspired the growth of nationalism throughout the Soviet Union.

"social organizations," including the Communist Party. Candidates also had to be approved by party-controlled election commissions. As a result, in 384 of the 1,500 districts, party-supported candidates ran unopposed.

Despite the restrictive rules, however, a space had been created in a monolithic political system. Yeltsin ran for a seat in the new parliament as a deputy from Moscow and found that his public humiliation at the hands of the party had made him a martyr. He defeated Yuri Brakov, director of the Zil truck factory, by thirteen to one. In Leningrad, the entire party leadership was rejected. In the restive Baltic republics, victory went to newly formed popular fronts.

In all, of 2,250 deputies elected to the new body, 300 to 400 were identifiable reformers. Gorbachev had created a power base independent of the party without allowing for the emergence of an alternative political force.

BY THE SPRING OF 1989, Gorbachev was ready to dominate both the parliament and the party, but the change to a semi-parliamentary system severely weakened the party. Most party leaders were simply unequal to real political competition and this was demonstrated almost immediately at the first Congress.

GALINA STAROVOITOVA, the only Russian in the Armenian delegation, entered the Palace of Congresses in the Kremlin for the opening session of the Congress. An ethnographer with the Soviet Academy of Sciences, she was elected a deputy almost by chance. She almost certainly would not have been but for her reaction to the events in Sumgait in February 1988.

(ON FEBRUARY 20, the council in Nagorny Karabach, a region in Azerbaijan with a majority Armenian population, voted to annex the region to Armenia. It was the first time that deputies elected in a one-candidate Soviet election had voted independently on a political issue. Eight days later, an anti-Armenian pogrom broke out in Sumgait, an Azerbaijani city on the Caspian Sea near Baku.)

"Where can I get a bus to Sumgait?" asked Andrei Shilkov, a reporter for the samizdat journal *Glasnost*, of a man outside the Baku railroad station.

"The buses to Sumgait have been canceled," said the man. It was March 9 and the hands of the station clock stood at 11 a.m. "The only way to get to Sumgait is in a taxi."

Shilkov asked several taxi drivers to take him but they refused. One of them asked why he was so anxious to go there. Andrei, a tall, blond-haired Russian whose appearance made him an obvious outsider in Baku, said that he had just been released from a labor camp near Makhachkala and wanted to see a friend. "There are no taxis to Sumgait," said the man suspiciously. "You'd better try to hitch a ride."

Shilkov walked to the main road, where he flagged down a car. He asked to be taken to Sumgait but the driver at first refused. He then said that he would take Andrei to the outskirts of Sumgait for thirty rubles, ten times the usual fare. Shilkov finally agreed. He was let off a mile from the city and hitched another ride into town.

The weather was warm but it was a gray day. There were police barricades in front of the ivy-covered, five-story oblast party headquarters. On a nearby boulevard there was a line of tanks, and on each corner there were soldiers and police auxiliaries. Andrei approached a young Azerbaijani who, for a fee of twenty-five rubles, agreed to drive him around the city.

As they got into his car, the Azerbaijani pointed to an apartment building facing the boulevard. "You see that house," he said. "They threw a naked girl out the fourth-story window."

For the next few hours, Shilkov rode through Sumgait secretly taking pictures of soldiers and armored cars. Finally, the driver stopped at a shopping arcade and Andrei got out of the car. He walked up to a line of people who were standing in front of a booth where a woman was selling cakes and began to ask about the "events." The people in the line refused to talk to him. Residents had been warned over the local radio and television that anyone repeating "rumors" about recent events would be prosecuted for "anti-Soviet propaganda." In the Soviet context, "rumors" could mean anything not printed officially by the government. Andrei finally walked into a nearby courtyard where he noticed a Slavic-looking woman of about forty sitting on a bench.

"Excuse me," he said, "I'm a recent arrival. They say there were some events here, something happened."

The woman studied Andrei for a minute and then said, "I live in

an apartment building on the other side of the courtyard. It was horrible. I've lived in Sumgait nearly all my life, and it's hard to believe
that such things could happen. Now, if you say that in Moscow they
boil children and eat them, I'll believe it."

The woman said that she was a Bulgarian married to an Armenian. On the night of February 29, she heard screams and the crashing in of doors in her building. Her husband called from a nearby
town and warned her to lock and bolt her door. At about 10 p.m.,
she looked out the window and saw that a ten-year-old girl was being
thrown out of the fifth-floor window of the apartment building directly across the courtyard. The girl landed on some bushes and began to move; a group of men then threw a dresser out the window,
which landed on top of her. The next morning, she learned from
neighbors that an Azerbaijani gang had murdered the whole family.

For the rest of that March 1 day, the woman drew her shades
and stayed indoors. That evening, she heard screams and the sound
of breaking glass as a crowd in the courtyard began breaking windows. At one point, she looked out and saw that a pile of furniture
in the courtyard was on fire. Finally, on the morning of March 2, she
left her apartment and met another of her neighbors, an Azerbaijani
woman who worked in a maternity home and was nearly hysterical.

"I can't go to work," she said. "These bandits are murdering
pregnant women."

The Azerbaijani woman said a gang of Azerbaijanis entered the
maternity ward where she worked and held a knife on the doctor and
told him to show them the Armenian women. Fearing for his life, the
doctor gave them the names and they murdered the women by slit-
ting them open and then pulling out and killing their infants, which
were still alive.

The Bulgarian woman urged Andrei to leave Sumgait before
dark to avoid being caught by the 10 p.m. curfew.

ON THE MAIN ROAD, Andrei was picked up by an Azerbaijani
and his passenger, a woman who appeared Russian. As Andrei sat in
the backseat, they discussed the events. "Those scoundrels had too
much hashish," the Azerbaijani said to the woman.

"If it was only hashish," said the woman, "how did they know
where to find the Armenians? There was a list with Armenian last
names in the hands of each of them."

Andrei got out in Baku and took a cab to the airport. As he waited for a flight to Yerevan, he noticed an unshaven Armenian in a black shirt, a sign of mourning. Andrei began to talk to the man, who said his nephew had been killed in the pogrom.

"He was home alone," said the Armenian. "They broke down the door and smashed his head with a hammer, then they dragged him down the steps by the legs so his head hit every step and then they threw his body on a garbage dump.

"My brother worked thirty-five years and all he had was destroyed, but he wouldn't have minded if only the boy had been left alive."

"Did anyone else die in your family?" Andrei asked.

"Why, wasn't this enough?"

Andrei apologized. He said that he was an independent journalist and was preparing to report on the events.

"They'll fix you so you forget how to report," the man said.

GALINA STAROVOITOVA had done research in the Caucasus in the 1980s, and when she got the first news of the killings in Sumgait, she sent a letter to the Armenian poetess Silva Kaputikian expressing her solidarity and grief. Starovoitova's letter was reproduced by the thousands and handed out in Yerevan's Theater Square. As a result, she became well known in Armenia. When elections took place, she was elected to the Congress as a deputy from Armenia.

It was the handful of independent deputies like Starovoitova who were to offer the first political competition to the party.

THE DEPUTIES FILED into the hall, finding their assigned places. Galina noticed that they were disciplined and immobile without being attentive. The session opened at 10 a.m. and it soon became obvious that the Congress was not completely controlled.

(At 4 a.m. on April 9, 1989, soldiers using poison gas and wielding sharpened shovels attacked a group of nonviolent demonstrators in the central square in Tbilisi, killing twenty-one persons and injuring hundreds of others. The demonstrators had been calling for independence for Georgia.)

The Congress turned to the question of electing a chairman. The choice of Gorbachev was a foregone conclusion, but the presence of the democratic deputies made a difference almost immediately. Marju Lauristan, the leader of the popular front in Estonia, asked Gorbachev when he had learned that army troops had attacked civilians in Tbilisi, saying, "Do you personally consider the use of the army for punitive operations against civilians to be compatible with democracy?"

Lauristan's straightforwardness inspired others. Finally, as the ballot was about to be approved, Alexander Obolensky, an engineer from Apatita, a town north of Leningrad, nominated himself for the post of chairman. His gesture threw the hall into confusion. When the Congress was asked to vote on putting Obolensky on the ballot, 689 deputies voted in favor (1,415 were opposed), many because they thought his candidacy was Gorbachev's idea.

The voting took place in the nearby St. George's Hall. Booths were set up and the deputies were given ballots. The only reason to stop in a booth, however, was to cross out Gorbachev's name, and the voting was being closely watched. The final result was 2,133 votes for Gorbachev and 87 against.

In the days that followed, a pattern began to emerge. Gorbachev controlled the hall with the help of the overwhelming conservative majority, and it was he, as chairman, who decided which deputies were allowed to speak. The speeches by members of the party majority were in the style of the totalitarian regime.

"Pluralism of opinions is obligatory but . . . in actions there should be unity!" E. N. Meshalkin, Novosibirsk.

"I do not remember a period when there was such a need for the consolidation of all forces of society. . . . Let's forsake meetings. To work! Now is the time to work!" V. S. Obraz, Poltava.

"What we need from everyone is order, order and discipline, democracy will only benefit from this. . . ." Leonid Kravchenko, Moscow.

The voting at the Congress was tightly controlled. When the Congress elected the 542 deputies who would serve in the Supreme Soviet, the working parliament, every well-known democratic deputy was defeated, including Yeltsin. The members of the territorial delegations were watched by their heads who, being high party officials, were in a position to retaliate economically for insubordination. At the same time, many of the deputies from the national republics did not speak Russian. Since there was no translation, they simply raised their hands at the same time as the heads of their delegations, giving rise to the saying, "All in favor, raise your *tubeteikas*."

The mere fact of open political discussion, however, changed the atmosphere in the country. When independent deputies did succeed in fighting their way to a microphone and being recognized, what they said had an effect. Yuri Chernichenko, a deputy from Moscow and a well-known journalist, attacked Ligachev, who had recently been given responsibility for agriculture. "Why, in a politically essential sector," he asked, "have they placed a man who understands nothing of [agriculture] and who has failed in ideology." Yuri Karyakin, a deputy from Moscow and a literary critic, appealed for the removal of Lenin's body from the mausoleum on Red Square. "Lenin himself wanted to be buried beside the grave of his mother at the Volkon Cemetery in St. Petersburg," he said. Starovoitova criticized the nomination of Anatoly Lukyanov, Gorbachev's longtime friend, to run unopposed for the post of deputy chairman and demanded to know why the army waited three days to intervene in Sumgait.

For the first time, Soviet citizens saw that it was possible for deputies to express dissenting views openly. Normal work stopped as people crowded around televisions in offices and factories, applauding and kissing the screen when a deputy expressed views they shared. Those who were unable to follow the debates at the Congress during the day stayed up until 2 a.m. watching the reruns on television.

By the fourth day of the Congress, the democratic deputies were being swamped by as many as a thousand telegrams a day. After each session, they were greeted by crowds of supporters as they left the Kremlin and walked across Red Square to their hotels. Opinion polls began to show that the democratic deputies, who constituted no more than 15 percent of the deputies in the hall, enjoyed the support of 70 percent of the population.

The most striking speech of the session was delivered by Yuri Vlasov, a former weightlifting champion, who denounced the KGB. "The KGB," he said, "is not a service but a real underground empire that has still not yielded its secrets, except for the graves [of Stalin's victims slain by the NKVD, predecessors of the KGB] that have been discovered."

Gorbachev was soon faced with a dilemma. He had created the

Congress of People's Deputies to weaken the party's ability to remove him and to resist reforms, not to surrender moral authority in the country to the democrats. The unexpected tide of public support for the democrats, however, showed that they could become a political force in their own right, and he and the majority decided to respond.

On June 2, the conservative deputies attacked Sakharov. Sergei Chervonopisky, a thirty-two-year-old former army major who had lost both legs in the Afghan war, denounced the physicist for saying, in an interview, that Soviet pilots had sometimes fired on Soviet soldiers to prevent them from being captured by rebels in Afghanistan. Chervonopisky then made a point that had occurred to others in the hall. "In this hall," he said, "more than 80 percent of the deputies are Communists. . . . But not from a single one of them have I heard the word *communism*. I am opposed to slogans, but I think that there are three words for which we should fight—state, motherland, and communism." Gorbachev, the Politburo, and almost the entire hall rose for a standing ovation.

Sakharov said that he had not intended to insult the Soviet army but wished to point out that the Afghanistan war was itself a crime. The majority of the deputies got out of their seats and, stamping their feet, shouted, "Shame! Away with Sakharov!" while a minority applauded.

BY THE BEGINNING OF 1990, power was being transferred steadily from the party apparatus to the Supreme Soviet, where the majority were party members. The party apparatus responded with attacks on Gorbachev's policies, which, in turn, prompted Gorbachev to take steps to free himself of the party by becoming the Soviet Union's first president.

THE 542-MEMBER Supreme Soviet began meeting and its votes reflected the inclinations of the party. The Supreme Soviet nonetheless was acting independently of the party and developing its own hierarchy and pattern of influence which did not reflect that of the party; so its ascendance inspired opposition to Gorbachev in the party.

By the end of 1989, the Central Committee was receiving floods of letters accusing Gorbachev of neglecting the party and allowing attacks on it to pass unanswered. Party leaders began to warn that perestroika could end in disaster. At the December 1989 plenum, one speaker said, "If the capitalists and the Pope praise us, it means that we are on the wrong track."

The vehemence of these attacks caused Gorbachev to give renewed attention to the possibility of creating a Soviet presidency.

Such a step, however, implied the elimination of article six of the constitution, which provided for the party's "leading role" in society since power would be invested in the president and not in the party. Gorbachev earlier rejected calls for the elimination of article six, but in January he changed his mind and endorsed the idea.

A short time later, he gave his tacit support to a demonstration in Moscow, scheduled for February 4, to demand an end to the party's political monopoly. Three days later, the Central Committee, bowing to Gorbachev's wishes, voted 249 to 1 in favor of eliminating article six. The vote was followed by a pro-democracy demonstration in Moscow, February 25, that attracted 500,000 demonstrators.

ON MARCH 12, 1990, the session of the Congress of People's Deputies opened in an atmosphere of nervous uncertainty. As the session got under way, Sergei Alexeev, a jurist and close Gorbachev ally, explained the need for a presidential system. "A purely parliamentary structure," he said, ". . . can block any decision. And . . . experience shows that a purely parliamentary structure . . . is most of all adapted to dictatorship."

After Alexeev had finished, debate focused on whether the president would be receiving too much power. Although Gorbachev was seeking a presidency to reduce his dependence on the party, party conservatives now backed the idea of creating a presidency in the hope that it would promote stability.

The members of the Inter-regional Group, who hoped to attract Gorbachev to their side, however, feared that the proposed legislation, by giving the president almost unlimited rights to rule by decree, would create a dictator.

In the meantime, there was growing doubt as to whether any type of leadership could control the situation completely.

The new political activism of Soviet citizens had been evident at the rally in Moscow only two weeks earlier.

At 11 a.m. on February 25, Olga Printseva, a Moscow biologist, approached the entrance to Gorky Park, where she saw that a vast crowd had filled the entire square.

All weekend long, the democratic opposition in Moscow had been organizing a demonstration to commemorate Russia's February 1917 revolution. In an effort to head it off, the authorities had spread rumors of plans to use force.

Olga, however, decided to go. Now she saw that thousands of others had also refused to be intimidated.

The scene resembled photographs of mass demonstrations in the last years of the tsarist regime. At the entrance to the park, there were tricolor Russian flags and signs reading DOWN WITH LIGACHEV and CPSU, AWAIT YOUR NUREMBERG. There were also the banners of a bewildering number of political parties. Olga had not realized that so many different parties had already been organized in the Soviet Union.

Olga joined a group from Democratic Russia, the main democratic opposition movement, and crossed the Krimsky Bridge. She passed crowds streaming out of the Park of Culture metro station and then became part of the giant demonstration on Zubovsky Boulevard. Demonstrators now filled all ten lanes of the ring road and Olga counted at least seventeen different types of flags and hundreds of placards.

As a meeting began in front of the headquarters of the Novosti Press Agency, it became obvious how subliminal doubts about communism had been brought to the surface with a vengeance under conditions of glasnost and relative freedom of speech.

Yuri Chernichenko described Communist rule in the Soviet Union as "seventy years of war with the people," and said that the Bolsheviks had begun to betray the people two months after taking power, when they dispersed the Constituent Assembly. He demanded that the collectivization of agriculture and the destruction of the peasantry be denounced as a crime.

Sergei Kuznetsov, an independent journalist from Sverdlovsk, said that many people were calling for talks between the party and the opposition. "But what is the purpose of holding a 'round table' with criminals?"

Oleg Rumyantsev, an organizer of the demonstration, warned that the party was getting ready to destroy the democratic gains that had been made in the country.

For years parades and demonstrations in the Soviet Union had been organized by the authorities, and so the march at first resembled the materialization of a spectre. Not only was the immense crowd serrated with the tricolor flags of the Russian empire but thousands of hand-painted signs reflected a people's newfound political creativity: COMMUNISTS, DON'T TEACH US HOW TO LIVE; PRIVATE PROPERTY IS FREEDOM; and WE'LL COVER YOUR NIGHTSTICKS WITH CONDOMS.

As the marchers neared Mayakovsky Square, an old woman on the sidewalk began screaming, "Stalin would have known what to do with you!" The marchers, however, buoyed by sheer numbers, ignored her.

At Mayakovsky Square, Olga looked back and could not see where the demonstration began, only a solid river of people framed by megalithic apartment blocks under the dome of a darkening sky. Watching this mass of humanity, she was sure that after so many years of silence and fear, something in the country had finally changed. For the first time, it occurred to her that there were millions of people in the Soviet Union who thought the way she did. She was no longer alone and, as a result, she could participate in the changes now sweeping the country.

ON MARCH 13, the second day of the Congress, the debate over a Soviet presidency became animated.

K. Makhkamov, the first secretary of the Communist Party of Tadjikistan, said that, to stop interethnic conflicts, "we need strong . . . civilized authority."

Ivan Polozkov, the first secretary of the Krasnodar regional party, said, "Our country . . . requires presidential power . . . otherwise the slipping of society into a swamp more viscous than the swamp of stagnation is inevitable."

However, N. T. Dabizh, a Moldavian writer, said, "[I]t is now our turn to defend Gorbachev from Gorbachev. The concentration of enormous power in the hands of one person represents a danger for the process of democratization. . . . Who among us is confident that after four years or nine years, there will not appear someone in the Soviet Union who wants to create socialism of the barracks type?"

With the conclusion of debate, the Congress proceeded to a vote. Under legislative rules, amendments were considered first and then a proposal was voted on as amended. In this case, however, Gorbachev put the proposal to a vote before it could be amended. The result was 1,771 in favor and 164 opposed. The reformers thought that this was a vote in principle. Gorbachev, however, announced that the proposal had been accepted as part of the constitution.

He next proposed that the first president be elected by the Congress. Polls showed that Soviet citizens were overwhelmingly in favor of voting directly for the president, but Gorbachev launched a campaign to convince the Congress that this would risk political instability. Dmitri Likhachev, an academician in his eighties, warned that the direct election of the president could lead to civil war. The proposal needed 1,497 positive votes. The final result was 1,542 for, 360 against, and 76 abstentions.

Gorbachev next ran for the presidency. Two other candidates, Ryzhkov and Vadim Bakatin, the interior minister, withdrew their candidacies so he ran unopposed. Nonetheless, Gorbachev lacked confidence in the outcome. Raisa Gorbachev urged female deputies to vote for her husband, assuring them that he was not a dictator. Selected intellectuals who attended the Congress as guests began to lobby democrats to vote for Gorbachev, arguing that if he was not elected, the presidency would go to a conservative like Ligachev.

Finally, the vote was held and 1,329 deputies voted in favor of Gorbachev and 495 against. There were also hundreds of unused votes. This was a way of voting no and a sign that hidden opposition to Gorbachev was rising almost as fast as his grab for power itself.

WITH HIS ELECTION as Soviet president, Gorbachev had accumulated more formal authority than any Soviet leader since Stalin. His political victories, however, ostensibly achieved in order to pave the way for significant economic reforms, were now leading not to reforms but to the destabilization of the Soviet system.

The election of Gorbachev as president was followed by the creation of a new system of presidential power. Gorbachev established an office in the Kremlin and took part of the Central Committee apparatus with him, where it became the core of the presidential apparatus.

The local and republican elections, which were held in February and March 1990, were a defeat for the party. The country had been changed by glasnost, and in the new atmosphere it was impossible to carry out the local elections with reserved places for "social organizations" and party-dominated election commissions. These institutions were eliminated and the number of independent candidates increased. Democrats won a majority in Moscow, Leningrad, and Sverdlovsk and nationalists swept to power in the Baltic states, Armenia, Moldavia, and Georgia. (On March 11, Lithuania declared itself independent.) Democrats also won a third of the seats in the Russian republic, preparing the way for Yeltsin to announce his candidacy for the leadership of the Russian parliament.

ON MAY 16, the first session of the Russian Congress of People's Deputies opened in the Great Kremlin Palace and the public deluged the deputies with letters and telegrams urging the election of Yeltsin. On May 23, Gorbachev addressed the Congress and accused Yeltsin of trying to separate Russia from socialism and of showing "crudity and intolerance." Gorbachev's speech and, in particular, the personal attack on Yeltsin, helped to ensure Yeltsin's victory. In the third round of voting, Yeltsin received 535 votes, four more than was required for victory. For the first time, the democratic forces in the country had an elected leader.

BY THE SUMMER OF 1990, the party's fall in the public's affections had led to deep fissures in its ranks, and there were large blocs of members whose programs were diametrically opposed. On June 19, a conference to organize a separate Russian Communist Party, which would be free of Gorbachev's control, opened in Moscow in an atmosphere of undisguised fury with the leader.

Ivan Osadchy, a conference organizer, accused Gorbachev of pushing the party to "suicide." General Albert Makashov said that the Soviet Union might cease to be a great power. Despite the strength of conservative and anti-Gorbachev sentiment at the Russian party conference, however, the conservatives could not prevail against Gorbachev in the party. This became clear shortly afterward at the Twenty-eighth Party Congress.

AS THE DELEGATES to the Party Congress entered the Kremlin Palace of Congresses on July 2, it was obvious that this was no longer the unified party of the past. The various factions all had recruiting tables in the corridors and the delegates separated into liberal and conservative groups that did not speak to or even greet each other.

Gorbachev opened the Congress with a two-and-a-half-hour speech in which he depicted himself as a reformer committed to the socialist system.

After Gorbachev, however, Vladimir Bludov, a delegate from the Magadan oblast, said the Congress should fire the existing Politburo and Central Committee. His speech was greeted with an ovation.

Ryzhkov, the first Politburo member to speak, was jeered. He was followed by Vadim Medvedev, the chief ideologist, who was interrupted by rhythmic clapping. The same fate would have awaited Yakovlev, but he went to the podium and spoke without stopping, depriving the delegates of the chance to begin their rhythmic clapping and stomping. The only Politburo member who received a warm reception was Ligachev. "All manner of ... improvisation ... hasn't given us much in the five years of perestroika," he said.

Finally, there was a motion to rate the individual Politburo members. The hall voted overwhelmingly in favor of the motion and Lukyanov, who was presiding, announced a break.

When the session of the Congress resumed, Gorbachev was in the chair. Yakovlev, sitting down next to Otto Latsis, a liberal communist journalist, told him that the politburo had voted to resign if the Congress tried to rate the politburo members individually. "Now I want to have a talk with you all," Gorbachev said. "If you want to split the party, if you want to bury it, then you are going about it the right way. The time has come to think and to think hard."

For the next hour, the delegates thought. Latsis realized that Gorbachev was using a brilliant tactic. Communists were committed to unity and anyone provoking a split would lose the sympathy of the rank and file. Since it was the conservatives who had provoked this conflict, the onus would be on them. As general secretary, Gorbachev also controlled the party's property. In the event of a split, the hard-liners would be left an impoverished rump group opposed not only to the party majority but to the new presidential structures.

Delegates began to take the floor to ask Gorbachev for the chance to reconsider. Finally, Gorbachev put the question of annulling the resolution to a vote and it passed by nearly the same margin as the vote in favor had passed a short time earlier.

The Congress prepared next for the election of a new general secretary. But Gorbachev's victory was now inevitable. He had demonstrated his ability to crush opposition and most of the delegates feared that if he was not reelected, he would use his power as president to persecute the party. The final vote showed 3,411 votes for Gorbachev against 501 votes for Teimuraz Avaliani, the party leader in the Western Siberian city of Kiselevsk and the only alternative candidate. There were 1,116 no votes for Gorbachev, a sign of strong opposition. Still, the full-scale revolt that had seemed to be a real possibility as recently as a month before did not take place.

BY THE SPRING OF 1991, Gorbachev's hold on the party had begun to resemble a death grip. The notion that it was possible to preserve a socialist state without the use of force was discredited as the command economy began to collapse and so did the imperial Soviet structure. As the crisis deepened, Gorbachev became less concerned with reform than with preserving his own power, maneuvering between the party-state apparatus and the new democratic forces, and finally triggering an attempt by the party to remove him at the April 1991 Central Committee plenum.

IN 1989, the consequences of removing the party from the management of the economy began to be felt. The rate of economic growth fell sharply and, in 1990, production started to decline. In a system of fixed prices, suppressed inflation led to the collapse of the consumer market. In the summer of 1989, of 211 food products, it was possible to buy freely only 23.

Gorbachev, however, made no move to introduce long-awaited market reforms. Soviet intellectuals noticed that he seemed to have lost direction. The popular movement had become strongly anti-Communist, and to preserve his influence with it while retaining control, he began advocating policies that contradicted each other, such as democratization and preservation of the empire, marketization and a ban on private property.

Finally, however, Gorbachev had little choice but to take decisive action of some kind. The attempt to introduce market reforms in an economy based on the abolition of the market had created economic chaos. At the same time, the republics, including Russia, began to declare their "sovereignty" (or independence) and to insist on the pri-

macy of their laws, leading to a "war of laws" with the union government. The combination of these forces led Gorbachev to agree with
Yeltsin to appoint Stanislaw Shatalin, a member of the presidential
council, to work out a strategy of serious economic reform.

The Shatalin plan, which was to be implemented in "five hundred days," called for the massive sale of state assets and putting tax-
ation in the hands of the republics. It was therefore actually a
prescription for dismantling the Soviet Union. On September 11,
Gorbachev tentatively endorsed the Shatalin plan before the Supreme Soviet. On September 21, however, he realized the plan's im-
plications and said that it could not be implemented. He then spent
several weeks trying to combine it with a plan developed by Ryzhkov
that provided for continued central planning before the Shatalin plan
was finally dropped.

THE REJECTION of the Shatalin plan introduced a period of reaction, as Gorbachev began to align himself with the army, police, and
KGB. On December 11, Kryuchkov, in a televised address, vowed
that the KGB would fight with all means at its disposal against anti-
Communist elements. Nine days later, Shevardnadze announced his
resignation at a session of the Congress of People's Deputies and said,
"A dictatorship is approaching."

THE FIRST RESULT of the change in policy was a crackdown in
Lithuania.

ON JANUARY 10, Gorbachev sent a message to the Lithuanian
government, accusing Lithuania of "flagrant violations" of the Soviet
constitution. The next morning, paratroopers, firing live ammunition
and accompanied by tanks, seized the main printing plant in the republic and a police anti-terrorism school. Later the same day, communists loyal to Moscow announced the creation of a "Committee of
National Salvation."

AT 12:30 A.M. on January 13, 1991, there was a holiday atmosphere in front of the Vilnius television tower. Teenagers danced to

music played on a portable tape recorder and vendors sold coffee and rolls.

Loreta Asanaviciute, a twenty-four-year-old factory worker, mingled with the crowd which was preparing to defend the television tower against seizure by Soviet troops.

At 1 a.m., however, the tension suddenly increased. Twenty Soviet tanks began moving down Kosmonauts Street and then pulled into the adjoining woods. Demonstrators linked arms as all eyes focused on the tanks, whose lights glowed amid the bare winter trees.

Suddenly, tracer bullets lit up the sky. The tanks, surrounded by soldiers, began moving toward the tower. The soldiers threw smoke bombs and as the defenders started to flee, the soldiers opened fire and the tanks accelerated, driving into the crowd.

Loreta began to run from the tower with a group of friends across a field shrouded in smoke and crisscrossed with the beams of searchlights. Suddenly, disoriented and partially blinded by the smoke, she found herself in the path of a tank. As her friends looked on in horror, she lost her footing and fell under the vehicle's treads.

After the tank passed over her, Loreta's friends carried her to an ambulance, where a doctor gave her an injection; the entire lower half of her body was crushed.

"Uncle," she asked, looking fearfully at her body, "if my legs are hurt badly, will I be able to marry?"

The doctor tried to comfort her, but she died a short time later.

In the meantime, with scores of demonstrators falling from bullets and being run over by tanks, a message began to be broadcast from a loudspeaker near the television tower: "Brothers and sisters, the bourgeois, fascist power in Lithuania has fallen. All power is now in the hands of the Committee for National Salvation."

WITH THE TELEVISION tower taken by Soviet troops, the demonstrators began massing in front of the Lithuanian parliament building.

News of the massacre spread rapidly and by daybreak, the area around the parliament building was a hive of activity. Giant coils of barbed wire were placed in front of the entrances and sandbags began to be piled up behind the windows. Heavy cranes lowered enormous concrete blocks into place around the building and, inside the parliament, volunteers and members of the newly formed Lithuanian self-defense force handed out hunting rifles, which began to arrive in a steady stream.

By noon, the basic fortifications were complete and there were nearly twenty thousand persons in the square, forming a human cordon around the building. The pictures of those killed at the television tower began to be displayed on wooden boards. One picture showed a young boy reaching out to touch the head of his father in a coffin. Funeral music was played over loudspeakers and everywhere yellow candles flickered at makeshift shrines.

Vilnius began to prepare for street battles. Ten-foot-high concrete barriers went up on Gediminas Street, blocking access to Parliament Square except for a narrow accessway. The central library was converted into a temporary hospital with a Red Cross flag fluttering over the entranceway, and for miles around the parliament building the windows of the city's apartment buildings were covered with crisscrossed bands of tape to reduce shattering in case of shooting or a tank battle.

On January 20, nearly five hundred thousand persons demonstrated in Moscow in protest over the killings at the television tower. In the evening, four persons were killed in Latvia as Soviet internal troops stormed the Latvian internal affairs ministry. Everything now appeared to be in readiness for the forcible dissolution of the Baltic parliaments and the imposition of direct Soviet rule. But, to the surprise of many, there was no order to attack.

On January 21, amid widespread confusion, preparations continued to defend the Lithuanian parliament building. But the next day the Lithuanian Committee of National Salvation and a similar committee in Latvia announced that they were suspending their activities. A short time later, paratroop units and internal troops that had been sent into the republic to hunt for draft evaders were withdrawn.

The threat to Lithuania and Latvia disappeared.

THE EVENTS in the Baltics were followed by a second attempt to crack down, this time in Moscow.

Gorbachev scheduled a referendum for March 17 on whether to preserve the Soviet Union. Yeltsin added a question in the Russian republic asking voters whether they wanted a directly elected Russian president. On February 19, Yeltsin called on Gorbachev to resign, and Communist deputies in the Russian parliament called for

Yeltsin's impeachment. An emergency session of the Congress of People's Deputies was called for March 28 to consider Yeltsin's fate.

The referendum took place on March 17. The proposition to preserve the union carried by 75 percent but the voters also approved a Russian presidency. As the date for the attempt to impeach Yeltsin neared, Democratic Russia began planning a massive demonstration for March 25 in support of Yeltsin. The Soviet government responded by announcing a three-week ban on demonstrations in Moscow. Pro-Yeltsin forces, however, said they would hold the demonstration anyway, and the government began moving thousands of troops into Moscow.

ON MARCH 28, the side streets and courtyards of central Moscow teemed with hundreds of military vehicles and thousands of soldiers. Under overcast skies, water ran down the drainpipes and old women with long-handled chippers split up layers of ice on the sidewalk, seemingly oblivious to the face off building around them.

In the Moscow City Council building, where Democratic Russia had its temporary headquarters, the phones were ringing constantly with reports of troop movements. Vladimir Boxer, a leader of the movement, was meeting with a group of colleagues to finalize plans for the day's rally. No one had expected such a show of force. A decision was finally made to proceed with the rally but, in order to avoid a possible provocation, to hold it in Arbat Square and in Mayakovsky Square, not, as first planned, in Manezh Square opposite the Kremlin, which was all but sealed off by police and troops.

The demonstrations were scheduled for 5:30 p.m., but crowds began forming in the early afternoon. Echo Moscow described the positions of troops on Gorky Street and around Manezh Square. Tass carried a warning from Vitaly Prilukov, the Moscow KGB chief, that the authorities would use "all means" to prevent demonstrations, and rows of ambulances stood ready near Red Square to carry away the injured.

At 3 p.m., fifty thousand Internal Ministry troops filled every street leading to Manezh Square.

As the number of persons taking part in the demonstration grew, however, the danger of an attack began to fade. There was no attempt to interfere with the crowd gathering in the two squares, and despite the armor on the streets, the soldiers and police were neutral or friendly. A woman asked the leader of a group of Internal troops near Mayakovsky Square, "Are you going to beat us?"

The officer said, "Besides epaulettes, I've got a conscience."

By 5:30 p.m., Arbat Square was a human sea. At 5:45 p.m., the speeches began. The attitude toward Gorbachev had changed radically as a result of the killings in Lithuania. "The biggest violator and biggest criminal in the country today is President Gorbachev," said Yuri Luchinsky, a Russian deputy.

Nikolai Travkin, leader of the Democratic Party of Russia, said, "We must get rid of the Communist Party. If we just detach the tip of the iceberg, the party will return in an even more reactionary form." From the windows of the nearby maternity hospital, doctors and nurses applauded the demonstrators while those in the square cheered them.

At Mayakovsky Square, the crowd grew quickly and it soon became obvious that the organizers had underestimated the capacity of the area. At 6 p.m., the square was completely full and tens of thousands, from the city's factories and enterprises, streamed out of the metro station to join the demonstration. Boxer, who was helping to organize the logistics, found that it took more than an hour to move only 1,500 feet. Speakers at the rally included Gavriil Popov, the mayor of Moscow, Yuri Afanasiev, Father Yakunin, and Starovoitova. Afanasiev said that the rally had demonstrated the strength and unity of the democratic forces. Their support for Yeltsin and reform would now be impossible to ignore.

As darkness fell, it began to snow steadily, and the first ranks of a column of fifty thousand demonstrators from Arbat Square came into view on the Sadovoye Ring Road. At the sight of the column, the throng in Mayakovsky Square burst into cheers and the two streams joined just as the streetlights came on and spotlights illumined the giant statue of Mayakovsky in the demonstrators' midst.

The number of people in Mayakovsky Square or near to it was well over 100,000, a record for a demonstration in Moscow on a weekday, and with the soldiers and police in stationary positions, it was now obvious that there would be no attempt by the authorities to use force.

The mood of the crowd was festive. There were chants of "Yeltsin! Yeltsin!" and "Gorbachev, go away!" The demonstrators carried hundreds of Russian flags and placards, some of which read: WOMEN—DON'T GIVE BIRTH TO COMMUNISTS;

CPSU—TO THE ASH HEAP OF HISTORY; BORIS, HOLD ON!; and ALL OF RUSSIA IS FOR BORIS. Finally, Father Yakunin, making himself heard over the shouts of "Yeltsin—President!" urged everyone to go home and warm up. Summing up the results of the rally, he said, "A great deed has been done." A short time later, with the victory of the demonstrators obvious and the streets starting to clear, the thousands of soldiers and their equipment which had poured into Moscow that morning began to be withdrawn.

THE CONFRONTATION ended with a complete victory for Yeltsin. The Russian Congress not only rejected the hard-liners' proposals to remove him but voted him new powers. The date of the Russian presidential elections was set for June 12.

Gorbachev now turned again to reform. On April 23, he met secretly with Yeltsin and the leaders of eight other republics in Novo-Ogarevo, a village outside of Moscow. After ten hours of negotiations, the participants signed a statement in which they called for a new union treaty and the drafting of a new constitution to be followed by elections throughout the union by 1992. The role of the union republics would be "fundamentally enhanced" and the six republics not represented at the meeting—the Baltic republics, Moldavia, Georgia, and Armenia—would be free to refuse to sign a new union treaty. Gorbachev had officially given up the effort to hold the Soviet Union together by force.

In the meantime, the party, outraged by Gorbachev's maneuvering, began to organize against him at the April 1991 plenum.

THE PLENUM OPENED in the Kremlin in an atmosphere of stunned disbelief. The members of the Central Committee, accustomed to thinking of Gorbachev and Yeltsin as rivals, were astounded by the Novo-Ogarevo statement and by the two leaders' apparent reconciliation.

At 3 p.m., there were introductory remarks by Gorbachev. "Let's speak frankly, comrades," he said. "It would be simply undignified to give the impression that the leadership does not notice that many in the party masses are disoriented and ... others, among party leaders, even give in to hysteria. This atmosphere is reminiscent of the ... period when V. I. Lenin turned the party and country sharply toward NEP [the New Economic Policy]."

Gorbachev said that now the complexity of the situation was similar: to foster enterprise, to defend workers, and to stand for the sovereignty of the republics while defending the union government.

His remarks evoked widespread confusion and only scattered applause. He was followed to the podium by Central Committee members whose speeches reflected incomprehension of events in the country as well as nostalgia for the recent past.

Stanislaw Gurenko, first secretary of the Ukrainian party, said, "People note with bitterness that in recent years damage was done to the country which could not have been done by our enemies. The economy was ruined, the society was split, and a large part of it was thrown below the threshold of poverty. Unemployment, strikes, and bloody interethnic conflicts have become a reality. . . . In short, we have quickly lost all that was accomplished by the . . . at times incredible efforts of all generations of Soviet people. . . ."

A. P. Rubiks, first secretary of the Latvian party, said, "People ask how many bags of resolutions is it necessary to send to Moscow before there are concrete measures to restore law enforcement in the country?"

A. M. Zaitsev, first secretary of the Kemerovo party, said, "The situation in the country has become practically unmanageable. The last six years have led to chaos and the collapse of government structures and organs of direction. . . . Anticommunism and capitalization of the economy have become the real policy of the Soviet Union. . . ."

Finally, Gorbachev lost his temper. Red-faced and shaking with fury, he said, "Okay, that's enough, now I'll answer everyone. . . . I suggest that the debate cease and the problem of the general secretary be dealt with—as well as who would take his place until the next party congress. Also, who would suit the two, three, or four parties in the hall. . . . I resign."

Gorbachev had now put the conservatives in a hopeless position.

Under party rules, he could only be replaced at a party congress. If he resigned before a new party congress could be organized, he would continue to function as general secretary, control party property, and even be in a position to create a new party. The conservatives would not retire Gorbachev. He would retire them.

The majority of the Central Committee members were opposed to Gorbachev, but they needed time to organize against him. By an overwhelming vote of 322 to 13, therefore, they took the question of his resignation off the agenda. The plenum continued with speeches about the economy and national conflicts. It was nonetheless clear to everyone that Gorbachev's removal as general secretary was a question for the near future.

BY THE SUMMER, the democratic forces Gorbachev had unleashed were threatening to overwhelm him. Unwilling to resort to mass repression and unable to save the Soviet system without it, he began to devote himself to preserving what he could of his position in a new political situation.

AS THE WEEKS PASSED, Gorbachev made steady progress with Yeltsin on a new union treaty which devolved a significant degree of power to the republics.

Gorbachev also prepared the draft of a new party program, which abandoned all traditional Communist positions. It condemned "the crimes of Stalinism," endorsed private property, and called for political pluralism, tolerance of religion, and the rule of law.

In June, Yeltsin was elected president of Russia by an overwhelming majority, and on July 10 he was officially installed as Russia's first president in the Palace of Congresses. Ten days later, he issued a decree banning Communist Party cells in the workplace. This order, which Gorbachev failed to countermand, threatened to deprive the party of its organizational base.

In the meantime, an atmosphere of gloom settled over the party. The corridors of the Central Committee building, never lively, began to empty of people. Typewriters started to be stolen from offices, and silverware and food products disappeared from the buffet.

At the July plenum, the party program was introduced and approved "for publication," which actually left some doubt as to its future. The most important question, however, was the scheduling of the party congress. Party conservatives were convinced that the only hope of saving the party and the Soviet Union was to remove Gorbachev, but this could only be done at a party congress, which they wanted to hold as soon as possible. Gorbachev, however, wanted to delay the congress so that he could solidify his alliance with Yeltsin, finalize a Union treaty, and split the party on his terms.

The conservatives suggested September as the date for the party congress but Gorbachev, citing the need to allow time for the harvest, insisted on December or January and the conservatives reluctantly agreed.

The conservatives were now convinced that Gorbachev's removal was imminent. On August 2, however, Gorbachev announced that Russia, Uzbekistan, and Kazakhstan were ready to sign the union treaty on August 20, effectively breaking up the Soviet Union. The announcement led to preparations by the army, KGB, and the government for a coup, which began, without the party's participation, seventeen days later.

AT 9:30 A.M. on August 19, tanks were already on the streets of Moscow. Oleg Sheinin—who was in charge of the party in the absence of Vladimir Ivashko, the deputy general secretary, then recuperating from a throat operation—called a meeting of the secretariat in the building on Old Square.

The secretaries asked questions about the health of Gorbachev, who at this point was a prisoner in his dacha at Foros. They were given vague replies. They were then provided with the text of a cipher telegram to be sent to local party organizations that recommended "enlisting Communists in the Emergency Committee's activities."

The atmosphere in the building became strangely calm. Many officials, left with nothing to do, began watching CNN broadcasts of the coup in their offices. They saw the first press conference given by the coup leaders and the crowds surrounding tanks on the Moscow streets. At 5 p.m., Ivashko was brought to Central Committee headquarters in an ambulance. On August 20, another telegram was sent from the secretariat to local party committees asking about the mood of the citizens. There were no further meetings, reactions, or explanations. Party officials, like millions of others, followed events on radio and television.

AS IT BECAME OBVIOUS that the coup was near collapse, however, the building on Old Square was seized by a wave of quiet fear.

The public was accustomed to the party's total domination of all aspects of Soviet life. It would almost certainly assume that the coup was the work of the party.

The order, August 23, to vacate Central Committee headquarters on Old Square, stunned members of the Central Committee. As the first officials left the building through the main entrance, they had their purses and briefcases searched by the police. All the exits from the building except the one on Kuibyshev Street were soon blocked. As the officials left the building, the crowd separated to form a "corridor of shame" one person wide and, held back by the police, shouted "Villains!" and "Scoundrels!" as the officials walked through.

As the Central Committee officials escaped from the angry crowd into the rainy streets of the city center, Gorbachev was entering the White House for a joint appearance with Yeltsin before the Russian Supreme Soviet. Inside the hall, Yeltsin forced Gorbachev to read the notes of the August 19 meeting of the Council of Ministers at which the ministers, all of whom were party members, overwhelmingly supported the coup.

Yeltsin next took out a document and said, "Now for a bit of relaxation, let me sign a decree banning the activity of the Russian Communist Party." Gorbachev said, "Boris Nikolaievich . . . I don't know what you are signing here. It's undemocratic to ban the entire party for the offenses of a few." Yeltsin paid no attention and signed the document to cheers from the deputies.

Gorbachev was now the only person in the Soviet Union in a position to defend the Soviet and Russian Communist Parties. He was still the Soviet president and he could cancel Yeltsin's decree and try to use the army and the KGB to take control of the country. In light of the experience of the coup plotters, however, he could not be confident of success. He decided to support Yeltsin.

On the morning of August 24, Soviet radio broadcast a statement by Gorbachev in which he said that in light of its inaction during the coup, the party should make the "difficult but honest decision to disband itself." He said that he was resigning as general secretary and ordered the state to seize all party property.

As he spoke, the police and Internal Ministry troops began sealing off all the major Communist Party buildings in Moscow, holding back angry crowds. In this way, seventy-three years after the Bolshevik seizure of power, the bloody, senseless, and surrealistic era of Communist rule in the Soviet Union finally came to an end.

4

Truth Seekers

To him that hath shall be given and from him that hath not shall be taken what little he hath.

—*Matthew 25:29*

MOSCOW, APRIL 1988

EVERY NIGHT, a large crowd fills Moscow's vast aerostation, the terminal for buses to the Moscow airports and one of the crossroads of the nation. In a country that spans eleven time zones, buses leave for the airports from the aerostation until late at night and then again in the predawn hours, and the glass-walled terminal with its arc lights, rows of leather chairs, and all-night restaurant and telegraph office is the scene of almost constant activity. Many in the crowd are passengers. They check their baggage on freight scales or queue up to get into the smoke-filled buffet as a large tableau over the double doors flashes the departure times of the internal flights. Besides the passengers, however, there is another category of people in the hall who are not going anywhere. They actually live in the aerostation, and some have lived there for a significant part of their lives.

The "residents" of the aerostation are "truth seekers," working people who arrive in Moscow to seek justice in the reception halls of government organizations, usually in response to an injustice committed in their collective.

The truth seeker usually begins his quest for justice by writing to the central authorities, sometimes to a Soviet newspaper. The letters are read, relevant information is extracted, and they are sent back to the local organization against which the truth seeker is complaining. This usually inspires a new wave of letters. "No, no, you didn't understand me. I already appealed to the local authorities. They won't help. THEY'RE ALL IN IT TOGETHER! THAT'S WHY I APPEALED TO YOU!!!" This second letter usually is not answered, and the truth seeker, no better off, is left defenseless to face the enraged local authorities. It is after the letters fail that most complainants come to Moscow.

When a complainant leaves a provincial city to seek truth in Moscow, he is taking a path littered with the discarded hopes of thousands of truth seekers before him. He is typically sent from one reception hall to the next, where he is asked to fill out ever more detailed forms. There will be long delays before it is possible to see any official, and each meeting will end with him being advised to see someone else. The process of going from office to office can be dragged out for months or even years. It can go on for as long as it takes before the truth seeker comes to understand that his quest for justice is futile in the Soviet system.

In the reception hall of the Communist Party Central Committee, a truth seeker talks to an official via a microphone through a wall of glass. Others sit in a row of hard chairs along the wall. One or two of them appear agitated, as if wrestling with an unseen enemy intent on ruining their lives.

In the reception hall of the all-Union procurator,* a woman says that her son was jailed on a falsified rape charge and sentenced to seven years in a labor camp after he tried to expose the financial manipulations of the chairman of their collective farm. She is crying and cannot bring herself to leave the waiting room even though her petition to reevaluate the case has been denied.

In the reception hall of the newspaper *Izvestiya*, Vladimir Magaric noticed that no sooner did a confused person from the provinces step into the reception hall than the staff members there began screaming, "Who are you? What are you doing here?"

A war invalid who walked with the help of canes asked Magaric if he had ever been in the army. Magaric said no.

"In the army," he said, motioning with his hand, "there is a won-

---

*The Soviet prosecutor.

derful thing called a Kalashnikov. You fire it from the stomach and then, right away, everyone . . ."

Truth seekers get off the trains from provincial cities, arriving at Moscow stations at the break of day, and walk the freezing streets of the capital for hours waiting impatiently for the reception halls to open their doors. They are the firmest believers in the justice of the Soviet system, which actually has no place for them.

THE BEGINNING OF GLASNOST, with its much freer flow of information and the new readiness to expose local corruption, did not improve the situation of truth seekers. A flood of desperate people descended on Moscow with fresh complaints. Others tried to reopen old cases. But everywhere they met with the same lack of success. On February 12, 1988, Abulfazfizza Aliskerova, a mother of four from Azerbaijan, poured gasoline over herself in the reception hall of the Supreme Soviet and set herself on fire. "For ten years, I've been coming here," she shouted. "For ten years, they don't receive me."

In time, often as a result of conversations in the reception halls, the truth seekers find the aerostation, and a life, of sorts, begins for them there. There are no metal separations between the leather chairs and so it is possible to lie down. Truth seekers often spread themselves out at night, covering themselves with their coats, resting their heads on bags of their things. For fifteen kopecks, they store their belongings in the metal boxes for luggage in the station's basement.

In many ways, the aerostation is the most tolerable shelter for truth seekers in the Soviet capital. It is cozier than the cavernous and unheated Kiev station. The chairs are more comfortable than the stiff, plastic seats in the Yaroslavl station. It is easier to wash up in the toilets than in the crowded toilets of the Leningrad station. The facilities make it possible for truth seekers to improvise and, in that way, survive.

In time, a truth seeker's life assumes a monotonous pattern. After a day spent writing out petitions on the counters in the central telegraph office and delivering them to the reception halls, he returns to the aerostation in the early evening to sit for hours watching the life of normal people swirling around him. As the weeks pass, he will get to know the other truth seekers as well as the informers who survey the hall for the KGB.

At night, the hall of the aerostation is noisy and flooded with light. The police circulate and they can easily arrest a truth seeker for "loitering."

On one occasion, they approached a woman who was sitting next to Valentina Romasheva and started to speak to her. The woman began screaming, "I'm a schoolteacher. I'm a respectable person. I'm fired, but . . ." The officers led the woman away. For some reason, they did not touch Romasheva, although she was in the same vulnerable position.

In early 1988, there began to be some liberalization. The truth seekers were allowed to sleep in the aerostation without periodic harassment.

THERE IS THE DUST of faraway places in the aerostation. But after a while most of the truth seekers barely notice their surroundings. As the weeks go by, they often sit lost in thought, absorbed with the struggle that brought them to Moscow in the first place.

THERE WERE TWO QUALITIES of Soviet society that led to the appearance of truth seekers: the powerlessness of Soviet citizens in their collectives, and the tendency of the administrative machine to treat individuals as interchangeable.

The collectives served to bind citizens to the Soviet system and, in fact, it was at the level of the collective that most repression occurred. If a citizen showed an unacceptable degree of independence, the first reaction was not from the KGB but from his collective, where he could be persecuted, fired, or forced to resign.

"The leader of a collective should educate the member of the collective so that he won't drink, won't steal, and, in general, will be a good Soviet citizen," said Johannes Tamme, a liberal Estonian ideological official, one afternoon in March 1988 in a café in Tallinn. "If you hit your wife, she can go to your factory and complain that they are not educating you properly.

"Generally, each level of the factory is responsible for educating those on the level below them. The director educates the shop bosses, the shop bosses educate the foremen, and the foremen educate the brigade leaders.

"If someone commits a crime, applies to emigrate, or fails to return from a trip abroad, this is seen not just as an individual decision but as a failure of collective instruction, and all levels of the collective can be punished for it."

The "responsibility" of the collective for its members gave it the right to interest itself in every aspect of an individual's life, from an extramarital affair to the abuse of alcohol and any incidents, friendships, or remarks that hinted at political disloyalty.

The individual was not only under the control of the collective, he was also completely dependent on it. Prized vacation packages were distributed through the collective. A worker's collective organized queues for furniture and private cars. Most important, it normally controlled the queue for apartments. Like any scarce good, apartments were an object of speculation, and even those who waited ten or fifteen years for an apartment could not be sure that their place in the queue would be respected.

A citizen was even dependent on his collective if he wanted to get another job. To apply for a job, he had to present his workbook, which contained details of his entire previous work history. In this way, a demotion, reprimand, or firing, no matter how unjustified, could ruin an individual's job prospects for the rest of his life.

ANOTHER FACTOR contributing to the appearance of truth seekers was the tendency of society's bureaucratic machine to treat individuals as interchangeable, which is reflected in society's dependence on documents.

As soon as a future citizen is conceived, his mother has to have the fact of pregnancy attested to. If a woman is pregnant and has no documents to prove it, she will not be excused from work to give birth no matter what she looks like. After the child is born, he is given a "medical passport" in which are listed the parents' names, birth dates, and nationalities. In this way, often before the child has a name, it has a passport.

At the age of sixteen, the citizen receives his internal passport and is officially accepted as a full member of Soviet society. The citizen is obliged to carry his passport at all times and the document itself is a striking example of the extent to which the individual is processed in the Soviet Union to fulfill the needs of society. Useless to its holder, it is designed to provide essential information to the police. There is a stamp that shows if the bearer is married or divorced. There is a place for a list of children and, most important, a registration stamp which indicates that the bearer has permission to live at a certain address.

The police are thus able to keep track of almost the entire population. If a citizen wants to move, he has to receive a stamp showing that he has been written out of his last place of residence. Without such a stamp, he is unable to register in the new location. Until 1990, if a Soviet citizen planned to visit another city for more than three days, he had to ask the police for a temporary registration.

When the time comes for a citizen to get married, he is once again dependent on documents. After a couple announce their intention to wed, the first step is to fill out questionnaires to qualify for a marriage license. When their documents are accepted, a stamp is put in the couple's passports that gives them the right to purchase rugs, shoes, and other clothing in a special wedding store. It also allows them to reserve a limousine.

After a citizen dies, the first obligation of the next of kin is to turn in his passport. The relative is then given the death certificate, which is needed in order to buy a coffin from the store in the district specializing in funeral supplies. The head of a household holds documents for two places in a cemetery. If the documents are lost, so are the places. After funeral arrangements are made, the next of kin takes the certificates to the district cemetery and the deceased is assigned a place. The type of gravestone that is permitted is specified and there are warnings that any monument that violates cemetery rules will be removed by officials.

At every stage in his life, the citizen is thus in the position of being processed by an administrative machine that defines him in terms of his social function and extends the standardization of bureaucracies to the most intimate and painful moments of human life.

THE TENDENCY OF the administrative machine to treat individuals as interchangeable often has tragic consequences.

In May 1971, a serial killer began to operate in the Vitebsk oblast of Belorussia on the country roads between the cities of Vitebsk and Polotsk. With each year, the number of victims increased until by

October 1985 it had reached thirty-seven. The bodies of murdered women were found in bushes, woods, in deserted areas, and occasionally on the outskirts of towns. In each case, the victim was strangled.

As the killer operated unimpeded year after year, the local police treated each murder as a separate event. In 1985, however, after the body of the thirty-sixth victim was found, Nikolai Ignatovich, a senior investigator with the Belorussian procuracy, was put in charge of the investigation. He began reading the case histories of all the unsolved murders of women in the area and came to the conclusion that the women had all been killed by the same man. The similarities in the cases were unmistakable. All were found strangled near little-traveled country roads and many were last seen accepting rides from a stranger. Many of the victims were raped, but there were no signs of a struggle, which suggested that the killer had intercourse with them while they were unconscious or after they were dead.

Finally, the police began looking for a single killer and the nature of the investigation changed. Fragmentary information from witnesses over the years indicated that a person who could be the killer was tall, powerfully built, and, by 1985, about forty. Ignatovich was seeking someone fitting that description who was in a position to have been killing women since 1971.

The investigators tried to match pauses in the murders with periods when known criminals from the area were in labor camps, but this proved fruitless. In late 1985, however, a witness saw one of the last victims getting into a red Zaporozhets automobile. Ignatovich found that there were 1,500 red Zaporozhetses registered in the Vitebsk oblast, and the police began stopping these cars and checking the identities of the drivers. The increased activity rattled the killer's nerves and he murdered a woman specifically to deceive the police. The woman was killed near Vitebsk and the murderer left a note in her mouth that read: "For infidelity, death. Death to Communists and police." This gave Ignatovich a copy of his handwriting.

Ignatovich drew a map of all of the killings of women in the area since 1971, identifying the places where the victims were last seen. The map showed that the victims either left the city of Polotsk in the morning or left other cities on their way to Polotsk at night. It was now obvious that the murderer lived near Polotsk, and Ignatovich presumed that the latest killing was perpetrated near Vitebsk to throw him off the trail.

He checked state auto records and found that there were thirty-five owners of red Zaporozhets automobiles in the Polotsk area. By comparing the owners to a presumptive profile of the killer, Ignatovich settled on Gennady Mikhasevich, the boss of a repair station for vehicles on the Dvina state farm two miles from Polotsk.

Mikhasevich was thirty-eight, married, and the father of two children. He was a Communist Party activist and was frequently written up in the local newspaper as an outstanding worker. When investigators went to question him, his neighbors were astonished. Nothing in his past appeared to link him to any crime. Investigators, however, took a copy of Mikhasevich's handwriting. It matched the script on the note found in the mouth of the last victim, and Mikhasevich was put under arrest.

During the fourteen years that Mikhasevich was murdering women on the roads of Belorussia, however, the wheels of justice had turned. Thirteen people were convicted for his crimes. Twelve were sentenced to long labor camp sentences and one was shot.

The first man sentenced was Alexander Garilov, who was arrested in 1971 after returning to the Vitebsk area illegally from a forced labor site, where he had been serving time for hooliganism. He was charged with the first of Mikhasevich's murders even though his only connection to the victim was that he was arrested on an unrelated charge shortly after the victim's body was found.

Garilov agreed to confess to the murder after the investigator, Mikhail Zhovnerovich, threatened him with the death penalty. At the last minute, however, Garilov began screaming that the charges were false and that Zhovnerovich was a scoundrel. The trial went ahead anyway and Garilov was sentenced to fifteen years.

Orel, a twenty-two-year-old worker, was also threatened with the death penalty. He was put in a cell that was full of lice and assured that, if he did not confess, he would be eaten alive. The lice allowed him no sleep and no rest. In the end, Orel confessed. Terenya, a vagrant, got drunk and committed a minor crime at a time when one of the early murders was being investigated. He was arrested and promised fifteen years if he admitted his guilt. Accustomed to prison and afraid of the death penalty, Terenya agreed. At one point in his trial, however, he interrupted the proceedings and said he did not kill anyone. He then waved his hand and repeated the version of the crime that the investigators had fed him. To Terenya's surprise, the court sentenced him to death. His request for commutation was refused and he was shot.

Terenya was in his thirties and he came from a village in the Vitebsk oblast. After Mikhasevich was arrested, Terenya's mother asked a Moscow investigator for help in retrieving her son's remains. The investigator called the Vitebsk prison and was told that Terenya had been buried in a common grave. He later told Igor Gamayunov, a journalist with *Literaturnaya Gazeta*, "I couldn't look at her. She stood there in her kerchief with tears in her eyes and my heart froze. I just told her, 'Your question is still being decided.' "

Blinov and Luzhkovsky were both arrested for the murder of their mistresses.

Blinov was difficult to intimidate but Zhovnerovich said to a police officer, "Blinov wants to drink. Take him to drink." The militiaman then led Blinov into the next room and beat him bloody so that the blood from his nose ran into his mouth. The investigator then asked, "Did you have enough to drink?"

Blinov was next sent to a psychiatric hospital where he was given injections and began talking uncontrollably. While he babbled, the doctors listened to hear if he revealed any details of his supposed crime—but he did not. Nonetheless, the doctors offered a conclusion consistent with guilt.

Adamov was a driver who operated a dump truck near where the body of one of the victims was found. He was arrested and interrogated ten times in fifteen days before confessing in order to avoid the death penalty. He was sentenced to fifteen years. He tried to hang himself while in confinement.

Kovalyev, a nineteen-year-old student in Vitebsk, was arrested after a witness reported that Kovalyev and his friends Yanchenko and Pashkevich had been playing volleyball near where the body of the latest victim was found. Kovalyev was sentenced to fifteen years while Yanchenko and Pashkevich each received twelve years.

After Mikhasevich was captured, Ignatovich sent one of his investigators to free Kovalyev, who by this time had spent thirteen years in confinement. Kovalyev's girlfriend at the time of his arrest refused to believe that he was a murderer. She went to the labor camp near Minsk where he was being held and registered their marriage. She was still waiting for him thirteen years later when he was released.

When Ignatovich entered the case, he was not even told that there were ten cases for which men had been convicted. It was only when he began to investigate and demanded to see, in addition to the records of the twenty-six officially unsolved murder cases, the records of these other cases that he realized the full scale of the killer's crimes.

By 1985, some of the convicted men had already served their terms and were at liberty. One of them was Garilov, who had served ten years of his fifteen-year sentence. When Ignatovich asked for information about him, he was told that Garilov lived in Vitebsk.

Ignatovich wrote to Garilov and asked him to come for an interview. A short time later, he received a call from Garilov's sister, who said he could not come. When Ignatovich asked her why, she said, "Come here and see for yourself."

Ignatovich went to an apartment in a dilapidated house on the edge of the city. Garilov was thirty-seven by this time but Ignatovich was introduced to an old man who was completely blind. The killer had not been captured but Ignatovich was already sure that Garilov was innocent and he told him, "I can't give you back your sight or the years you lost in the camps, but I can give you back your good name."

Garilov began to cry and said, "At least give me back that, so the neighbors will not think that I'm a murderer."

Garilov's father also cried and it was all Ignatovich could do to keep from crying himself.

In the end, six men were freed by Ignatovich. The others had served their terms and Terenya had been executed. Some cried when they were freed, others cursed.

Most of the freed men accepted their fate and returned quietly to civilian life. This was true even of those who were the most bitter. Glushakov, who served time in a camp in the Far North, said that the only thing that kept him going was the desire to kill Zhovnerovich. Ignatovich, however, met Glushakov accidentally about six months after he was released and asked him whether he still intended to kill Zhovnerovich. "He'll croak on his own," Glushakov said. "I have a life to organize."

THE COMBINATION OF the helplessness of the individual in his collective and a bureaucratic machine that treated individuals as interchangeable created millions of victims and thousands of truth seekers. Soviet society had laws to protect the individual in his collective, but they were not enforced because the judges and procurators took orders from the local party. In light of this situation, most citizens did not take the stated law seriously. The truth seekers, however, could not reconcile themselves to the difference between the stated law and actual practices. They left for Moscow to insist on enforcement of the law, which, in case after case, proved to be a road to oblivion.

IF THE SOVIET UNION had really been the democracy it pretended to be, the Central Committee of the party, the Supreme Soviet, the procuracy, and the other institutions that received citizens' complaints would have been ready to defend the rights of individuals who had suffered injustices in their collectives. Truth seekers quickly discovered, however, that the institutions for handling their complaints were a fiction, and this discovery, in many cases, gave them their first real insight into the Soviet system.

On a quiet summer afternoon in 1987, Valentina Romasheva entered the main telegraph office on Gorky Street and saw a group of truth seekers studying an article that had appeared in *Moskovskaya Pravda*. The article criticized a man named Sergei Grigoriants, the editor of the journal *Glasnost*, and accused him of using a state photocopying machine for nongovernmental purposes.

"Where is this *Glasnost?*" one of the truth seekers asked. "Where can we find it?"

A week went by and the truth seekers got their answer. The telephone number of the journal began to be broadcast by Western radio stations. Romasheva called the journal and got the address and arrived a short time later only to find that a dozen other truth seekers had arrived before her.

Romasheva grew up in Gorky and moved to Moscow in 1979 after agreeing to work in Psychiatric Clinic 27, a mental hospital for persons abandoned by their relatives. In order to live in Moscow, she had agreed to become a "limitchik," a person who is registered temporarily in the capital in return for working in a labor-short industry. Limitchiks are very vulnerable because although they can be given a permanent registration, or *propiska*, after three to five years, a permanent residency permit is not guaranteed. It depends on the approval of the head of the collective.

In February 1980, Romasheva began work at the clinic and was immediately struck by the bad conditions. The patients walked around barefoot and in rags and there was no attempt to provide activities for them. Instead, psychotropic drugs, such as haloperidol and aminazine, were used to keep them quiet. When the patients were not confined to their wards, with the windows left open in the freezing cold to dissipate the bad air, they were often assigned to heavy work, such as carrying pails of water and piles of wet linen. After coming in filthy and exhausted, they were left to wander for hours in freezing corridors in soaking-wet clothing.

More disturbing for Romasheva than the bad conditions, however, were the signs of corruption. Alexander Chuprakov, the director, had a chauffeur and personal chef paid for by the clinic, and there were people listed as employees of the clinic with salaries of eight hundred rubles a month who did not work there. At the same time, there was only one doctor for six hundred patients and each nurse was assigned to care for one hundred twenty patients per shift. Deprived of timely medical help, the clinic's patients died like flies.

Romasheva was bothered by what she saw but, aware of how vulnerable she was, said nothing. Finally, in June 1981, she learned, to her surprise, that Mikhail Korsakov, the clinic's medical director, had sent a letter to the Ministry of Internal Affairs charging Chuprakov with corruption. A short time later, a criminal case was opened and Chuprakov began summoning employees to his office and demanding that they sign statements against Korsakov. He asked Romasheva to write a statement accusing Korsakov of speculation, but she refused.

After six months of uncertainty, Alla Nizovtseva, the raion first secretary, intervened and the investigation was closed. Chuprakov then reasserted his authority, and Korsakov was forced out. So was Naira Stepanova, the clinic's pharmacist. Others who, like Romasheva, had refused to testify against Korsakov also left, but Romasheva could not leave. As a limitchik, if she gave up her job at the clinic, she would lose her right to live in Moscow. She had no place to go.

With the close of the investigation, life at the clinic returned to normal. Trucks arrived with materials that were to be used in building Chuprakov's dacha. Some of the female inmates became pregnant and had abortions and, on one occasion, the nurses found Pyotr Yegorov, one of Chuprakov's cronies, naked in a closet with one of the deranged female patients.

Romasheva devoted herself to her job, trying to prevent patients from harassing each other and eating and drinking themselves to death. Chuprakov docked her pay and deprived her of bonuses, but what worried her most was the possibility that he might refuse to approve a Moscow *propiska* for her at the end of her contract.

Finally, in September 1984, Chuprakov called Romasheva into his office and told her that in return for his agreement to a permanent *propiska*, he expected a bribe. "Without money, you won't live in Moscow," he told her. "Think of the last five years of your life."

Romasheva knew she needed Chuprakov's approval to receive a Moscow residency permit, but she refused to comply.

She went to the local police station, where she was received by Nikolai Novikov, the head of the passport department.

"We know that Chuprakov is a thief," Novikov said, "but you have to settle the situation with him, only with him."

"But how?"

"Any way you want," he said, "but remember, you have no rights."

"What do you mean? It's written in the constitution that we have the right to work and no one can deprive us of this."

"I'll tell you again. You have no rights, none at all."

Chuprakov began stopping Romasheva in the corridor and demanding money. When this did not work, he ordered her to vacate her room in the clinic's dormitory and move into a transit room that was located between two others. When she refused, he put a violent hoodlum in the room next to hers in the dormitory, and the head of the clinic's trade union organized a meeting at which the dormitory residents demanded that Romasheva be expelled.

On December 25, 1984, Romasheva's registration expired, yet she still refused to offer a bribe. In January, she gave her passport to Chuprakov and he wrote her out of Moscow. On February 18, she was fired on the grounds that her work agreement had ended.

Romasheva knew that without a registration she could not remain long in Moscow without being stopped, but she refused to accept being victimized by Chuprakov. She decided to seek justice in the reception halls. She petitioned the Supreme Soviet, the Central Committee of the Communist Party, the Soviet trade union organization, the Soviet procurator, and the Ministry of Social Welfare, walking a well-worn path from one reception hall to the next.

For a long time, she had been seeing Vladimir Izotov, a worker in the Oktyabrsky streetcar depot, and he suggested that they get married so that she would have a legal right to remain in the capital. After considering her situation, Romasheva reluctantly agreed.

Once she was registered, Romasheva no longer had to fear being stopped on the street, but she had another worry. She found a place to stay with Alevtina Kotsabuch, a former colleague at Clinic 27. If it became known that she was living with Kotsabuch and not with Izotov, however, she could be expelled from Moscow for having entered into a fictitious marriage. This danger became more serious when Viktor Saraev, a former suitor, learned where she was living and threatened to denounce her.

In the meantime, Mikhail Gorbachev had come to power, and in February 1986, Romasheva heard references to perestroika and was intrigued by promises that people would be punished for their crimes whatever their rank. She wondered if it was possible that times were changing.

Romasheva went from one reception hall to the next. She traveled frequently between Gorodets, where she stayed with her mother, and Moscow, where she pursued her complaints, surviving on money from her mother. Eventually, she quarreled with Kotsabuch and, unwilling to move in with Izotov, went to live in the railroad stations. From every official tribune, they were announcing perestroika and the fight against bribery. But no one seemed interested in doing anything about any particular case of bribery.

The scenes in the reception halls were striking in their surrealism. As the newspapers filled with detailed exposés of bribery and corruption, truth seekers arrived full of hope, only to find that they were treated with rudeness and condescension and their complaints were ignored. In the reception hall of *Izvestiya*, truth seekers were ridiculed for believing what they read in the press.

The Soviet procurator told Romasheva that her complaint of extortion had been investigated and found to be without merit, although Chuprakov's attempts to force her to give him a bribe were well known in the clinic. The Soviet trade union organization said that there was no basis for restoring Romasheva to her previous job, although where extortion is concerned, even limitchiks are entitled to trade union protection. A woman at the journal *Man and the Law* told Romasheva, "If you are a limitchik, you were treated properly. The purpose of the journal is not to help individuals but to explain Soviet laws."

Other Soviet newspapers declined to interest themselves in Romasheva's case. Only the central television station showed some sympathy. They advised her to give up her struggle and leave the matter on the conscience of the law enforcement agencies.

After Romasheva had been petitioning for more than a year, she was received in Moscow party headquarters by an official named Tropin. He told her that he had investigated her claims with "special methods" and had established that no crime had been committed against her. He then said that Naira Stepanova, whom Romasheva had mentioned in her statement, did not exist.

"Excuse me," Romasheva said, "she hasn't died yet. If you're going to tell me she doesn't exist, further conversation with you doesn't make sense."

"In that case, goodbye," Tropin said, evidently glad to finish the conversation.

Romasheva tried to understand what was going on in the country. It seemed obvious to her that the authorities wanted change, but as far as she could see, all of the bribe takers and swindlers continued to be protected by their party connections.

In the meantime, news reached her that Saraev had informed the police that she and Izotov did not live together. Saraev knew of Romasheva's conflict in Clinic 27, and some of her former colleagues told her he had enlisted Chuprakov as an ally.

A short time later, a summons arrived for Romasheva at Izotov's apartment and she went to see the chief of police. He asked her if she lived with her husband and whether or not they had sexual relations. "I'm sure there are no sexual relations," he said.

"Behave yourself decently," Romasheva said, "and don't try to enter a person's soul with your leather boots."

Romasheva finally collected all the replies she had received and prepared to take them to the Supreme Soviet to show the kind of perestroika that was taking place in the country. When she went to the central telegraph office to write out a new statement, however, another truth seeker approached her and asked where she was going with her petition. When she said the Supreme Soviet, the woman said, "Don't go there alone. They are dragging people out of there and taking them to psychiatric hospitals. If you go, go with someone else."

Romasheva decided not to go. After her years working in a psychiatric clinic, she knew what could happen to a person in a Soviet mental hospital, and she regarded the threat of being seized and committed as entirely realistic.

Romasheva's struggle to find justice was finally beginning to take its toll. She had become immersed in her fight to defend her rights, living for weeks on end in the railroad stations and exhausting herself writing petitions and fighting for appointments but achieving nothing. She finally came to the conclusion that her only hope was to appeal to the United Nations. She learned from another truth seeker that there was a U.N. office on Lunacharsky Lane.

Romasheva went to the U.N. office and saw that the employees were Soviet. Nonetheless, she handed in her letter. She did not expect an immediate reply, so she left to spend the summer with her mother in Gorodets. When she returned to Moscow, she found a letter from the United Nations waiting for her care of poste restante. It said the United Nations had no authority in her case and advised her to appeal to the relevant Soviet organs.

After the reply from the U.N., Romasheva decided that her cause was lost.

Before she did anything else, however, she went to the central telegraph office, where, by chance, she met the group of truth seekers who were studying the article in *Moskovskaya Pravda* that referred to the new "unofficial" journal. The mention of an independent journal was a ray of hope.

Romasheva told her story to the editors of *Glasnost* and they published it in the sixteenth issue of the magazine. She started again to visit the reception halls and she noticed that there were changes.

The liberalization in the country was finally reaching the reception halls, and by early 1988, the militia were no longer seizing people and taking them to psychiatric hospitals. One day, a friend of Romasheva's took her to meet a truth seeker, Yekaterina Arseniev, who had been circulating a petition protesting the refusal of the authorities to consider complaints seriously. In a matter of weeks, she had collected five hundred signatures.

Romasheva added her name to the petition and, a few days later, joined a demonstration of truth seekers at the Council of Ministers. An official there agreed to set up meetings for them. The meetings took place on the following day and to the truth seekers' surprise, the officials proved very accommodating.

As the weeks passed, however, there was no word from the Council of Ministers. Finally, Romasheva received a card which said that her complaint had been investigated and found to be without merit. A similar card was received by each of the others who took part in the demonstration.

After her failure to find justice at the Council of Ministers, Romasheva decided to take a much-needed rest.

On October 16, however, she received a postcard ordering her to appear in court. Saraev had continued to bombard official organizations with letters claiming that Romasheva's marriage was fictitious, and although the authorities showed little interest in her charges of extortion against Chuprakov, they were more than willing to pursue the possibility that to stay in Moscow she had entered into a fictitious marriage.

One morning, Izotov met Romasheva at the *Glasnost* office and warned her that the police had come to his apartment looking for her, and that she was the object of an all-Union search. With that, she ended her efforts to find justice in the reception halls.

Romasheva's fight for justice was a matter of principle, but now she faced a more immediate threat. In November, the Zhdanov *raion* court invalidated her marriage. She appealed to the city court, which returned the case to the raion court. Izotov wrote out a statement in which he insisted that he and Romasheva were legitimately married. The raion court, however, ignored it and prepared to try the case and, possibly, expel Romasheva from Moscow.

ONE AFTERNOON IN MARCH 1981, Nadezhda Martovaya was working at her knitting machine in the Dnepryanka knitted goods factory in Dnepropetrovsk when one of her coworkers stopped at her machine and informed her that she was wanted in the assembly hall for a meeting of the factory's trade union committee.

Martovaya got up from her machine and walked down a long corridor to the assembly hall, where the leaders of the collective, including Olga Fyodorova, the factory director, and Vsevolod Ryasuy, the trade union leader, were waiting for her. Six years earlier, Martovaya had become the object of a campaign of harassment in the factory after she insisted on her right to a large, separate apartment as the mother of four children.

Once Martovaya was seated, Fyodorova began to speak. She said she had received a letter from the oblast council asking her to give Martovaya an apartment.

"I've considered doing this," she said, "but I am not going to because Martovaya is a thief and she is constantly writing complaints. We can't work because of her. Martovaya has to be fired, not given an apartment."

Ryasuy spoke next. "Martovaya is entitled to a large apartment," he said. "She has a large family and her son is a Soviet officer. But we won't give it to her because she constantly complains. In Poland, there are strikes. People don't want to work there. We have people like that here. We will not tolerate such people. We will liquidate them."

The denunciation of Martovaya was the end result of a long process that grew out of her determination to better herself. Shortly after she began work as a machine minder at the Dnepryanka plant, Martovaya was told by Boris Chernyavsky, the director, that a four-room apartment for a large family that was going to be transferred to the factory would be assigned to her. At the time, she, her children, and her second husband, Vasily Sitikh, a retired coal miner, lived in two tiny rooms and a kitchen.

Not long after his meeting with Martovaya, however, Chernyavsky retired and was replaced as director by his former mistress, Fyodorova.

The months passed and Martovaya heard nothing about the promised apartment. She finally decided to inquire in the factory trade union office, but every time she asked, she was put off. Finally, she inquired at the Dnepropetrovsk City Council, where she learned the apartment was already in the hands of the factory.

This news made Martovaya very uneasy. If the apartment had been given to the factory, it should have been assigned to her, and she began to suspect that someone else had taken it. A short time later, she was told by another worker that the apartment had been appropriated by Fyodorova.

Martovaya was overcome with a sense of helplessness. Nonetheless, she went to see Fyodorova. Trying to keep her emotions under control, she told Fyodorova that the apartment had been intended for her as the mother of a large family. Fyodorova, however, was unimpressed.

"Whose fault is it," she asked, "that you produce so many children and multiply poverty in the Soviet Union?"

Martovaya tried to decide what to do. Six people could not live forever in two tiny rooms, but she feared the revenge of Fyodorova if she tried to defend her rights.

The only hope seemed to be to take the matter outside the factory, perhaps to some national organization in Moscow, but she had no idea whether such an appeal for justice would be successful.

For the next few months, Martovaya weighed the possible costs of challenging Fyodorova, and in the end, she decided to seek justice in Moscow. What persuaded her was the experience of another knitter, Tatyana Urazbayeva.

Urazbayeva was one of those who had helped to build the Dnepryanka plant. She had taken a job in construction in 1969 and was promised early access to a separate apartment. After she began working as a knitter at the factory, however, Urazbayeva found that the official queue for housing was being ignored. She went to Moscow and complained to the Ministry of Light Industry. The ministry sent a commission to check on the situation and, in a rare victory over the administration, a number of workers, including Urazbayeva, received apartments.

Martovaya knew that Urazbayeva's success was exceptional, but several weeks after her conversation with Fyodorova, she asked for an unpaid leave and left for Moscow.

She had no idea where to go in the city and finally decided on the Defense Ministry since one of her sons had just been inducted into the army. In the reception hall, she explained her complaint and was taken to an adjoining office. She was then escorted out of the reception hall and, to her astonishment, taken to see Dmitri Ustinov, the Soviet defense minister. Martovaya told Ustinov her story and he promised to send an inquiry to the local authorities in Dnepropetrovsk, expressing the ministry's interest in her case.

Martovaya returned home, but she soon found that the only effect of the Defense Ministry's inquiry had been to enrage the leaders of the factory. One night after she had worked a double shift, she was stopped by the guard, who asked to see her purse. A few days later, she was summoned to the local police and told that a roll of stolen cloth had been found in her bag.

For the next eight months, Zhuravleva, an investigator with the *raion* procurator and a friend of Fyodorova's, summoned Martovaya by telephone to the police station every day, demanding that she admit to stealing the material.

The investigation used up all of Martovaya's free time. The matter was closed only after she complained to the all-Union procurator.

The procuracy in the oblast checked on Zhuravleva's activities and had her removed.

Martovaya then began writing letters to officials in the Dnepropetrovsk oblast, asking to be given the promised apartment. She appealed to the trade union, the city council, and the party organizations. She soon found, however, that she was fighting an entire local mafia.

According to the law, all four of her children had to be counted in determining her eligibility for a larger apartment, even though one son was in the army and a second son was studying in Odessa. Yet every organization in the Dnepropetrovsk oblast told her that she was not entitled to the larger apartment because she had only two children. Martovaya quickly realized that the local officials were simply telephoning each other and repeating the same answer.

As the months passed, the strain of the fight began to affect Sitikh, who became apathetic. He and Martovaya quarreled over things that had never been important before. The children got in his way and he in theirs, and one day, Martovaya came home from work and found that Sitikh was gone.

Sitikh's departure left Martovaya deeply depressed. Nonetheless, she refused to give up her struggle. She found support from Urazbayeva, who not only encouraged her but often backed her up tangibly, cosigning her complaints.

Years went by and Martovaya became a familiar figure in the halls of the Dnepropetrovsk City Council and in the trade union organization, but, after a time, her efforts took on a purely ritual quality. Fyodorova was settled in her apartment and Martovaya had given up hope.

In December 1980, however, something unexpected occurred. In response to one of her petitions, Vladimir Boyko, the head of the Dnepropetrovsk oblast council, assigned a commission to look into Martovaya's complaint and, to her astonishment, the commission concluded that she was entitled to a large apartment.

The decision was the first positive official response she had received in five years, and it filled her with hope. But it only set the stage for her final confrontation with Fyodorova.

As long as Martovaya had fought alone, Fyodorova had no need to be concerned about her. All this changed once she was supported by Boyko. As head of the Dnepropetrovsk oblast council Boyko had the option of trying to enforce the law, and if he ruled that Martovaya was entitled to a large apartment as the mother of a large family, it would be an acknowledgment that she had been denied such a place wrongfully, and that someone should be punished, possibly Ryasuy and Fyodorova herself.

The first hint that Fyodorova was preparing to take decisive action against the "dissidents" in her collective came on January 22, 1981, when Martovaya and Urazbayeva arrived for work. The foreman called the workers together and announced that a piece of material had been cut away from a roll of cloth.

Thefts were not unusual in the factory, but the public announcement was unprecedented. For the next two weeks, rumors were rampant about what was to happen next. On February 6, Urazbayeva was called in for questioning about the stolen material and found that the investigator was Zhuravleva, who had been reinstated in her position. After being questioned, Urazbayeva was allowed to leave, but on February 18, a general meeting was called at the factory at which Zhuravleva accused Urazbayeva of theft.

"She is guilty," said Valentina Talyan, Urazbayeva's superior. "She steals every day."

On February 20, in an atmosphere of rising tension, Zhuravleva burst into the shop accompanied by two women in heavy overcoats. The women ran up to Urazbayeva and Zhuravleva shouted, "Grab her!" Urazbayeva started screaming. She shook herself free and ran out of the shop.

Zhuravleva ran to the phone to call the police and Urazbayeva headed for the factory exit. But when she arrived at the exit, the guard shouted, "Hide yourself. They've got the factory surrounded!"

Urazbayeva ran in the opposite direction, finally hiding in an area of the factory that was still under construction. Martovaya, meanwhile, got dressed and left the factory through the main exit. But when she stepped out on the street, she was grabbed by the police and forced into a waiting car.

Martovaya was driven to the police station and taken in past the same two women who had tried to seize Urazbayeva. She saw that under their outer garments they were wearing white coats.

A policeman took Martovaya in to see Zhuravleva. "I don't need you," Zhuravleva said. "I need Urazbayeva. You are here as a witness to sign a statement that you saw her cut this material."

"I will not sign," said Martovaya. "I refuse to sign a lie."

"You will next time," said Zhuravleva. "We'll make you. As for Urazbayeva, she's going to a crazy house because she's insane."

At 3 p.m., when the shift changed, Urazbayeva left her hiding place and went to Martovaya's apartment, where Martovaya arrived a short time later. The two women were badly shaken. It was obvious to them that only Urazbayeva's timely escape had prevented one or possibly both of them from being put in a mental hospital. But neither knew what to do next. They decided that, for the moment, they had no choice but to continue to report for work.

For the next few days, there was an eerie calm in the factory. But on March 9, a new attempt was made to seize Urazbayeva. On that day, a police car was waiting near the factory door.

At 3 p.m., when Urazbayeva left work, three men grabbed her by the arms and took her to a detention room. They then went out to arrest Martovaya. As it happened, however, Martovaya's son Stanislaw was home from the army on leave.

After she was seized, Urazbayeva used the few minutes that she was alone in the detention room to call Stanislaw and tell him to go to the local police station. When the guards discovered what Urazbayeva was doing, they disconnected the entire factory telephone system.

When Martovaya arrived for the second shift, she was stopped by the police, and she and Urazbayeva were then taken to the police station, where they were brought in to see Zhuravleva.

While the women were being questioned by Zhuravleva, however, Urazbayeva pushed open the door of the interrogation room and saw Martovaya's son, who had arrived moments earlier.

"Stasili! Stasili!" she shouted.

When Zhuravleva realized that this was Martovaya's son, she allowed the women to go.

This second failed attempt to seize the women, however, did nothing to calm their nerves. On March 11, Stanislaw returned to his unit and the persecution began again almost immediately. Martovaya was called to the meeting of the trade union committee where she was denounced as a thief by Fyodorova.

Martovaya asked when she would be informed in writing that she was a thief and would not get an apartment. She was told that she would know on March 16 or 17.

The situation was now critical. Police cars waited outside the factory every day, and Martovaya was afraid that she and Urazbayeva would be put in a mental hospital or that Fyodorova would have her killed to free herself of Boyko and settle the apartment question once and for all. On the whole, it seemed most likely that she would be put in a mental hospital.

Martovaya and Urazbayeva decided not to wait to be seized. They left for Moscow to seek help in the reception halls. On arrival in the capital, the two women went to the reception hall of the Communist Party Central Committee, where they were received by Rudakov, who spoke with them for three hours and seemed sympathetic. He called someone in the Dnepropetrovsk party organization and said, "How long can this go on? Do something or we'll send a commission."

In fact, Martovaya and Urazbayeva put little faith in Rudakov's assurances, but they did not have the money to remain in Moscow and so returned to Dnepropetrovsk on April 6.

To rid herself of Martovaya and Urazbayeva, Fyodorova needed only an excuse for firing them, and although Martovaya and Urazbayeva had fled Dnepropetrovsk to avoid being put in a mental hospital, their unsanctioned absence gave Fyodorova the pretext she required.

On April 14, the two women were told to attend a meeting of the factory trade union committee the next day that would take up the question of their dismissal.

Martovaya and Urazbayeva stayed away from work. They knew that they could not be fired in their absence. In the meantime, they tried to think of who might be able to offer them help, and finally decided to see Boyko.

The two women went to the oblast council. Just as they entered the reception hall, Boyko emerged from his office. Martovaya broke away from Urazbayeva and ran toward Boyko. "They don't let me see you," she said. But when Boyko spotted her, he turned away.

Martovaya now lost all faith in Boyko. She saw that he was not willing to challenge the entire local party mafia over a point of law. She and Urazbayeva were now completely without hope.

Out of sheer desperation, they decided to return to Moscow.

This time, however, they vowed to contact foreign correspondents, and during this, their last trip to Moscow, they were introduced to me on the sidewalk in front of my office on Kutuzovsky Prospekt. In all, Martovaya and Urazbayeva spent three weeks in Moscow, but they had no success in the reception halls, and the trips to Moscow were beginning to lose their point, particularly as the two women had families to support and nothing to live on.

I later met with the women in the apartment of one of Urazbayeva's distant relatives, and they told me their story. There was little I could do to help, and, in the end, they finally had no choice but to return to Dnepropetrovsk and to the Dnepryanka factory, where they were fired shortly thereafter. They told me by telephone that they appealed to the court in the Industrialny *raion*, where the factory was located, but the court refused to hear their case.

The two women's story breaks off with them selling their belongings to a pawnbroker in Dnepropetrovsk in order to have enough to live on. They did not come back to Moscow or return my telephone calls, so their fate is unknown.

ON A QUIET spring day, Pyotr Reznichenko entered the office of the egg factory in Pervomaiskoe, a village thirty-five miles from Odessa, and handed the personnel manager a work assignment from a *raion* party committee in Odessa. Reznichenko needed a job and, inasmuch as he had a work order from a local party committee, the woman could not refuse to accept him. Still, it was clear from her expression that she wished he would disappear.

She told Reznichenko he could not start work without instruction in technical safety and the engineer responsible for the subject was out of town. But until he began working, he could not stay in the dormitory. Under the circumstances, Reznichenko had no choice but to wait idly for a week, sleeping in the fields. When the engineer returned, he signed Reznichenko's documents without instructing him. "You'll learn the rules as you work," he said.

When Reznichenko returned with the signed documents, the woman asked, "Where is the photograph for your gate pass?"

"I don't have any photograph," Reznichenko said.

"In that case, you'll have to go to Odessa and get a photograph."

Reznichenko was now beside himself with rage. For seven days he had waited for the engineer to return, and during that time the personnel manager had never mentioned that he needed photographs. "Little one," he said, "you are an illiterate, tactless woman."

The woman bristled with fury. "You are not going to work here," she said, "no matter what."

When Reznichenko returned from Odessa with the photographs, the woman's assistant nonetheless signed him up for a job and he was given a bed in the dormitory so he had a place to stay.

He was assigned to service the conveyer that carried eggs from the chicken cages to the collection points. He noticed, however, that six of the cages had no wiring to catch the eggs, so they dropped on the floor.

A day passed and a thick layer of smashed eggs formed on the floor. When Reznichenko asked the foreman why no one repaired the wiring, the foreman told him to clean up the eggs.

"Why don't you fix the cages?" Reznichenko suggested.

"I've got a backache," the foreman said.

"What do you get paid for?" Reznichenko asked. "For being an informer or just a lackey?"

On the following day, Reznichenko repaired the cages in his work area himself.

Later that afternoon, inspired by the debacle with the eggs, he began to talk to some of the workers about the difference between the Soviet Union and the United States.

"In the capitalist world, not a single boss would keep you," he said. "But here you show that you're a lackey and they keep you at the expense of me and everyone else."

"What do you know about the capitalist world?" asked a young worker. Reznichenko asked the worker how much he earned. The worker said 130 rubles. "In America, you would earn $2,500 to $3,000 a month," Reznichenko said. "Then you have to consider the difference between what you can buy for a ruble and what you can buy for a dollar."

The workers seemed impressed.

"Just turn to me for answers to all questions," Reznichenko said.

On Reznichenko's fourth day at the egg factory, Ignatiev, the chief mechanic, saw him and started bellowing, "Who are you commanding?" Reznichenko had repaired the wiring in his area, but eggs were still smashing on the floor from other bins throughout the shop.

Reznichenko took Ignatiev and led him to a pile of smashed eggs on the floor. "Take a look at this," he said.

"Get out of the shop," Ignatiev said furiously.

Reznichenko had no choice but to leave and return to the dormitory. That night, a note was slipped under his door ordering him to appear the next morning before a commission of the egg factory.

The next morning, Reznichenko appeared before the commission. It was chaired by the deputy director, who asked Reznichenko why he had left work. Reznichenko said that he was ordered to leave the factory by Ignatiev and he described what happened after he showed Ignatiev the eggs that were smashing on the floor.

The deputy director told Reznichenko that he was fired.

"In that case," Reznichenko said, "I'll try to find justice through the legal system."

"Go ahead. I've fired hundreds like you and nothing happened."

Reznichenko sank into despair, but a short time later he learned that the chairman of the trade union had not sanctioned his dismissal, which made it illegal. He appealed to the raion court, which agreed to hear his case. The deputy director, however, ordered Reznichenko to leave the dormitory. In fact, Reznichenko had a right to remain there while his case was being considered, but the administration controlled access to the building and repeatedly tried to prevent him from entering. In the end, he decided to leave the dormitory. A court hearing was now certain to be avoided because once he left the dormitory, Reznichenko had no way of receiving the postcard with the notification of the court date.

Reznichenko decided to leave the area to seek justice in Moscow. He went first to the Supreme Soviet. An official there, Fyodor Davydov, said he would refer his complaint to the procurator for the Odessa oblast and told him to return to the egg factory and stay in the dormitory.

When Reznichenko returned to the egg factory, however, the bosses, as he expected, barred him from the dormitory. Reznichenko's court date passed. He went to the local procurator, who told him that his case could be reopened if he explained why he failed to appear in court.

Sleeping again in the fields, Reznichenko appealed to the oblast directorate of justice, where he was received by Korovkin. He said that he had been instructed to explain why he had not been in court. "That's right," Korovkin replied, "if you have an acceptable reason why you were not in court, we'll schedule another hearing."

Reznichenko told Korovkin that he was in Moscow discussing his case with an official of the Supreme Soviet when the postcard with the court date arrived. But Korovkin acted as if he had not heard him. "Present an acceptable reason why you weren't in court and we'll investigate," he said. Reznichenko asked for a document at-testing to what he had just been told.

"I'm not giving you any document," Korovkin said.

At that moment, Reznichenko understood that he was not going to get any help in Odessa, and so he left Korovkin's office and again got on a train for Moscow. This time, at the Supreme Soviet, he was received by Sovkov, who had taken over from Davydov.

"Who received you in the Odessa directorate of justice?" Sovkov asked.

"Korovkin, the boss," Reznichenko said.

Sovkov called Odessa and got Korovkin on the line. He asked him about Reznichenko's case and listened, with what seemed like impatience, to an apparent denial. He finally began screaming, "You hold a hearing!" He then slammed down the phone and told Reznichenko to go back to Odessa.

Reznichenko slept in the Odessa station until he was received again by Korovkin. This time, however, Korovkin told him that his case had been reexamined and it had been determined that he had been fired justifiably. How this could have been decided without a court hearing was a mystery to Reznichenko. He left again for Moscow and, again, was received by Sovkov.

Sovkov read Reznichenko's documents and drummed the table.

"Well, do you like coming to Moscow?" he said finally.

"Maybe I should smash you in the face," said Reznichenko.

Sovkov leaned back in his chair and pushed a button. Almost immediately, the door opened and a policeman entered.

Sovkov then got on the phone to Odessa and in hysteria screamed, "I said, hold a hearing!" He then turned to Reznichenko and said, "Go back to Odessa!"

But this time Reznichenko did not go back to Odessa. As he left the reception hall, he saw two people sitting on a bench opposite the office. One of them was Vera Travkina, who worked in a newspaper kiosk in Kiev; the other was an engineer from Tashkent.

"You spoke so bravely," said Vera, who with the engineer had heard everything through the door, "we were stunned. How is it that you are not afraid to talk to them that way?"

"If you're afraid of wolves, don't go into the forest," Reznichenko said.

Travkina whispered, "Listen, they're forming an organization here." She gave Reznichenko the name of Valentin Poplavsky and an address in Klimovsk. Reznichenko took an electric train to Klimovsk and met Poplavsky, who described the organization as one that would defend the rights of workers. He told Reznichenko that if he was interested, he should meet him the next day at the Pushkin Square metro station at 9 a.m.

The two men met the following day as planned and then walked to the Kuznetsky Most metro station near KGB headquarters on Dzerzhinsky Square. Reznichenko saw a small group of men whom he recognized immediately as truth seekers by their determined expressions and provincial clothing. Among them was one whose self-confident, businesslike attitude set him apart—Vladimir Klebanov, a coal miner from Makeyevka in the Donbass.

After Reznichenko explained what had happened to him, Klebanov asked if he was interested in joining the group. He said the goal of the group was action on their complaints. If their demands were not satisfied, they would form an independent trade union and organize a press conference for foreign correspondents. If that didn't help, they would demand a collective exit from the Soviet Union because they did not have the rights of Soviet citizens.

Reznichenko was impressed with Klebanov immediately. The idea of organizing an independent trade union struck him as excellent. He said that he wanted to participate. Klebanov welcomed him into the group and said that the first order of business would be the organization of collective letters. Reznichenko began to work with other members of the group turning out letters and documents, including complaints to *Pravda, Izvestiya, Ogonyek,* the popular journal *Man and the Law,* and the Central Committee, procurator, and the Supreme Soviet.

The members of the group began meeting every morning at 9 a.m. on Gorky Street in front of the central post office. Klebanov, Reznichenko, and others also began making their first contacts with foreign correspondents, including me and Hal Piper of the *Baltimore Sun.*

Emissaries visited the stations and reception halls, rapidly gathering more signatures. After months, and in some cases years, of frustration, the members of the group at last began to feel that there was some hope.

The authorities did not respond to the collective petitions, and finally, a date for a press conference was set and Hal, David Shipler of the *New York Times,* and I met Klebanov and Poplavsky in the center of Moscow. Together, with other members of the group, we took the subway to the Tekstilshchiki metro station on the outskirts of Moscow and went to an apartment nearby.

Several other members of the Klebanov group were waiting for us. Klebanov began by describing his experiences. He said that in 1968, after becoming a shift foreman in the Bazhanova mine in Makeyevka, he began to refuse to send miners into the mine when safety equipment was missing or broken and, as a result, he was persecuted by the bosses of the mine.

Poplavsky said he had been the head of the maintenance department of a concrete plant in Klimovsk when he was fired for refusing to write a reprimand into the work record of a woman who protested against the use of company funds for drinking.

Anatoly Poznyakov said that he had worked as a locksmith in Moscow for seventy-five rubles a month. When he asked for a raise, he was told that his destiny in life was "to eat from a pig's trough." When he continued to appeal for a raise, he was fired and was now forced to live on a semi-disability pension of twenty-one rubles a month.

Nadezhda Kurakin said that she had worked for twenty-five years in a restaurant in Volgograd. The restaurant managers were docking her pay and that of other waitresses for fictitious broken crockery and then ordering new crockery for themselves. In 1975, Kurakin protested against this practice publicly and was fired for shirking.

The press conference continued until well into the evening. Reznichenko did not speak, but his case was described in the documents of the group.

About a week after the press conference, Klebanov was seized on the street and taken to a police station near Pushkin Square. From there, he was removed by KGB men to Kursk station and put on a train to Donetsk with two MVD officers. At KGB headquarters in Donetsk, he was told that his conflict with the mine bosses in Makeyevka would be settled. The KGB asked only that he not return to Moscow. Klebanov agreed and he was set free, although two KGB men followed him. A short time later, Klebanov managed to elude them and escaped to a nearby city. Two days later, he appeared on the sidewalk outside the central post office.

In January, Klebanov held another press conference at which he announced the official formation of the Independent Free Trade

Union. By now the group had collected the signatures of seventy persons who were ready to join the new union, and there was strong support in the reception halls even on the part of those who were afraid.

News of the creation of the new union was broadcast back to the country on foreign radio stations and hundreds of letters began to arrive at the central post office in the name of Klebanov, care of K-9, which was general delivery.

At this point, however, the KGB started to make arrests. On January 20, Reznichenko was sitting in Kiev station with a meal of lard and bread spread out on a copy of *Pravda* when he noticed two policemen coming toward him. They checked his documents and then arrested him and took him to the Lyublinsky special detention center where inmates were packed twenty to a cell. After three weeks, he was taken back to the Kiev station and transported under guard in an ordinary passenger car to Odessa.

When the train arrived in Odessa at 5 a.m., Reznichenko was taken by KGB agents back to the egg factory, where he was allowed to work but not given a bed in the dormitory. He spent three days in the dormitory sleeping on half of a bed that he shared with a friend. On the fourth day, he sold his watch and went back to Moscow.

On arrival in Moscow, Reznichenko went back to Kursk station and, from there, took an electric train to Klimovsk, where he hoped to find Poplavsky. When Reznichenko got off the train in Klimovsk, however, he saw Varvara Kucherenko, a member of the group, on the platform. She said that she had been given her job back in a pickling plant in Makhachkala and urged Reznichenko to quit the movement. Reznichenko, however, refused to listen.

He found Poplavsky, who told him that Klebanov had been arrested in February.

With Klebanov behind bars, Reznichenko and Poplavsky began answering the letters for Klebanov that were arriving at K-9. Working separately, they looked for new recruits. In the railroad stations, Reznichenko searched the crowd for men who were shaking their fists or women who were crying. There had been seventy people in the original trade union, but within a few weeks of the arrest of Klebanov, almost all of them had been sent home under threat of arrest. Reznichenko and Poplavsky signed up seventy more.

On March 13, however, the KGB closed in. Reznichenko and

Poplavsky had agreed to meet at 10 a.m. at the Kuznetsky Most metro station, but Poplavsky did not show up. After waiting for almost an hour, Reznichenko went to the central telegraph building and was arrested by KGB agents. He was then taken to Domodedovo airport, where he was put on a plane under guard and sent back to Odessa. In Odessa, the KGB got him a room for the night, and on the following day, he was driven back to the egg factory and taken to the dormitory. When Reznichenko entered the room with his KGB escort, however, he saw that there was blood on the sheets and the floor was sticky. The remains of food were on the small tables and the room was filled with swarms of flies.

The KGB man protested to the director, who had the room cleaned. Reznichenko spent part of the night there, but at 2 a.m. he gathered all his things, leaving his radio on for the benefit of the police guard at the door, and left through the first-floor window.

For three days he traveled only at night, crossing fields and avoiding the roads. He finally arrived at a rural settlement and got on an electric train and rode without paying to Donetsk. From there, he traveled by electric train to Voronezh, then to Michurinsk, and, finally, to Ryazan, where he lived in the park and on the street for almost two months.

In Ryazan, Reznichenko subsisted on bread and salt, earning money by cashing in empty bottles. He also wrote out an eight-page statement to Brezhnev as well as statements to President Jimmy Carter and Kurt Waldheim. He finally left for Moscow and, from there, went to Klimovsk, where he went to the apartment of Poplavsky.

Poplavsky's wife said he had been arrested and convicted of vagrancy and sentenced to a year in prison.

Reznichenko returned to Moscow and took up residence in the Lenin Stadium. For two months, Reznichenko was the only inhabitant of the stadium, which made him feel like Robinson Crusoe. He was to remember those months in the Stadium fondly when he was in prison.

When fall came and the weather got cold, Reznichenko moved back into Kiev station, where he was arrested on October 8 by the same policeman who had arrested him previously. The police were preparing to take Reznichenko to the local police station when Feoktistov, the duty officer, asked Reznichenko if he had brought anything with him. Reznichenko showed him the statement to

Brezhnev that he had written while in Ryazan. In it, Reznichenko spoke of the "shame of the red fascists" and the "shame of the red murderers." He also renounced his Soviet citizenship and said that he considered Jimmy Carter to be his president.

When he finished reading the statement, Feoktistov told Reznichenko that he liked it very much. He then gave it to his boss, the chief of the station, who also told Reznichenko how much he liked it. Feoktistov said that he would shortly be visiting the Ministry of Internal Affairs and that he would, without fail, give the statement to Mikhail Shchelokov, the minister, who would give it to Brezhnev.

Reznichenko was taken back to Odessa and then to the police station near the egg factory. An investigation was started on charges of vagrancy and violation of the passport regulations.

He refused to cooperate with the investigation, explaining, "I don't trust red fascists." He was finally sentenced on December 21, 1978, to two years for vagrancy and taken to a labor camp in the Voroshilovgrad oblast to serve out his term.

5

The Workers

All previous historical movements were movements of minorities, or in the interests of minorities. The proletarian movement is the self-conscious, independent movement of the immense majority, in the interests of the immense majority.

—*Karl Marx,* The Communist Manifesto

THE KUZBASS REGION, 1989

FOR MONTHS, in the antediluvian coal mines of Kuzbass, there was a feeling that something was about to happen. The miners in the smoky, polluted region had long been angry about food shortages that got worse with every year. Then, in early 1989, the stores ran out of laundry powder, toothpaste, and soap. At the Shevyakova mine in Mezhdurechensk, forty miles from Novokuznetsk, feelings ran particularly high. The miners had written to the television program "Projector of Perestroika" in December 1988 asking for better food supplies and transport and extra pay for evening and night work, but the letter was referred to the official trade union organization and they never got a reply.

In the spring, the mine bosses announced that, in addition to the shortages of soap in the city stores, there was now no soap in the mine. Instead, after a long shift underground, the men were given a washing-up liquid that was used for cleaning engines and caused their hair to fall out. As the taps broke on the showers, four men were forced to wash under one shower.

Finally, Valery Kokorin, one of the miners, began circulating a petition with a set of demands, including a raise in the pay for work in difficult conditions, increases in food supplies, and improvements in medical care. By July 8, the petition had been signed by five hundred miners, but the bosses seemed indifferent. When Kokorin presented it to them, he received no response.

On the morning of July 11, the Shevyakova miners' patience finally ran out. As the sun rose over the forested hills behind the mine, three hundred men arrived for the morning shift and put on their lanterns and batteries but refused to go into the mine. When miners arrived for the afternoon and evening shifts, they also changed into workclothes but refused to work. By the end of the day, hundreds of militant miners were massed in front of the mine.

As dusk fell, the miners began sending emissaries to the other mines in Mezhdurechensk asking for support. They arrived there at midnight, in time for the shift change, and the events at the Shevyakova mine were repeated. The miners, to a man, declined to enter the mines. The action continued to spread the next morning as miners arrived for the morning shift and strikers went to the auto depots and recruited the truck drivers who hauled away the freshly mined coal to join the work stoppage.

By the afternoon of July 12, every major enterprise in the city was on strike.

Mezhdurechensk soon began to resemble a city under siege. Miners marched in long columns from the mines, which were located in the surrounding valleys, into Mezhdurechensk, encamping in front of the four-story party headquarters in the central square. By nightfall, there were up to thirty thousand people in the square and authority in the city had passed from the local Communist Party to the miners' strike committees. The miners organized their own militia to close liquor stores, and the police agreed to cooperate with the workers' militia in keeping order.

The local authorities, afraid that the striking miners would ransack the town, gave them microphones and loudspeakers. As speakers began denouncing conditions in the city from a makeshift platform, the miners, joined on the square by their wives and children, built fires to warm themselves as they prepared to spend the night.

The revolt of Soviet coal miners was sudden and dramatic. But the shaking off of fear did not come all at once. For Soviet workers, fear characterized an entire era.

DONETSK, 1980

Kevin Klose of the *Washington Post* and I arrived at a dilapidated miners' village in the Panfilov district and went to a lonely apartment building that stood on the edge of a weedy field. Across the road from the building were chalk-colored cottages and rusting metal sheds, and looming in the background were enormous coal tips wreathed in fog.

It began to rain and the bare winter branches of the trees, the rolling gray clouds, and the crows cawing and wheeling amid the telegraph lines added to the ominousness of the scene and its desolation.

Kevin and I entered the building and walked up to the fourth floor, where we were admitted to the apartment of Alexei Nikitin, a Donetsk coal miner, by his sister, Lyubov Poludnyak.

Poludnyak said Nikitin had not returned home. "I'm afraid they're going to grab him," she told us.

She led us into Nikitin's room, where we waited for a few minutes but became increasingly worried. Finally, we went back downstairs and stood in the entryway.

The air smelled of coal dust, and the black-clad women standing with pails at a hand pump were a portrait of nineteenth-century exploitation extended inexplicably into the twentieth.

A growing number of cars began arriving, and KGB agents stationed themselves under the eaves of metal sheds at points all around us. Several of Nikitin's neighbors joined us in front of the entryway.

Finally, I asked one of them, a small hunchbacked woman with a wrinkled face and watery eyes, to try to see whether Nikitin was anywhere in the area. She agreed and limped slowly through the rain to the end of the road past the waiting KGB agents. She turned the corner and looked around behind the houses. She returned fifteen minutes later and said she had seen no trace of Nikitin. This was bad news. I was sure his only hope of avoiding arrest was being able to join us before he was seized.

Suddenly, a middle-aged woman told me to look in the opposite direction. I turned and was surprised to notice, coming out of a nearby field, a small figure dressed in green and wearing a large hat that all but covered his face. As the figure drew closer, I saw that he was grinning and I understood, with a twinge of horror, that this was a KGB agent who had come to tell us that Nikitin had been arrested.

When the figure came closer, however, I took a better look.

"Ha, ha, ha," Nikitin said, removing the hat. "Oh, they're stupid. Look at them. I've fooled those KGB men so many times that I've come to the conclusion that they ought to fire 70 percent of them. They're just in it for the money."

We shook hands with Nikitin and pounded him on the back. A group of KGB agents were now standing at the end of the road, looking on silently. "Oh, a lot of people are going to be fired because of this," Nikitin said. "I defeated them good, those bastards. They harassed me, tortured me. Now let them think about how I fooled them. They won't fire people for refusing to give me a job, but for failing to prevent us from meeting, they'll fire them for that.

"They're wolves in human skin," he continued, savoring his victory. "They wanted to grab me at the railroad station and take me straight to a mental hospital. They were waiting at the station with a truck that had a red cross on it, but I circled around behind the train and went to stay with a friend who gave me fresh clothing."

In this fashion, Alexei Vasilievich Nikitin returned safely home in Donetsk from Moscow—and established contact on his home ground with two foreign correspondents.

NIKITIN'S CONFRONTATION with the Communist authorities dated back many years.

He went to work as a miner in the late 1950s in the Butovka-Donetsk mine. He joined the Communist Party, determined to fight against "shortcomings" in the interest of Soviet power and, at first, was seen by the mine bosses as a possible Communist leader. While working in the ventilation department, however, he became concerned about safety violations—in particular, ventilators placed too deep in the mine shaft—and began warning about a possible explosion.

For a time, the mine bosses tolerated Nikitin because of his loyalty and hard work, but in June 1969, an event took place that changed the course of his life.

The miners at Butovka-Donetsk were fearful and powerless. For several months, Viktor Savitch, the director, had been taking extra coal mined on Sundays and applying it against the following month's plan target to avoid paying workers their bonuses—and this angered them.

The sheer arbitrariness of Savitch's actions began to inspire a rebellion. Knowing Nikitin's willingness to speak out, several miners approached him about the problem and he suggested they form a delegation. A short time later, a group of miners led by Nikitin went to see Savitch.

"The miners are literate men," Nikitin said. "They can read the graphs and they know how much coal they are loading each day. They know to the kopeck how much they have coming to them and they know that they are entitled to a 15 percent bonus."

Savitch said that he would pay whatever he wanted to pay and threw the miners out of his office. The workers, under the direction of Nikitin, then took the usual step of signing a collective letter of complaint, which was sent to the Communist Party Central Committee.

Several months later, Vladimir Dyekhtyarev, the party first secretary in the oblast, arrived at the mine and ordered Nikitin expelled from the party. The other miners were forced to renounce their signatures.

Nikitin, a loyal Communist, appealed for reinstatement, but he quickly discovered that the party in Donetsk not only had no interest in the rights of workers but considered activism on the part of miners to be a direct threat.

At a meeting of the Donetsk city Party Committee, Kubishkin, the first secretary, said, "You defend the people. You are a literate fellow. You've read history. Well, in history it is written that those who tried to lead the masses ended up having their heads cut off."

Eight months after being expelled from the party, Nikitin was fired from his job, marking the beginning of a long search for work. There were forty-eight coal mines in Donetsk and each of them needed miners, but Nikitin soon found that he had been blacklisted by all of them.

His thoughts began to move in an unexpected direction. What if, he wondered, the Communists were only pretending to build communism but were really creating some kind of society of hangmen? What if the legal system was only a facade and behind that facade was a country ruled by a gang of fascist, Pinochet thugs?

Nikitin did not like this idea, but he could not dismiss it either. After all, the people who were persecuting him for defending the workers called themselves Communists. He began working part-time as a bricklayer. He also traveled to Moscow to seek justice in the reception halls of government organizations.

Nikitin went to Moscow five times in the course of two years and came to recognize those who, like him, returned to the reception halls repeatedly. He saw that not one of these people, in the time that he was seeking justice in Moscow, ever left because the authorities had satisfied his complaint.

Instead, they were shuttled between the Central Committee, the Supreme Soviet, and the procurator and forced at every stage to fill out ever more voluminous documents until, exhausted, frantic, and confused, they were sent back to the local authorities, against whom they were complaining in the first place.

Nikitin tried to decide what to do. He could attempt to survive with the help of odd jobs and forget the injustice that had been committed against him, but this meant submitting to the local mafia—an idea that made him physically ill.

He decided, instead, to carry the battle one step further.

ON APRIL 15, 1971, Nikitin strolled around the center of Moscow, studying the guarded entryways to the various embassies. The West German embassy was difficult to approach. The Turkish embassy looked easier, but he wanted to explore further. Finally, he passed the Norwegian embassy and noticed that the Soviet guard was looking in the other direction. He seized the moment and ran in through the gate.

Nikitin was met by a young diplomat, who interviewed him and gave him the telephone number of the American embassy. He then left the building, called the American embassy, and spoke to a diplomat who promised to send him an invitation care of the post office on Gorky Street.

As he hung up the phone, Nikitin felt a surge of relief. His first thought was that if the American embassy was ready to help him, the United Nations would almost certainly come to his aid. He felt that he was practically a free man.

The first sign to the contrary came when Nikitin went to the post office to pick up his invitation. There was a long queue and when he reached the counter, he gave the clerk his name and asked if there was a letter for him. She told him, to his surprise, that there was only a package.

Nikitin said he was expecting a letter, not a package. That was strange, she said, there was a parcel for him from Novocherkassk but no letter. The threat implied by the point of origin struck Nikitin immediately. Novocherkassk was the scene of a massacre of protesting workers in 1962.

Nikitin left the post office and came back a short time later. The woman again insisted that there was a package for him.

"No," Nikitin said. "My twin is living here in Moscow. The package is for him. I'm waiting for a letter from the American embassy."

Two days later, he returned again to the post office and asked for his letter. This time the clerk said that there was no package and no letter. Confused and very apprehensive, Nikitin walked out of the post office and, as the double doors swung shut behind him, he was grabbed from behind by two men and forced into a waiting car. He was then driven to a nearby police station and taken from there to a psychiatric hospital, where he was questioned by the KGB before being allowed to return to Donetsk.

In the months to come, Nikitin took odd jobs as an agricultural laborer on the collective farms near Donetsk, but he was closely shadowed by the KGB, which often posted agents in cars outside his apartment building.

As the net tightened around him, Nikitin's friends began to avoid him. It seemed to him that his arrest was only a matter of time.

For several months, however, Nikitin was not touched. The danger remained vague and undefined. It only crystallized when, on the morning of December 22, 1971, an explosion ripped through the Butovka-Donetsk mine at the time of the shift change.

The explosion devastated the mine. Seven workers were killed and more than a hundred injured, many of them severely. In the aftermath of the blast, angry miners gathered in front of the mine, shouting "Nikitin warned you!" The area was soon flooded with a hundred cars and five hundred KGB men and police. In the face of such a show of force, the miners slowly dispersed, shaking their fists but risking nothing more than angry shouts.

When Nikitin learned about the explosion, he realized that his fate was sealed. He was sure that the local authorities would not allow him to become a rallying point for the angry miners. Three weeks later, he was seized and put in the Donetsk jail, where he was charged with anti-Soviet propaganda. He spent five months in prison without trial until, one night, he was suddenly put in a truck and taken to a prison train.

Nikitin had experienced many shocks in the years since he first confronted Savitch in the Butovka-Donetsk mine, but nothing prepared him for what was to happen next.

The train left Donetsk and arrived in the dead of night in Dnepropetrovsk, where Nikitin and other prisoners were taken in a truck to a fortresslike building surrounded by high walls and barbed wire. Nikitin was then led to a basement, where there were some baths.

He could see that he was in some type of prison, but he was puzzled because, although he had been charged with anti-Soviet propaganda, there had not been any kind of trial and he had not been convicted of anything.

The first clue to his situation came from an orderly who began making a list of his belongings.

"You won't need these, dear Comrade," the orderly said, "because you're going to be here for life."

"For life?" Nikitin repeated. "How do you know that this is for life?"

"Little friend." The orderly laughed. "They've decided you're a fool and you've got a political offense. So don't worry about your things, you're here for life."

Nikitin was next led to the baths. After he finished washing up, he was given a black prison uniform and taken upstairs to a corridor with a long row of locked doors.

An orderly escorting him unlocked one of the doors and, when he opened it, Nikitin was seized with a wave of revulsion and fear. Facing him were thirty inmates with yellow faces and wildly contorted limbs. Some sat with their tongues hanging out, staring blankly, others were unable to look at anything because their faces were disfigured by horrible tics. The air in the chamber was so poisoned by the smell of unwashed bodies and the noxious, chemical breath of men who had been treated with powerful drugs that it was all Nikitin could do to keep from vomiting.

Nikitin realized that he was not in a prison. They had put him in a hospital.

THE DNEPROPETROVSK Special Psychiatric Hospital was to be Nikitin's home for the next three years.

On the day after his arrival, Nikitin was examined by the doctors, and after two weeks, he was diagnosed as suffering from "psychopathology, simple form."

He quickly learned that the purpose of the hospital was to reform the inmates' behavior with the help of drugs. He saw that ten milligrams of haloperidol could turn a man into a suffering mass with no power to resist, and the doctors prescribed ten tablets at a time, ten times the normal dose.

He also learned about sulfazine, a preparation of purified sulfur that sent temperatures up over 104 degrees and caused excruciating pain that got worse and worse—like a drill boring into a man's body—until it was more than a person could bear.

To Nikitin's surprise, however, the treatment assigned to him was rather mild. He was given a drug called majeptil, which caused internal pressure and contortion of movements but did not cause unbearable pain.

As the weeks passed, Nikitin saw that while many inmates in the hospital were clearly deranged, others were incarcerated on political charges. He met Alexander Polezhayev, a Soviet marine who, while serving in Egypt, tried to escape to Israel; Vasily Serry, a teacher from Odessa who attempted to hijack a plane; and a Ukrainian student who was declared mentally incompetent for displaying a Ukrainian flag.

During the day, the patients were given their injections, and although some patients were left in no condition to work, those who could were assigned to sewing sacks or washing the floor.

It was only at night, however, that life in the hospital achieved its full Dantean possibilities. At that time, all the inmates were locked in their rooms and the patients who had been injected with drugs lay on their narrow beds, groaning in agony, twitching uncontrollably, or going through horrible convulsions. The lamp which burned through the night from the high ceiling to prevent suicides cast the inmates' shadows on the walls and, as Nikitin watched in horror, patients in the grip of paroxysms induced by the drugs used the last of their strength to curse the psychiatrists and Soviet power.

After two years, during which Nikitin worked as a carpenter and stone mason but was forced to continue taking majeptil, he was made an orderly and then, after nine more months, he was transferred to a Donetsk psychiatric hospital before finally being released on March 26, 1976.

When he got out, Nikitin went to live with his sister in the Panfilov district. Four and a half years had passed since his arrest, and in that time, Savitch, Kubishkin, and Dyekhtyarev had all lost their posts amid talk of speculation in apartments. As the weeks went by, however, it became obvious that none of these changes affected Nikitin. No mine would hire him and the local authorities refused to give him any help in finding a job.

Nikitin survived with the help of odd jobs. He also traveled to Moscow to seek help in the reception halls, not to right an injustice this time but simply to get regular work.

In fact he found no help, but his appeals to Moscow infuriated the local authorities, who retaliated by stationing two policemen in the corridor of his sister's communal flat.

"We'll lock you up," one of the policeman said. "Not right now, but we'll find a way."

Nikitin finally decided that he had to take decisive action. On February 20, 1977, he left his sister's apartment at 5 a.m. to avoid being seen by the police and took a bus to the nearby city of Makeyevka, where he boarded a train for Moscow. Two days after his arrival in Moscow, he again entered the Norwegian embassy, where he was received by a gray-haired man with a thin face and a sharp nose.

Nikitin explained that he wanted political asylum.

"We can't give you political asylum," the diplomat said. "We can only do that on Norwegian territory."

Nikitin tried to control a wave of panic. "But what about the Helsinki agreements that oblige you to give asylum to a person in a critical situation?"

"I'm sorry," the diplomat said, "you can only receive political asylum in Norway."

Nikitin got up and the diplomat escorted him to the door. Nikitin stepped out into the subzero weather, where a KGB agent in a military uniform arrested him. As he looked up at the embassy from the street, Nikitin saw people in every window, watching him.

He was taken to a nearby police station and then sent back to the Dnepropetrovsk Special Psychiatric Hospital, where he was immediately given three drugs: triftazin, tisercin, and chlorprothixene, which made it difficult for him to walk.

Nikitin had feared being sent back to that hospital, but, to his surprise, his second stay was to prove not that different from his first.

The hospital officials recalled Nikitin's skill as a handyman and carpenter and assigned him to work on various construction projects. In the meantime, his drug treatment was suspended.

Soon, Nikitin was treated almost like a free employee. There was one occasion, however, when he was reminded of his status. One day, while he was doing some repair work, he stopped to talk to Serry, the plane hijacker. Politicals were strictly forbidden to speak to each other, and when the orderlies saw Nikitin and Serry in the corridor they grabbed them, pulled them into separate rooms, and began injecting them with haloperidol and aminazine. Nikitin received two injections, three times a day, until there was no longer any place in his buttocks to stick a needle.

After the series of injections was over, Nikitin returned to his work. In October 1979, he was transferred to Psychiatric Hospital Number 2 in Donetsk and was released seven months later, on May 5, 1980.

Once he was free, Nikitin again moved into his sister's apartment, but he still could not get a job.

While a patient at Dnepropetrovsk, Nikitin heard from other inmates about an organization called the Working Commission on the Abuse of Psychiatry for Political Goals, which had been created by dissidents in Moscow. After his release, he went to Moscow at the first opportunity to meet Felix Serebrov, a member of the commission, whose address he had learned from a foreign radio broadcast.

Nikitin told Serebrov his story and, for the first time in his long struggle, he realized he had met someone in Moscow who was ready to listen to him with sympathy and understanding. Serebrov decided to call me.

Felix lived in a new, proletarian section of Moscow not far from the Olympic Village, and I arrived at an hour when the area was alive with the aimless activity of one of Moscow's new districts on a warm midsummer night. About fifteen minutes after I arrived, the doorbell rang and Felix opened the door. The man in the doorway was short and stocky. He was wearing a checkered jacket with a badge marked "engineer" in his lapel. His fleshy face, keen blue eyes under barely discernible eyebrows, and double chin gave him a faint resemblance to a younger Nikita Khrushchev.

Nikitin had just been examined by Anatoly Koryagin, a Kharkov psychiatrist and consultant to the commission, who had pronounced him sane. At my request, Nikitin began to tell me his story, and three months after we became acquainted, he invited me to accompany him to Donetsk to learn about the real conditions of Soviet workers. I recruited Kevin Klose to accompany me and agreed to make the trip.

NIKITIN'S RUSE had foiled the KGB—at least temporarily—and we went up to his apartment. Nikitin changed his clothes and, in a victorious mood, we tried to make plans for the next few days.

Nikitin said it would be easiest to talk to coal miners during one of the shift changes, so we decided to postpone our first visit to Butovka-Donetsk until dawn of the following day.

The rain had stopped but the weather remained overcast and the miners' district seemed desolate and neglected, a set of dilapidated buildings before a railroad embankment under the arch of a white, featureless sky.

Our first priority was to speak to coal miners, but even with Nikitin's help, it was not clear how this could be done. Foreign correspondents were a rarity in Donetsk, and any miner could rightly fear that the price of a conversation with a foreign correspondent would be the loss of his job. At the same time, the whole country was on edge over the labor crisis in Poland and the constant denunciations in the Soviet press of the Polish workers as "anti-socialist" elements.

We decided to try to visit people Nikitin knew. We left the miners' village and made our way to a main highway, where we caught a cab and traveled across the city, followed everywhere by a car with four KGB agents.

We arrived at the apartment of a friend who had worked with

Nikitin in the late 1960s. He claimed to be busy. Next, we went to the apartment of a woman whom Nikitin had met while seeking truth in Moscow, but she did not want to talk.

Nikitin finally decided to take us to visit his former neighbors, who lived in Yuzovka, a district named after John Hughes, the English capitalist who helped finance early coal mining in Donetsk.

We reached Yuzovka at about 8 p.m., and in the moon's silvery light it was easy to imagine that we were in an English suburb. Yuzovka was founded as a model community for Russian miners and it consisted of two-story, white plaster houses with red-tile roofs set on spacious lots behind neat wooden fences. The well-paved streets were lined with spreading trees and in the yards were small "summer kitchens," where, in mild weather, families could take their meals outdoors.

Nikitin led us into the backyard of one of the houses. The collection of doorbells and mailboxes, as well as the hanging laundry in the windows, made it clear that the house was now occupied by six to eight Soviet families.

We crossed the yard and knocked on the door of the small summer kitchen and were welcomed by Nikolai, a carpenter at Butovka-Donetsk, and Zina, his wife, a sorter.

For the next few hours, we were given a description of what it was like to work in a mine like Butovka-Donetsk.

Zina said that after the coal is mined, it is brought to the surface on a conveyor along with a lot of rock. About ten women per shift work as sorters removing the rock by hand from the conveyor and dropping it into a hole leading to the dumps of three-wheeled cars. The bosses try to keep the process going at all times and the women must lean over the conveyor, sorting out the rock as fast as possible.

The sorters inhaled coal dust, but there was no extra pay for the danger of silicosis. The sorters also were not given specific times when they could take breaks. Their movements were subordinated to the movement of the conveyor; if a sorter complained of feeling ill, she was sent to the medical section and her temperature was taken. In many cases, sorters were forced to work with fevers of up to 100 degrees. Ill and exhausted, they could easily fall onto the conveyor belt.

Nikolai said the miners long ago became accustomed to a six-day week as well as working on Sunday although, according to the law, miners can only be asked to work on Sundays twice a month and, if

asked, have the right to refuse. In November 1980, the miners at
Butovka-Donetsk worked all five Sundays and any miner daring to
invoke his legal right to refuse would have been fired.

Compensatory time off for Sunday work was given at a time of
the bosses' choosing, and a miner's hours could be changed when-
ever needed to suit the demands of production. In the course of
a single month, a miner could work the night shift (10 p.m. to
6 a.m.), the morning shift (6 a.m. to 2 p.m.), and then the second
shift (2 p.m. to 10 p.m.) with no compensation for the disruption and
only an extra twenty-two kopecks a day for night work.

The miners lived, in effect, in a state of perpetual mobilization.
Nikitin said that bosses in Donetsk could control the workers because
they had split the working class.

At Butovka-Donetsk, all of the mining brigades worked with
identical combines, but for efficiency a brigade also needed wagons
for loading, ventilation equipment, materials for reinforcing the mine
shaft, water, and spare parts. The necessary supplies were assured
only to "shock workers," who could be relied on to stand up at factory meetings and defend management. As a result, the shock workers regularly mined more coal. Since salaries were calculated on the
basis of production, they earned more than twice as much as members of ordinary brigades for the same work.

I asked Nikolai and Zina why there were not more miners who
were willing to defend workers' rights.

"The workers are afraid to challenge the bosses," said Zina. "In
this country, they don't love the truth."

Zina said that most miners had to wait fifteen to twenty years for
a separate apartment. As a result, they learned to avoid all conflicts,
hoping to keep their job and assure that their place in the queue was
respected.

Besides controlling apartments, the mine bosses also determined
the miners' vacation schedules, which gave them tremendous power
over people who spent all year underground.

IT GREW LATE and we got up to go. But before returning with
Nikitin to his apartment, we went with Zina and Nikolai from the
summer kitchen to their apartment in the main house.

The apartment was located in a corner of the house and consisted of a dimly lit small room, crowded with furniture, and a porch,

which was separated from the room by a curtain. The family shared a bathroom at the end of the corridor with three other families.

Nikitin said that the majority of mining families in Donetsk lived in conditions like these as they waited for up to fifteen years to receive a separate apartment. If they alienated the mine bosses, they could live in such conditions until the end of their lives.

By the time we left Zina and Nikolai's apartment, the streetlamps were glowing and the city was covered with a light fog. We walked to a main avenue, caught a cab, and returned to Nikitin's apartment, followed closely by a white car with four men in it.

In front of Nikitin's building, I saw other men standing around on the sidewalk or sitting in parked cars.

Poludnyak prepared dinner for us. Shortly after 11 p.m., I walked over to the window and pulled back the curtain. Outside, two cars were parked opposite the building. Under these circumstances, I felt that our presence offered Nikitin some protection, and we decided not to return to our hotel. Poludnyak made up a couch for Kevin and a bed for me and Nikitin went to sleep on a bed in his sister's small room.

Day 2

We were awakened by the alarm clock at 4:30 a.m. We then dressed, had breakfast, left Nikitin's apartment, and walked through the silent streets on the way to the Butovka-Donetsk mine.

The weather had gotten warmer and a fine rain was falling. Smoke rose from the small chimneys of the one-story, white plaster houses. We arrived at the bus stop, where small knots of men waited, the blue smoke of their cigarettes visible in the morning air. The bus pulled up and about twenty minutes later we arrived at the Butovka-Donetsk mine.

The mine was a collection of coal chutes and redbrick buildings. We went with Nikitin to the entryway of the bathhouse, where streetlamps created coronas of light in the smoky haze. One by one, the miners emerged in street clothes on their way to catch buses to their homes.

Many of the miners recognized Nikitin and shook his hand, asking where he had been. Yet when he tried to strike up conversations, he had little success.

The situation aroused the miners' suspicions. Nikitin pointed to us and said that we represented the "two most influential newspapers in the world" and explained that he was helping us to write about the conditions of miners in Donetsk.

This type of introduction, however, did us little good. The miners probably feared that Nikitin was being watched. At the same time, some of them undoubtedly knew that Nikitin had been in a psychiatric hospital and were not anxious to share his fate.

Eventually, the bathhouse emptied and we crossed the street and tried to talk to the miners at the bus stop. When Nikitin mentioned who we were, however, they either fell silent or changed the subject and remarked that the bus was late.

Gradually, the last miners left the bus stop. The mine's motors began operating, gently vibrating the ground. The chance to talk to miners at Butovka-Donetsk that morning was lost.

We left the mine and began to travel across Donetsk. We went to shopping areas, cafés, and bus stops outside of mines during the afternoon shift change, but we had almost no success in speaking to people. I recalled the remark of a woman in Moscow who told me that in forty years in Donetsk, she had never heard "a free thought, freely expressed." As the hours passed, I began to wonder if the effort to talk to miners had even been worthwhile.

At length, Nikitin had an idea. He said that some of the pensioners from Butovka-Donetsk lived in a community known as the New Colony; unlike active miners, they might be willing to talk to us because they would have less to lose.

After a forty-minute cab ride, we arrived at a group of apartment buildings on the edge of a windswept plain. Nikitin walked up to an old woman on a weedy path leading to the first building and asked her if we could see her apartment. To our surprise, she invited us in.

The woman's name was Matriona Dmitrieva and she led us into a room where wet laundry hung from the ceiling and the chairs and cupboards were crowded together and covered with dust. Other women peered in through the open door and Dmitrieva invited them in to meet her "guests."

I asked Dmitrieva if she could tell us about her life and she seemed flattered by the request.

She said that she worked as an attendant in the bathhouse at the Butovka mine and that she, her husband, Tikhon, an invalid, and Vitaly, their son, had lived in this room and a corner of the communal kitchen since 1945. Her son slept on the couch and she slept on a bed near the wall. Her husband, who was eighty years old and had lost his legs in 1938 when he fell under the wheels of a wagon on a slag heap, slept on a bed in the kitchen.

Dmitrieva said there was no running water in the building so it was necessary to walk to the well and to the outdoor toilets, which were more than a quarter of a mile away. Tikhon, who could not leave his bed, used a bucket as a chamber bowl.

She described her job as a machinist, running a conveyor at the Butovka mine, her husband's accident, and the situation of her son, who had little prospect of ever leaving this room in which he had lived for all forty-one years of his life.

I asked her if she had tried to improve her living conditions. Dmitrieva said that she requested a separate apartment in a letter to Anatoly Dyuba, who succeeded Savitch as director of the Butovka mine, citing her husband's condition and his advanced age. Dyuba wrote back saying that her request was being referred to his deputy for housing conditions. But that was the last she ever heard about it.

By the time Dmitrieva finished speaking, the room was nearly full and her neighbors added their own complaints about their living conditions. They said that pensioners were always pushed to the back of the queue for apartments while mine officials gave apartments illegally to their relatives and friends.

I asked the pensioners to tell about their experiences and they began standing up one by one to describe their fate.

Lydia Belozorova, seventy-eight years old, said she had worked for eighteen years turning coal cars around with her own back at the bottom of an incline until, finally exhausted from her work, she retired on a small pension, living in the kitchen of a communal flat. In 1979, she went to see a mine official to ask for a one-room apartment and showed him a certificate she had received in recognition of her years of hard work. The official said, "You worked for your order. Take it. There is nothing I can do for you."

Olga Famina, eighty years old, said she had worked as a coal sorter and retired on a pension of twenty-four rubles a month, which did not leave her enough money for milk. In desperation, she went to the district council to ask for help.

"You have a bed?" an official asked.

"Yes."

"A stove?"

"Yes."

"That's enough for you. Now get out of here."

Famina burst into tears. "I won't come back here anymore," she said.

Other residents of the New Colony described the closet-sized rooms and kitchens in which they lived. Finally, we got up to leave and Belozorova accompanied us outside. The gray sky grew dark, and with the temperature dropping rapidly, it began to rain.

We spent the next few hours traveling in cabs across Donetsk, trying to find various people that Nikitin remembered but again without success. During the years of persecution, Nikitin had apparently lost touch with many people he once knew.

We finally decided to return to Nikitin's home. By the time we got to the Panfilov district, it had turned cold, the wind had died down, and smoke from several chimneys rose slowly in the frigid air. We went up the stairs to Nikitin's apartment, where Poludnyak was busy in the kitchen preparing a meal. It had been a long day. We had crisscrossed the city for almost seventeen hours and had succeeded principally in talking to a group of old-age pensioners. The working people of the city had concealed their feelings behind a veil of silence.

At 11:30 p.m., Poludnyak served us dinner and Nikitin gave me some things he had written, including appeals to the World Federation of Labor and to the British Trade Union Council in which he asked them for help in organizing an independent Soviet trade union. As I read them, I was impressed not only by his courage but by his phenomenal will to fight. Poludnyak brought us some tea and some freshly made *vareniye,* and a somber mood came over us.

For the first time all day, I began to think about what the consequences of this trip would be for Nikitin. I walked to the window and pulled back the curtain. A half moon cast a faint glow over the railroad tracks and sheds, and as I watched, men in dark coats and fur hats emerged from the shadows.

When I returned, Nikitin asked when we would be leaving Donetsk. I said we would probably go on Monday.

"I guess they'll grab me as soon as you leave," he said calmly.

There was another period of silence as I made some notes and we drank the tea, mixing it with the berry *vareniye,* which dyed it red.

As the gravity of Nikitin's situation began to sink in, I tried to imagine some way of getting him back to Moscow with us. The KGB would prevent Aeroflot from selling him a plane ticket to Moscow, but it might be possible to get on a train. Thinking aloud, I told Nikitin that he should lose himself in the crowd in Moscow for a few days and then get back in touch with me through Serebrov. We would then decide what to do.

"You could take me in your car," he said.

"My car?" I repeated, not sure what he meant.

"Into the embassy," he said. "I'll lie down in the backseat. You just drive in past the guards and I'll get out and ask for political asylum."

"In the American embassy?"

"That's right. Just like those Pentecostalists* who are living there now."

"But what would you do there?"

"I could do anything. I'm an electrician, a carpenter. I can repair anything. I'm a bricklayer. There is nothing that they could want done that I couldn't do."

"But you could be in the American embassy for the rest of your life," I said.

"That's better than being tortured to death in a mental hospital," he replied.

The atmosphere of gloom deepened. The condensation on the inside of the windows had frosted over, a sign of a deep freeze. Kevin turned off the portable tape recorder that he had used to tape our conversations.

"Taking a Soviet citizen into a foreign embassy," I began cautiously, "is against the law here. Despite everything, we have to operate within the law. If I took you into the American embassy, I could be arrested. The best I could hope for is that I would be expelled immediately."

I fell silent. For a long time Nikitin said nothing.

"That's all right," he said, finally. "I'll find my own way in." He drank deeply from his cup of tea, which had become cold.

"Those obscurantists," he said, referring to the KGB agents who were waiting in the cold outside. "I paid them back good. All those years, they tortured me and humiliated me. . . ."

---

*In June 1978, seven Pentecostalists from Siberia who were seeking to emigrate ran past the guards outside the U. S. embassy in Moscow and asked for asylum in the embassy. They were allowed to remain there and lived in a one-room apartment in the embassy for five years until finally being permitted to emigrate in 1983.

His mind seemed to wander. "I'm not worried," he said. "I'll find a way out of this."

He looked at his hands, which were folded on the table, and then looked up at us. "Yes," he said firmly, "for every situation, there is a way out."

Suddenly ashamed for having thought of my own expulsion, I told Nikitin that the important thing was to get him back to Moscow, but the whole idea of going there and relying on a foreign embassy now seemed to displease him. He said that there were some dense woods at the back of one of the Donetsk coal tips. We would go after dark on Sunday night, Kevin and I would stand together for about fifteen minutes facing the wooded area, protecting Nikitin from the view of the KGB agents. When we turned around to walk back toward a main road, he would be gone.

I got up and walked again to the window, but this time I could see no one, although I had no doubt they were there. We didn't talk anymore that night. But Kevin and I for the second night in a row slept at Nikitin's apartment.

The previous night, I had managed to sleep without much trouble, but this night, I was bothered by the cold. As I lay awake, I thought about Nikitin's future. I assumed that he could make good his escape. But what would he do after that? He had no money and no documents. And without a job or a place to live, wasn't it just a matter of time before he was captured?

Day 3

We again rose early. I pulled back the curtain and saw that the ground and the roofs outside were covered with patches of freshly fallen snow. In the predawn darkness, a small streetlamp cast a dim glow. We got dressed, had breakfast, and walked out to the main road and caught a cab to our hotel. A short time later, we went to the Aeroflot office in Donetsk and picked up tickets for a Monday flight.

With little left to do, we took a walk through the center of the city. Although we had given up hope of contacting many more people in Donetsk, there was one person, the wife of a political prisoner Nikitin had known in the Dnepropetrovsk psychiatric hospital, whom we still hoped to be able to meet. When we rang her doorbell, however, she was not at home.

In the end, we spent the entire day strolling more or less aimlessly through the freezing city, and it was only by chance, at the end of the afternoon, that Nikitin noticed the woman we were seeking getting off a streetcar. The brief encounter that followed was symbolic of the difficulties we had had in Donetsk.

When Nikitin saw the woman, he approached her and she seemed happy to see him. Nikitin pointed in our direction. I saw her shaking her head while Nikitin continued speaking to her. Finally, she turned abruptly and walked away. Nikitin returned and explained that she had not wanted to talk to us for fear of doing something to worsen her husband's situation.

On the way back to Nikitin's apartment, we stopped again at the apartment of Nikolai and Zina. Nikitin knocked on the door of the summer kitchen where we had spent the evening on Friday. This time, however, Zina opened the door only a crack. When she saw Nikitin, she told him angrily to go away. She said that she and Nikolai had been interrogated by the KGB for the entire previous day.

We returned to Nikitin's apartment and, again, Poludnyak prepared a generous dinner for us. Nikitin answered some of my questions about his past life, but as we talked, the question in the back of my mind was whether we would soon be helping him to make good his escape.

After we finished eating, Nikitin told me he had decided to stay behind to settle some matters in Donetsk and would come up to Moscow later. What he meant, of course, was that he had decided to face the KGB alone.

Day 4

On our last morning in Donetsk, we checked out of our hotel and caught a cab to Nikitin's apartment. We had not succeeded in talking to many people during our stay, but we had learned enough to see that the conditions for the labor unrest convulsing Poland also existed in the Soviet Union. We walked up to Nikitin's apartment and found him hard at work repairing the lock and installing a peephole in his door. He said he had slept soundly for the first time in days.

We went together to his room and his sister brought out some tea. Nikitin's manner became brisk and businesslike. "If I am arrested," he said, "I will immediately declare a hunger strike, and if they put me in a psychiatric hospital, I will refuse to take any kind of behavior modification drugs. I want to remind you that I have been pronounced sane by Dr. Anatoly Koryagin."

I told Nikitin that I understood, but I emphasized that he should come to Moscow as soon as possible.

There was nothing else to do. We shook hands and then said goodbye to Poludnyak, who, drying her hands, came out from the kitchen to say goodbye to us. I thanked her. She said that she was sorry that she had received us so modestly. We agreed that Nikitin would call me that evening at 8 p.m. from the Donetsk central post office, so that I would know he was safe. Nikitin decided not to walk with us to the car. He went with us to the door, waved goodbye, and as we started down the steps, closed the door behind us.

Alone again in Donetsk, Nikitin busied himself in his apartment and then, after a few hours had passed, he began leaving the apartment for short walks. When he went outside for the first time, he was pleasantly surprised to see that the KGB agents who had surrounded the building were gone, and that he was free to come and go as he liked.

I waited in my office each night for Nikitin's call, but there was no word from him.

Finally, on Friday, Nikitin phoned Vera Serebrova. He told her that everything was fine and he was moving around freely. Vera passed this message on to me.

After calling Serebrova, Nikitin returned home. A short time later, an ambulance pulled up silently in front of his apartment building. Moments later, there was a knock at the door. When Poludnyak opened it, the apartment was flooded with seven or eight plainclothes KGB men who pushed her to one side and rushed into Nikitin's room.

A struggle ensued and Poludnyak started screaming. One of the KGB men said to her, "Shut up, or you'll end up in the hospital, too." She looked through the open door and saw, to her horror, that her brother was being given an injection. He fell limp and was then wrapped in a blanket like a corpse. In that state, he was carried out of the apartment.

Several hours after Serebrova called me with the news that Nikitin was free, she called again to tell me he had been arrested. I asked her for details, but she said that the man who phoned was so frightened that it was all he could do to pass on the fact of the arrest.

．　．　．

SEVERAL NIGHTS after Nikitin's arrest, I had dinner with Felix
Serebrov.

I asked him what he thought would happen to Nikitin.

"Most likely he'll be put in a mental hospital," Serebrov said.

"And treated?"

"Probably."

I hesitated for a moment.

"Do you think our visit determined his fate?"

"His fate would have been the same regardless," Serebrov said.
"Sooner or later he would have ended up back in a mental hospital.
To have avoided that he would have had to merge once again with
that gray mass that he had left behind forever."

Serebrov rolled a cigarette and began to smoke.

"What happened to Nikitin," he said, "was what happens to a lot
of people in his position. He started out by sensing that there was an
injustice and embarked on a series of actions, the consequences of
which convinced him that his instincts had been accurate. But instead of it being just an injustice in the mine where he worked or in
one city, he gradually learned that it was the injustice of a whole system, and it was only by forgetting about that completely that he
could have hoped to remain free."

"So he could not have saved himself?"

"The only way would have been for him to have gone crawling
back to the authorities and to have begged their forgiveness, but he
had suffered too much for that.

"Alexei used to refer to himself as a 'simple worker.' He used to
say, 'I'm just a simple worker,' because he knew that he was already
someone out of the ordinary.

"He had passed the point beyond which he could give up the
struggle with them, and he was ready for whatever they would do
to him."

There was a moment's silence, and Serebrov and I realized that
we had been talking about Nikitin in the past tense.

THE DAYS PASSED with no further word of Nikitin until Vera
Serebrova received a terse phone call from someone in Donetsk who
said that Nikitin had been taken to Donetsk Psychiatric Hospital

Number 2. The caller reported that Nikitin had been visited by his sister and other relatives. He was running a very high fever, as a result of a series of injections, probably with sulfazine, and was in great pain.

In the meantime, the KGB net was closing around Serebrov. On the morning of January 8, agents arrived at his apartment and began a search. When the search was concluded, he was arrested and taken to Lefortovo.

Serebrov was the last Moscow member of the Working Commission on the Abuse of Psychiatry for Political Goals to be arrested.

WITH NIKITIN ONCE AGAIN in a psychiatric hospital, I decided I had to do something to defend him. On January 17, I went to Kharkov to meet Koryagin. A message had reached me that Nikitin had been transferred to the Dnepropetrovsk Special Psychiatric Hospital. It was Koryagin who had pronounced Nikitin sane, and I decided to ask him to reaffirm his diagnosis so that I could write an article for the *Financial Times* demonstrating the unjustified nature of Nikitin's confinement. Koryagin received me and Tony Barbieri of the *Baltimore Sun* at his apartment where Galina Koryagina had prepared an elaborate banquet in our honor.

After we finished eating, I asked Koryasin if he would be willing to repeat his diagnosis of Nikitin for publication in the *Financial Times* and the *Baltimore Sun*.

He nodded his head vigorously.

"I don't have to tell you," I said, "that this conversation carries a serious risk for you."

"Just go ahead with your questions."

I turned on a tape recorder and asked him to speak into the microphone.

"Were you familiar with Alexei Nikitin?" I asked.

"Yes."

"How would you describe him?"

"I examined Alexei Nikitin in September 1980, and on the basis of that examination, I would say that he is energetic, active, the kind of person who can prosper in any society, regardless of the social system."

"Did you notice any symptoms of mental illness?"

"No, he showed no symptoms of schizophrenia, which is normally accompanied by a lowering of the patient's level of activity, or of paranoia, although he did have a negative attitude toward his surroundings following years of conflict with the local authorities. He had no difficulty in speaking and he was capable of reasoning deeply and expressing his conclusions quickly and with concision."

"The information I now have suggests that Nikitin has been put in a mental hospital," I said. "Can you imagine any legitimate basis for this?"

"I came to the conclusion," Koryagin said, "after examining Nikitin, that his two previous spells in psychiatric hospitals were without foundation. I am inclined to think that his present hospitalization also has this character."

Koryagin's public affirmation of Nikitin's sanity was a source of support for Nikitin, but it virtually guaranteed the arrest of Koryagin.

On February 13, the Koryagins were seated in a compartment of the Kharkov-Moscow train when two policemen and three plainclothes KGB agents burst into the compartment, looking for a "criminal." They had a photograph with them and when they saw Koryagin, they placed him under arrest.

When the train stopped at Belgorod, the first stop on the way to Moscow, Anatoly and Galina were taken off the train and Anatoly was led away.

Nikitin, in the meantime, remained trapped in the shadowy world of Soviet psychiatric hospitals.

On May 18, Lyuba Poludnyak went to Dnepropetrovsk and was refused permission to see her brother, but was assured by a doctor that he would be "cured."

Finally, in December 1981, Poludnyak was allowed to visit Nikitin. Although he could not speak frankly to his sister in the presence of guards, he appeared cheerful and in reasonable health. It is possible that Nikitin would have been allowed to spend another period in confinement with relatively little drug treatment, but in early 1982 there was a toughening of the attitude toward dissent in the country. Yuri Andropov, the head of the KGB, began a campaign to wrest power from the dying Leonid Brezhnev.

In January 1982, Nikitin was transferred to the special psychiatric hospital in Talgar, Kazakhstan, and for the next two years virtually nothing could be learned about his fate. The curtain of silence was only broken in early 1984, when Nikitin was transferred back to Donetsk Psychiatric Hospital Number 2. By this time, however, he did not represent a threat to anyone. He was dying of stomach cancer and barely able to rise from his bed.

The doctors in the hospital detained him until just a few days before his death, when he was finally released home to his sister, where he died.

After Nikitin's death, Poludnyak declined to meet with people who tried to learn about his last days; she did, however, answer a letter from Viktor Davydov, a former victim of psychiatric terror:

Dear Mr. Davydov,
Thank you for your letter. Unfortunately, there is bad news. Alexei was my favorite brother and he died, January 21. I can't write anything else because even as it is, they won't let me live.
Lyuba V. Poludnyak

NOVOKUZNETSK, 1989

In Novokuznetsk, the coal capital of the Kuzbass region, word was spreading rapidly that the miners in Mezhdurechensk were striking.

As a result of the policy of glasnost, news of strikes was not being suppressed, and a short report on the stoppage was broadcast over "Pulse," the regional news program on the evening of July 11.

The following morning, miners traveling to their jobs on electric trains and buses talked about nothing but the strike in Mezhdurechensk. There had never been a walkout in the Kuzbass coal mines before, but now nearly everyone was sure that a strike in Novokuznetsk, the Soviet Union's largest coal-producing city, was imminent.

In front of the mines, miners began massing at the time of the shift changes urging support for the workers of Mezhdurechensk, arguing that if they were not supported, they would be suppressed. The only difficulty was that no one knew what the Mezhdurechensk miners were demanding. Almost all of them were in the square, so it was impossible to reach them. After a day of mounting tension, marked by conflicting rumors and wild speculation, miners in Novokuznetsk began to commandeer vehicles that belonged to the mine and drove to Mezhdurechensk themselves.

One of the miners who left for Mezhdurechensk was Nikolai

Ocherednoi, a miner at the Yesaulskaya mine, who arrived in Mezh-durechensk at 3 a.m. What he saw before him was a workers' revolution in the Soviet Union. The entire square in Mezhdurechensk was filled with people, and lights burned in every window of the surrounding apartment buildings.

From an improvised stand in front of the party headquarters, one speaker after another denounced the situation in the city. Miners spoke about dangerous working conditions and the failure to observe safety regulations. Doctors denounced inadequate supplies of medicine. Hairdressers demanded set days off so they could spend time with their husbands. Housewives asked for better food supplies.

Ocherednoi waded through the crowd, past mothers and children, milling knots of miners, and tea brewing over open fires before making his way to the speakers' area, where Valery Kokorin and other strike leaders had congregated. Ocherednoi asked the miners what their demands were. The strikers showed him a list of forty-two demands, including calls for higher pay, increased food deliveries, and better facilities for the city, including a new hospital and a sports stadium. He promised they could count on support from the miners of Novokuznetsk.

As dawn broke on July 13, the Novokuznetsk miners were seized by strike fever, and fear of a walkout swept the local administration. At the Polosukhinskaya mine, Viktor Pishenko, the director, met the miners arriving for the morning shift and warned them against going out on strike. At that moment, however, Ocherednoi pulled up in front of the mine in a minibus he had commandeered, scrambled out, and ran up the steps in front of the bathhouse.

"I've just come back from Mezhdurechensk," he said.

The crowd of almost three hundred men in uniforms and helmets surged around him. "The miners in Mezhdurechensk are demanding satisfaction of their demands," Ocherednoi said. "They have asked for our support."

"We'll strike!" shouted voices from the crowd.

With that, the die was cast. For decades, the Communist Party had monopolized all forms of organized life in the Kuzbass region, and now the long-suppressed anger of years exploded in an unstoppable chain reaction. In minutes, the miners elected a twenty-member strike committee that took over the mine offices. Its leaders immediately began calling other mines. They learned that strike committees had been formed spontaneously in mines all over the city.

At 10 a.m., members of the strike committees from a dozen mines gathered in the large assembly hall of the Abashevskaya mine and elected a raion strike committee. By the middle of the day, every mine in Novokuznetsk was on strike and the committee had expanded to embrace the whole city.

FOR YEARS, the Kuzbass had been one of the most passive and beaten-down regions in a silent and fearful country. It was taken for granted that the plan for coal had to be fulfilled at any cost, and nothing human was allowed to interfere with the relentless exploiting of the earth.

The official ideology held that the workers were the real "owners" of the country and that rule by the party was the political expression of their success. Disagreement between the workers and the party was precluded because the party was not alien to the working class but only its "most conscious part," and independent trade unions were unnecessary because Soviet workers needed no defense against their own representatives.

At the same time, strikes were an absurdity because the workers would only be striking against themselves.

The imposition—with the help of police terror—of this view of reality cut the ground out from under the workers' feet. Everywhere, there were signs such as THE WORKERS ARE THE OWNERS OF THE COUNTRY and GLORY TO THE WORKING CLASS. On the front pages of newspapers workers were pictured pouring molten steel and mining ore. They figured as heroes in films. Yet there was never an uncontrolled word in public from the workers themselves, and in every specific situation, workers were treated like children whose every thought was expressed by the regime.

All this changed, however, with the beginning of glasnost and freer access to information. Glasnost opened the miners' eyes to their real conditions and undermined the justification for the entire structure of power.

GLASNOST WAS A BREAK in the system," said Anatoly Malikhin, a coal miner. "As a result of glasnost, it became possible to speak up at a meeting. Earlier, it would have been dangerous. The system discriminated against the individual as a personality. Two years ago, a person could not express his opinion or defend his personal dignity. But every person has a wife and children whom he educates, and insofar as he educates them, he is a personality.

"We began to read about how the local bosses in Uzbekistan falsified the results of the cotton harvest. The miners knew that mine directors did the same with coal production in the Kuzbass.

"The process of liberation ripened and soon everyone knew that we were in a prestrike situation. The only question was who would be first."

"If we had met ten years ago," said Vladimir Lapin, a mining engineer, "I would have been different. I trusted the Soviet information media. I thought that the press might remain silent about some issues, but I excluded the possibility of outright lies.

"As far as the radio broadcasts from the West, I assumed they took truthful information and fabricated various plausible versions.

"We lived our whole life surrounded by enemies. American imperialism threatened us with nuclear war. We were the only good ones and for that reason we had to build up our military strength. If we lived worse than the West in some respects, it was because we had to have a good army, otherwise the Western countries would strangle socialism, which was dangerous for them.

"When people spoke about freedom of speech, I said it doesn't exist anywhere. In America, they have the freedom of speech which is convenient to them. I considered free enterprise to be speculation and could not imagine that it could exist in industry.

"When glasnost started, I began to clip articles from the newspapers. For years, our press had been full of stories about the sad fate of workers in the West, but we suddenly saw that everything was not as bad in the West as we had thought.

"I learned for the first time that less than one percent of those who emigrated eventually returned to the Soviet Union, and of those who did come back, most wanted to return to the West after only a few months. All this began to be printed in our newspapers.

"From the time I was a student, there was an expression, 'about this it is impossible to speak.' This was the norm. Glasnost opened our eyes.

"For me, the greatest surprise came when I saw an interview on Soviet television with an American who worked as a translator for

Progress Publishers. She said that for a few months she was unemployed and she received unemployment compensation. She said that it was enough to live on but she felt uncomfortable not having a job. I had thought that the unemployed in America lived on the streets and begged."

"For years, there was no way to compare our situation with the West," said Sergei Sukhov, a doctor with the Novokuznetsk ambulance service. "Everything was presented in a distorted form. In the U.S., Negroes are lynched. There is no freedom. Only the rich have the chance to live well. As a result of glasnost, we now know that this was far from the truth.

"Recently, there was a program on Soviet television called 'Rural America' that showed conditions on American farms. We saw veterinarians riding out in medical vans to give injections to pigs with disposable syringes. In Novokuznetsk, we don't even have disposable syringes for human beings."

"When I saw all this, I began to ask myself, 'Why is there such poverty? Why are these powerful mines and enormous steel mills unable to guarantee the most minimal services?' "

AS THOUSANDS OF OTHERS began to ask the same question, the stage was set in Novokuznetsk and in other coal-mining cities for a social explosion.

By the afternoon of July 13, the strike committee had relocated to the Mayakovsky House of Culture, which was made available by Valery Komarov, the director, who was also a former miner. The members crowded into the director's office and used the only phone line to call each of the city's forty mines and organize the setting up of pickets. At the same time, hundreds of miners began arriving in the square in front of the building to defend the committee, if necessary with their own bodies, and to lend it moral support.

At first, there were sixty people on the committee, but as the strike spread to embrace truck depots, construction sites, and factories, new representatives arrived and the membership of the committee swelled. As work stopped all over the city and large crowds gathered outside their headquarters in the square, however, the leaders were haunted by fear. They knew that the miners could easily be suppressed, and no one had forgotten the massacre of striking workers in 1962 in Novocherkassk.

The leaders agreed that the greatest danger was that a fight or drunken brawl would give the authorities an excuse to use force against them. To prevent this, they agreed on their first official act, to close the liquor stores. Miners in the square were recruited to form patrols. They sewed on red armbands and traveled around the city closing the liquor stores and taking drunks to the sobering-up station.

In the meantime, the strike committee struggled to formulate its demands. The miners had long compared the vast amount of coal that left Kuzbass with the paltry portions of food, medicine, and clothing that were shipped in. The first and most important demand was therefore to give economic independence to mines so that workers could use profits from the coal they mined to buy food products and needed goods and, in that way, cease being forced to live in poverty at the whim of central planners. They also asked for more vacation time, better pensions, and a higher coefficient on pay for work in the region, as well as a limit of about 70 percent on "state orders," thereby giving enterprises more latitude to engage in independent economic activity.

Amid the commotion in the director's office, Lapin, who had been named to the strike committee from the Polosukhinskaya mine, thought back over the events that led to the strike.

Life in Novokuznetsk had always been hard, but on the eve of the strike it had grown much worse. The mines ran out of soap. It became impossible to buy shoes. Miners had to travel to Moscow to buy basic goods, and in the airport they were forced to sleep on spread-out newspapers, waiting days for a flight.

What bothered Lapin most, however, was a sense that the hardships of life in Novokuznetsk were not equally shared. During the Brezhnev period, he witnessed the growth of a rigid caste system that was particularly noticeable in the mines.

In 1982, Lapin went to work in the Listyansky open-face mine in the village of Listvyagi. He shared an apartment with his mother in Novokuznetsk but most of the other miners lived in communal apartments without gas, heat, or running water.

In the fall of 1983, it was announced that apartments would soon be available for miners in the open-face mine in a new nine-story building. Many miners had been waiting fifteen years for a separate apartment, and each of them knew his place in the queue. At the same time the apartment block was being built for the open-face mine, however, an identical apartment block was being erected alongside it for the nearby Bungurskaya mine. This building was due to be finished somewhat later.

Shortly after the apartment block for the open-face mine was completed, a list of those who were to receive apartments was posted in the mine office. To the surprise of nearly everyone, instead of the sixty-seven miners who were scheduled to receive apartments, the list contained the names of only fifty-two. The bosses explained that fifteen apartments had been given to the Bungurskaya mine, and miners who worked in the open-face mine would be able to take apartments in the Bungurskaya mine's new block once it was finished.

Those who were assigned their apartments took them and those who were told to wait waited. But when, finally, the building of the Bungurskaya mine was completed and the fifteen extra apartments became available, there was no announcement and the apartments were given not to the miners in the queue but to the relatives, mistresses, and political allies of the bosses of the open-face mine.

Months passed and the fifteen miners who expected apartments began to ask when they were going to get them. The trade union officials, who organized the manipulation, offered a series of complicated explanations, and, lacking detailed information, the miners did not know how to reply. At the same time, each of the miners felt his vulnerability. The men who were supposed to receive the new apartments worked in different sections, some of them separated by up to six miles, and on different shifts. They visited the mine's office only occasionally and had no way of knowing who else had been victimized. Each was aware that if he protested too much, he could lose not only his apartment but also his job.

A short time later, Lapin learned what had happened at the Bungurskaya mine. Having received fifteen apartments in the Listyansky building before their own apartment complex was ready, the bosses filled them with their friends and relatives, saying nothing to the workers. Because these apartments were in the building of another mine, the Bungurskaya miners found it difficult to check on them, and when the mine's own building was finished, the bosses simply announced that they had fifty-two apartments to distribute instead of sixty-seven because they had been given apartments by the open-face mine and had to return them.

In both places, for an ordinary miner to challenge the ability of the bosses to reward their relatives and friends was absolutely impossible.

LAPIN LEFT THE OPEN-FACE MINE in 1986 and went to work at the Polosukhinskaya mine, where he found another example of the inequality in the mines—this one in the form of the system known as "model workers."

In the Polosukhinskaya mine, the "model worker" was Yegor Drozdetsky, a Hero of Socialist Labor. So successful was Drozdetsky that a bronze statue of him was put up in the center of Novokuznetsk.

In every mine, there is a *mayak*, or "rudder." The *mayak* is supposed to serve as an inspiration to the other workers. Drozdetsky was selected as a *mayak* because he was sober, married, and, most important, politically reliable. The local authorities needed an example of successful work, and, in short order, Drozdetsky was assigned to direct the exploitation of a promising coal vein that was ten feet thick and very close to the surface. To make his work easier, he was given a new conveyor, new supports for reinforcing the walls of the mine, new combines, and four telephones in his section of the mine so he would not have to waste time traveling long distances to a telephone in the event of problems.

To the surprise of no one, Drozdetsky and his brigade began to mine enormous amounts of coal, and since pay was calculated on a piece basis, the members of the privileged brigade began to earn a thousand rubles a month—twice the pay of other miners, who worked with obsolete equipment in difficult geological conditions. Drozdetsky appeared on television, promising to use his own "special methods" to achieve even greater labor victories in the future. In the early Gorbachev period, the policy of the party was "acceleration," and Drozdetsky vowed that in his brigade there would be "genuine acceleration."

Lapin, like virtually every other ordinary miner, hated Drozdetsky and considered these broadcasts to be "information for fools."

FOR YEARS, the citizens of Novokuznetsk had been accustomed to a certain order, which seemed as changeless as the sun. If anything moved in the city, it was on orders of the local party committee. As workers struck all over the city, however, the orders of the party committee ceased to be operative. The workers were willing to carry out the orders only of the strike committee.

Valery Demidov of the Abashevskaya mine was elected the head of the strike committee. From its headquarters in the House of Culture, the committee authorized the delivery of coal to the power stations, so that electricity in the city would be maintained, and agreed to supply coal to the steel mills to prevent the coke ovens from cooling. The committee also approved the continuation of essential work in the mines, such as the operation of the ventilation systems.

At the same time, the residents of Novokuznetsk came to the strike committee in a steady stream with their complaints. They brought evidence of corruption in the distribution of apartments, and machinations in determining the rate of pay. One group of desperate visitors were the city's diabetics. Novokuznetsk had run out of insulin and, in the heat, the diabetics had trouble breathing. The committee immediately demanded emergency shipments of insulin.

Throughout the second day of the strike, the frightened heads of enterprises, particularly steel mills and pharmaceutical factories, also converged on the House of Culture to plead to be excluded from the strike.

With production in Novokuznetsk paralyzed, the local party authorities showed signs of complete disarray. Instead of threatening to suppress the strikes, they said nothing or confined themselves, in meetings with members of the strike committee, to saying that the strikes showed "ideological nearsightedness." Albert Lensky, the party first secretary, arrived at the strike committee headquarters at midnight and, after silently reading some of the committee's preliminary demands, said, "Lads, I see in your work the sprouts of worker self-management."

As they realized that allegiance to the strike was virtually unanimous, the members of the strike committee began to lose their fear. They started calling the city party committee to request cars, and in every case the party complied. The committee summoned party officials to explain to them how much food was being delivered to the city, how many apartment buildings were going up, and how much medicine was in the hospitals, and the committee soon began receiving the records of all the local government institutions, particularly the Department of Health and the Directorate of Trade, which was responsible for all the goods sold in the stores. Stunned by the strike's success, the local party leaders treated the committee's every wish as a command.

People from all walks of life in Novokuznetsk watched the strike with fascination, but few were more interested than Sergei Sukhov, a doctor with the ambulance service.

Sukhov grew up near Novokuznetsk, studied medicine in the Siberian city of Krasnoyarsk, and then returned home in the mid-1980s. He became convinced that something had to be done to improve health care after answering a call one night from a mother whose eleven-month-old baby was suffering from pneumonia. Sukhov took the child to Children's Hospital Number 4, entered the building, and fell through the rotten floorboards, nearly dropping the child.

It seemed to Sukhov that the central authorities had no respect for the people of Novokuznetsk. In a city of 600,000, there were twenty-nine hospitals, all of them in barracks that were more than fifty years old. The cloud of industrial smoke that covered the city contributed to widespread breathing problems and skin allergies, but there were almost no dermatologists or eye, ear, nose, and throat doctors. In the Zavodsky raion, there was one eye, ear, nose, and throat physician for 40,000 children. He examined 13 patients an hour.

What bothered Sukhov most of all, however, was the negligent attitude of doctors who did not do everything they could to save their patients' lives. When Sukhov rushed patients to hospitals, he often found, in addition to a shortage of oxygen equipment and hospital beds, that the sufferers were met with laziness and indifference on the part of medical personnel. This was particularly obvious in the treatment of children.

Sukhov began to work in the Novokuznetsk ambulance service in June 1986, and one night during his first week he answered a call from a woman whose four-year-old son was having an asthma attack. Sukhov took her to a children's hospital and as she entered the building, carrying her son, one of the doctors shouted, "Where are you going in your street clothes?" The woman became hysterical and began screaming at the doctor, who started screaming back.

Most children in Novokuznetsk were asthmatic, and they had their worst attacks in the hours between midnight and 4 a.m., when the factories were free to pour pollutants into the air without any restrictions.

The doctor, seeing that the child's condition was not critical and it was only 10 p.m., refused to examine him and, to Sukhov's astonishment, complained that the woman had brought the child in too early. It was obvious that his real concern was to avoid extra work.

Seeing this attitude, the woman immediately lost faith in the doctor and threatened to take her son back home. It was only Sukhov's intervention that forced the doctor to look at the child and persuaded the woman to stay.

Two years later, Sukhov was exposed to another case of medical indifference.

On the night of April 17, 1988, at 6 p.m., Andrei Golovey, the ten-year-old son of a Novokuznetsk teacher, was brought to Children's Hospital Number 4 by his father, suffering from a severe attack of bronchial asthma. Golovey warned that his son's condition was serious, but the doctors ignored him.

Although the boy was having trouble breathing, the doctors forced him to walk up two flights of stairs. He was then locked in an office and left there until 10 p.m., by which time he was turning violet and crying that he could not breathe. Finally, he was taken to a reanimation ward, but was left without treatment even there.

The hours passed and the boy's condition grew steadily worse until, at 3 a.m., he lost consciousness. Despite this, he did not begin to receive treatment until 9 a.m. By this time, however, it was too late. He died two hours later.

AT THE STRIKE headquarters in the House of Culture, the phones rang off the hook as unshaved miners, working in clouds of cigarette smoke, argued through the night about tactics and what demands to present to the government. Most of the calls were from citizens protesting against speculation in food or asking for help in righting injustices.

On the third day, however, a call came from Mikhail Shadov, the Soviet minister of coal, who had arrived in the city from Mezhdurechensk to try to negotiate an end to the work stoppage that had now spread from Novokuznetsk to the entire Kuzbass region and threatened to touch off strikes in Donetsk, Vorkuta, and Karaganda. Shadov invited the miners to send representatives to see him in the raion party committee.

"Shadov is confused," said Demidov. "He doesn't invite us. We invite him."

The committee sent a representative to deliver this message, and ten minutes later, Shadov arrived at the House of Culture to begin negotiations. Exhausted and barely able to talk after his experience in Mezhdurechensk, he smiled warmly when he entered the strike headquarters, shook hands with everyone, and put his arm around several members of the committee.

In Mezhdurechensk, Shadov had tried, without success, to persuade the crowd that the miners should return to work in exchange for thousands of tons of increased deliveries of food products, soap, and detergents. In Novokuznetsk, he abandoned this tactic and tried to make use of outright deception.

Alexander Melnikov, the Kemerovo oblast first secretary who accompanied Shadov to Novokuznetsk, produced a telegram that he claimed to have just received, saying that the Mezhdurechensk miners had gone back to work. When members of the committee tried to call Mezhdurechensk, they found that the code for the city was blocked. Meanwhile, in Mezhdurechensk, a rumor was spread that strikers were returning to work in Novokuznetsk. The Mezhdurechensk miners, in turn, found it impossible to phone Novokuznetsk.

The confusion was resolved only when three miners from Mezhdurechensk arrived at the House of Culture and asked if Novokuznetsk was still on strike. They said that the information in Melnikov's telegram—that Mezhdurechensk had gone back to work—was false. While they spoke, Shadov sat staring down at his papers.

When the negotiations resumed, Shadov and his entourage tried another tactic. He began approving one demand after another. "What do you want?" he asked. "Cars? We'll give them to you. Products? We'll give them to you. You want self-sufficiency? Take it. Why raise a fuss?"

The miners then noticed that Shadov was signing his approval of the miners' demands on ordinary paper instead of official stationery. When they asked him why, he said that he had no official forms with him. The mines then inquired into whether Shadov even had the authority to approve their demands. He admitted he did not.

"Why are you signing documents for questions you are not qualified to decide?" asked Malikhin.

"I can't decide these questions, but I can give you my signature," Shadov said.

A messenger informed the miners that a government commission headed by Nikolai Slyunkov, a member of the Politburo, was on its way to Novokuznetsk. The miners broke off their negotiations with Shadov and decided to wait for Slyunkov.

One of the most militant members of the strike committee was Yuri Komarov, who believed that miners risked their lives needlessly because of the pressure to fulfill the plan. He was haunted by the way death followed the Novokuznetsk miners around, either as a result of accidents in the mines or negligence in the hospitals. After a while, he lost count of all the men that had died.

The risks in the Kuzbass mines were substantial, in part, because of natural conditions. Kuzbass coal generates a very high quantity of methane gas, up to fifteen thousand cubic meters per one thousand tons of mined coal. At the same time, since the region is rich in coal, the ministry makes up for the low level of technology by racing to open new deposits. Necessary safety features, such as guard rails and extra ventilation shafts, were often ignored.

The most serious problem, however, was the organization of work. If miners fell just short of the plan target in a given month, they received only 350 rubles, but if they fulfilled the plan, they received nearly twice as much.

Under these conditions, safety regulations were often ignored by the miners themselves. Meters that measured the amount of methane in the mine and could turn off the electricity if there was too much gas or too little air, were sometimes disabled by the miners to avoid the possibility of unwelcome delays, with the result that the miners often worked unaware that there was a dangerous buildup of gas.

Komarov was exposed to accidents almost from the moment he began to work as a miner in 1981. The first serious incident he witnessed occurred in the Badaevskaya mine in 1982. An improperly fastened hydraulic jack that was being hauled to the surface in a cart slipped free. There were no guard rails. The cart raced 2,500 feet down an incline and collided with an electric generating station that fell on four miners who were eating breakfast, cutting off their legs. One of them later died.

In 1985, while he was working as a miner on Spitzbergen, Komarov received a letter from his wife telling him that there had been an accident in his section of the mine. Sixteen miners had been killed, including four who worked in Komarov's brigade. Two had been crushed to death. The others, including a father of two children, had been burned alive.

One night, Komarov was working underground in the Badaevskaya mine when he noticed a tiny blue flame dancing along the roof of the mine shaft. As he watched the flame, he felt his hair stand on end. He knew that if that flame hit a pocket of gas, there would be an explosion and everyone in its path would be burned alive. Finally, however, the flame disappeared and he got to the surface safely.

The incident that convinced Komarov that something had to be done about the conditions in the mine occurred on February 25, 1989, by which time he was working at the Abashevskaya mine. One of Komarov's friends in the mine was Ivan Vlasov, whose job was to reinforce the mine. On the day of the accident, Vlasov was in a distant section of the mine putting up supports when suddenly the roof caved in on him. The accident set off an alarm. Eighteen men dug for sixteen hours before they finally reached Vlasov, and it was Komarov who pulled him out.

Days before, he had urged Vlasov, who was forty-eight, to retire. Vlasov had already bought a house in the country where he wanted to live with his wife and two daughters, but he said that he was not yet ready to retire. He needed to work two more years to receive his full pension.

Komarov felt particularly bitter about Vlasov, who was cheated by fate of a few years of rest. But he saw that even if a miner lived long enough to retire, all he could count on was a certificate of honor from management. He had invariably left his health in the mine.

AFTER SHADOV LEFT the House of Culture, plans were made for a meeting of representatives of the strike committees in all of the coal cities of the Kuzbass. The various strike committees had been acting separately, and this gave rise to fears that the authorities could find a way to turn them against each other.

Representatives of the striking miners in Prokopievsk, Ovsiniki, Kiselevsk, Mezhdurechensk, and Lenin-Kuznetsk began to arrive at the House of Culture in Novokuznetsk. Anticipating the arrival of Slyunkov, they discussed drawing up demands for the entire region.

Finally, each committee elected two representatives to an oblast strike committee. This committee then began to codify all of the various economic, ecological, and medical proposals into a single document.

On July 16, the oblast committee held its first meeting in Prokopievsk, in the headquarters of Gidrougol, one of the area's giant coal trusts. The committee, however, proved unwieldy. When disagreements arose, the discussion became chaotic because the miners lacked a frame of reference. Finally, Yuri Rudolph, a representative of the Prokopievsk strike committee, suggested that the miners turn over chairmanship of the strike committee to a qualified economist.

"Why look for him? He's sitting in the hall," said one of the miners. He pointed to Teimuraz Avaliani, a people's deputy who was in the audience.

Avaliani had once written a critical letter to Brezhnev on the state of the Soviet economy and, in the aftermath, had nearly been put in a psychiatric hospital. This gave him a reputation as a local dissident. The members of the committee elected Avaliani as chairman although he was not a miner and had not participated in the strike. Under Avaliani's direction, the committee prepared regional demands, including one for economic independence for the entire region.

On the night of June 17, the government delegation arrived in Prokopievsk, and negotiations began the next day. Slyunkov was accompanied by Sergei Shalayev, chairman of the Soviet trade unions, and Leonid Voronin, a deputy prime minister. Slyunkov seemed to be a man in a hurry.

"Comrades," he said to the oblast strike committee, "why are you sitting here? Why aren't you working?"

The workers reacted with irritation.

"Whom do you represent?" asked Yuri Gerold, deputy chairman of the oblast strike committee.

This reply surprised the numerous aides accompanying Slyunkov. It was unprecedented for an ordinary worker to talk to a member of the Politburo like that. But Slyunkov simply replied, "The Communist Party of the Soviet Union and the Council of Ministers."

Despite the fact that the strike by now had paralyzed coal mining throughout the whole country, the Soviet leaders continued to think of the workers as their subordinates.

The two sides worked virtually around the clock. When the

discussion concerned practical concessions—higher pay, better deliveries—agreement was possible. Any matter of regional autonomy and self-management for the mines, however, was lost in a fog of words.

Slyunkov, like Shadov before him, did not want to take the demand for the economic autonomy of the Kuzbass region seriously. He was ready only to promise increased supplies.

At 1 a.m. on July 19, Slyunkov left the talks and went to the central square in Prokopievsk, where between eight thousand and ten thousand miners and their families were waiting for news of the negotiations.

Slyunkov wanted to calm the crowd and win them over to the government's side. He promised that by the new year there would be more goods in the stores.

The square erupted in jeers.

"The hell with you," the crowd yelled, "don't try to shut our mouths with sausages."

AS THE DETAILS of the negotiations in Prokopievsk were reported over local television, Irina Gladkova, a student in the Novokuznetsk Pedagogical Institute and the divorced mother of a young son, felt a surge of hope. For the first time, she thought it was possible that life in Novokuznetsk might one day get better.

It was not surprising that Soviet officials dangled the prospect of increased food deliveries before the miners, because food had become an obsession for people in Novokuznetsk, particularly if they had small children.

In the months preceding the strike, Irina had had a recurring dream in which something was being sold and she had to rush with her ration card in order to buy it. By the time she arrived, however, all she found was an enormous line and empty counters. The dream bothered Irina. But by the summer of 1989, it had become a reasonable reflection of reality.

There had been no meat in the state stores of Novokuznetsk since the 1960s, but in the 1980s, with the beginning of the Afghan war, sausage disappeared as well. There began to be problems with milk, eggs, butter, and cheese and, as the decade wore on, the interruptions in deliveries became more frequent and lasted for longer periods. In 1989, sugar disappeared and hard candies also vanished, along with all types of cheap medicine, particularly headache remedies, and toothpaste, laundry powder, and soap.

The result was a mass hysteria as people began to fear that everything was disappearing and started to buy up anything in the stores, including dry products like noodles, flour, and rice, and even salt, until these products too became unattainable. Finally, potatoes started to disappear or soar in price on the free market, although many persons were saved by the fact that they raised potatoes on small personal plots.

The severe shortages in Novokuznetsk finally inspired rationing. This gave each person a chance of gaining access to basic supplies. But the unremitting struggle to find necessary food products drained Irina of energy.

NO ONE COULD BE SURE of the quality of the food products, even if they were obtained.

At one point, Irina took a job working as a loader in a bread store at night to supplement her income of 80 rubles a month in alimony and a student's stipend. Most of the store's employees were women—either students or pensioners—and they unloaded two large trucks full of twenty-two-pound boxes of bread every night.

Shortly after she started working, Irina noticed that there was something strange about the bread she was unloading. At first, she thought it was flecked with flour, but, on closer examination, she realized that the loaves of bread had actually been fouled with bird droppings.

Irina asked her supervisor the reason for the fouled bread and he said that the warehouse for the bakery which served Novokuznetsk was actually a large, semi-open hangar and that birds gathered in the rafters and, from a height of fifty feet, defecated on the bread.

The containers of bread could have been protected by covering them with polyethylene, but no one bothered to do it. Irina began to watch carefully for fouled loaves, although this was not easy because the bread was packed in the containers in rows. When she did find fouled bread, she wrote it off and it was sent back to the bakery as ruined. But this was not the end of the story.

After working at the bread store for several months, Irina was told by a driver that the fouled bread was delivered back to the bakery but, contrary to what she had assumed, it was not thrown out.

Instead, it was ground up and mixed with the flour for fresh bread, which was then redelivered to the stores.

THE NEGOTIATIONS BETWEEN the striking miners and Slyunkov, Shalayev, and Voronin went on for two days.

Agreement was reached on the demands concerning pay, pensions, vacations, and increased food supplies. There was even concurrence on the miners' most important demands: economic independence for enterprises and regional self-financing for the entire Kuzbass region.

The understanding on economic independence, however, was vaguely worded. It called for "full economic and juridical independence" for the mines and enterprises of the Kuzbass region, but there was no clear explanation of what that would mean.

The authorities committed themselves to granting a 30 percent increase in pay and a 40 percent raise for night work. They agreed to give forty-five working days of paid vacation to those who worked underground and promised an increase in deliveries in the Kuzbass region, including: 6,500 tons of meat, 5,000 tons of butter, 10,000 tons of sugar, and 3,000 tons of soap.

The agreement gave enterprises the right to sell production above the level of state orders for free prices both in the country and to foreign countries. The problem was that the share of production taken by state orders was often nearly 100 percent.

The workers were not completely satisfied with the outcome of the talks. Most of their demands had been met, but they had no way of being sure that the accords would be respected by the authorities. Nonetheless, on July 19, the workers' representatives announced that agreement had been reached, and at dawn of the following day, they returned to their mines to explain the accords to the workers. Later that day, Slyunkov spoke before members of the workers' committee, and his speech was broadcast to the crowd outside the House of Culture. He said that the government understood the just demands of the Kuzbass workers and would do everything possible to satisfy them.

Some members of the audience asked Slyunkov what they should do if the local authorities tried to interfere with the agreement's implementation.

"In that case," he said, "call me or the Central Committee."
On July 21, the workers returned to work.

Five Months Later

IN THE FADING LIGHT of a December afternoon, Anatoly
Malikhin, Valery Komarov, and Yuri Komarov got out of a ramshackle bus, walked into the Ziryanovskaya mine and announced a
meeting of the miners in the assembly hall. Ten minutes later, the
hall was filled with miners who had just finished working the day
shift. Standing under a white bust of Lenin, Malikhin began to take
questions.

The strike committee had become a workers' committee whose
job it was to monitor the fulfillment of the July agreement. Each
committee member had his salary paid out of donations from his fellow miners, and they, in turn, traveled regularly to the mines to inform the workers about the situation in Novokuznetsk or the progress
of their continuing negotiations.

Outside, darkness enveloped the birch trees and snow-covered
hills.

"I want to know," said one miner, "in the four or five months
since the strike, what has changed?"

In fact, almost nothing had changed. The deliveries of laundry
detergent, soap, and food products stopped almost immediately and
no new deliveries took their place. It began to seem that Novokuznetsk had finally solved the problems of queues because, in many
stores, there was now absolutely nothing to buy. At the same time,
work in the mines continued to be dominated by the drive to fulfill
the plan.

"What is your suggestion?" Malikhin asked.

"I think we should go back on strike."

Another miner described a recent incident in the mine. In one
section, the miners had been told they would be paid a three-ruble-
a-ton bonus for mining coal in difficult geological conditions. After
the coal was mined, however, the miners were informed in the cashier's office that there was not enough money to pay their bonuses,
and each miner received two hundred rubles less than he had been

expecting. When the miners complained, the chief accountant said that there were big problems in the country and the Ministry of Coal did not have any money. "You asked for self-sufficiency," he said, "now you've got it."

The miners asked about the strike in Vorkuta, where workers in the Vorshagorskaya mine were striking on behalf of political demands, including the removal of article six from the Soviet constitution, which guaranteed the Communist Party the leading role in society.

The miners in Novokuznetsk had collected money for the striking miners, and they were anxious to hear about what was happening in Vorkuta.

Yuri Komarov, who had just returned from Vorkuta, said that of the eighteen demands put forth by the miners, seventeen were political, including one for the resignation of the government.

"I asked one miner after another," Komarov said, " 'Do you have an apartment?' 'No.' 'Do you have a car?' 'No.' 'So what do you care about article six?' "

"The fact is," Malikhin said, "if we try to change the situation without the cooperation of the Communist Party, there will be bloodshed."

As if to illustrate Malikhin's point, Alexander Volkov, the secretary of the party organization in the mine, hurried into the hall and said, "Who said that you have permission to be here? I'll lock the door to the assembly hall and expel everyone in here."

"Okay," said Malikhin, "let's leave it to the workers. We'll see who they want to hear. I think they'll carry you out by your feet."

By the time the commotion subsided, Volkov had sat down and the meeting continued.

ALTHOUGH THE STRIKES had demonstrated the miners' ability to stop production, they did nothing to change the Soviet system.

Once the authorities no longer felt the pressure of a massive strike, they were ready to ignore many of the provisions of the agreement. And in the Soviet system, there was no way to force them to adhere to it. The spontaneity that allowed the strikes to spread like a chain reaction was also their weakness. Once the strikes were over, the miners found they were still beholden to a hostile bureaucracy that dominated every aspect of their lives.

In the months after the end of the strikes, delegations of Kuzbass workers traveled to Moscow eighteen times, but they had no success in compelling the government to comply with the agreement that ended the strike.

The government set up meetings with different groups of miners in different organizations. The Donetsk miners went to the official trade unions, a group from Vorkuta to the Council of Ministers, a delegation from Novokuznetsk to the Ministry of Coal.

At the same time, government representatives tried to drown discussions with the Kuzbass miners in detail, taking up one narrow question after another, such as an increase in food deliveries or new supplies of detergent, while avoiding the principal question, which was the economic independence of the whole region.

In some cases, when the workers arrived for meetings in the offices of government organizations, they were not even allowed in.

Tabeyev, Voronin's deputy, received a miners' delegation that included Yuri Komarov. The miners told him that they wanted full economic independence for each enterprise and the establishment of free cities that would have the ability to negotiate with suppliers.

Tabeyev said, "Boys, you demand economic independence and direct links with foreign firms. If we gave that to you, in five years it would bring the whole union to its knees."

The government's refusal to consider a new system of economic relations, even though this had been agreed to in the July accords, gave rise to widespread discontent. The workers' committees, consulting with economists, continually refined their proposals for the establishment of economic independence for the Kuzbass and forwarded them to Moscow, but government agencies did not even consider them.

The deadline for working out a plan for Kuzbass economic independence was January 1, but the date passed and no action was taken. In the meantime, despite an agreement to begin the reconstruction of the Kemerovo steel mill, no action was taken to reconstruct any factory or to improve the ecology or infrastructure of the region.

On January 2, 1990, the workers' committees' patience finally ran out. They informed the government that if they did not send a representative to the region immediately, the government would bear full responsibility for the resulting destabilization.

This message made an impression, and a short time later, Lev Ryabev, the first deputy prime minister, was sent to the Kuzbass.

Ryabev's mission was to last two weeks, and in that time he gave not only the workers' committee but also the population of the Kuzbass at large an example of the government's bad faith.

When Ryabev arrived in Novokuznetsk on January 16, he said, "I'm ready to discuss any question except the overthrow of Soviet power." But when the meetings actually commenced, he tried to convince the miners that the country was in crisis and there were limits to what the government could do to implement its own accord.

The workers showed Ryabev a plan for turning the Kuzbass into a free enterprise zone and called on him to endorse it.

He refused. "The country is in a very difficult condition," he said. "We can't do without Kuzbass steel, coal, and chemicals."

For two weeks, Ryabev traveled from city to city, trying to avoid a meeting with a workers' committee representing the region as a whole. In one place, he promised there would be money for a new school. In another, he said there would be an increase in food supplies or the reconstruction of an obsolete factory.

In some areas, he met with success because he was well informed about pressing local needs and promised to satisfy them. Every time the discussion strayed from the concrete question of extra deliveries to the deeper question of changes in the system, however, the thread of the conversation was lost.

While the strike committees were running into a stone wall in their dealings with the central authorities, they also found themselves challenged by the local party organizations, which worked to undercut their support among the population.

The local party had been discredited by the strikes, which temporarily neutralized its authority, but it still controlled the enterprises, the courts, the police, and the local branches of the ministries. It determined what was built and where, who held management posts, and, in cooperation with the central authorities, implemented vital economic decisions based on the centrally determined price of coal.

Against this background, the local leaders called on the workers' committees to "unite" with the party. At the same time, however, they carried out active propaganda against strikes. Party leaders calculated for Novokuznetsk audiences how much money was lost as a result of a strike and translated it into losses of apartment buildings, hospital beds, and schools. The newspapers printed letters from supposed "war veterans" and "pensioners" denouncing the activities of the workers' committees as harmful to the country, but the committees were given no opportunity to reply.

Perhaps more important, party officials did not give the workers an opportunity to print a newspaper of their own. Since they controlled the newsprint, the kiosks, and printing presses, this made it impossible for the workers' movement to have an independent voice.

The result of this situation was an uneasy impasse. The workers were powerless to control the bureaucracy, but they now could strike, a possibility that was excluded under conditions of total police repression.

To preserve their standing with the workers, the workers' committee regularly visited every mine in the area and kept the miners informed of their activities. The members also continued the practice of trying to defend ordinary citizens who came to them with complaints and requests.

Malikhin, who was in charge of the workers' committee in the Ordzhonikidze raion, received requests that reflected the region's utter poverty. He was asked to help three construction workers obtain shoes in large sizes. He was asked for help in getting a washing machine for four gravely ill invalids who could not leave their apartments, and for aid in obtaining a washing machine for a kindergarten, without which it could not open.

The workers' committees functioned as an unofficial government in the eyes of the population, but the whole region was seized by a feeling that the strike had accomplished nothing, and this led to an effort to expand the committee into a labor organization that would include all of the working people in the area.

In November 1989, the Kuzbass strike committees gathered to organize a Union of Toilers of the Kuzbass region, which accepted members from every collective in the area, not just from mines and factories.

The leaders of the strike committees hoped that this would lead to the creation of unions of workers in Donetsk, Vorkuta, and Karaganda and eventually throughout the Soviet Union.

At a meeting of the Novokuznetsk workers' committee in its new headquarters in the House of Political Education, Viktor Dolgov explained the rationale for creating the new organization.

"We raised three generations of loafers who don't know how to do anything but receive money in a bureaucracy. For so many years, they have deceived us, telling us that we had it so good. Well, now the rose-colored glasses have been removed."

6

The Economy

The free workman is paid, but he does his work quicker than the slave; and rapidity of execution is one of the great elements of economy . . . the free workman receives his wages in money; the slave in education in food in care and in clothing . . . in the end, the slave has cost more than the free servant and his labor is less productive.

—*Alexis de Tocqueville*, Democracy in America

IN JULY 1989, Dmitri Barabashov, an official in the department of the chemical industry of the Communist Party Central Committee, entered party headquarters on Old Square after a long absence and was taken aback by the nearly empty corridors and the apparent lack of work.

It was a peaceful summer morning, the kind of day when, in the past, the department had been the scene of frantic activity as officials prepared for the upcoming harvest. There was always an enormous increase in the use of fuel during the harvest, especially gas and diesel fuel, and it was the job of Barabashov and his colleagues to see to it that the country's oil processing plants worked at full capacity and that cisterns reached their intended destinations. If cisterns were delayed, for example, on a railroad siding in the Astrakhan oblast, the oil processing plant in Kuibyshev which was waiting for them had no way to force the boss of the Astrakhan railroad yard to send them further. But the boss there was a party member, and a Central Committee official could *order* him to dispatch the cisterns to Kuibyshev.

Normally, instructors like Barabashov manned the telephones from 9 a.m. to 9 p.m. during this period, and there were officials on duty all night maintaining contact with the major oil refineries and railroad yards, assuring that fuel moved to the refineries where it was needed.

Yet on the day Barabashov returned to Old Square, most officials were absent, secretaries sat idly at their desks, and the phones were nearly silent. At the end of 1988, there had been a sharp cut in the central party apparatus. Of the forty-two people who had worked in the chemical industry department, only nine were left, and they had been told not to "interfere" in the economy.

When the harvest got under way, the officials who remained in the department made a few desultory calls, but they did not know what was expected of them. Instead of giving orders, they wrote reports which were ignored.

"THE COMMODITIES EXCHANGE exists to help the enterprise solve its problems," said Alexander Solntsev to the director of a Kazan refrigerator factory in June 1991. "Before, you had to rely on the department of supplies in your factory to acquire needed materials, but we can get them for you quickly, painlessly, and effectively." As the system of central planning came unraveled, commodity exchanges sprang up all over the country. Solntsev was a member of the Nizhny Novogorod commodities exchange, which, with a turnover of millions of rubles a day, had become the richest commercial structure in the oblast.

The factory director was becoming irritated. "You're a trickster," he said. "And the exchange is a collection of upstarts."

"The exchange is a source of raw materials and a new outlet for sales," Solntsev said. "You need both. The question is whether this society will be able to exist on the basis of common sense. I think it will. Otherwise, I wouldn't be doing this."

ON A SUNNY AFTERNOON in June 1991, Pavel Lebedev, the director of the silicate factory in Bor, passed out fact sheets to the employees as they crowded into the factory assembly hall to discuss a new idea: privatization.

"This factory is very profitable," Lebedev said, "but, right now,

94 percent of the profit is taken by the ministry. If we become owners, those profits can be shared."

Although factories in the Soviet Union were supposed to belong
to the workers, the idea of sharing profits was new. The workers tried
to understand what privatization would mean.

"How will we get what we need?" asked one of the workers at
the meeting. "The state provides us with supplies."

"We produce 150 million silicate bricks a year and bricks are
a deficit item," Lebedev said. "We have a deficit item and they have
deficit items, so we'll trade our deficit for theirs."

Lebedev was well aware of problems in the operation of the factory. It wasted enormous amounts of gas, electricity, and raw materials so that its allocation would not be cut. At the same time, the
workers were indifferent. When equipment broke, no one bothered
to repair it. The brick factory ranked third in the city for the number
of employees picked up on the street drunk each month and taken to
a sobering-up station.

What convinced Lebedev that privatization was necessary, however, was the constant interference in the operation of the factory by
the party.

In late August 1990, he was ordered to send forty workers to a
nearby collective farm to dig potatoes. Two weeks later, on September 1, he was summoned to the local party headquarters, where the
first secretary told him to send sixty workers to help finish construction of a nearby apartment building by September 30. Lebedev explained that he could not spare sixty workers after having sent forty
to harvest potatoes.

"I'm not here to listen to excuses," the first secretary said.

"In that case," said Lebedev. "I resign."

The next morning, Lebedev was called back to party headquarters. "You were very disrespectful to the first secretary yesterday,"
said one of the local party officials. "But he has decided nonetheless
to relieve you of responsibility for potatoes as long as the work on the
apartment building is completed on time."

The incident was the last straw for Lebedev. When state enterprises began to be privatized, he decided that his factory would be
the first in line.

"When we privatize," Lebedev told the workers, "we are on our
own. The only thing we will have to pay to the state is taxes."

"But what if we lose money?" asked one of the workers.

"It will become our job and your job," Lebedev said, "to make sure that doesn't happen."

THE REDUCTION OF CONTROL and the appearance of free economic activity and privatization marked the beginning of the attempt to break up the planned economy.

Marx wrote that the root of evil in the modern world was private ownership of the means of production. The Soviet system of central planning, therefore, was organized to realize the aspiration to eliminate private owners and to run the entire economy by command. This was largely accomplished. With the help of plan targets, the central authorities directed the life of thousands of factories and enterprises, deciding which regions to starve and which to favor, which industries to develop and which to neglect without paying the slightest attention to the wishes of those who lived in those regions or worked in those industries.

The factory director or collective farm chairman was told what to produce, from whom to receive materials, what prices should be charged, the number of workers to be hired, the amount of wages to be paid, and how the workers' labor should be distributed.

By subjecting economic relations to the circular logic of a closed intellectual system, however, central planning destroyed individual initiative. When the goal is not to produce a usable product but only to fulfill a predetermined plan, the focus shifts from the character of the article being manufactured to quantities—units, tons, kilometers—the only means through which plan fulfillment can be assessed. In the process, workers are turned into robots. If gross output is calculated in rubles, they add useless, expensive details; if it is calculated in weight, they use the heaviest materials; if it is measured in kilometer-hours, they send transports back and forth between distant cities.

Under these circumstances, the transition to a market economy is not just a matter of removing central direction and breaking up the remaining monopolistic system. It is, to a greater extent, a question of creating openings for individual initiative after three generations of working according to a plan.

The stifling effect of a command economy was evident for decades in every factory and collective farm in the Soviet Union.

.   .   .

The Factories

VLADIMIR TANCHUK took a job at the Moscow Pipe Factory on Barklaya Street because he wanted to see how the economy functioned at the level of an individual factory. Two things caught his attention immediately: the way the shop floor was covered with enormous piles of various materials, and the fact that nearly everyone who worked in the factory was drunk.

The working day began at 8 a.m. and almost all of the workers came to work on time. Despite this, there was often nothing to do when the workers arrived, and they started the day waiting for materials.

The first event of any consequence was the "all-Union smoking break" at 10 a.m. When Tanchuk started at the pipe factory, he tried to work during the smoking break, but the other workers told him it was obligatory to take a break, and one worker explained that there was a law to the effect that for every two hours of work, the workers were entitled to a twenty-minute break. There was a room for smoking during the shift, which included a big table, benches, and signs on the wall warning against drunkenness. There was also a red ribbon strung out across the wall with white letters urging the workers to obey the rules of technical safety. Workers at the pipe factory tended to sleep under the posters and, when drunk, to wipe their hands on the ribbon.

After the 10 a.m. smoking break, the workers thought only about food. There was another break at 11 a.m. At 11:25 a.m., the pace of work began to slow, and at 11:45 a.m., everyone left the workplace and went to lunch.

There was a canteen at the pipe factory, but many of the workers did not eat there. The line was long and the canteen smelled of Soviet soap, the steam of communal cooking, and disinfectant. This made it impossible for many workers even to enter the place. They brought their own food and spent the lunch hour in the dressing room playing dominoes. Typically, someone appeared with a bottle of beer or wine even though alcohol was not allowed in the factory. So the workers often had a lot to drink by the time they finished eating.

When the lunch break was over, the workers stayed where they were until a foreman came into the dressing room and urged them to get up.

The appearance of the foreman often led to lengthy discussions. The workers loved to argue with him over whether necessary materials had arrived, because this stretched out the lunch break. When the workers finally did get up, they rose one by one and as slowly as possible. They put on their work gloves and, as the foreman walked back and forth impatiently, filed into the shop.

By 1:30 p.m., work had begun again, but at two there was another smoking break. It was usually after the afternoon break that the workers began to feel the need for more alcohol, and someone was sent out to get vodka.

By 3 p.m., the bosses of the pipe factory sometimes came out specifically to make sure that no one was drinking on the job, and freshly obtained bottles were quickly hidden. If a boss saw a bulge in the belt of one of the workers, he might slap it. If he discovered a bottle, he normally began screaming and deprived the worker of his bonus.

After nearly everyone had had something to drink in the afternoon, the pace of work in the factory slowed markedly. Some of the workers began to sway and, to prevent themselves from falling, those who had had the most to drink tightened the vise at their workbench on parts of their shirts.

At the same time, the workers did their work.

The machines in the pipe factory were foreign-made, which should have made them easier to use. Nonetheless, they were misused. One of the jobs in the factory was to cut the pipes into five-meter sections. Cutting the pipe itself was not complicated. It only required pushing a button at the right moment. But each worker was expected, at the same time, to check the pipe as it was being processed and eliminate spoiled production. This required paying attention, and as they watched for defects, the workers cut many of the pipes either a half-meter too short or a half-meter too long, leading to an enormous waste of metal.

The cutting also required applying pressure to the button evenly. This, too, was often done incorrectly, with the result that lead remnants frequently protruded inside the pipe, making it necessary for the recipient of the pipes to cut them again at both ends, leading to a further waste of metal.

. . .

AS WORK CONTINUED, the shop floor was submerged under
enormous piles of various materials. Everywhere Tanchuk turned,
there were stacks of crates, metal parts, boxes, tools, and supplies.
Workers were often reduced to taking an object from one pile, performing an operation on it, and throwing it on another pile until the
workers seemed less to be using the materials than servicing the piles.

The loaders at the factory loaded two types of pipe: ordinary
pipes, which had to be coated with oil to prevent corrosion, and special, noncorrosible pipes, which had to be kept away from oil because
the oil ruined them immediately. The different characteristics of the
two types would have seemed to require that they be loaded separately, but the workers packed them together, with the predictable result that oil from the ordinary pipes coated the stainless-steel pipes
and ruined them.

The workers did this in order to fulfill the plan. Orders for the
stainless-steel pipes were usually small, and there were not enough of
them to fill a railroad car, but plan fulfillment was measured exclusively in terms of how many railroad cars were loaded. In some
cases, the stainless-steel pipes had already rusted through exposure to
the air, but it did not help to pack them with oil-covered pipes. The
workers also stepped on the stainless-steel pipes in oil-covered boots.
They laughed about this, wondering why they should not step on the
pipes if the pipes were going to be loaded into a railroad car with ordinary steel pipes that were covered with oil anyway.

In the end, the pipes were sent to a conserving plant in
Moldavia, where they were used in the production of tomato juice,
which came out tasting like rust.

In those moments when there was no work to do, perhaps due to
one of the frequent interruptions in deliveries, the workers who were
still relatively sober tried to do something for themselves on the territory of the factory.

At such moments, Tanchuk used to go to the foundry to work on
a stand for a bicycle. Others performed odd jobs—for example, unloading a truck for five rubles. If they were called back to work, they
unloaded the truck so rapidly that someone familiar with their normal manner of working would have thought it was impossible.

At 4 p.m., the workers began to wrap up in paper whatever they
wanted to take home with them—screwdrivers, nails, pencils,

notebooks—and left the packages on the floor of the dressing room. Someone entering the dressing room at that time would have seen the piles of rolled paper on the floor, and no one could have explained what they were doing there. In fact, hardly a day went by without a worker taking something from the factory home with him in his coat pocket or under his arm.

The workers also frequently stole articles for their friends. Perhaps the friend worked at a plant where the needed item was not available, so he could not steal it himself. The attitude of the workers was that everything was communal, so it belonged to them.

The workday ended at 5:30 p.m. People began to change clothes and were gone by 5:45 p.m. At 6 p.m., the pipe factory was taken over by the night shift, where work went on in the absence of the bosses.

If productivity was low during the day shift, at night it fell off completely. Workers drank during working hours as did workers on the day shift, but, unlike members of the day shift, the night workers normally arrived drunk. Most of the night workers were loaders. The only management representative during those hours was a duty officer who supervised several shops and spent most of his time sleeping.

At night, heavy loads of sliding pipes were carried from place to place by men who were nearly blind from drunkenness. The woman who operated a crane on the shop floor screamed, "Petka, get out of there," as a worker, smiling stupidly, looked up at her from under a load of pipes that was suspended over his head.

"Don't worry, Marusya," he said, "everything is in order"—and then fell down.

Sometimes, the night shift was enlivened by philosophical discussion.

"You're drunk," one worker said, "the police should grab you and take you to a sobering-up station."

"They won't do anything to me," the second worker replied, "I'm loyal. Vladimir Mayakovsky said, 'My police guard me.' "

"Well, what about Mayakovsky. He did the wrong thing. He shot himself. No Christian would have done that."

"Do you believe in God?"

There was a moment's hesitation as conversation was drowned out by the crash of pipes rolling off a forklift and the screeching of pulleys overhead.

"There is no God," he said, "but there is something."

"Do you force your children to believe in God?"

"They should believe in their own forces, maybe in God if that's what they believe in."

The night shift was the scene of frequent accidents. One night, while Tanchuk was the shift boss, a worker lost part of his finger. He had put it in a pipe that was lifted suddenly by a crane.

Moments after the accident occurred, the worker, who was in a drunken stupor, walked over to Tanchuk and, pointing to the exposed bone, said, "Look at this," behaving as if he had damaged a piece of equipment instead of his own body.

Tanchuk wanted to take the worker to the medical point, but he was stopped by his deputy. If the accident was registered, the worker would not get any sick pay because he was drunk when the accident occurred. Tanchuk would be blamed for having allowed him to work while intoxicated. The fact was that Tanchuk had no choice but to take on drunken workers at night if he wanted to have enough men, but he eventually followed his deputy's advice and did not register the accident.

After the worker had received first aid, he came to Tanchuk with his mangled finger and said, "I raised two children in the spirit of devotion to the people." There was nothing in his tone to suggest that anything out of the ordinary had happened to him.

"This was why Hitler lost the war," Tanchuk told me afterward. "He [the worker] did not look at the appendage as his finger. It was all government-issue."

When accidents were registered, it was usually in situations where the circumstances left the administration with little choice. One night, a deaf cleaning woman in the factory fell in the dark on a slippery floor and landed under a train. Afterward, her body was so mangled that it was impossible at first to distinguish who the victim had been. Still, there was no way to conceal the fact that there had been a victim. In time, her identity was established and the accident was recorded.

THE LOADERS WORKED only when railroad cars were available and ready to be packed with finished pipes. As a matter of principle, they did not do anything to prepare pipes for the next morning. When railroad cars arrived at night and it was no longer possible for the work to be delayed, they worked and they did their work properly. As soon as the job was done, however, they sat down again and began drinking either vodka or *chifir*—a powerful narcotic drink made with an entire packet of tea added to boiling water in a small glass—and, in a state of high inebriation, waited for the day shift.

AT THE ARSENAL machine building factory in Moscow, the goal also seemed to be to avoid work. Sergei Malyutin got a job there as a machine operator and the first thing he noticed was the constant verbal abuse of workers and the way they responded by doing as little as possible.

The day began at 8 a.m. As long as there was a steady flow of supplies, the operators were tied to their machines by the rhythm of the work. Usually, they remained at their places until 11 a.m., when it was time for lunch. If something went wrong with one of the machines, however, the operators did nothing. They either sat at their machines or went out for a smoke.

In addition to the machine operators, there were a large number of auxiliary personnel, including loaders and packers, forklift operators, maintenance and repair crews, and a large white-collar administrative staff, including engineers, accountants, and managers. The maintenance men spent most of the day sitting on benches and smoking. If a machine needed to be repaired, the shop boss wrote out a work order and gave it to a maintenance man, who did not fulfill it. When the boss asked why the work had not been done, the worker typically explained that he had another assignment, that there were no spare parts, or that someone had stolen his toolcase. In the end, it was hours or even days before he responded to the boss's request.

The situation was slightly different with the administrative employees. They often simply punched in, left the factory for long periods, and then returned to punch out.

At 11 a.m., the cacophony in the factory ceased as the workers turned off their machines and went to lunch. Although the break was a full hour, the workers invariably returned to their machines as late as possible.

For the rest of the day, the workers were concerned with drinking. Vodka was the principal solace in life for the factory workers, and it was possible to get vodka in the factory at any time, day or night, for fifteen rubles, ten rubles above the street price. The worst scenes in the factory took place twice a month, on payday. The workers swayed at their workplaces, but they were left alone. The police simply did not have the vehicles or manpower to carry away all the drunks.

In fact, vodka in the Soviet Union often took on a purely mystical significance. In a country that denied God and promised an earthly paradise, which it did not deliver, vodka was the only way for a worker, amid the hardships of daily life, to enter that paradise on his own.

The workers were also keenly attentive to what they could steal, often taking parts from the finished machines that were turned out by the factory. The operator responsible for adding a critical detail to a machine knew where it was and could easily sneak into the warehouse and quietly remove it. These thefts were often not discovered because the workers stole parts whose absence was not evident until the machine was used.

In fact, workers took home whatever was lying around in a factory where there was little effort to put anything away. Loaders, freight handlers, and forklift operators stole instruments, materials, and tools. The workers often dropped crates, breaking the packaging, and then scooped up the parts from the crates as they scattered over the floor. They took home the spare parts for their own equipment and when the machines ceased to function, they just sat at their places stolidly, waiting for the bosses to supply new spare parts to replace those they had stolen.

The Arsenal factory employed six thousand workers, and because of its size, the greatest potential difficulty was interruption in the delivery of materials and spare parts. To deal with this problem, the factory relied on an army of *tolkachi*, or "pushers," who were authorized to use any means, from bribery to threats and harassment, to ensure that the factory received needed supplies.

On one occasion, Malyutin fell into a conversation with a *tolkach* who was about to leave for Novokuznetsk to try to obtain supplies that had been assigned to the Arsenal factory under the plan. The *tolkach* explained that for months, Arsenal had been waiting for a consignment of light metal from Zapsib, a giant Novokuznetsk steel mill and one of the largest producers of rolled steel in the Soviet Union. At first, when the necessary metal did not arrive, the factory, drawing on its reserves, built with heavier metal than was necessary. This led to waste, which did not bother anyone because the use of heavier metal helped the plant overfulfill the plan for weight and entitled everyone to a bonus.

If Zapsib did not send the necessary consignment by the end of the year, however, it would become obvious that the plan could be fulfilled without it, and the consignment for the factory would be reduced by that amount for the following year.

Arsenal's director wrote to Zapsib and demanded to know why they had not received the metal. He received a letter that said, "It will be sent." This was a bad sign because there was no indication of when the metal would be sent. It was then that the director decided to dispatch the *tolkach*. The trip was written up as undertaken "to agree on deliveries of materials," although there was nothing to agree about. What was necessary was to bully Zapsib into sending the metal that was provided for in the plan.

The *tolkach* said that in this situation, the best course of action would have been to bring a gift. Factories in the Caucasus often sent crates of cognac. Factories that produced something desirable, for example furniture or dishes, tried to send their products.

How much difficulty the *tolkach* encountered in his mission depended on the quantity of supplies being withheld and the influence of his factory, which had a critical effect on his ability to make trouble for the supplier. Sometimes it was enough simply to take a warehouse boss out to dinner and buy him a big meal with vodka, wine, and the best hors d'oeuvres. But if enticements didn't work, the *tolkach* was obliged to resort to pressure. This was usually applied through the *raion* committee, which was motivated to act by threatening to complain to the Central Committee while waving an entire pile of letters and demanding the goods. The idea was to harass a local party secretary until he could not bear to listen any longer and ordered that something be done to satisfy the *tolkach*'s complaints.

The *tolkach* was seeking 320 tons of metal from Zapsib, which was an enormous combine that turned out millions of tons of steel a year. He probably needed only to speak to the warehouse boss, but he was not bringing any gifts and he had a speech defect, so it was unlikely that anyone would listen to him. The situation demanded creativity and he had a plan.

He explained to Malyutin that he was going to tell the Zapsib warehouse boss that the head of the industrial section at *Izvestiya* was a close relative of his and was interested in why Zapsib had not made its required deliveries. The *tolkach* had no idea whether this "actor's approach" was going to work, but no Soviet organization wants to be criticized in *Izvestiya*. So he thought it possible that Zapsib would release the goods rather than run the risk, however remote, that he was telling the truth.

But the *tolkach* said that even if Zapsib released the metal, his work would not be over. It would still be necessary to reach an agreement with the railroad, which meant going to speak to the boss of the station or one of his deputies and trying to persuade or bully him into delivering the goods.

If bribes and threats didn't work, the *tolkach* said that it was often necessary just to sit in the office of the station manager and refuse to leave, interrupting what he was doing, until he understood that it would cost him less effort to comply than to continue to hold on to the goods.

In this way goods necessary for the functioning of industry were exchanged, despite the absence of a market, across the length and breadth of the Soviet Union.

ANATOLY PAPP WORKED for two years at a metal-cutting machine in a factory that employed three hundred workers in the southern Ukrainian city of Genichesk.

The factory was one of several belonging to the Ministry of Chemical Machine Building that produced parts for cranes that laid oil and gas pipelines. Unlike the other factories, however, the factory in Genichesk used Swiss metal-cutting machines. As a result, its production was of higher quality than that of the other factories, although it still was not very good.

The workday began at 8 a.m. and it was immediately evident that the metal cutters were the only people who did any real work. Papp's job was to cut metal cylinders into spindles. He fed the cylinders into his machine and regulated the machine as it cut the metal, controlling the cutting while removing waste metal and, when necessary, replacing the machine's oil. There were seventy metal cutters among the factory's three hundred employees, and, as it happened, they had little choice but to work hard because almost 30 percent of their pay depended on their fulfilling the plan for spindles.

The most serious problem was that the operators were obliged constantly to interrupt the cutting of spindles to repair their own machines. There were workers in the repair shop who were responsible for fixing the machines, but they were busy with private jobs. They fashioned exhaust pipes, hot-water tanks, and the borders for graves—all of which they sold privately. The bosses did not object, because they received a cut of the proceeds.

The metal used for details produced by the factory was a brass alloy that was often imprecisely combined. Partially, as a result, it was of uneven consistency and when the cylinders were fed into overworked machines, the machines jammed. In Switzerland, an operator was able to supervise five cutting machines; Anatoly found that he exhausted himself running two.

During the morning hours, the work went better because the operators were fresher. Nonetheless, Anatoly was obliged frequently to stop the flow of work and repair his machine. By the end of the day, he was sometimes stopping to mend his machine every five minutes, and the pace of work slowed to a crawl. Working effectively under these conditions, Anatoly estimated that he might have been able to cut one thousand accurate spindles a month, but the plan called for him to cut ten thousand.

The constant interruptions took a toll on the quality of Anatoly's work. The spindles came out too short, too long, too thick, and too thin, but they were considered waste only when they could not be fitted into the cranes. The factory that assembled the cranes was dissatisfied with the Genichesk production, but it accepted the spindles anyway, knowing that if it exercised its right to refuse, it would not get anything. In fact, the conditions in the Genichesk factory were no different from those in other factories, and, as a result, Soviet machines built with hundreds of faulty components were always of poor quality and often did not work at all.

The Collective Farms

WHEN EVGENY POLYAKOV, a Moscow archivist, began visiting the "Zarya" collective farm, in the Kaluga oblast near Moscow, to audit its books, it seemed to him that the farmers there resembled nothing so much as a group of forced laborers looking for a way to flee.

The day began at 5 a.m., when a sleepy milkmaid left her home to milk cows. A single light burned in the collective farm headquarters and the only sound was that of a dog barking in the distance. On her way to the cow barn, the milkmaid passed giant posters with pictures of Lenin and drawings of muscular heroes of socialist labor.

The cow barn was full of uncollected excrement and it was possible to locate it by the smell. The milkmaids worked hard, but there was constant uncertainty because the electricity provided by an erratic generator could go off at any moment, panicking the cows and forcing the milkmaids to milk them by hand.

At 7:30 a.m., the collective farm bosses met in the office of the chairman to plot their battle strategy for the day. Among those present were the chief animal breeder and the chief agronomist, but it was the chairman who decided which tractors would work in which fields, how many men would plow, how many would fertilize, and how many would spend the day pulling weeds.

Once the decisions were made, the chairman's instructions were radioed directly to the groups of farmers waiting at muddy rural crossroads, and the work of the brigades was divided among the individual collective farmers.

AS THE SUN ROSE over the distant horizon, the collective farm came to life and, across its territory, groups of farmers began performing their assigned tasks.

In the vast common fields, fleets of tractors fanned out to begin the plowing. Plan fulfillment was calculated on the basis of hectares worked, and so it was to the drivers' advantage to cover as much territory as quickly as possible. The drivers started by cutting deep furrows around the edge of the fields. As they moved deeper into the fields, however, they began to lift the blade of the plow and race the tractor, and the furrows became progressively shallower. The first furrows were nine to ten inches deep. A little farther from the road, they were five to six inches deep, and in the center of the field, where the tractor drivers were certain that no one would check on them, the furrows were as little as two inches deep. Usually, no one discovered that the furrows were so shallow in the middle of the field until it became obvious that something was wrong from the stunted nature of the crop.

While the plowing was going on, other farmers were occupying themselves with fertilization.

The cow manure on the farm was gathered sporadically and left out in the open, where it was exposed to the rain. When the first downpour came, it was moistened and began to run off into a nearby stream. Of the remaining manure, part of it was spread on the fields from carts that were pulled by tractors. This work was disagreeable and tiresome. More important, it was difficult to check. The fertilization often only continued for a few hours, and the majority of the fertilizer was then taken to a remote area of the farm and burned to conceal the fact that it had never been spread.

Without proper fertilization, the soil was quickly exhausted. The farmers also ignored crop rotation, planting potatoes year after year in one field even though rotation was essential to protect against fungus and disease. The five-year plan called for fields to be planted with potatoes one year and then cereals, onions, or cabbages the next. But after each change of crops, it was also necessary to rework the soil. The field had to be cleared of weeds and there needed to be a deep plowing with the further addition of organic fertilizer. There were very few farmers who were willing to go to that much trouble.

In yet another part of the collective farm, women worked in the chicken house, located in the central village of the farm, looking after the poultry. The women working there had to scrape up congealed dung from the asphalt floor with shovels and load it into the backs of trucks. The dust this raised in the chicken house created a fog. The women wore gauze masks, but these offered little protection. Each truck was loaded in thirty minutes, and the women could rest for no more than five or ten minutes between trucks.

The work was no easier for women who worked as inseminators. They chased a grown turkey, which weighed as much as twenty-five pounds, into a corner and placed barriers around it. Two women then entered the closed-off area and grabbed the bird by the wings, trying to hold it immobile for two or three minutes while a third person inseminated it. While the turkey was being held, it tore at the women's clothing with its claws, scratching and bruising them. If the bird succeeded in freeing one of its wings, it could slap one of the inseminators in the face, possibly blinding her. The inseminators received one pair of work clothes a year and the birds ripped their clothes mercilessly. After a few hours, the inseminators were covered with bruises and filthy from the dust, but there was nowhere for them to wash.

· · ·

MANY OF THE FARMERS began to drift away from their work shortly after lunch. If the farm chairman arrived unexpectedly and asked where everyone was, the answer was that one farmer had left to turn in reports and the others had gone to get a shovel.

By 2 or 3 p.m., it was hard to find anyone in the collective farm. They were already asleep in the fields, at home drunk, or snoring in a haystack.

In fact, the atmosphere on the collective farm was that of a permanent general strike. The farmers were drunk at least half of the time, and each one did everything possible to avoid work while taking a keen interest in the shirking of others. There was a tradition of envy and jealousy, and the farmers collected material on one another and on the foreman.

In this situation, the foreman found it difficult to compel the farmers to work, as they were fully aware of his sins, and too much pressure on them could result in an anonymous letter denouncing him to the authorities for, for example, the theft of collective farm property. The chairman was also in a difficult position. He knew that every one of his employees deserved to be fired. But he also knew that he could not afford to get rid of anyone because, even as it was, there were not enough people to do the work. If a farmer was called to account for his unwillingness to work seriously, he stood silently in front of the chairman and muttered something unintelligible. He knew that, no matter what, the chairman would not throw him out.

THE ISKRA COLLECTIVE farm was located in the Kalinin oblast near the city of Staritsa and its principal products were milk and grain.

Alexander Lyakin, an icon painter, lived on the collective farm and he considered the indifference he witnessed there a product of the Communist destruction of Russia. The villages were dilapidated and half of the houses were boarded up and abandoned. The tractor repair station was littered with discarded parts and rusting agricultural machinery and so deep in mud that, even with boots on, it was difficult to walk there. In the fields, ragged clumps of uncut crops were still standing long after the harvest, sometimes partly submerged by the snow.

Conversations among the collective farmers proceeded almost entirely in profanity, and the collective farmers seemed to have no interest in the outside world. Indolent to a fault, they became active only when it was a matter of drinking or stealing.

The bosses reported for work promptly at 7:30 a.m. and decided on the day's work assignments. After about an hour, however, it was difficult to find them.

Shortly after 9 a.m. tractors appeared on the rutted roads. A sign on the machines read, DON'T TAKE PEOPLE, but this was ignored. Almost all of the tractors were pulling wagons that had several workers in them. There were many cases of wagons overturning and people being killed, especially when the driver was drunk.

It soon was possible to see small groups of people at work in various parts of the farm, but there was a desultory quality to the way they worked. In the fields, five or six women might be picking potatoes by hand while lying next to them was a man who was completely drunk.

By 10 a.m., Lyakin typically came upon ten or fifteen people standing around near a construction project discussing where to find vodka and whether there would be advances on their pay. The men usually had the concentrated expressions of those who were hard at work, but they did not seem to be doing anything, and they became angry if anyone interrupted them to ask a question.

The group drinking usually began a short time later as the collective farmers gathered in the woods or behind bushes or in a garage where the tractors were being repaired. Elsewhere on the territory, tractor drivers met in the fields to drink. Life on the collective farm soon fell under an alcoholic cloud as scores of people swayed as they walked through the villages, and there were violent scenes in the stores. Work came to a standstill as most collective farmers abandoned their posts while others went to work and collapsed. Sometimes outraged wives pulled their husbands away from the places of collective drinking, but many women on the farm were alcoholics themselves.

By midafternoon, however, the collective farmers, even if they were drunk, were already at work on their private plots. Collective farmers were not paid a living wage for their work on the common fields, so food they raised on their private plots allowed them to make up the difference. Mechanization was almost nonexistent, and it was sometimes possible to see a husband and wife on their private plot, strapped together pulling harrows and wooden plows with ropes. Other work was carried out using shovels, sickles, and scythes.

To support their private plots, farmers engaged in constant stealing. Adults stole, as did their children. It was possible to stand in a collective farmer's house surrounded by wire, hammer, nails, wheels, machine oil, and lumber, only to realize that not a single item had been purchased.

The collective farmers lived with the psychology that he who does not steal from the state, steals from his family and in some respects, stealing was forced on them. The collective farmers could not buy feed for the animals they raised on their private plots, so they stole it from the cattle barn. They could not buy tools, so they stole them from the collective farm's repair shop. Most important, the collective farmers stole as much as possible of the food that, with their help, the collective was able to produce.

The milkmaids, for example, stole between half a pail and a full pail of milk every day. The mechanics who operated the machinery that cleaned out the dung in the cow barn also stole milk, as did the wagon drivers who picked up the canisters. Lyakin estimated that the loss to the collective farm from pilferage was about 10 percent of daily production, which was concealed by topping the milk off with water. (Later, in the stores, the milk was watered down a second time.)

If a milkmaid was caught taking milk, the milk was poured back into the canister and the jar or pail in which the milk had been hidden was smashed. This stealing, like that of other collective farmers, was generally tolerated, having long since become part of the system.

THE SEMPITERNAL RHYTHMS of the Iskra collective farm continued unchanged for many years. Then, in the late 1980s, an event took place that disturbed the normal quiet of the area. One morning in the spring of 1988, Vladimir Kardanov, a tractor driver, was told to report to the office of Alexei Durnov, the chairman of the collective farm in Pankovo. Kardanov, a Cherkass, had arrived at the farm the previous November, having fled a conflict in his native Caucasus, and he proved to be a conscientious worker.

By 1987, a new wind was blowing in the country and Durnov was under pressure, in keeping with Gorbachev's scheme to create a class of rural leaseholders, to find a collective farmer who was willing to rent land.

The problem was that Gorbachev's new renting scheme involved a commitment to hard work. It was this that made Durnov turn to a newcomer like Kardanov. Durnov promised Kardanov good conditions, including favorable terms for repaying a credit to cover the cost of a tractor, cows and cow barn, and a low rent, and Kardanov agreed to become the collective farm's first renter. He selected twenty-five cows, took possession of a tractor, and was assigned a piece of land and a cow barn.

Kardanov began his career as a renter with high hopes, partially inspired by the propaganda campaign waged in the central press on behalf of renters. Problems, however, began almost immediately. On May 1, when he took over his cow barn, he discovered that the collective farm had neglected to turn on the electricity, and for two months he and his wife had to milk the cows by hand. He also had problems getting feed for his animals. Once the electricity had been turned on and the feed problem had been solved, the Baltic republics issued declarations of sovereignty and promulgated the right to "private property." This frightened the local authorities, who rewrote Kardanov's contract. If, in the earlier version, the cows, cow barn, and tractor, once they were paid off, were to become his property, the contract now said, once paid off, they were to remain the property of the collective farm.

Despite these setbacks, however, Kardanov threw himself into the effort to make his enterprise a success. Inspired by the possibility of financial rewards, he began to work almost around the clock, sometimes sleeping as little as four hours a night. The care he lavished on his cows began to have an effect. In the space of a few months, Kardanov's cows became the most productive on the collective farm. He soon collected twelve liters per cow a day compared with the average for the farm of eight liters per cow a day. Kardanov's cows also produced higher-quality milk. The fat content of his milk was 3.9 percent compared to 2.8 percent for the collective farm as a whole. He began earning as much as 1,500 rubles a month.

Kardanov's success stunned the other collective farmers. At first, they watched his progress in silence, but soon the spectacle of him becoming rich began to inspire hatred.

The first tensions arose in the cashier's office where the collective farmers lined up to receive their pay. They watched greedily as Kardanov's salary was counted out for him. It had been a rule on the collective farm that everyone was paid more or less equally no matter how badly they worked. Now, Kardanov was earning three times as much as anyone else.

Kardanov quickly became the object of denunciations. The collective farmers complained that Kardanov's cows escaped and trampled the clover fields and demanded that he be fined. They accused him of using tricks to increase his milk's fat content. A commission arrived and tested the milk and found it to be legitimately high in fat.

A condition for Kardanov becoming a renter was that the collective farm would provide him with assistance, but his fellow farmers began to demand money from him for every service. When he asked to borrow a harrow, he was told by a foreman, "I'm not giving you anything. You are making a lot of money. You can buy it yourself."

The neighbors began to insult Kardanov's children. Their children hit them in the face and stole their bicycles. When Kardanov's wife complained, the parents defended their children, saying that they did the right thing. When Kardanov went to investigate, he was told to "go fuck yourself."

As the harvest got under way, Kardanov was exposed to open aggression. A member of the collective farm who had a heavy tractor began to drive it across Kardanov's fields, ruining them for grazing. When Kardanov asked him not to drive across his field, he told Kardanov to "go fuck yourself."

In November, on a frosty morning, Kardanov saw that one of his neighbors was busy plowing up one of his fields. Kardanov ran out and told the neighbor that the land belonged to him.

The neighbor replied, "I was born here and you've lived here less than a year, so this land is mine."

One by one all of Kardanov's neighbors broke off relations with him. It became impossible to get spare parts for his tractor or help with loading and construction. In December, a fire broke out in Kardanov's cow barn, leaving it in ruins. Kardanov claimed that the fire was set deliberately. There was no proof of this, but once the barn was destroyed, Kardanov found it difficult to get help in rebuilding it. He bought cement and rented a cement mixer, but the mixer was stolen, and the workers who had agreed to help in the new construction did not show up.

Finally, surrounded by resentment and unable to do his work, Kardanov decided to give up his attempt to become a renter. On a cold winter night, he packed up his family and left the collective farm for good.

7

The Border

"Do you have tigers in Greece?"
"Yes."
"How about lions?"
"We also have lions."
"In Russia, there is nothing and in Greece, they have everything."
—Anton Chekhov, The Wedding

"WHEN A SOVIET CITIZEN comes out of customs at Shereme-tevo Airport," said Andrei Koveshnikov, a cab driver in his late twenties, "he resembles a hunted animal. He is loaded down with suitcases and bags and it is obvious that he is afraid that someone is waiting to grab his belongings. As he tries to find a taxi, he is nervous and constantly asking himself who will try to trick him next. With a foreigner, it's different. He is calm, smiling. He has a life-affirming face. As he looks around, it is evident that this is his first time in the Soviet Union, but he is not suspicious. You speak to him in broken English and his reaction is friendly. He is polite and says thank-you.

"Watching this scene day by day, I got my first exposure to the West.

"I was finally invited to visit Germany by my friend, a former Soviet German who was living in St. Augustine near Cologne. The first thing that struck me about Germany was the road from the Cologne airport. It was as if the road was polished. There were no potholes. All the signs were visible from a distance, and it seemed to me that it would have been difficult to get lost even if you did not know the language.

"On Friday, I ended up in a large store. There were three floors of groceries, and in two hours, I was only able to see half of the first floor. My friends bought all that they needed. I compared the prices to our prices, and in relation to pay the prices in Germany were lower.

"There were dozens of different types of bread. I never in my life saw such abundance and I felt pain for my country. I began to think that only fools live in Russia. My father and mother never saw such abundance and my relatives never saw it and never will see it.

"I began to work in a [German] factory where one of my friends was a foreman. It was a furniture factory and most of the workers spent time cutting boards.

"In Germany, if a person works, he works for the entire eight hours. I worked carrying and arranging the boards. It was heavy and monotonous. I got very tired and could not drink or smoke. In Russia, no one works like that. The workday started at 6 a.m. and we worked until 9 a.m. From 9 a.m. to 9:15 a.m., there was a fifteen-minute break. In other words, we worked for three hours without once going to the corridor to smoke. No foreman came and shouted abuse at us and the Germans did not complain.

"I immediately realized that it would have been possible to steal a lot of wood. There were also many tools—electric saws, drills, and hammers—lying around, but no one tried to steal anything.

"The relations were very businesslike. The shop was very clean. There were no piles of materials. No one was standing over us. Wood was being cut everywhere, but I saw no dust. The strips were all put accurately in garbage cans. If there was no work to discuss, there was no conversation.

"If there was a break in the work because something went wrong with the conveyor, people began immediately to find things to do on their own. They took out garbage. They cleaned tools. For a Russian, this was insanity, but this attitude toward work was the reason they lived so well."

ON A WARM NIGHT in May 1990, Igor Yerofeev knocked on the door of the apartment of Nikolai Fyodorov, an official in the Gas Ministry, in a building on Komsomolsky Prospekt. The door opened and he was greeted by Fyodorov, who had a strangely wandering gaze.

"Don't pay attention to him," said Fyodorov's wife, who appeared moments later. "He's been in this condition for a week, ever since he got back from the United States."

Fyodorov invited Igor to sit in the living room while his wife went to make tea.

"What did I live for, what did I work for, what did I achieve?" Fyodorov asked, only barely noticing Igor's presence. It was obvious to Igor that Fyodorov was in a state of shock.

"Do you know Sasha Ivanov?" Fyodorov asked, referring to a chess grandmaster who had married a Jewish woman and emigrated, and was now living in Boston.

"Yes."

"Can you imagine him at the wheel of a car?"

"No, honestly speaking, I can't," Igor said. Ivanov had earned very little in Moscow and had always dressed modestly.

"He has a car nine meters long."

Fyodorov continued, ". . . fifteen years in a queue to get an apartment, five years in a queue for a car, now in line for a dacha with only two years before pension. . . ."

"THE FIRST THING that struck me," said Sergei Melkumov, a mechanic at the ice-skating rink in the Dynamo Stadium, "was the organization of work on a French farm.

"In one of the cow barns near Beauvais, where I was visiting a friend, there were ten cows attached to an automatic milking machine. A tender pushed a button and, suddenly, streams of milk began to pour through transparent rubber tubes into an enormous noncorrosible steel vat.

"A truck immediately arrived and was connected to the vat with a hose and drew milk that was measured automatically on a meter.

"Watching this, I thought about our own dairy maids, putting cows in place and milking them with dirty hands.

"Nearby, I saw a pasture. The grass was rich and the area was fenced off with concrete pillars and barbed wire. It was all very exact. I thought: This is one person's land. It is his and cannot be touched. Each cow had a number and I realized that with the help of these numbers, they kept track of each cow, how much it ate, how much milk it gave, and how much it weighed. With the help of the numbers, they could make an inventory with the highest level of accuracy.

"I knew rural life in Russia and to see this made me feel ill.

"The first time I ate French cakes, I was stunned. I could not get over the fact they were so tasty. I had bought six cakes for seventy-two francs.

"I began to compare the cost of the cakes as a percent of a French worker's pay with the relative cost of the cakes in Russia. It was about the same percentage, but the quality in France was much higher.

"My friend was a tennis instructor. I went with him to work in the Paris suburb of Sourcelles, where he taught at the Maccabee Club. He organized a small tournament for children eight to twelve years old. I saw how he worked with the children and how the parents thanked him. I was struck by the excited attitude of the children and their gratitude to the Russian teacher.

"In Russia, such clubs are not possible. Children are trained only for professional sports, in order to make money.

"Everything about France intrigued me. In Russia, if you turn to someone to get directions or information, there is no guarantee that you'll receive a fully expressed answer. In France, you'll get it."

WITH THE BEGINNING of the reform process in the Soviet Union, thousands of Soviet citizens for the first time received permission to travel abroad and were shocked by their exposure to the outside world.

Arriving in the West, which for years had been described to them principally in terms of squalor and exploitation, they saw lights, colors, prosperity, and the absence of queues.

Their shock, however, was not merely a reaction to surface appearances. During decades of totalitarian rule, citizens lost the sense that the outside world had relevance. In a situation in which the regime attempted to impose a delusionary ideology, only access to the outside world could give Soviet citizens an external point of reference capable of restoring their sense of reality. But such access was tightly controlled.

The Soviet border was no ordinary barrier but a line of demarcation between two different states of consciousness, the impenetrable dividing line between the West, where reality is given, and the Soviet Union, where reality is made. In this situation, Soviet citizens became interlopers in normal life.

This was why they reacted with such shock to their first exposure to the outside world. The difference in consciousness, however, was demonstrated in its pure form under totalitarian rule in the experience of those individuals who tried to escape from the Soviet Union on their own.

ON A CALM summer night, Anatoly Butko, a gynecologist from Artemovsk in the Donetsk oblast, entered his cabin on board the diesel ship *Latvia* in the port at Batumi, took off his shoes and, without undressing, lay down on his bunk and pretended to sleep. Around him, the three other passengers arranged their suitcases, apparently not noticing that Butko had entered the cabin without any belongings.

At 10:10 p.m., the engines of the *Latvia*, the only ship plying the eastern Black Sea route at night, started up and the ship pulled out of the harbor to begin its voyage to Sukhumi and then Sochi.

The corridor and cabins were quiet. After the last of his fellow passengers began breathing heavily, Butko sat up and put on his shoes. As a precaution, he said, in a loud voice, "I think I'll take a walk on the deck." None of the other passengers stirred. He then wrapped his watch in cellophane, stepped into the empty corridor and went to a box for fire equipment, where he had hidden an umbrella, which, in case of necessity, he could use as a sail; a bag with several bars of chocolate; a small container of water; and a rubber life preserver. He took these things up to the deck.

On the rippled surface of the water, the moonlight was reflected in silver bars. It was nearly midnight and Butko noticed that the deck was empty except for two lovers leaning over a railing and a young man who Butko assumed was a KGB agent, standing alone with his hands in his jacket pockets. Butko lit a cigarette and the young man, after studying him casually for a few minutes, turned away and walked toward the ship's bow. Seeing this, Butko calmly threw away the cigarette and walked toward the ship's stern. On reaching the stern, he looked behind him and saw that the deck was empty. He then climbed over the railing and dived thirty feet into the water below.

Butko's actions that night were the product of years of disillusion-
ment with the Soviet regime. In the 1950s, after his army service on
Sakhalin Island, Butko traveled across the Soviet Union to his home
in the Donbass and saw rows of labor camps in Siberia. Starving collective farmers in the Baikal region begged for grain. In the 1960s, he
was beaten by the police when he was taken, while drunk, to a
sobering-up station; his head was shaved after he called the police
"fascists." Even at that time, he knew he would have to leave his
homeland, but personal ties kept him in the Soviet Union. After his
marriage broke up, he decided it was time to try to escape to the
West.

Butko began to study the problem of crossing the Soviet border.
He learned that the border was, in all cases, preceded by a "zone of
heightened vigilance" at least nine miles in depth. In the border
zone, the police guarded all roads and any nonresident found there
without authorization was subject to immediate arrest. Residents
were screened for "loyalty" and received rewards for reporting the
presence of a stranger. At the same time, anyone who seemed out of
place in an area as much as thirty miles from the border could be
stopped and asked to explain his mission.

He also learned from a neighbor whose son was a guard that the
border was directly preceded, in most areas, by electrified barbed-
wire fences, watchtowers, and broad control strips of smoothed-over
earth, which were constantly raked and checked for footprints.

The Soviet Union was surrounded by "friendly" countries—
Finland, the socialist nations, and Iran—which handed back border
crossers to the Soviet authorities. Turkey did not return border crossers but, in light of security in the border zones, Butko doubted that
it would be possible to cross into Turkey on foot. He considered
making a balloon, but found that there was no way to get the necessary hydrogen. He had marine experience and was a strong swim-
mer. He decided he would try to swim.

Butko had timed his escape well. The water was warm, and after
he recovered his breath he put on his life preserver and watched as
the *Latvia* turned north toward Sukhumi. He began to take powerful,
rhythmic strokes. It was a clear night and a warm breeze rippled the
surface of the water. He felt utterly alone, making a passage to another planet under a canopy of stars. The *Latvia* disappeared over the
horizon and, in the distance, Butko noticed that the lights of Soviet
cities were yellow but that lights in Turkey were different colors. He

wondered if this was advertising. Butko saw occasional Soviet patrol boats on the water and, at points along the coast, searchlights blinked ominously, lighting up the shore. He tried to maintain a steady pace and he could see that with each passing hour, he was getting closer to the Turkish shore.

As he swam, Butko wondered what he would do in the West. He was a doctor and he assumed that there would always be a need for his skills. He felt a sense of euphoria, the sensation that, for the first time in his life, he was a free man.

The sun rose in the east. Butko used his watch to read its position and concluded that he was about four hours from the Turkish coast. Soon, however, the breeze abated and Butko heard the sound of distant thunder and noticed patches of lightning in the sky. Suddenly, the current became stronger and Butko found it harder and harder to swim. A heavy fog rolled in and he could no longer distinguish the shore. He tried to orient toward the Turkish coast but became unsure of his direction. Suddenly, he collided with a piece of gelatinous garbage, experienced a terrible shock, and blacked out.

When Butko regained consciousness, the sea was being raked with heavy rain and he could not move. He realized that he had been stung by a jellyfish. Kept afloat by his life preserver, he began to be carried backward by the strong current. The current carried him all that day and all the next night. By the time he finally overcame the shock and recovered his strength, he had been carried back to where he had jumped ship, and he realized that, in several more hours, he would be carried back to the Soviet shore.

Butko was without food or water. The weather had changed and the sea was now turbulent. There was a strong wind and waves splashed over him, but fighting the current, he began swimming toward Turkey. Bending every effort, he swam for hours and, as the current became more and more powerful, he came to within a mile and a half of the coast, close enough to see houses on the shore. Yet at the moment, when success was within his grasp, he realized with a sickening certainty that he could not fight the current any longer. Totally exhausted, he was swept back out to sea.

For the next thirty hours, Butko was carried by the waves until, finally, after more than three days in the water, he was washed up, half-conscious, in the city of Poti, on the Soviet coast.

At first, Butko lay on the beach in a daze, unsure of where he was. Finally, however, he discerned watchtowers and realized that he was in the Soviet Union. A passerby, seeing his life preserver, summoned the border guards. Too weak to flee, Butko was arrested and taken first to the police station in Poti and then to the KGB isolator in Batumi.

In Batumi, Butko was interviewed by a KGB major who told him that for attempting to cross the Soviet border illegally, he could expect twelve to fifteen years in a labor camp. If it could be shown that he was mentally ill (and what sane person would want to leave the Soviet Union?), the punishment might be lighter.

Given the alternative, Butko decided to agree he was mentally ill. He told a psychiatrist, "Find something wrong with me." He was finally diagnosed as suffering from "psychopathy with grandiose ideas." He was sent to a mental hospital in Gukovo in the Rostov oblast, where he was held for thirteen months, an extremely short period for an unsuccessful border crosser.

When I met Butko at the apartment of Felix Serebrov in Moscow in 1980, he was living quietly in Alushta in the Crimea. After his release from the mental hospital, he had begun writing poetry, including a poem entitled "S.O.S.," in which he called on people to recognize reality.

FROM HIS CELL in the prison of a small Finnish city, Alexander Shatravka heard the sound of several cars pulling up to the prison entrance. He then heard the sound of keys in the main door of the prison one floor below and activity in the corridor. Finally, two guards opened the door of his cell. Shatravka was handcuffed and led outside.

In front of the prison, Shatravka saw the three other men who had successfully crossed the Soviet-Finnish border with him—his brother, Mikhail; Anatoly Romanchuk, a former border guard; and his friend, Boris Sivkov—seated in various cars. Shatravka was then put in a blue police car and, after a brief delay, the column left the city and started moving in a southerly direction.

"Where are they taking us?" Shatravka thought. "The Soviet border is east of us but we're heading south. Maybe we're heading for the regional center? Or maybe they're getting ready to hand us over." For an instant, Shatravka considered seizing the driver, who was sitting in front of him. But he thought better of it. It seemed to him that they were heading for another Finnish city.

From the window of the car, Shatravka looked out at a wooded landscape. Coming toward them from the opposite direction was a long line of cars, some of which had camping trailers attached. The people in the cars were, for the most part, young, and Shatravka envied them. Suddenly, the column of cars made a sharp turn onto a narrow asphalted road that headed east into a deep forest. The cars slowed and then drove onto the territory of a Finnish border post, a well-built house surrounded by a wire fence.

The four border crossers got out of the cars and Shatravka saw Sivkov ahead of him.

Suddenly, Shatravka could see from his erratic movements that Boris was becoming agitated.

"Sanya," he screamed, "they're handing us back."

The Finnish guards began to force the Soviet border crossers back into the cars, but before Shatravka could sit down, he felt a hand grabbing his right hand through the open door and shaking it. Turning sharply, he saw the apologetic face of the Finnish investigator who had interrogated him. Shatravka became infuriated and pulled his hand away.

Shatravka's decision to try to escape from the Soviet Union was a reaction to coercion. As a student in the auto school in Krivoi Rog, where he was studying to become a chauffeur, he had moderately long hair. The instructors began demanding that students get their hair cut and Shatravka began to protest. A short time later, he was called to the *raion* party committee, where Panchenko, a propaganda official, said, "There are five hundred people in Krivoi Rog with hair like yours. If we could, we would shoot every one of you."

Shatravka left the auto school and went to Krasnovodsk to work on a fishing boat and decided to ask a "jurist" (juridical consultant) how to leave the country. The jurist reported the conversation to the KGB, and a short time later, Shatravka was summoned to KGB headquarters in Krasnovodsk, where he was interrogated by Major Bober, the deputy chief of the KGB, about his plans to cross the border.

"You are a son of Russia," Bober said, "why would you want to leave your motherland?"

"I hate this country," Shatravka said, becoming emotional. "I don't want to die on this land."

"All right," Bober said, "if you want to sell this country, head for the border and get a bullet in the back."

Shatravka left Krasnovodsk and returned to Krivoi Rog. But shortly after his arrival, he was ordered to report to the military commissariat for induction into the army. Shatravka, however, had no intention of going into the army and went to the induction center with a concealed knife. At the center, he pointed to the red line on a map that delineated the Soviet border and said to the commandant, "You see that line? I give you my word that one day I'm going to be on the other side of it."

"You're a coward," the commandant said.

"So you think I'm a coward," Shatravka screamed. He then ran out of the room into the yard, pulled off his shirt, and began slashing himself. Shatravka returned home. A few hours later, he was picked up and taken to the psychiatric hospital in Igim near Dnepropetrovsk.

A short time later, Shatravka was written out of the army on grounds of signs of psychopathology, and he began to make definitive plans to escape to the west.

Shatravka and his brother, Mikhail, traveled around the Soviet Union to survey possible sites for the attempt. They wanted to flee by boat, but saw in Yalta that the shore was guarded with searchlights and patrol boats. They considered commandeering an air taxi from Simferopol, but learned that all of them had been removed from the border areas after a successful escape to Turkey by two Lithuanian hijackers some years earlier. They went to the Western Ukraine, but gave up the idea of escaping through Hungary to Yugoslavia and Italy because they'd have to cross too many borders. The best chance seemed to be to try to cross the border on foot into Finland.

One of Shatravka's neighbors in Krivoi Rog, Anatoly Romanchuk, had served as a border guard. He told Shatravka that it would be possible to cross in the area west of Chupa. At first, Shatravka was skeptical of Romanchuk, but three years had passed since his conflict at the auto school and he was now anxious to begin life in the West.

Shatravka took a job at a Krivoi Rog steel mill to earn money, but soon quit. Then he, Mikhail, Romanchuk, and his friend Boris Sivkov caught a train to Leningrad. In Leningrad, they changed trains for Murmansk, and at 2 a.m. they got off the train at the isolated forest station of Chupa. They then walked past several log houses and entered the woods by the light of the midnight sun.

Romanchuk had assured them that there was no need for a compass because he knew the terrain, but they were soon lost in a wilderness of forests, swamps, and endless lakes. Mosquitoes swarmed around them in clouds. They had no petroleum jelly to protect their hands or faces. They perspired under their jeans, and when they lay down in exhaustion, gnats crawled up under their clothes.

For six days and six nights, they wandered. On the seventh day, they came upon a party of geophysicists who fed them and took them on their supply plane to Louchi, which was about eighty-five miles away.

Normally, border crossers pay for their mistakes by being captured, but fate had apparently decreed that the four voyagers would have a second chance. For eight days, they worked at odd jobs in Louchi and then bought petroleum jelly, boots, and a compass. They took buses to a spot about fifty miles from the border and, having decided not to listen to Romanchuk and to navigate only with the compass, they set out again.

This time they made steady progress toward the border. They were at last able to appreciate the beauty of nature and slept with pleasure in the woods, protected by the vaseline.

At first, they followed well-marked paths, but as they neared the border, they left the paths and began to pick their way through the woods. On their eighth day in the forest they came to a broad, plowed strip of earth that had been smoothed over to pick up footprints. They crossed the strip, leaving their footprints. They now knew they were near the border, but instead of showing greater caution, they began to run, abandoning themselves to the thought of getting to the border as quickly as possible.

Suddenly, the forest broke and they found themselves on the bank of a swift-flowing river, the boundary between the Soviet Union and Finland. They ran down the bank, jumped into the river and swam across to the Finnish side. On the opposite shore, they clambered up the riverbank and ran past a long row of blue and white border posts with the lion and saber emblem of Finland.

Years later, Shatravka was to remember those first moments in Finland as among the happiest of his life. Exhausted but drunk with joy, he began singing a nonsensical song. In their euphoria, the border crossers lost the sensation of being tired. They ran, and as they ran, they no longer felt the earth under their feet.

The four of them walked for two hours as if they had arrived on a strange planet, stopping to examine every discarded box or can. In the distance, they saw a dilapidated, abandoned house on the shore of a lake. Too euphoric to be concerned about any potential danger, the border crossers decided to camp in the abandoned house.

When they reached the cabin, Romanchuk told the others that the Finns would not try hard to catch them. Their only worry was the local police, whom it would be easy to avoid.

Sivkov and Romanchuk lay down on the floor and fell asleep. Shatravka and his brother, overcome with fatigue, also soon fell into a deep sleep on the wooden floor.

A short time later, Shatravka was woken by the loud noise of a helicopter flying overhead.

"Where did a helicopter come from?" he asked sleepily.

"Go back to sleep," Romanchuk said, "that's just the fire brigade helicopter. They're checking the forests."

They all went back to sleep, but after a few minutes, they were awakened again by Romanchuk's voice, this time less confident. "Someone's coming," he said.

The door burst open. A man in khaki with an automatic over his shoulder, holding a straining dog on a short leash, addressed them in Finnish. Not receiving any kind of answer, he calmly stepped back out, slamming the door after him.

"We should have avoided this house," Sivkov said. "I knew that something bad was going to happen."

The others tried to decide what to do. All of their efforts had been directed at escaping from the Soviet Union. It had hardly occurred to them that they might have a problem with the Finns.

They decided first to hide all their Soviet documents under the floor with the idea that they would tell the Finns that they were Canadians of Ukrainian origin who were seeking a way of entering the Soviet Union illegally. After some discussion, they lost hope that the Finns would find this a convincing explanation.

"They're going to call for help," Romanchuk said.

The border crossers decided to leave the cabin, but when they appeared outside, the Finnish guards, who had been sitting on the grass, jumped up and gestured to them to put up their hands. They then went and frisked each of their captives. They removed knives from their pockets, but didn't seem to attach much importance to them, handing them back. Having convinced themselves that Shatravka and his companions had no firearms, the Finns went back and sat down again on the grass.

At that, Shatravka and the others decided to sit down on the grass, too, and engage the Finns in a friendly conversation.

The Finns offered them cigarettes and they spread out a detailed map of the immediate area and showed their Soviet guests the exact spot where they had crossed the border and, at the same time, an empty pack of Tuluki Estonian cigarettes that they had discarded along the way.

"Where are we going now?" Shatravka asked as best he could. "Two kilometers by the road," one of the Finns said, pronouncing the words softly in Russian. He pointed on the map to the city of Kusamo.

"Us, to Russia, will we go to Russia?" Shatravka asked in what he presumed to be English.

"Ya, ya, Russland," one of the Finns said, pointing to Shatravka and the others and then in the direction of the Soviet border.

Shatravka tried to explain to them that prison awaited them in the Soviet Union, crossing his fingers to indicate prison bars. The Finns apparently understood what this meant because they began to converse among themselves, shaking their heads in apparent sympathy.

At that moment, a helicopter appeared overhead and landed nearby. An older, beefy Finn in a hat emerged from the helicopter and without paying any attention to the border crossers, went straight into the cabin. When he came out, no more than a minute later, he was carrying in his hands the documents they had carefully hidden under the floor.

He gave a command to the guards and jumped back into the helicopter. The helicopter immediately lifted off and disappeared.

Shortly afterward, the group left the cabin. The skies filled with thick, gray clouds and it began to rain. The column spread out, with a Finn who had a compass in the lead. At last, Shatravka and his companions, accompanied by the guards, emerged onto a wet asphalt highway. From around a corner, three cars appeared, two Volvos and a Volkswagen. Behind the cars, completing the column, was a minibus. Shatravka got into a green Volvo with two border guards. In front of him, he could see Sivkov in the red Volvo and behind him was a yellow Volkswagen followed by the minibus, with his brother and Romanchuk.

As they rode down the wet highway, Shatravka was astounded by how different Finland was from Soviet Karelia, even though the climate and topography were the same. The farmhouses were neat and painted in bright yellow and brown. There were barns as well as asphalted lots for agricultural machinery such as tractors. The highway did not have a single crack or pothole and along the side of the road, milk canisters had been left on wooden platforms, which seemed to imply that there was no stealing.

Finally, they came to a small city. The main street was filled with cars in every color of the rainbow. The store windows were so clean that they gleamed in the sun's light. The stores seemed to be full of products and everywhere there were patches of flowers, as well as brightly painted houses surrounded by fences. Shatravka was so hypnotized he could not take his eyes off the storefronts and did not notice that the car in which he was riding had turned into an area cordoned off by a wire-mesh fence.

It had stopped raining and the sun had come out. The four border crossers were led into an army barracks and placed in separate rooms. Shatravka lay down on a cot and quickly fell asleep. The next thing he knew, someone was shaking him angrily. He got up and followed a Finn, who led him to a room where a thin man in a Finnish military uniform sat behind a desk. The officer asked Shatravka if he knew any foreign languages and received a negative reply. He then began to speak in broken Russian.

"Why did you cross the Soviet-Finnish border?" he asked. "Did you know that Finland has a treaty with the Soviet Union on the return of border crossers?"

"We were going to Sweden. We want political asylum. But since we're here in Finland, I ask you to give us the opportunity to meet with the official representatives of the United States," Shatravka said.

"Very well, we'll see about that," said the Finn, "but now I ask you to select, out of this pile of documents, only your own."

It was not difficult for Shatravka to find his papers and the Finn, after checking to make sure that he had picked up what looked like the right documents, allowed him to go back to his room.

The border crossers spent the day in the barracks and that night they were put in cars and driven out through the sleeping town. Shatravka and Romanchuk rode together. Romanchuk asked the Russian-speaking guard who sat in the front seat with the driver, "Are you going to hand us back?"

"I can't say exactly," he replied. "That will be clear on Monday, after two days."

The car drove up to a two-story building and Shatravka and Romanchuk were led inside. This was the town prison. The border crossers were met by a red-bearded Finn who seemed to be in charge, and they were taken to their cells. Shatravka lay down on his cot but did not want to sleep. He looked out the window, which was divided by thick, vertical bars. After a time, he saw the red-bearded Finn on the street in front of the prison, walking toward a yellow house in the distance. Gradually, lights went out in the houses and the town became quiet. Only a small dog ran along the fence in front of the prison, keeping vigil with the four sojourners from the Soviet Union.

The border crossers spoke through the cell doors and compared their impressions. They all were astounded by the beauty of Finland and agreed that they would be ready to stay and live there for the rest of their lives. When the conversation turned to the possibility of being handed back to the Soviet authorities, there was also unanimity. They preferred to remain forever in the cells of the prison than to return to the Soviet Union.

The next morning, the red-bearded Finn entered their cells and served each of them a small breakfast. Shortly afterward, the Finns began the interrogations. Shatravka was questioned by a friendly young man with flax-colored hair. An older man, a teacher of Russian at a local school, served as the translator.

The investigator asked questions, typing continuously on the typewriter as Shatravka gave his answers. Shatravka told how he had sought the advice of a jurist on leaving the Soviet Union legally, how he had struggled to stay out of the army, how he had slashed himself, and how he had been incarcerated in a mental hospital.

"So you see," Shatravka said to the investigator, who continued to type, "if you hand us back, a mental hospital for me is guaranteed."

The investigator asked Shatravka why he was so anxious to leave the Soviet Union. "You have so many beautiful women there, especially in Leningrad," he said, smiling.

"There were many reasons," Shatravka said, completely seriously, "the daily Communist propaganda from which it is almost impossible to escape, the slander and persecution of honest and decent men, for example the campaign against Academician Andrei Dmitrievich Sakharov, low wages and the threat of being imprisoned for refusing to work for the state—in other words, legalized slavery—

the fact that closed borders make the country resemble a large concentration camp."

The investigator seemed impressed with Shatravka's answer.

"Are you going to hand us back?" Shatravka asked.

"We have no choice," said the investigator. "We have a treaty with the Soviet Union on the return of border crossers. If you had been a tourist and had asked for political asylum, we could have given it to you."

Finally, the investigator handed a document to Shatravka, which was typed in Finnish, and asked him to sign it. Shatravka signed and was taken back to his cell. The next day, he and the three others were taken from the prison to the Soviet-Finnish border.

AFTER SHATRAVKA ANGRILY PULLED his hand away from the Finnish investigator, the door of the minibus was closed behind him. Once he and the others were seated, the cars drove another couple of hundred meters into the woods. The column pulled up to the barrier marking the Soviet border and a Finnish officer with several border guards approached the red Volvo in which Sivkov was riding. Sivkov emerged clumsily from the car. The first barrier gate was lifted and then the second barrier and he was on the other side.

Overcome with fury, Shatravka got up and kicked out the window of the minibus, which flew onto the asphalt together with its rubber border. The Finns in the minibus remained calm, as if nothing had happened. "Suomi schwein!" Shatravka screamed, and then began spitting out of the open window space. But after his outburst of fury, he seemed unable to do anything further to resist the inevitable.

An officer came to the minibus and said, "Let's go." He left the minibus and, escorted by the Finns, crossed the border back into the Soviet Union, leaving Finland and the West behind him.

"What is your last name?" asked a thin Soviet colonel who met Shatravka. He was joined by a small, porcine major and two groups of three border guards with Kalashnikovs.

"I don't know. I've forgotten," said Shatravka calmly.

"What is your last name?" the colonel said, repeating the question.

"I don't know," Shatravka shouted, and then began cursing him uncontrollably.

The Finnish officer who was standing nearby said, in broken Russian, "His last name is . . ."

"Shut up, lackey," Shatravka shouted, and then, trying to imagine some way to irritate the Soviet officers even more, he said, "My name is Ian Smith."

"His last name is Shatravka," said the Finn.

"Stop clowning," said the colonel. "We'll write up a report on you for insulting the Finnish representatives."

"Shut up, you Soviet son of a bitch. I couldn't care less what you write," Shatravka said.

"Grab the schizophrenic!" said the major in a voice loud enough to be audible to Mikhail, who was still on Finnish territory.

The Soviet border guards grabbed Shatravka and exchanged his loose Finnish handcuffs for narrow Soviet ones, which were fastened as tightly as possible, causing him excruciating pain. Shatravka was put in the rear seat of a small truck that smelled of gasoline. As the truck pulled out, he began to bait the guards seated around him.

"You know," he said, "Finland is a country intended for human beings. In fact, it is better to be a prisoner in Finland than to live as a free man in the Soviet Union."

The guards told him that he would soon be put on trial.

"It's useless, all the same, I'll sit out my three years and try to cross the border again. One way or another, I'm going to break out of this Communist hell."

"What are you talking about, three years?" said a young lieutenant. "You'll get fifteen years."

Four small trucks bearing the fugitives followed a small dirt road in the woods, around a small lake, and stopped near a house in the forest.

Shatravka was escorted into a lighted room with a long table covered with a red tablecloth. On one side of the table were Finnish officers. On the other side were Soviets. A Soviet colonel invited Shatravka to sit down and explained that he had been invited to witness the handing over of his documents by the Finnish authorities. He would be asked to sign for each document.

"That's clear," said Shatravka, "but first, can you remove the handcuffs? Otherwise, I can't sign."

The colonel ordered the handcuffs removed. The almost intolerable pain that had reached his elbows began to disappear, but Shatravka still found it difficult to move his fingers.

"Your handcuffs are better than the Soviet kind," Shatravka said to the Finns, who smiled, acknowledging the compliment.

He finally indicated that he was ready and began to sign for his documents. When this was complete, an officer refastened the handcuffs.

"Is it possible not to put the handcuffs on so tightly?" Shatravka asked in a loud voice.

"Don't fasten them tightly," the colonel said.

Shatravka was escorted out and his brother was called in.

VALERY ZERN, A YOUNG Soviet German, stood in the crowded railway station at Chernovtsy and studied the schedule of departures on an overhead tableau, trying to decide whether to board the diesel train for Vadul-Siret, a town on the Soviet-Romanian border. Vadul-Siret was deep in the restricted border zone, so traveling there without authorization was risky. But he hoped that from Vadul-Siret it would be possible to cross into Romania on foot.

It was a humid, muggy summer evening and Zern was wracked by indecision. He had made friends with dissidents in Moscow and was aware that unsuccessful border crossers ended up in labor camps or psychiatric hospitals. At the same time, the atmosphere of lying in the Soviet Union was becoming unbearable. He watched a group of German tourists parting with their Intourist guide and getting on a train to Bucharest.

"Strange," he thought to himself. "In a few hours, they will be across the border. Romania is a communist country, but at least they penetrate that border."

The train for Vadul-Siret was scheduled to leave at midnight. Finally, at 11:30 p.m., Zern steeled himself and entered one of the cars, sitting down on a wooden bench across from an obese woman in a flowered shawl who eyed him knowingly. "If you're caught in Vadul-Siret without permission, you'll be arrested immediately," she said.

Zern looked up at her and said, "I've got nothing to worry about, I'm local."

At midnight, the train left the station.

. . .

ZERN LIVED IN KHARTSISK in the Ukraine, and he first began seriously thinking about crossing the border when he was persecuted while in the Soviet army for protesting against the description of West Germany in political lectures as a "capitalist hell." What finally convinced him to make the attempt, however, was the rejection of his application to emigrate to West Germany.

Zern's first idea was to cross the border into Turkey. When he went to Batumi, however, and saw the watchtowers along the water, he became convinced that he would have little chance of success. He next went to Kishinev. There he boarded an electric train for Ungeni, on the Romanian border. When the train entered the border zone, however, the doors suddenly locked automatically and there was no way to get out. Zern finally got off the train in Oknitsa in northern Moldavia.

Zern was now unsure what to do. At last, after washing up in a local bathhouse, he walked along the railroad tracks in the direction of the border, arriving at the end of the day at the station of Voskantsy in the Chernovtsy oblast. He noticed a woman standing with a cow in front of a house near the station and asked her in Ukrainian for a piece of bread. "Go to Papa," she said. "He'll give you something." Zern spent the night in the station and the next morning hitched a ride with a truck driver to another rural station, where he caught a local train to Chernovtsy.

AT 2:30 A.M., the train for Vadul-Siret arrived in Glibokaya, the last stop before the border zone. The train was not due to leave again until 4 a.m., and Zern walked out into the empty central square of the city. It was a moonless night, and the thought now struck him that instead of continuing on to Vadul-Siret, it would be less risky to try to reach the border from Glibokaya on foot. He left the central square, walked a short distance to a nearby freight yard, and plunged into the woods.

For two hours, Zern walked through woods thick with acacia trees and dense shrubbery, picking his way through bushes and branches and trying to follow the tracks while listening for the sounds of trains. At length, he saw a railroad station bathed in floodlights and, beyond it, searchlights and watchtowers. He realized that this was Vadul-Siret.

Avoiding the station, Zern turned down a dirt road which led in the direction of the border. When the first streaks of dawn appeared in the sky, however, he was surprised by a man approaching him on a bicycle. Shaken, he left the road and dived into the nearby woods, where he decided to spend the day, with the idea of crossing the border that night.

It began to get lighter and Zern could feel that it would be a hot day. He emerged from the woods briefly and studied the watchtowers which loomed in front of him. In a nearby field, a tractor began working. He lay down in the forest and, after hanging up his wet shoes, took a pocket atlas out of his pocket and studied the map of Romania. It became hotter and he began to perspire freely. The stagnant water of a nearby swamp emitted a sulfurous smell and the atmosphere became suffocating. The last time he had had a drink was in Chernovtsy twenty-four hours earlier. Finally, he crawled out of the woods and emerged in a clearing, where he ate some wheat grains off the plants.

The hours wore on and Zern's thirst became overwhelming. Occasionally, he crept out of the woods and surveyed the fields and an asphalt road leading to Romania. On the road, he could see foreign cars.

Finally, however, under the pressure of hunger and thirst, he began to reconsider the wisdom of what he was doing. He began to feel that it had been a stupid idea to try to cross the border into Romania, of all countries.

At last, Zern decided that he could not go on without water any longer and he got up, left the woods, and walked to a nearby village, where he asked the first person he saw where he could get some water. The man directed him to a factory, and there Zern was directed to a well where he pulled up the pail and, oblivious to the impression he was making, drank greedily before dropping the pail back into the well and walking to the road.

Apparently, it had not taken long for someone to inform the authorities of his presence. As he stood on the road, Zern saw a jeep approaching with an officer and three soldiers. Zern make no attempt to flee and the jeep stopped in front of him. The border guards got out and asked to see his documents.

"I lost my way," Zern said.

"Get in the car," the officer said, "so you won't get lost anymore."

Zern was taken to a border post and interrogated for six hours.

He was then taken to Chernovtsy, where he spent the night in a cell with a mattress and a pillow. Zern was told that the reason for the good conditions was that foreigners were sometimes held there.

The next morning, Zern was interrogated again and taken to the border and ordered to retrace his steps. The guards followed him with a dog and he showed them every place that he had stopped so they would be able to seal off the route in the future.

To Zern's surprise, Captain Kucherenko, the arresting officer, displayed a friendly attitude toward him. He told him that he was a fool to have thought of crossing the Romanian border, since the Romanians would only have handed him back.

Kucherenko said that people had the wrong attitude about border guards. "The KGB treats us badly, and the people are skeptical toward us, but we do useful work." In the end, Zern was lucky. He had a disability as a result of his army service, and he had been caught in the border zone but not on the border. These facts were counted in his favor. He was held for a month in special detention, jammed into a tiny cell with twenty-five persons, mostly drunks and vagrants. He was then released with a warning that if he were ever seen in a border zone again, he would be charged with a serious crime.

8

The KGB

Never speak to strangers.
—*Mikhail Bulgakov,* The Master and Margarita

ON THE MORNING of October 27, 1990, the citizens of Moscow woke up to discover an unexpected article on the front page of the newspaper *Komsomolskaya Pravda*. Despite glasnost, the KGB was seldom mentioned in the Soviet press, but on this particular morning, the attention of every reader was attracted to a photograph of Katya Mayorova, a striking, dark-haired woman in her early twenties who was putting on a bulletproof vest.

Under the headline "Katya Mayorova—Miss KGB," the article began to describe Mayorova, depicting the KGB as an organization which, like any normal organization, has its own beauty queen. Mayorova, the newspaper said, wears her bulletproof vest with the "sophisticated softness" of a Pierre Cardin model. "But nothing underscores Katya's innocent charm, in the opinion of her colleagues, like the ability to deliver a karate kick to the head of an adversary."

After the article in *Komsomolskaya Pravda* appeared, David Remnick of the *Washington Post* called the KGB press center and asked if he could interview Mayorova. He had expected to be laughed at, but ten minutes later, the call came back, confirming an interview.

"May I bring a camera?" he asked.

"We would expect you to."

A short time later, Remnick arrived at one of the buildings in the

KGB complex in central Moscow and met Mayorova, who arrived in an angora sweater and a pair of tight jeans.

Mayorova did not reveal anything about the inner workings of the KGB, but she did say that she loved the Beatles, played the guitar, and did not necessarily date only KGB men. She posed for a photo next to a statue of Dzerzhinsky and said that she had been trained in pistol shooting. She explained: "They try to give us all-around skills."

The naming of a Miss KGB was only part of a broad effort to change the organization's image. Vladimir Kryuchkov, the head of the KGB, began to make himself available for interviews in which he spoke about himself and gave a curious version of the agency's past. "Violence, inhumanity, and the violation of human rights," he told the Italian newspaper *L'Unita*, "have always been alien to the work of our secret services." Although the Brezhnev era was "not the best in our lives," the KGB during that period acted in compliance with existing legislation.

The KGB also started to conduct tours of its headquarters on Dzerzhinsky Square. The tours included visits to the third-floor office of former chairman Yuri Andropov and the museum, which, in addition to halls commemorating Lenin and Dzerzhinsky, also contains a hall describing successful operations carried out in recent years.

The KGB created a public relations department headed by General Alexander Karbayinov, who told a Western journalist that his department existed to explain to the world that "The purpose of the KGB is to serve society and not the other way around."

In this way, the KGB tried to alter its image in the eyes of the Soviet population, doing so not by undertaking real change but rather by creating a mirage.

The KGB was the invisible animating force responsible for everything in the Soviet Union that appeared to occur automatically, from the votes by acclamation in factory meetings to the all-pervasive silence that provided the backdrop for them.

All dictatorial regimes insist that their citizens are happy, but the Soviet regime tried to force its citizens to demonstrate their "happiness." These demonstrations, in turn, far from being frivolous, were vital to the regime's survival, because the claim to have created a society characterized by voluntary unanimity is what justified the regime's total concentration of power.

The KGB achieved its goal of forcing Soviet citizens to play their assigned roles in the country's ideological play by performing two separate functions: It created the general conditions for imposing conformity on the population by placing everyone under surveillance with the help of a network of informers so dense that there was not a club, apartment building, or work brigade without one, and making sure that anyone showing political independence was fired from his job. At the same time, camouflaging its actions by pretending to act within the framework of a "democratic" ideology, the KGB took whatever measures were necessary to suppress the handful of exceptions who had the courage publicly to dissent.

The two functions were, of course, related. In a country determined to impose a false version of reality, if the minority is not suppressed, the conformity of the majority soon begins to unravel.

THE KGB'S PROCLIVITY for creating illusions was not a harmless eccentricity. The mirage of unanimity produced by monolithic conformity exerted powerful psychological pressure. In a situation in which everyone seems to agree, the individual who does not agree loses hope that he can defend his individuality and may even start to question his own sanity. At the very least, he becomes convinced that he is isolated totally.

For decades, the drive of the KGB to create reality was reflected in individual fates.

IN MAY 1977, two months after Anatoly Shcharansky was arrested, Viktor Brailovsky, a longtime Jewish refusenik, noticed he was being followed. The shadowing continued for several days both on foot and from cars and it was very tight. On one occasion, men in dark coats walked a little in front of Brailovsky and a little behind him, exactly as in a prearrest situation. Finally, Brailovsky was called to the Lefortovo KGB investigative prison, where he was interrogated by Alexander Solonchevko, a KGB senior lieutenant.

"I have enough material here to accuse you of treason," said Solonchevko, as he rustled through some papers. "But we are very humanistic. If you agree to give evidence, we won't take any action against you."

Solonchevko then took out a handwritten appeal to foreign Jewish organizations. "A handwriting expert has concluded that this anti-Soviet document was written by you," he said. He showed the document to Brailovsky and studied him intently. Brailovsky, however, refused to react. Solonchevko put down the document and began to ask about other Jewish appeals and meetings, in particular about a meeting between Jewish refuseniks and a group of U.S. senators in 1975. Brailovsky again refused to answer. Finally, Solonchevko took out a second appeal and asked Brailovsky whether he had signed it. "This is an investigation of Shcharansky," Brailovsky said, "but you are using my position as a witness to try to prepare a case against me."

To Brailovsky's surprise, Solonchevko stopped asking questions and launched into a lengthy speech. Walking around the room, he discussed the Russian-language broadcasts of the Voice of America and the BBC, gave his views about various dissidents including Sakharov, and tried to demonstrate to Brailovsky that Yuri Orlov was a paid Western agent and that support in the West for the dissidents was diminishing.

"Soon we'll be able to do whatever we want with you," he said.

When he finished his speech, Solonchevko again took out the second appeal and asked Brailovsky whether he had signed it. "I can charge you with article sixty-four in five minutes," he said. "If you don't answer the questions, I will call the soldiers and they will arrest you immediately."

Brailovsky, however, again refused to respond, and Solonchevko began a new speech, which consisted of a renewed analysis of the world situation.

The hours passed and Solonchevko appeared inexhaustible, delivering rambling analyses of the domestic and international situation and interrupting himself only to ask Brailovsky again about his signature on the Jewish petition.

"This petition is completely innocuous and your signature on it would not involve you in anything illegal," he said. "I urge you to answer this question."

Nonetheless, Brailovsky continued to refuse.

At 8 p.m., it began to get dark. Lights went on in the apartment buildings across the street.

"Viktor Lvovich," Solonchevko said, "you understand and I understand that this is an innocent document and an absolutely innocent question. Why have you refused to answer this question for eleven hours?"

"I understand and you understand that this is a perfectly innocent document and an absolutely innocent question," said Brailovsky.
"So why have you been asking me this question for eleven hours?"

On the second day of the interrogation, Solonchevko repeated
his warning that Brailovsky could be charged with treason, and he
returned to the first handwritten document he had shown the day before. Solonchevko repeated that KGB handwriting experts had concluded that it had been written by Brailovsky. Again, Brailovsky
declined to respond, and Solonchevko started a new speech, which
dealt this time with the tragic fate of Jews who left the Soviet Union.
Solonchevko tried to show that Jews who emigrated were egoists and
lived miserable lives in the West. The interrogation lasted for ten
hours, with Brailovsky again refusing to cooperate.

On the third day, Brailovsky said he wanted to make a statement.
Solonchevko gave him the document and Brailovsky wrote: "I refuse
to give any evidence in the Shcharansky case."

Solonchevko then left the room and returned a short time later
with a senior KGB investigator, who took a chair while Solonchevko
stood at attention.

The senior investigator addressed Brailovsky with a grave expression. "You are making a great mistake if you think that you will not
be punished," he said.

"You will get some years in a labor camp, not very many perhaps, but we know you are not healthy and Soviet labor camps are
not rest homes. You will have very little chance to survive. I suggest
that you take two or three days to think about it and if, after that,
you still refuse to give evidence, that will decide your fate."

Brailovsky was not called again to give evidence until four weeks
later. When he appeared before Solonchevko, however, the interrogator was a changed man. "Viktor Lvovich," Solonchevko said, shaking his head in apparent sadness, "you have done a very bad thing.
You have broken the law, the law that a witness must give evidence.
As you know, the dissident movement insists on operating in accord-
ance with Soviet law. Viktor Lvovich, out of respect to the dissident
movement, you are obliged to give evidence."

Brailovsky's hair stood on end. He later told his wife, "I was
ready for anything, but not this." Nonetheless, he continued to refuse
to give evidence.

Brailovsky was not called back to Lefortovo until November. This
time there was a new interrogator—Koval.

"Viktor Lvovich," Koval said, "I want to know why you are not giving evidence. Perhaps the previous interrogator did not satisfy you? Solonchevko is still very young. But let's talk seriously. You are waiting for an exit visa. We cannot give you an exit visa unless you give evidence. . . ."

Brailovsky nonetheless again refused to give evidence against Shcharansky, and at last he was allowed to leave.

GALINA KREMEN was interrogated by Major Skalov, who began with a long speech on the subject of President Carter's human rights campaign, which he delivered without a break. At first, Kremen interrupted Skalov with sarcastic remarks, but, gradually, she fell silent. This was her first interrogation and, in spite of herself, she found Skalov's speech interesting.

Skalov denounced the refuseniks, who he said were trying to intimidate the authorities. He vowed that their tactics would not work. "We aren't afraid of the policy of Carter," he said, "and we aren't going to make any concessions to the refuseniks to please Carter."

Finally, at 11 a.m., Kremen interrupted him and asked, "When do we break for lunch?"

"Lunch is at 1 p.m.," Skalov said, taken aback by the question.

"I'm sorry," Kremen said, "it's time for my second breakfast." She then removed an apple and a sandwich she had carried in her purse and began eating in Skalov's presence. Flustered, Skalov left the room; he returned thirty minutes later.

When the interrogation resumed, Skalov asked Kremen whether she knew Shcharansky.

"Unfortunately, I don't," she said.

"Why 'unfortunately'?" Skalov asked.

"To you, he's a criminal, but I don't consider him that," she said.

Skalov asked Kremen what she knew about how a list of refuseniks and their work addresses got to the West. He asked her what Shcharansky's role was in sending the list and what role he played in organizing demonstrations. To all such questions, Kremen said she could not answer. Skalov then showed Kremen various petitions that had been signed by herself and Shcharansky. He asked her if she had signed them. She said that she had.

Skalov asked her if she had seen the film *Buyers of Souls*, a film about Soviet Jewish activists, including Shcharansky, that was shown on Soviet television.

"I saw it," Kremen said, "and found it disgusting."

The window of Skalov's office was open and it faced the courtyard of the prison. Suddenly, Kremen heard a scream. She asked Skalov what it was. He said it was a television film in another office. He added that if people didn't give evidence voluntarily, they could become prisoners in this prison.

"What did you hear from your husband about Shcharansky?" Skalov asked.

"I can't say anything about my husband," she said.

"What did you hear about Shcharansky's ties with the CIA?"

"I didn't know Shcharansky."

"Did you know the first wife or the second wife of Shcharansky?" Skalov asked.

"I thought he had only one wife."

"Do you think that after all your petitions, more refuseniks will receive permission to leave?"

"This has no relation to the case."

"Shcharansky is arrogant," said Skalov. "He walks around like a head of state." Skalov then began stamping around the room trying to imitate the way Shcharansky walked.

Finally, Skalov returned to his desk and said, "I think Alexander Lunts [an early leader of the Jewish emigration movement] was cleverer than Shcharansky. Lunts left and Shcharansky is in prison. Maybe in science, Shcharansky is intelligent, but in life, he's a fool."

ARKADY MAY, a retired historian and scientist, was also interrogated by Major Skalov. For a member of May's generation, there was a certain psychological pressure simply in being called to Lefortovo, from which so many people during the 1930s never returned.

In the morning session, Skalov asked no direct questions about Shcharansky, whom, in any case, May did not know very well. He asked May instead about his pension and about what was being written to him by his relatives in Israel. May said his pension was not relevant to the case. As for the letters from his relatives, it was certainly no secret from the KGB since they were reading all his mail.

Skalov laughed heartily.

"Why all these questions?" May asked.

"We just want to know you better," he said.

After lunch, Skalov began to question May about the activities of Shcharansky.

"I want to know what are the charges against Shcharansky," May said.

Instead of answering, however, Skalov began a long speech, the point of which was that it was necessary for the KGB and the refuseniks to collaborate for the good of the investigation.

"From my point of view," May said, "this isn't a collaboration but rather a struggle between you and me."

"What do you mean?" Skalov asked. "A class struggle?"

May again asked Skalov what Shcharansky had been charged with.

Skalov hesitated a moment but finally said, "Shcharansky delivered secret information to Western correspondents."

"But how was it possible?" May asked. "Shcharansky met with correspondents openly."

"It was done in matchboxes," Skalov said.

Skalov asked May what he thought about Shcharansky's meetings with congressmen and senators.

"Why do you ask me this? I was not there."

"Yes, that's right, we know everyone who was there," Skalov said.

"So why do you ask me?" May said.

"We want to know your opinion."

"My opinion is not important to the case."

At one point, Skalov went out of the room and returned with some documents, including a copy of a Russian-language Israeli newspaper, some letters, and several photocopies. He asked May if Shcharansky was the author of a letter to the Israeli paper about the beating of some Soviet Jewish demonstrators. "You must know who wrote the letter," Skalov said, "because your name is mentioned."

"I'm not going to talk about this because it is a newspaper article and not a document. Besides, my name is misspelled."

Skalov showed May several photocopies of Jewish collective letters, but May also refused to comment on these. "Never show copies to a historian," he said. "There are many examples of falsification in history." May then began a lengthy discourse on the subject, citing a number of examples of successful forgeries, including the case of the

Sheremetovs, who falsified the documents that made them the owners of great estates in the seventeenth century.

"The forgery was so convincing," May said, as Skalov tried helplessly to interrupt, "that it was not identified until the twentieth century."

"Did you sign any of these collective letters?" Skalov asked, referring to some of the documents.

"Is it a crime?" May asked.

"What do you know about Shcharansky's spying?"

"Nothing, I think the charge is an absurdity."

May watched as Skalov wrote the reply "Nothing" on the document. Noticing that Skalov was not including his entire reply, May insisted that he add the words "I think the charge is an absurdity," as well as the remarks Skalov had made about Shcharansky passing information to foreign correspondents in matchboxes. Skalov refused.

VLADIMIR SLEPAK knew Shcharansky better than many of the other refuseniks, but he was interrogated after the others, perhaps because the KGB recognized that there was little hope of gaining his cooperation unless others had been induced to cooperate first.

Slepak began by asking Koval, his interrogator, to tell him the charge against Shcharansky. Koval said that Shcharansky was charged with Article 64, "betrayal of the motherland."

"There are a lot of paragraphs in Article Sixty-four," Slepak said. "For example, there is refusal to return from abroad, espionage, fleeing the Soviet Union. Under which paragraph is Shcharansky being charged?" Koval said that that was a secret of the investigation. "You have to tell me the specific accusation against Shcharansky," Slepak said. "If you don't, I will assume that the investigation is not objective and will refuse to testify."

To Slepak's surprise, Koval became emotional. "We want to know the truth," he said. "If the truth will be for Shcharansky, it will be better for him. Why don't you want to help Shcharansky?"

"You can change what I say," Slepak said. "If I say something for Shcharansky, you can use it against him."

Koval tried to persuade Slepak that the KGB conducted its investigations with strict respect for legality, but after years of being prevented from leaving for Israel "legally," Slepak was impossible to convince.

"I know many examples where innocent people were sent to prison camps or to their deaths by your organization," he said.

"That was thirty years ago," Koval said.

"Nothing has changed."

"You say that nothing has changed," Koval said, "but we are not beating you now, we are not putting needles under your fingernails."

"Many of those who committed crimes during the Stalin era are free now, without ever having been prosecuted," Slepak said. "Stalin is becoming a hero again."

"He did a lot for this country," Koval said.

Slepak then took out a statement he had written denouncing the investigation and asked Koval to include it in the file. Koval refused.

"Where is your objectivity?" Slepak asked. "I tried to give testimony for Shcharansky and you refused to accept it."

Slepak then wrote out another statement and asked Koval to give it to the chief of investigations in the KGB, but Koval again declined, adding, "If I refused to take it, he'll also refuse to take it." On the way out, Slepak tried to give his statement to the guard at the entrance, but he also refused, explaining, "I never take any papers."

IN THE END, of the more than two hundred refuseniks who were interrogated in the Shcharansky case, not a single person gave evidence against Shcharansky, a significant feat of resistance. The behavior of the refuseniks was possible because they treated the investigation not as an attempt to learn the truth, but rather as a charade staged to make a predetermined verdict seem plausible. One person who did give important evidence was not a refusenik at all but Robert Toth, Moscow correspondent of the *Los Angeles Times*, who made the mistake of taking the investigation seriously.

Toth's direct involvement began on Saturday, June 11, 1977, when he was seized by KGB agents on the street while accepting an article on parapsychology from its author, Valery Petukhov, a Moscow biophysicist. Toth was taken to the Lefortovo KGB investigative prison and released after being told that he was under investigation on charges of espionage and could not leave the country. Toth was finishing his assignment in Moscow and had tickets for a flight on June 17, only six days later.

The interrogation of Toth began on the following Monday and it dealt not with the article he received from Petukhov but exclusively with his ties to Shcharansky. With an espionage accusation hanging over his head, Toth gave the interrogators detailed information about his ties with Shcharansky. Shcharansky had been one of Toth's principal sources and the reporter spoke in detail about their relations on the assumption, valid in an American context, that he had nothing to hide. On the advice of the American embassy, Toth signed a protocol of the interrogation even though it was written in Russian, a language Toth did not understand.

The KGB's possibilities for fabrication were endless, but, in the end, it was Toth's testimony that helped the KGB to make the case against Shcharansky that they presented in July 1978. A list of secret enterprises supposedly taken by a janitor from a garbage can in the courtyard of the building where Toth lived was connected to Shcharansky, who was convicted of treason and sentenced to twelve years in a labor camp.

ON A BLEAK December afternoon, Vasily Baratz, a member of the Soviet general staff, was summoned to the office of Colonel Kozhevnikov, the head of the psychiatric department of the staff clinic.

Baratz had asked to leave the army a month earlier and he and Kozhevnikov had agreed that the stated reason would be that he suffered from "a complex of fear." In fact, as Kozhevnikov knew, the real reason was that Baratz could no longer work for the general staff because the KGB had begun to investigate him as an English spy.

Baratz acknowledged the message, got up from his desk, and went to see Kozhevnikov immediately.

"I'm sorry," Kozhevnikov said when Baratz entered his office, "your application to leave the army hasn't been confirmed. You're going to have to go back to Burdenko Hospital."

Baratz began shaking his head. "I'm not going back there," he said. Kozhevnikov looked at Baratz sympathetically. "If you don't go," he said, "they'll take you there by force."

Suddenly, Kozhevnikov got up and ran out into the corridor and began shouting for the orderlies. Every psychiatrist has a key with which he can lock in a patient; however, Kozhevnikov had left the door open. Baratz, realizing what that meant, ran out of the office and down two flights of stairs. He ducked into the clinic's pharmacy and burst out of the service entrance onto the street. He then began running down the parkway in the middle of Gogolevsky Boulevard in the direction of Kropotkinskaya Square.

It was a raw winter day, and seeing that no one was following him, Baratz jumped over the iron fence lining the parkway, crossed the street, and plunged into the maze of small lanes behind the Old Arbat, eventually making his way to the giant outdoor swimming pool that had been built on the site of the former Christ the Savior Cathedral. Desperate, he tried to think about what to do next and finally went to the home of a friend, where he spent the night.

Baratz's escape from the clinic was only the latest incident in a nightmare that had begun years before. In the 1960s, while a student at the Higher Military Engineering Academy in Kiev, Baratz suggested at a Komsomol *sobraniye* that an alcoholic named Fedotov be expelled. Fedotov was expelled, but after he finished his studies, Baratz went to work for the computer division of the Soviet general staff, where the chief of personnel was Fedotov's uncle and Fedotov's father was the head of Baratz's sector. Baratz soon also quarreled with Anatoly Tishin, the KGB man in charge of counterintelligence in the computer division. Tishin seemed to have something personal against soldiers. He referred to them in Baratz's presence as "garbage," and this almost led to a fight between Baratz and Tishin.

A few months after the near-fight with Tishin, strange things started to happen to Baratz. He took an exam in German in Moscow, which was given by three civilians and two officers in uniform. The examiners asked questions for half an hour in German and, when they were finished, they told Baratz that he had passed with a "5," the highest grade. To his surprise, however, one of the military examiners then began to speak to Baratz in English. Baratz could only stand there smiling foolishly, because he did not understand what he was saying.

Finally, one of the men in civilian clothing said in Russian, "Why are you hiding your knowledge of English?"

"I'm sorry," Baratz said, "I don't know English."

"Of course you know it," replied the civilian. "You don't simply speak English, you speak it superbly, better than I do."

Baratz was incredulous. He repeated that he did not speak English.

"You do," said the second officer. "You know English, but for some reason, you want to hide it."

About ten days later, Baratz bumped into the chief political officer in his unit, Colonel Lyevkin. "Why do you hide the fact that you speak English?" Lyevkin asked him. "What are you afraid of? You should be proud. Who among us speaks a foreign language?" Baratz explained that he did not speak English, but Lyevkin looked at him with obvious disapproval and then walked away.

Baratz was always very neat and he made it a point at his workplace to arrange his papers in a specific order. Now, he began to find that every time he came back to his desk, they were rearranged. For no apparent reason, his colleagues began to refer to him as a "Banderite," a reference to the anti-Communist Ukrainian partisan leader Stepan Bandera. Baratz was, in fact, from the area in the Carpathians where the Banderites had been active. It was therefore in a state of perplexity that, in the summer of 1973, Baratz went to spend his vacation in the Carpathians, where he met his future wife, Galina Kochan, who apparently was also under surveillance by the KGB.

IN 1968 Kochan's uncle, Mikhail Dyamko-Davis, traveled from his home in Beverly Hills, California, to the Soviet Union to visit his family. Dyamko-Davis had emigrated before the First World War and had returned to the Carpathians only in 1931, for his father's funeral. He met his sister and Galina in Uzhgorod, and when he learned how they were living, he decided to buy them a car. Dyamko-Davis went to a hard-currency store and ordered a Volga export model for his sister. The export model was more expensive and had more chrome and a better engine than a standard car. But it was impossible for Galina to take delivery while Dyamko-Davis was in the country because the car had to be ordered from Kiev.

Dyamko-Davis therefore left the country when his visa expired. When Galina finally went to pick up the car, she was given an ordinary Volga. When she refused to accept it, she was told she had no choice.

Several months later, Kochan was driving the car when Slepichev, an officer of the State Auto Inspection, who had been present at the sale, passed her in a police car on an empty stretch of country road. Kochan pulled into a gas station. Slepichev made a U-turn and also stopped at the gas station. He got out of his car and began a conversation with her. He told Kochan she had been robbed of her car and promised to meet her and tell her how to write a letter to the proper authorities explaining how it had been done. Two

weeks later, however, Kochan read that Slepichev had died "tragi-
cally." People said he had been murdered but no one knew the details. Later, Kochan heard a rumor that her Volga had gone to
Luchok, who, at the time of the sale, was the police chief in the oblast and had since been named deputy chief of the Uzhgorod KGB.
When she heard this news, Kochan felt faint and, from that point on,
she lived in fear of the Uzhgorod KGB.

After the death of Slepichev, there were signs that Kochan was
being watched. In the village of Ust-Chernaya, where she taught
school, she had petty conflicts with the other teachers, and on one
occasion, when she was preparing to drive to her mother's village,
160 miles away, a mechanic looked under the hood of her car and
said, "Look what they are trying to do to you." The axle had been
almost filed through so that if the car had built up speed it would
have broken.

In 1970, Galina Kochan entered the graduate school at Uzhgorod University, where she also sensed that she was being watched
by informers. A party member since 1963, she was criticized at party
meetings for "painting her eyelashes, wearing pants, traveling in a
car, and advertising the American way of life."

The incident that convinced her she was being pursued by the
KGB, however, took place in May 1972 in Moscow. Kochan had
gone there to do research and was staying in the University Hotel.
During the second week of her stay, she was given a roommate, a
young nurse from Kalinin, who introduced herself as Albina. From
the beginning, Albina's situation struck Kochan as strange. It had
been difficult enough for her to get a place in the hotel, which is intended primarily for academics, even with full documentation from
Uzhgorod; yet Albina, who lived within commuting distance of Moscow, was able to reside in the hotel indefinitely, apparently without
difficulty. She also never seemed to leave the room. Albina was
asleep when Kochan left and in the room when she returned.

On several occasions, Kochan returned and realized that someone had been going through her belongings. She always arranged
her things very carefully, yet she found everything crumpled and dis-
arranged. Once she returned after having forgotten something and
found Albina going through her suitcase. Kochan noticed that her
soap, toothpaste, and lipstick had been somehow interfered with.
There was a strange smell, as if they had been mixed with something, and her underclothes were damp.

One morning ten days after Albina moved into the room, Kochan awoke and noticed red spots on her arms and face. The curtains were open at 8 a.m. and the room was filled with light. Albina was already up and dressed. Kochan felt weak, and she noticed that the spots on her body were covered with tiny pimples, like gooseflesh. Kochan knew that Albina was a nurse, so she asked her what she saw on her body.

"Hee, hee, hee . . . well, at last," Albina said, hissing with laughter.

Kochan was filled with a wild terror. She grabbed Albina and dragged her to the window. "Tell me what you are doing here. Tell me what this means or I'll throw us both out of this window." Kochan held Albina in an iron grip and opened the window. The noise from Vernadsky Prospekt filled the room. It would have made any scream inaudible. She started to lift Albina up in order to throw her out and Albina realized that Kochan was serious about killing her.

"Wait," she screamed, "I'll tell you."

Kochan put Albina down and led her to the bathroom. Albina turned on the water in the bath all the way. The blood drained from her face and her lips and mouth turned blue. Her voice changed and seemed to become thin and reedlike with an almost dying effort from the center of her chest.

"I beg you not to tell anyone," Albina said. "If they ever learn that I told you, they'll kill me, too. I know such cases." Albina said she had been sent to infect Kochan with some kind of contamination. She didn't know what kind. "How could you do this?" Kochan asked. "What did I ever do to you?"

"They forced me," Albina said. "If I had not done it, it would have been someone else." She said it was the work of the KGB. Albina then fell into the same state of shock that had overcome Kochan. She repeated that Kochan must not tell anyone, that she would try to cure her, that Kochan could ruin her but she would be ruined as well.

"I can't talk to you," Kochan said. "You've done what you had to do." Albina left the room and Kochan sat on her bed for what seemed like an hour or two; she didn't know what to do or think. Finally, she left the hotel and started walking around the city. It was a beautiful spring day and trucks were cleaning the roads and repairing the curbs in preparation for the visit of President Richard Nixon, which was to mark the start of the détente era. Kochan remembered the case of Boris Spivak, a historian at Uzhgorod University, who had been found dead in the same hotel a year earlier. The official explanation was that he died of a heart ailment, but no one in the Carpathians believed it. As soon as he was buried, the local authorities took away the apartment where his wife lived with their two children.

GALINA KOCHAN decided to stay in Moscow for the full amount of time that was expected of her and then return to Uzhgorod to seek medical help from a doctor she knew she could trust. In fact, by the time she returned to Uzhgorod two weeks later, the symptoms had disappeared and she gave a report in the university on the research she had carried out in Moscow. She was examined in Uzhgorod by the doctor she knew. He told her she was ill and needed to be treated, but he did not give her any details. Instead, he gave her the address of a doctor in Kiev. A month later, Kochan went to Kiev and the doctor to whom she had been referred said she had an elevated white blood cell count.

He gave her a prescription for some tablets and told her to come back in a month. When she returned, however, she learned that he had been transferred to Karaganda in Kazakhstan. For months afterward, she searched for the tablets but could not find them in any store.

A short time later, at a sanitorium attached to the Perechinsky chemical factory, Kochan met Baratz, who was introduced to her as a member of the Soviet general staff by Stepan Malitsky, a friend of Kochan's who was the chief doctor.

Baratz suggested that they have a cup of coffee together, but at first, Kochan was reluctant. She was afraid that contact with her might spoil Baratz's career. After Malitsky left them alone, Kochan told Baratz about Slepichev and the car and a few other details of her situation. Baratz listened to her attentively but didn't appear to take her situation seriously.

"If Moscow investigates, they'll see that this is the action of the local KGB," he said, "and it will be all cleared up." He then added, "In fact, I've had some problems with the KGB myself. It's always possible to put these agents in their place."

Finally, Kochan agreed to go out with Baratz, and a week later, they had dinner in the Mirror Hall in Uzhgorod, where, surrounded by their own images, they spoke in detail about the things that had been happening to them. They saw each other a few more times in Uzhgorod, and when Kochan returned to Moscow in December to do research in the dissertation hall of the Lenin Library, Baratz met the train. They were married a month later in the home of Baratz's parents in Perechin, a village in the Carpathians.

Despite the suspicion that he knew English and was concealing it, Baratz, shortly after his marriage, was given a portfolio pass by the head of counterintelligence for the computer division. This meant that he could carry a portfolio into any building of the Ministry of Defense without leaving it with the wardrobe attendant, a privilege normally accorded to only the highest-ranking military men. At the same time, he was escorted everywhere while at work and Galina began to be followed.

In the autumn of 1973, Baratz started to run high temperatures and was hospitalized for two months. To his surprise, however, he was not treated. At one point, when he complained about the lack of treatment, he asked jokingly what he was supposed to confess to.

Baratz was finally released from the hospital, but in the spring of 1974, his health once more deteriorated and he was again hospitalized. This time he was put in the Burdenko Military Hospital, where he was interviewed by Captain Vladimir Iutin, a psychiatrist who first suggested that he be examined in the hospital's psychiatric division and then made it clear that he had little choice. In the psychiatric division, Baratz was told by Colonel Grigory Kolupaev that he was weak and needed glucose and vitamins. He was given eighteen injections in as many days plus various tablets, which he later learned were sampoax and seduxen. The result of this treatment was that Baratz began talking uncontrollably. When he was transferred out of the psychiatric hospital after eighteen days, he could not walk under his own power, the right side of his body was partially paralyzed, and his memory had deteriorated. When he was finally released, he was not allowed to return to his former job as a computer engineer but was assigned, like an ordinary soldier, to repair work and loading.

Realizing that his military career was over, Baratz went to see Colonel Kozhevnikov in the psychiatric department of the clinic of the army general staff, and asked if he could be discharged on medical grounds. This is when Kozhevnikov agreed that Baratz would write a statement asking to leave the army owing to a "complex of fear."

As it happened, however, there was a delay in his discharge while the army psychiatrists argued over whether he was mentally ill. Kozhevnikov told Baratz he would have to go back to the Burdenko Hospital; shaken by this news, Baratz fled.

From his hiding place in a friend's apartment, Baratz understood the gravity of his situation. If he did not return to work, he was a deserter. If he did go back, he would be taken to a mental hospital. He finally called Kozhevnikov from a pay phone and then returned to his office, where he was interviewed by eight psychiatrists. He was next sent to the neurological division of the third central military hospital in Krasnogorsk, where Colonel Oleg Lumonov, the chief doctor, examined him and found him sane. Baratz then went to the Burdenko Hospital accompanied by Lumonov, where he was pronounced physically unfit for service and released from the army on health grounds.

With his discharge, Baratz hoped that his troubles with the KGB were at an end. In March 1975, he went to work in the computer center of the Forestry Ministry, but the same pattern of harassment continued. Baratz found himself surrounded by people who were constantly asking him questions about his political views, and the eighty-year-old woman who cleaned up told him that men were entering the office at night.

Nonetheless, there were no overt incidents for more than a year, during which time Kochan was given a job as a junior scientific worker in the history department at Moscow State University. In the summer of 1976, the Baratzes decided to spend their summer vacation in the Carpathians. One night they were walking in the village of Obava, a small hamlet set in a valley between wooded hills, when they were suddenly attacked with sticks and rocks by ten young men. They fell to the ground and started screaming for help. As the beating went on and their screaming continued, a light went on in a nearby house and the attackers fled.

When they got up, Vasily and Galina were both covered with blood. They also noticed that, around the corner from where they were attacked, a local KGB agent, who was known to them, was watching the scene from a motorcycle. They asked him why he had not tried to help, to which he said, "They don't beat good people."

When Baratz returned to his job, he found that the atmosphere had worsened. Informers initiated anti-Soviet conversations and his work materials began to disappear. One night, he asked Dmitri

Chereshkin, the deputy director of the computer center, with whom he was friendly, for help. "Vasya," Chereshkin said, "there is nothing I can do. This is the end for you. Your head should be on a platter by the end of the year."

In December 1976, a coworker gave Baratz a copy of Solzhenitsyn's *One Day in the Life of Ivan Denisovich.* A short time later, at lunchtime, his briefcase was stolen, and at 5 p.m., a party meeting was called to discuss allegations that Baratz had lost some type of forbidden literature. In the end, Baratz was saved when the workers at the meeting complained that management was wasting the employees' time with nonsense. In early 1977, however, Baratz was demoted by three ranks, his salary falling from 200 rubles a month to 130. Shortly afterward, he was asked to go to Kiev on a business trip with Viktor Astakhov, a deputy to the chief of the department, but before the trip took place, Astakhov called him to his office and told him he had learned that Baratz was an English spy and had wanted to use him as cover.

"We're not going anywhere," he told Baratz. "You wanted to spread a network for your spying goals. Well, we caught you."

At that moment, Baratz realized that the KGB would not leave him in peace. The only thing he did not know was whether he would be arrested or fired.

In early May, Baratz was fired. He was told he was being let go in a staff reduction, but in fact the staff was being increased, which made the dismissal illegal. Nonetheless, the trade union at the computer center confirmed it.

The shock of losing his job in the ministry convinced Baratz that there was no hope for him in the Soviet system. In an attempt to be reinstated in his job, he appealed directly to the ministry and even to the regional KGB. Kochan appealed to Yuri Andropov, but it was all to no avail. Finally, Baratz decided that there was nowhere else to turn, so on July 4, 1977, he sent a letter to Brezhnev announcing that he and Galina were renouncing their citizenship and applying to leave the Soviet Union. He listed as the reason for his request years of baseless persecution by the KGB.

Shortly after the Baratzes sent the letter, Kochan was demoted from her job as a teacher of Communist Party history at Moscow State University at 105 rubles a month and made a groundskeeper at 75 rubles a month.

The Baratzes applied formally to emigrate and were received at the headquarters of the Moscow visa office by a female official who told them they did not have a sufficiently detailed basis for leaving the country.

This line of reasoning bewildered Baratz. "We're fleeing from repression," he said.

The woman only repeated, "You have to have a firmer basis."

As the months passed, the Baratzes began to run out of money. Vasily, in this period, learned to prepare a meal for fifty kopecks a day. A kilogram of bread cost twenty kopecks, a small piece of cabbage cost ten to fifteen kopecks, and the rest of the money could be used to buy potatoes, sunflower oil, onions, and dried mushrooms, all of which could be put into soup. At the end of 1977, Vasily began to sell his books.

Finally, the Baratzes contacted Robert Pringle, a consul at the American embassy, about the possibility of getting an invitation to the United States. A few days after their meeting with Pringle, however, Baratz was summoned to the local police station, where he was met by the police chief, the prosecutor, a woman named Pechkina, and a man in plainclothes who Baratz assumed was from the KGB.

They asked Baratz why he did not work and threatened him with charges of vagrancy. Finally, at a second meeting, they gave him a work order and, on June 1, 1978, he reported to a laundry, where he was put to work as a handyman for 105 rubles a month.

During the next two years, the Baratzes continued their efforts to emigrate but made no progress. Finally, after an attempt to get help from a Moscow party official—who at first had seemed sympathetic—failed, Baratz decided that their only hope of getting permission to emigrate was in becoming dissidents. With the help of Jewish contacts, Baratz became acquainted with other non-Jews who were trying to leave the country and organized a Committee on the Right to Emigrate.

I was introduced to Baratz by other members of the committee, and during our first meeting he told me his story in detail. He tried to explain that his experiences were not as unusual as they seemed.

"Anyone can be suspected by the KGB of being a foreign spy," he said, "because the KGB is always looking for them. A KGB agent may begin investigating someone as a foreign spy to repay an insult, ruin a rival, or take personal, petty revenge. But once a case is opened, it is difficult to close. Every move the suspected spy makes is seen as supporting the original accusation. If he takes reasonable

steps to protect himself from persecution by avoiding informers or re-
sisting provocations, he is seen as behaving like a spy. As a result, the
case grows."

I was to cooperate with the Baratzes in publicizing the cases of
some of the people who had turned to their committee for help, and
experience repeatedly confirmed their reliability. In the course of
their years of harassment, however, the Baratzes had been affected
by the total environment that the KGB was able to create around
them.

Baratz, in particular, lived in a world infested with informers and
spies. He was quick to accuse others of being KGB informers, often
accurately, and he prided himself on being able to know when he
was under surveillance. Baratz told me that listening devices had
been put in the room of the next apartment, which was separated
from the Baratzes' by a single wall.

Baratz recalled that when he and his wife first moved into their
room, there had been a Soviet family in the adjoining apartment
who liked to drink, dance, and play the harmonica. Some time later,
however, the adjoining apartment fell silent and remained so for the
next three years, except for the sound of a transmitter being switched
on every morning at 6 a.m. Baratz said that on hot summer days,
when the front windows of his room were open against the heat, as
were those of the neighboring apartment, it was possible to look inside the apartment with the help of a mirror attached to a long stick.
Baratz saw an empty room and a large metal apparatus. There were
times when he spotted the KGB agent who was operating it.

Baratz believed that he and Galina were also being spied upon
from the room directly beneath them, and that the KGB was even
watching from an observation post across the street. One night he
took me to the window and pointed to a small point of light emanat-
ing from the attic area directly under the eaves of the darkened
building across the street. He said that that was the place from which
the KGB was watching them.

The Committee on the Right to Emigrate concerned itself with
the attempts to emigrate of a wide variety of people—Jews, Russians,
ordinary workers, and people suffering religious persecution. Besides
cultivating foreign journalists and working days at the laundry,
Baratz compiled a journal called "Leaves," which contained detailed
case histories of people who had been refused permission to leave the
country, as well as Baratz's commentary.

The group, however, was destined to be short-lived, as Baratz and the other members traded accusations of being KGB informers. When the group broke up, the Baratzes became involved with the Pentecostalists, the Protestants who were the most active in their efforts to secure the right to leave the country.

With the change in their activities, however, it began to be difficult to find the Baratzes. They would disappear for weeks at a time, traveling in Kochan's car to the Baltics or to cities in the Ukraine and refusing to talk about where they had been. Having courted foreign correspondents for a time, Baratz became elusive and I saw less and less of him. His struggle ended, finally, on August 9, 1982, in the city of Rovno, where, as he was preparing to board a plane, he was seized by the KGB and beaten. When Kochan flew to Rovno to try to find out what had happened to him, the local authorities refused even to confirm that Baratz was in Rovno. On her third trip to Rovno on August 23, she was finally told that he was being held in Rostov-on-Don. Kochan was herself arrested in that city on March 9, 1983. The two suspected spies were charged not with espionage but with anti-Soviet agitation.

ONE AFTERNOON IN JUNE 1980, Viktor Blok, a Moscow physicist, and two of his friends at the Institute of Organic Semi-products, Yuri Khronopoulo and Gennady Krochik, also physicists, took their places in the viewing hall of the Makarenko Club in central Moscow and waited for a film about India to begin. At that moment, they heard sirens and cars pulling up to the curb. A moment later, twenty uniformed and plainclothes police burst into the hall and started shouting, "Stay in your places. No one gave you permission to show this film." The police then took the names of the persons in the audience and the group broke up.

Four months passed and Khronopoulo, Blok, and Krochik did not attend any more movies. But they did frequent the laboratory of bioelectronics on Furmanny Lane, which was conducting experiments in parapsychology. In response to their involvement at the laboratory, Khronopoulo was called before the party committee in his institute, where, in addition to the institute's party members, there were three strangers, a young man who was obviously from the KGB, an instructor from the raion party committee, and an Old Bolshevik.

The meeting began in typical Soviet fashion.

"Why do you think we called you here?" the KGB agent asked.

"I don't know why you called me here," Khronopoulo said. "You tell me."

"All right," said the KGB man, "tell us, do you take an interest in parapsychology?"

"Yes, I do."

"Do you visit the laboratory of bioelectronics on Furmanny Lane?"

"Yes, I've even filled out an application to join the laboratory."

"You filled out an application," the Old Bolshevik interrupted, repeating the words with heavy irony. "And don't you think that your biographical data now lies on the table of American intelligence?"

"My biographical information is in every journal where I've ever published my scientific work," Khronopoulo said.

"What about that film?" asked the instructor. "What was it about?"

"I don't know," Khronopoulo said. "I never got a chance to see it."

"Well, what was the name of the film?"

"I don't even know that."

"You are a doctor of sciences," the Old Bolshevik said, "and you are not ashamed to be deceived into joining a sect? What was the name of it . . . ?"

"The Society of Krishtana," the instructor said, although he appeared unsure of his information.

"I don't know of any such group," Khronopoulo said.

For some reason, this statement made the Old Bolshevik angry. "You should occupy yourself with science!" he shouted.

"Are you trying to tell me that I can't take an interest in parapsychology in my spare time?"

"Of course you can," the KGB man said, for some reason trying to calm the atmosphere, "but beware of any provocation. They may try to draw you into a religious sect."

A short time later, Blok was called in by the director of the institute.

"You go to the laboratory of bioelectronics," he said, "and the KGB is not happy. I'm advising you that if you continue to go there, a situation could arise in which I'll be forced to fire you."

Khronopoulo and Krochik received similar warnings and, as a result, all three stopped going.

Blok's involvement in parapsychology began in 1962 when he decided to visit a laboratory for bioinformation near the Kursk station that was reported to be conducting experiments in telepathy. Blok had heard that the laboratory operated on Wednesdays, and when he arrived at the building for the first time, he walked down the steps to the basement and entered a dimly lit room. A small, good-natured man in his forties sat behind a table busily writing. Blok said he wanted to observe the work of the laboratory, and the man shook Blok's hand vigorously and gave him a membership card.

When Blok returned on the following Wednesday, there was no table in the basement room and the man who had given him his membership card was gone. Blok tried to strike up a conversation with some of the people who were standing around in the basement, but when he asked about the man who had been sitting at the table the previous week, one of them said, "We don't know who he was either."

Blok did not return to the laboratory, but in 1968, while in his last year at the physical technical institute, he conducted some experiments in telepathy with friends in the dormitory. One person concentrated on one of five cards that were face up on a table and another tried to read his thoughts from a distance of thirty feet.

In his last year at the physical technical institute, Blok attended a lecture by Yuri Kaminsky on experiments he had conducted in telepathy, sending and receiving signals from Karl Nikolaev, an actor. The lecture was held in a club. There was no sign outside to indicate that it was taking place, but the hall was full. Besides describing his own experiments, Kaminsky spoke about a wide variety of cases, including those involving a psychic in Austria who sought lost children and investigated crimes.

Blok continued to be interested in research into parapsychology but could find no published material on the subject. There were constant rumors that experiments were taking place, but he could only guess at the scale of work being carried out.

After he graduated from the physical technical institute, Blok went to work at the Institute of Radio Technology in Moscow and continued his experiments in parapsychology with his friends. One day, he met a woman who had studied with him; she gave him a ticket to the Third All-Union Congress of Parapsychology, which was to be held in the Institute of Civil Aviation in Moscow. Blok was struck by the fact that there could be such a thing as an All-Union Congress of Parapsychology in the Soviet Union, insofar as, according to Marxism-Leninism, parapyschology did not exist.

On the way to the institute, Blok met a short, gray-haired man in his fifties. Blok asked him if he knew the way to the Institute of Civil Aviation and the man replied that he was also going there. "My name is Alexander Spirkin," he said, extending his hand. "You probably read my textbook on Marxist-Leninist philosophy."

"Who doesn't know your textbook?" said Blok, taken completely aback. "But doesn't Marxist-Leninist philosophy prevent you from taking an interest in mysticism?"

"Not at all," said Spirkin good-naturedly. "Dialectical philosophy has the advantage that you can include in it today everything that you denied yesterday, including mysticism."

There were about four hundred people at the congress and the hall was absolutely full even though there were no notices advertising the event. The first speaker was Gennady Sergeev, a doctor of science from Leningrad, who spoke of experiments with Kulagin, one of the few extrasensors in the Soviet Union who could move objects. A biophysicist from Novosibirsk described how white mice could be guided through a labyrinth by an extrasensor. He also said that the presence of a mouse that had already gone through the labyrinth once, and then went through the maze with an inexperienced mouse, had an effect on the inexperienced mouse, helping the inexperienced mouse to move through the labyrinth more quickly.

A speaker from the laboratory of bioinformation, which Blok had visited years earlier, described attempts to guess the contents of closed boxes.

At the end of the day a speaker said, "We hope to gather again next year." But nothing was said about when the next congress would be held, or where. Blok never learned who organized the congress, what happened at the first and second congresses, or whether there was ever a fourth or fifth congress. He also never saw any publications describing the work that was discussed at the congress.

Some time passed and Blok began to lose hope of being able to pursue his interest in parapsychology. Just as he was about to give up on the idea he was introduced to Valery Sergeievich Averyanov, a Moscow mystic also known as Var Avera.

One day, Blok was visited by his friend Igor Stepankov, who was working as a janitor while immersing himself in the study of yoga and Spengler's *The Decline of the West.* Stepankov frequently talked to Blok about yoga but, on this particular day, he wanted his friend to meet his new teacher. Blok agreed. They left Blok's apartment together and went to a basement apartment in a shabby, two-story brick building in the center of Moscow. It was there that Stepankov introduced Blok to Averyanov.

Averyanov had blond hair and crude but expressive features in a wedge-shaped face. In his room was a small desk, which was piled high with manuscripts and books; a cupboard with a few personal things; and a long wooden bench, which was apparently for guests. On the wall there were two large pictures; one of them was an abstract painting that suggested a war in the cosmos, the other a realistic painting of a woman. There were also two of Averyanov's students in the room, Valera and Natasha.

Averyanov asked Blok what he thought was the significance of the paintings. Blok hesitated and then said he saw the aspiration to unite motherhood and cosmic struggle.

Averyanov was delighted with the answer.

"You are the first person who recognized the meaning of these paintings." He introduced the others in the room. "Valera here is the god of war," he said. "Igor is a higher divinity. You will be the god of wisdom."

Blok soon learned that Averyanov and his disciples practiced what they called "space karate," the inflicting of pain from a distance. Averyanov explained the natural movement of energy in the body, how to gather it and direct it, and how it could be dispersed. When he struggled against someone, his pupils got together and meditated on the person they wanted to destroy. Igor told Blok later that Averyanov had succeeded in inducing a heart attack in one of Moscow's leading yogis.

"Yogis write that you must prevent the development of jealousy and hatred," Averyanov said, "but this is nonsense. We must develop hatred. We won the war over the fascists only through hatred. Hatred is the source of force and energy." Averyanov said the greatest threats to Russians came from the Chinese and the national minorities, and it was necessary to destroy the Chinese. "The secret is to get inside people's minds. If I had seventy-five pupils, together we could change the aggressive nature of the Chinese by reeducating them mystically to do whatever we want. We can study the process by working out our methods on the Buryats."*

Averyanov said the KGB persecuted Jews in the Soviet Union and this was good, but it was necessary to do it more effectively. He also made it clear that he hated all national minorities. Over the years, Averyanov had been periodically confined in mental hospitals, and in his opinion, after national minorities, the biggest enemy was psychiatrists, who put him in psychiatric hospitals when it was obvious that he was the most normal of all. The only place where he was treated with respect and his explanation of space karate was treated with utter seriousness, he said, was the KGB.

Averyanov said that his pupils were trained to fulfill his every order. "If I tell them to undress and go out in the street and scream something, they'll do it," he said.

On the subject of what was required in order to practice space karate, he said, "If I see in your eyes that you have some idea of your own, you will never learn the method. You must know how to subordinate yourself."

Blok had no further contact with Averyanov, but he continued to hear about him because Moscow was flooded with his books, booklets, and brochures. Most of them were between a hundred and two hundred pages, and they were reproduced in excellent photocopies. Averyanov wrote about his personal experiences and his philosophy, the Chinese menace, and the need to destroy national minorities. He always signed his name to the publications, so the KGB could have stopped them at any time, but his work multiplied and circulated. This was a clear sign of KGB interest in his activities, and confirmation of his claim that the KGB were the only ones who took his ideas seriously.

In one of Averyanov's booklets, "The Theory and Practice of Psycho-energetic Struggle with Universal Chinese Expansionism," he answered the questions of two of his pupils. In it, he explained the methods for the preparation of adepts in space karate and said that the adept must "bring his brain to a state in which it is a clean magnetic tape on which can be inscribed only our ideas—brief and to the point, like military commands." The book ended with Averyanov's

*A Mongoloid people who live in Siberia on the eastern shore of Lake Baikal.

pupils challenging Chinese mystics to a fight and concluding, "They will learn our force. It will be their final knowledge."

Sometime after meeting Averyanov, Blok went to work at the Institute of Organic Semi-products, where he was soon joined by Khronopoulo and Krochik, who had been attending, in Moscow, occasional lectures on parapsychology, which they heard about through word of mouth. On one occasion, they attended a lecture by Sergeev on "biopoles" at the Society of Historians. Sergeev said it was possible for a biopole to indicate in what century an event took place. He showed a small dark box, about the size of a transistor radio, which had an antenna and a dial with an arrow. When he brought the device near someone, the indicator moved across the dial. When a spear from the twelfth century was brought to the machine, the device reacted to the spear, giving a reading. The historians nodded their heads in approval.

After the lecture, Khronopoulo and Krochik asked if they could see a plan of the instrument. Sergeev invited them to his next lecture at the Zoological Museum at Moscow University. Khronopoulo and Krochik mentioned this to Blok and suggested he join them. After this lecture, Sergeev gave the three physicists a plan of the device he had demonstrated earlier and explained its ability to register the biopole. It seemed to them, however, that his reasoning was unsound scientifically. They tried to explain certain basic physical principles to him, but he kept repeating himself like a broken phonograph record. They found it impossible to discuss anything with him and stopped meeting him.

In early 1980, Blok, Khronopoulo, and Krochik heard from scientists at the Lebedev Physical Institute that a group was being formed in the Institute of Physical Culture to conduct experiments in parapsychology, and they joined the group. Others who joined had also heard about the group through the grapevine. They were all to be taught the principles of parapsychology. In the first semester, the students learned how to use their hands to perceive the biological field around a person. In the second semester, they studied the organs of the body and how to distinguish between a healthy organ and a sick one.

When the three physicists found that they really could feel the signals given off by the body, they decided to try to prove the existence of the biopole scientifically. They wondered if there was some connection between the biopole and the existence of chakras, the source of poles according to yoga. Yoga teaches that there are sounds, mantras, which cause a response in these chakras. The physicists pronounced these sounds and verified with their hands that they excited the chakras, but they wanted to see if they could verify this result with instruments. Some of the doctors in the group had parallel interests. They wondered if parapsychologists could affect the places that were acted upon by acupuncture.

The teacher of the physicists and the organizer of the group at the Institute of Physical Culture was Sergei Mitrofanov, a radio engineer, who was also a member of the laboratory of bioinformation that Blok had visited eighteen years earlier. Khronopoulo and Krochik went to the laboratory, where entry was now by special pass, and groups of people waited outside asking for help in being cured. At frequent intervals, someone came out of the laboratory and asked these people to disperse. Mitrofanov introduced Khronopoulo and Krochik to Spirkin, whose interest in parapsychology had not waned over the years, and they met Nikolai Nosov, the head of the laboratory and a colonel in the army technical services.

The atmosphere in the laboratory was very secretive. The only way to gain entry was to be brought in by a member. Passersby were barred. Strange personalities who were not members of the laboratory read lectures about yoga, healing, and theories of the construction of the universe. Some of those in the laboratory were scientists, others were mystics. When a visitor asked what kind of work the laboratory was doing, he was told, "Become a member and you'll find out."

Khronopoulo and Krochik, now joined by Blok, went to the weekly seminar, where they presented their proposal to about forty people. They said they wanted to use ultrasonic waves to act on the chakras of people and to measure whatever changed in the electrical field near that person's body. They needed equipment to conduct the experiments and hoped they could get this from the laboratory. Among other things, they required an extremely sensitive electronic electrometer.

The reactions of the people in the audience were mixed. Nosov was abusive. "What are you doing here?" he shouted. "What did you come here for?" Others were more positive. Several persons from Moscow scientific institutes who participated in the work of the laboratory reacted with enthusiasm. But it soon became clear that to obtain the necessary equipment would require such an enormous expenditure of energy that they would have little time for anything else.

The physicists attended seminars on three Tuesdays in a row, trying to interest people in their idea, but they soon learned that their presence was not appreciated. To become a member of the laboratory, it was necessary to fill out a questionnaire, provide a photograph, and be examined by psychics to determine "suitability." Khronopoulo, Blok, and Krochik had not done any of this. When they arrived for a seminar on the fourth week, they were abruptly told to leave.

While Blok, Khronopoulo, and Krochik were trying to interest the laboratory of bioelectronics in their proposal, efforts were being made by some Soviet officials to close the laboratory on the grounds that it did not have a materialistic basis. The future of the laboratory was discussed several times in the hierarchy of the Popov Scientific Technical Society, and it was finally decided to rid the laboratory of unscientific practices. Khronopoulo, Blok, and Krochik were finally definitively barred from the laboratory after the police raid on the film at the Makarenko Club and the official warnings at their institute.

The three continued to study parapsychology with Mitrofanov at the Institute of Physical Culture until, in January 1981, the party committee at the institute changed its attitude toward the parapsychology classes. Mitrofanov was called in and told that parapsychology was not a Marxist science and mysticism could lead people to a religious worldview. One evening, Mitrofanov gathered together the members of the parapsychology class and said, "We've been forbidden to meet here. We'll continue to meet, but it will have to be privately."

Many members of the group did continue the private meetings, but it was much more difficult to carry out the work with fewer people and without an organized structure. At the same time, the authorities began to harass those who had demonstrated an interest in parapsychology.

Khronopoulo was called in again at his institute, this time by the deputy director, who warned him that the KGB was upset that he continued to meet with parapsychologists. He was warned that this could ruin his career. He was also asked to step down as laboratory director. The deputy director explained that "only people who share our ideology should be in management positions."

A short time later, however, a strange thing happened. The colleague from Khronopoulo's institute who had originally invited Blok to the film in the Makarenko Club came up to Khronopoulo at work and said, "Yuri Georgevich, what would you say if someone suggested to you working with parapsychology in a closed establishment?"

Khronopoulo asked him why he wanted to know.

"The question interests me purely theoretically," he said.

"I don't want to work in a closed institute," he said. "I don't want to add parapsychology to the instruments of war."

Khronopoulo's colleague approached him several more times. "Listen," he said to Khronopoulo, "if you worked in a closed institute, at least you could pursue your interest."

"It is better not to have anything to do with it," Khronopoulo said, and his colleague made no further approach.

In the aftermath of their experience, Khronopoulo, Blok, and Krochik understood that although the KGB persecuted parapsychology, the authorities wanted to make full use of it, particularly if there was some way it could be used to serve military purposes. Parapsychology was banned, but the laboratory on Furmanny Lane was allowed to operate, in order to attract anyone interested in the subject and to find who among them would be ready to work for the Soviet military.

In addition to their interest in parapsychology, Blok and Khronopoulo had long been interested in spiritualism. Blok participated in his first séance in the 1960s in Yaroslavl.

The method the two men used in communicating with spirits was similar to that employed by spiritualists all over the world. They painted an arrow on a plate after heating it over a candle and then wrote letters on a sheet in a semicircle. Setting the plate on the sheet and putting their hands on the plate as lightly as possible, they then followed the movement of the plate to get answers to questions.

One December evening, they were invited to a meeting in the apartment of a forty-five-year-old parapsychologist who was doing research into ways of growing younger. They were told they could expect to meet some interesting people.

The apartment where the meeting took place was crowded with books on the occult, astrology, and parapsychology. In the kitchen, there was a system of pipes connected by a crane to a purification apparatus, which included a mechanism for the ionization of water with silver. The water also passed through "activated coal" and a system of magnets. The apartment owner explained he had combined every method of water purification that had ever been described in any journal into a single system. He froze the result in his freezer and then melted it before drinking it. He said the final product had helped him become younger, and he was indeed active and vigorous although a little paranoid.

After Blok and Khronopoulo seated themselves in the living room, they were presented to two men they had never seen before. They introduced themselves by name and patronymic but did not give their family names or say where they worked. They said they would not ask Blok and Khronopoulo for their names and did not want to be asked for theirs. Despite this expressed willingness to allow Blok and Khronopoulo to remain anonymous, however, the two men showed that they knew a lot about them and seemed to have a healthy respect for their abilities. They began talking about parapsychology and the problems of communicating information. Finally, the smaller and more active of the two said they were interested in carrying out an experiment with the help of a plate because they were interested in the answer to a very important question. The men said that they had information that a Czech parapsychologist by the name of Pavlita had developed a means of creating a biological pole without a person by using some type of apparatus. They said this discovery was potentially very interesting to them and they needed to find Pavlita; unfortunately, he had vanished two years before and had not been heard from since.

"If he died," the more talkative of the two said, "he is not buried in any cemetery. We checked every cemetery in Czechoslovakia."

Blok and Khronopoulo suddenly lost all desire to participate in this experiment. There was only one organization capable of checking every cemetery in Czechoslovakia.

"As a rule," Blok said, trying to extricate himself from the situation, "such questions are not answered." But the two men urged them to make the attempt, and after heating the plate, they asked the question and received a foggy answer. Finally, Blok asked the two men, "If you want to find this man, why don't you ask the Czech government?"

"The Czechs might not tell us," the quieter of the two said. "They might keep whatever they are doing to themselves. We don't trust them."

"We believe that mysticism is a channel of information," said the other man.

"What do you mean by a channel of information?" Blok asked.

"Take a woman with bare knees. She doesn't see you but she begins to cover her knees when you start to look at her. This is telepathic communication between people that could also become a means of gathering information. It might be possible to develop a kind of telepathic transmission that would be sent only to one person and could not be intercepted by anyone else."

Blok said he and Khronopoulo were interested only in studying the mechanism for the transmission of information and in diagnostics and healing. The more vocal man said they were not interested in how the mechanism worked, only in how to use it.

When Blok and Khronopoulo got ready to leave, the two men addressed them correctly by name and patronymic, although they had only given their first names, and said that they worked in the Institute of Distant Communications, which is a largely closed, military institute. They invited them to a seminar, which was to be held in a basement of one of the regional offices of the GAI, the state traffic police.

Khronopoulo did not want to go. He felt it was dangerous to have any further contact, but Blok did attend and listened to a philosopher speak about his theory of paraphenomena, including telepathy, and saw a healer demonstrate her diagnostic skills. There was also a demonstration by Zharikov, a professor of Marxism-Leninism, who was able to move objects. Zharikov was scheduled to give a more detailed demonstration at the next seminar. One of the two men who invited them had given Blok his telephone number, but when Blok called to learn the place and the date of the Zharikov demonstration, he was told that it would not take place. He later learned that the demonstration did occur, but he and Khronopoulo had shown by their reluctance to cooperate that they were not of real interest to the Soviet Union's principal patrons of mysticism and parapsychology.

9

Internal
Policy

Under conditions of terror, most people will comply but some people will not. Humanly speaking, no more is required and no more can reasonably be asked, for this planet to remain a place fit for human habitation.

—*Hannah Arendt*, Eichmann in Jerusalem

MOSCOW, FEBRUARY 6, 1987

THE LOW-LYING NORTHERN SUN lit the facades of the rows of five-story apartment buildings, casting the sides of the buildings in deep blue shadow as laundry stiff from the cold swayed in balconies on ice-covered lines and a strong wind blew up clouds of snow.

For weeks, the endless winter had brought out the monotony and dreariness of life in the Yugo-Zapadny section of Moscow, contributing to the sense that nothing in the Soviet Union could ever change. But on this particular morning, as buses plied the roads and bundled women walked between scattered birch trees along paths of hardened snow, a meeting was taking place in one of the buildings that showed that something in the Soviet Union had changed, and that the change was important enough to affect the course of millions of lives.

As steam from a teapot clouded the double-glazed windows, Rostislav Yevdokimov and Lev Volokhonsky, who had just been released from a political labor camp, waited while a woman friend placed a call to a Soviet émigré in the West. "Hello," said the woman, after a long delay, "I'm calling from home. Volokhonsky and Yevdokimov are sitting next to me. They arrived yesterday from the train."

The conversation then continued.

"That's impossible," said the émigré.

"Wait a minute. I'll hand Volokhonsky the phone."

"Hello."

"Levka! This cannot be."

"That's what I think," said Volokhonsky. "I think this is some kind of mirage. But we arrived here with half a wagon of political prisoners. They photographed all of us in one tie, one shirt, and one jacket, and then issued certificates of release. In our thirty-fifth zone, they insist that there are no more political prisoners."

Yevdokimov took the phone.

"We don't know what the situation is in the thirty-sixth zone," he said. "It seems that the order on liberation does not apply there. But maybe there is a different order. In any case, they aren't freeing people from the special zone."

"But what is the decree?"

"No one knows," said Yevdokimov, "especially since there is more than one decree. Of the prisoners who traveled with us, some were freed under decree 6463 and some under 6462. How these decrees differ from one another no one knows."

"One thing is sure," said Volokhonsky, "they now do not have enough political prisoners to fill three camps. Apparently they are going to close either one or two camps. I think they will preserve the thirty-fifth zone."

"And they freed you directly," asked the émigré, "instead of by way of the investigative isolator?"

"Yes, yes," said Volokhonsky.

"On what conditions?"

"For everyone they were the same. We had to say that we will not engage in antistate activity, although no one acknowledged that he had ever engaged in antistate activity. Then it was said that the procurator, in the name of the Supreme Soviet, would issue pardons, and we were asked what we would do after being freed. Here each prisoner had his own version.

"They took us to Chusovoy. The station was completely surrounded but we were allowed to enter freely and then we were put on a train."

The Moscow woman took the phone.

"I came home," she said, "and was told, 'Sit down, don't fall over, Volokhonsky is waiting for you.'"

"I think," said Yevdokimov, "that this is the very beginning of a process. We just have to be reasonable and hope for the best...."

THE PHONE CALL of Volokhonsky and Yevdokimov was a harbinger of the end of the Soviet system.

Unlike other tyrannies, which demanded little more than obedience, the Soviet system created a world of false appearances that then became a powerful instrument of mental domination and made it possible for the regime to rule with a minimum of brute force.

ON MAY DAY in Red Square, the loudspeakers poured out martial music as a column of demonstrators entered the square bearing letters spelling out the message, "We Will Fulfill the Decisions of the 25th Party Congress!" They were followed by rows of gymnasts carrying flags and paper flowers. When the rows were in place, the area became momentarily quiet. The members of the Politburo mounted the steps of the Lenin mausoleum and the young people twirled their flags and gave rising and falling cheers until all the members of the Politburo had reached the top of the reviewing stand. At that point, the demonstrators beat time with a thousand red flags and chanted, "Glory, glory to the Soviet Union," "Glory, glory to the Soviet people." Then, marching in step and waving the flags in syncopated time, they passed out of the square, followed by floats from area factories and marchers carrying flags, flowers, balloons, and portraits of Lenin and Brezhnev.

The May Day demonstration showed how, in the Soviet Union, myth was always being turned into reality and reality dissolved into myth. The demonstration was tightly controlled, but in the clear morning light it was easy to imagine that it was the spontaneous show of support for the regime it pretended to be.

UNTIL THE creation of the Soviet Union, it was accepted universally that the only way to verify a scientific hypothesis was empirically. With the attempt to treat Marxism-Leninism as a science, however, the situation changed. Instead of ideology being compared to observable reality, reality began to be falsified to conform to ideology, a process completely consistent with a cosmology in which concepts, far from deriving permanent meaning from a transcendent sphere, were treated as merely a reflection of the ever-changing "needs" of the working class.

The regime was able to create a fictitious world because it was dealing with people who carried within them a hidden kernel of fear that made them afraid to dissent openly. In this respect, it did not matter that there was no longer mass terror. Every citizen knew that free expression was punished, and this was enough to influence behavior where, in the absence of reliable rights, each person felt himself to be at the mercy of the authorities.

When the regime released political prisoners in 1987, it, in effect, began to liberate people from fear. As a result, the world of false appearances that engendered a mirage of unanimity began to be violated; once violated, it began to unravel, making its collapse and that of the system it justified a virtual inevitability.

VOLOGDA, OCTOBER 1981

The illusion of unanimity was created in every Soviet city. Andrew Nagorski of *Newsweek* and I left the train station and walked across a square to the Hotel Vologda, where we checked in. After unpacking our things, we began to stroll around Vologda, which was a mixture of old and new. Five-story concrete housing blocks were interspersed with dilapidated log houses in fields of birch trees and tall weeds.

After about ten minutes, we reached the center, which resembled a turn-of-the-century amusement park, its main street lined with gabled storefronts, adorned with bas reliefs, pillars, and columns. The center, however, was nearly empty on this Sunday morning, so we decided to take a taxi to the Kirillov-Belotserkovsky monastery, which was about two hours away. From there, we drove into Kirillov, which was separated from the monastery by a small park.

We had decided to visit Vologda because it was the home of "Vologda butter," the best butter in the Soviet Union, and a logical place from which to write about food shortages in Russia. The people of northern Russia also had a reputation for patience. We wanted to see if their patience was holding up in the face of an apparently worsening situation.

In Kirillov, we turned down a street and, at length, came to an unwashed, two-story brick shopping arcade and entered a store that had a sign over the entryway that said "Meat." In the dim light, old women waited with string bags in long lines in front of counters where there was no meat on sale, only sprats—a small herring—frozen together in large blocks. There was no butter at the butter counter, only a few packs of margarine.

I asked an old woman in line if there was any butter.

"Butter?" she said, in amazement. "What kind of butter? There is no butter."

Suddenly there were shouts from somewhere behind us. "Who said there is no butter?" The old lady turned pale and I began writing down what was happening. "What are you writing?" said a man in a black leather jacket who was now standing between us.

"Why don't you get out of here?" I suggested unpleasantly.

"I'll go away and call the police," he said, furious. He then turned and walked out of the store.

We tried to speak again to the old woman, but she was now terrified. "I don't know anything," she said.

We went to the vegetable store, where there were no fresh vegetables on sale, only carrots in large bins and cabbage, onions, and beets. We looked for someone to interview when another man in a black leather jacket entered the store. Rather than risk another confrontation, we decided to leave.

Outside it was getting dark. Snow flurries danced over the surrounding fields. The temperature fell and, in the sky, dark clouds were outlined by the orange glow of a setting sun. We walked for a time down a street that was little better than a river of mud and came to a store where milk was being ladled out to people who stood in line with canisters. I asked an old woman in the line if there was any butter on sale in the store.

"Not butter, little son," she said, smiling sweetly, "margarine."

Suddenly, a middle-aged man appeared out of nowhere and began swearing, repeating the words *sour cream*. We decided to leave the store rather than create problems for the woman.

With nothing further to learn in Kirillov, we left for Vologda.

· · ·

MONDAY MORNING was overcast. There were crowds on the street as Andy and I began to visit stores to get some idea of the state of food supplies. A store on Peace Prospekt had no meat, no butter, and no milk. I asked a salesgirl if there would be butter.

"Sometimes we have it," she said thoughtfully. "It's rare, but sometimes we have it. Come back later."

At the collective farmers' market, small amounts of pork and bacon were on sale. I talked to some collective farmers and Andy photographed them. Then, two seedy-looking young men suddenly appeared and started to block Andy. The collective farmers quickly broke off the conversation.

On the way back to the hotel, we spoke to an elderly saleswoman in the central bookstore. "Yes, there are problems," she said, sighing slightly. "But Moscow wasn't built in a day. We're optimists. This was the first socialist country in the world. There are problems, but we think there is no problem that cannot be overcome."

That night we had dinner in the hotel restaurant and were joined by Lyuba, a teacher of English. We asked her about the food situation in Vologda.

"There are problems of a temporary nature," she said, "but compared to what we experienced during the war, a few disruptions in deliveries don't worry anyone."

THE FOLLOWING MORNING we walked back to the center of Vologda, where we tried, without much success, to engage more passersby in conversation. Finally, we decided to go to Cherepovets, the site of a vast steel complex, about eighty miles away.

On the way, we talked to our driver, who, in response to questions about the food situation, pointed out that if people wanted meat they could go to Moscow for it. He said that the factories organized "sausage trips." The official purpose was to visit museums or Lenin's tomb, but people just spent their time shopping.

"Isn't it strange to travel to Moscow to buy meat produced in your own region?" I asked.

"The capital is the capital," he replied.

We drove into Cherepovets, past islands of grimy wooden houses framed by coal dumps and railroad yards. We finally stopped in an area of five-story apartment blocks and entered a store where we asked the salesgirl if she expected any butter.

"We don't get butter anymore," she said nostalgically. I asked her about meat. She shook her head and said, "We don't receive meat at all." In another store, milk was available for infants between the ages of one and two, but the saleswoman said that there was nowhere in Cherepovets to buy milk freely after 11 a.m.

None of this, however, seemed to bother people.

"We manage," said a woman on the street. "One person gets food at the market, another at a canteen, a third from acquaintances. In the West, the stores are full but, at home, there is nothing. Here, there is nothing in the stores but, at home, everything is there."

THE NEXT MORNING in Vologda was cloudy. I left the hotel early to take a walk, and as I stopped to watch workmen placing logs from a derelict house on a smoky fire, I was approached by a stranger who shouted that I had come to Vologda to "throw dirt."

When I returned to the hotel, Andy told me that a passerby had berated him, too.

Later, as Andy prepared to take a picture in front of a long queue outside a milk store, a young man stepped in front of his camera. The more Andy tried to slip around him, the more the young man maneuvered to block the photo.

We left the store and went to the city hall, where we were received by Vladimir Parmyenov, Vologda's mayor. He admitted there were shortages, but he blamed bad weather conditions that had ruined the harvest, and the tense international situation.

"Our people understand that miracles don't exist," he said. "Our people remember World War II, when not a single family did not have someone to cry over. No country in the world suffered like the Soviet Union."

After leaving City Hall, we again went for a walk and came to a cobblestone square where we stopped two elderly sisters and asked where we could buy Vologda butter. They said it was not on sale and then, noticing our accents, asked us where we were from. We said we were American correspondents.

"Why does America threaten us?" one of them asked.

"America doesn't threaten you," I said.

"Then why are you building the neutron bomb?"

At that moment, a sleazy teenager approached and stepped between Andy and me and the two women. "If you want information, you should go over there," he said, pointing to the city hall.

Noticing the self-confidence with which the teenager was addressing us, the women brought the conversation to a rapid close.

That evening we packed and went to the train station; the scene there reinforced the impression of cosmic passivity. In the hazy light of the waiting room, the only flash of color was the red of Soviet army epaulettes. In the straight-backed chairs, people sat with their hands folded, sacks of potatoes at their feet, their eyes closed, resembling not passengers but human freight being sent to the next destination by some unseen force they could neither control nor understand.

THE ILLUSION OF UNANIMITY in Vologda was typical of every city in the Soviet Union, and the impression that no one disagreed reinforced the notion that the boundaries of consciousness were those set by the regime. The core of the process of creating reality, however, remained repression in the labor camps and the psychiatric hospitals.

Spread out across a vast country, the places of detention constituted an unseen world that was nonetheless familiar to everyone and shaped the nature of the visible world in cities like Vologda.

The Labor Camps

The first pole of the unseen world was the political labor camps, where prisoners were exhausted with forced labor and subjected to constant moral harassment. For the slightest attempt to protest mistreatment, a prisoner was put in a punishment cell, a stone box where the food ration amounted to slow starvation.

Because any free-thinking person had the potential to ruin the mirage of unanimity that was the ultimate guarantee of the state's stability, the goal of the camps was not just to punish dissenters but to force them to renounce their political activities. The prisoners usually resisted, but the pressure to recant was unrelenting.

．　．　．

ON A RAINY AUTUMN MORNING, Galina Koryagina left the village of Polovinka in the Ural Mountains. Carrying two bags full of food in her arms and a rucksack on her back, she began walking along a dirt road up a hill. She walked slowly, stopping frequently and putting her bags down in the mud. Finally, she reached the top of the hill; in the distance, she could see the towers of an abandoned mine rising above the forest.

Next to that abandoned mine was the labor camp where her husband, Anatoly, was a prisoner. Nine months had passed since he was arrested, and this was to be her first meeting with him since then.

Koryagina paused to catch her breath. Suddenly, she heard a knocking sound coming from somewhere behind her. She turned and saw that she was being overtaken by an old man with a horse and a wagon. He was carrying a set of canisters to the camp, apparently to collect the garbage. The old man pulled up alongside Koryagina and she asked if she could have a ride as far as the camp. He agreed and, getting down from the wagon, helped her with her bags.

"From where do the Russian women get their strength?" he said. "People say that women are the weak sex. But you see how many bags and up a hill. And with shoes with heels. Are you going for a visit?"

"Yes," Koryagina answered.

"Your husband?"

"Yes."

"Is he in for politics?"

"Not exactly. I don't know how to explain it."

"He probably sought truth and proved something where it wasn't necessary. They don't like that. There are lots of smart people in this camp and there have been a lot of them. They call them democrats here. They did everything for truth. Only to whom are you going to prove the truth? How many years did they give him?"

"Seven and five exile."

"There, there. So much water flows away. Your years aren't returned to you. Yes, and health, from here not a one ever left healthy. And you have so much grief, yes. . . . Do you have any children?"

"Three sons."

"Three? What was his work?"

"Psychiatrist."

The old man looked at Koryagina in bewilderment.

"What did he lack that he had to seek truth?"

"He sought the truth and he spoke the truth, Uncle. He said that psychologically healthy people were put in special psychiatric hospitals, that they mocked them and treated them as if they were ill."

"Why would they put them there?"

"So they don't have to put them on trial—as you say, for politics and for telling the truth. They consider that psychologically normal people cannot say anything against the authorities, that this can be done only by people who are mentally ill. There are no politically discontented people, just people who are sick."

The old man seemed puzzled. "But what did he prove? He's been sentenced to twelve years and they say that exile is worse than camp."

"All I can say is that any deed which is done by a man for the good of another man does not pass in vain, all the less so if it's done unselfishly, according to the commands of the heart."

The old man fell silent, and then, as they descended the hill through the thick forest, he spoke about himself. He said that in the village, no one cared about anything. Everywhere he looked there was negligence and drunkenness. His neighbors drank and fought constantly.

Koryagina was taken to the headquarters of the Perm 37 Labor Camp, where she was received by a representative of the KGB.

"I consider it important," the KGB man said, "that we try to persuade Anatoly Ivanovich to take the path of correction. I think if he does this, we could reconsider his sentence and maybe send him to work in 'chemicals' [forced labor in a labor-short industry].

"Think about the long separation from your husband and the effect on your children and Anatoly's mother."

"How do you expect me to persuade him?" Koryagina asked.

"You're a woman," he said.

"I did not come here to agitate my husband to repent some nonexistent sins," she said. "And I have no intention of blackmailing him with an appeal to feminine weakness. Anatoly has nothing to repent."

Seeing that he would be unable to persuade her to help him, the KGB officer allowed her to leave and she met with Koryagin a short time later.

Anatoly was overcome when he saw his wife and could barely

speak. Galina found that she could not stop crying. Finally, when they both had calmed down, Anatoly talked about the conditions in the camp. He said that the authorities did everything possible to provoke the prisoners into acts that would formally justify punishment. He said the bread was made from unused crusts that were ground up and rebaked. The prisoners ate as little of it as possible, aware that it had no nutritional value. All summer long there was virtually no fruit or vegetables, not even onions or garlic. Those in the camp for more than a year suffered from stomach and kidney ailments, with terrible vitamin deficiencies.

Anatoly said that the camp authorities had singled him out for special treatment. He was forced to wear a striped uniform and to clean up in the forbidden zone between the camp walls, where, for any false move, he could be shot without warning.

"I didn't try to achieve any great goal," he said. "I just felt that I had a responsibility as a doctor, which was to prevent unnecessary torment. I couldn't bear the thought that the profession that I belonged to was not used for humane purposes but as a way to punish people.

"Now they do everything they can to break my will. If they can even begin to break me, it will be the end. I could not live with myself."

Not long after Koryagina's visit, Anatoly's situation sharply deteriorated. In late October, Oleg Mikhailov, a plane hijacker, began to assault other prisoners, often beating them savagely. No action was taken when the men protested, and it soon became clear that Mikhailov was simply a tool in the hands of the administration.

Koryagin decided to organize a strike in the camp factory to demand that Mikhailov be removed. The strike lasted two weeks. In response, Koryagin and ten other prisoners were put in the penalty isolator. The isolator in Perm 37 was a freezing concrete box 3.2 meters square.

For fifteen days, hunger gnawed away at Koryagin and he stumbled around in a sleepless daze. He sometimes dropped off to sleep for fifteen minutes but was jolted awake by the cold. At the end of his term in the isolator, Koryagin was summoned to the camp headquarters to talk to two KGB representatives. "Anatoly Ivanovich," said one of the agents, "you had good work, a family and children. What made you get involved in anti-Sovietism? You made a mistake.

If you will admit your mistake, this whole situation can be taken care of."

"I don't talk to KGB agents," Koryagin said, "and I advise you not to try to talk to me again."

Koryagin was next put in the camp prison for six months. The conditions were better than in the isolator. He was held in a cell rather than a concrete box and there was a cot instead of boards. There was also a little more food. With the exception of a brief exercise period, however, he could not leave his cell.

In April 1982, Koryagin finished his term in the prison, but he was not released to the camp. Instead, he was given two extra terms in the isolator for refusing to talk to the KGB. He was finally released to the camp in May.

When Koryagin returned to the camp, he found that the work norms in the factory had increased and prisoners were being thrown into the isolator on the slightest pretext. When the prisoners responded with hunger strikes, Koryagin also participated, and this led the administration to increase the pressure on him. On July 13, 1982, he was put on trial for insubordination and sentenced to three years in the Chistopol prison.

Koryagin was put on a prison train and a week later arrived in Chistopol. Soon after his arrival, the boss of the prison told him, "If you conduct yourself here the way you did in the zone, life won't be sweet for you."

Despite the warning, however, Anatoly refused to abide by the prison rules. He was assigned to knitting nets, but he did this only to kill time. He refused to fulfill the norm. As punishment, he was put in the isolator, and when he was severely beaten by guards, he announced an indefinite hunger strike.

Koryagin's hunger strike was to become a six-and-a-half-month ordeal. For two weeks, he remained in the isolator without food. Time passed slowly. He thought about his home and his children, about human life and its physical limits. Each morning, the guards who had beaten him entered the isolator and asked him, "How is everything? How do you feel? When will you take food? Why are you doing this?" Finally, Koryagin was removed to a cell in the prison where he was force-fed. A clamp was inserted between his teeth and his jaws were forced open. A hose was inserted down his windpipe and food was poured through the pipe into his stomach.

This procedure was carried out every four or five days, so Koryagin constantly had the sensation of beginning a new hunger strike. Gradually, he lost strength, until he could no longer rise from his cot.

Once this happened, the guards began to employ various forms of psychological torture. They turned on the official radio to full volume so that Koryagin was forced to listen all day to Soviet propaganda. They also opened control valves in the plumbing so that water roared through the toilets and he had the impression that he was lying under Niagara Falls. Unable to stand, he was taken to the baths on a stretcher. On his way, the guards in the corridor cursed him. Some said, "That scoundrel, he should be taken out of here and thrown on a garbage heap." Others said, "Why carry him? We should shoot him and get the problem over with once and for all."

In the bathhouse, Koryagin was undressed and doused with warm water. The guards frequently opened the doors to the street and the icy cold air spread along the floor. They also would wash him and then leave him on a stretcher in the middle of the prison yard, perhaps hoping he would catch pneumonia and die a natural death.

The guards prepared meals and put them inches from his face. Finally, after Koryagin had been on a hunger strike for six weeks, he was visited in his cell by a KGB representative.

"Anatoly Ivanovich," the officer said, "how is it that you drive yourself to this state? You're emaciated. You may even die. Why don't you stop all this. Let's talk and try to find a common language. When you were free, what did you lack? What prevented you from living peacefully in freedom? You were a doctor. If you are here, it is because you want to be here. If you change your behavior, I assure you that the attitude toward you will change. Everything depends on you."

The KGB agent waited for an answer for nearly half an hour, but Koryagin refused to speak.

After two or three months, Koryagin had lost 40 percent of his body weight despite the force-feedings. He survived the ordeal but he weakened steadily, until he was little more than skin and bones, a starving bag of water covered with albugineous edemas.

By this time, though, a campaign in his defense had begun in the West, and he had been elected an honorary member of the World Psychiatric Association. For the first time, the KGB had a reason to keep him alive, and knowing that many of his fellow prisoners were afraid he would die, they, in the seventh month of Koryagin's hunger strike, allowed Genrikh Altunyan, a friend from Kharkov and a fellow political prisoner, into Koryagin's cell. Altunyan told Koryagin that all the political prisoners insisted that he stop his hunger strike. Koryagin did not agree immediately, but after two or three days, he presented the prison administration with three conditions for stopping his hunger strike: that he be given a meeting with his family, that he be removed from the hunger strike according to safe medical procedures, and that Altunyan be allowed to remain in his cell. The prison authorities agreed to his conditions and, in this case, they kept their word.

Koryagin's meeting two weeks later with his wife was his first in two years, and she was horrified by the change in his appearance. They communicated through a glass partition and Galina thought she was looking at a ghost.

Anatoly asked about events in Kharkov, but when he tried to say something about his condition, the guard interrupted and said, "Anatoly Ivanovich, if you speak about confinement or how you live here, we will break off the meeting." At one point, Anatoly pointed toward his throat in an attempt to show that he had been force-fed, but the guard shouted, "We already agreed about this, Anatoly Ivanovich."

It was only at the end of the two-hour visit that Galina managed to tell Anatoly that Western psychiatrists were rallying to his support.

AFTER TWO MONTHS in the prison hospital recovering from his hunger strike, Koryagin was released to the prison. The test of wills, however, was not over.

On March 21, 1984, the political prisoners at Chistopol called a one-day hunger strike to protest harassment, and several were thrown in the punishment cell, including Koryagin. He immediately announced that he would go on a hunger strike and refuse all food until the end of his prison term, fourteen months later.

The same sequence repeated itself. Within two weeks, Koryagin was fed with a hose that was inserted into his stomach, and, by the third month, his life again hung in the balance.

At this point, a KGB agent entered his cell and told him that his son, Ivan, had been involved in a fight in Kharkov and the police were preparing to charge him with hooliganism. "We're going to put your son on trial," the KGB agent said. "His fate depends on the way you behave. Let's speak on this theme."

But Koryagin continued to refuse to talk to the KGB.

Six months after the beginning of his second hunger strike, the guards who were force-feeding Koryagin fastened self-tightening handcuffs around his forearm, which was skin and bones. This caused excruciating pain and Koryagin spat in the guard's face. He was immediately charged with resistance and the authorities prepared to put him on trial.

As it happened, however, the prospect of a trial saved his life. Prisoners were routinely examined by a doctor before being put on trial, and the doctor who looked Koryagin over ordered that he be force-fed twice a day so that he would seem to be in normal condition when he appeared in court. At the trial, Koryagin was sentenced to two additional years in the labor camp; afterward, the guards resumed feeding him every four or five days. As a result of the extra food he had before his trial, however, his life was no longer threatened.

Finally, in June 1985, having served his prison sentence, Koryagin was brought to the Perm 35 Labor Camp. He canceled his hunger strike and was put in the camp hospital, where he met Vasily Ovsienko, a Ukrainian nationalist. Ovsienko told Koryagin that he had heard about his long hunger strikes and informed him about the deaths of Vasily Stus, Olexander Tikhy, and Valery Marchenko, all of whom died after long periods in the punishment cell. "I don't advise you to continue declaring hunger strikes," Ovsienko said. "Save your life. There has got to be someone to testify."

BY THE SECOND HALF of 1986, the pressure on the political prisoners in Perm 35 increased sharply. The authorities began throwing prisoners into the penalty cells for the slightest violation of the rules. At the same time, prisoners continued to die of medical neglect. In June 1986, Mikhail Furasov, a political prisoner from Kiev, died of acute uremia after being denied timely medical care, provoking hunger strikes by many of his fellow prisoners.

Everything was being done to extort "confessions" from the prisoners and to persuade them to cooperate with the KGB, but then, suddenly, the pressure eased and there were rumors in the camps about impending liberations.

The guards started telling prisoners to sign a statement asking to be liberated. "Why should you stay?" they asked. "All you have to do is sign and you can go."

The informers repeated the same thing.

"There is perestroika now. You've got to sign. Why not?"

Finally, on January 17, 1987, Koryagin and two other prisoners were taken to the city of Perm, where the procurator told him that the authorities had decided he could now be freed. All he had to do was sign a statement saying that he would not participate in his former activities.

"On the contrary," Koryagin said, "I promise that if you free me, on the very next day, I'll resume my former activities."

From Perm, Koryagin was removed to Kiev, where he was held in the KGB investigative prison. The same proposition was made to him. He again refused. "I consider the suggestion disgusting and don't plan to write a single word," Koryagin said.

On February 12, he began a new hunger strike. On February 15, he was called again to the procurator, who told him that his case would be settled in a week. On February 18, he was taken from his cell and put in a car and driven to the railroad station. One of the guards then got out of the car with him and escorted him to the station entrance.

"Go home," he said. "You are freed."

JANIS BARKANS, a Latvian nationalist, arrived at a labor camp in Latvia on an icy winter day. He was registered and led to a wooden barracks where he saw, to his horror, that the other prisoners resembled inmates in a Nazi concentration camp.

Barkans had been arrested by the KGB in Vyborg for trying to cross the Soviet-Finnish border and sentenced to eighteen months at hard labor. The Latvian camp was for ordinary criminals, but he remained under the supervision of the KGB.

After a few days, Barkans was put to work as a loader. The labor camp produced metal plates and the work went on sixteen hours a day, seven days a week. At the same time, the food was so poor that the prisoners ferreted in the garbage and ate maggots or grass. After working under these conditions for several months, Barkans wrote a poem entitled "Down with Communists," which he read to several fellow prisoners, one of whom denounced him. He was immediately put in the isolation cell, where, once a KGB officer gave his consent, he began to be beaten.

On the first day, Barkans was beaten and kicked. On the following day, he was beaten by a guard and doused with cold water. "So you don't like Soviet power?!" the guard shouted.

Barkans was then taken to a warehouse for his beatings. The guards explained, "We're going for a political information session."

Each day, he was beaten and kicked until, after the fifteenth day in the isolation cell, he was transferred to the internal camp prison for six months.

In the camp prison, Barkans was given penalty rations and had to sew sacks, but he was nonetheless able to relax. After a few days, however, Barkans was asked if he was ready to be "loyal" to Soviet power. When he responded "no," he was sent back to the isolation cell and the transfer marked the beginning of outright terror.

• On the first night, Barkans overheard an inmate in his cell saying that he had been told by camp officials to continue beating Barkans and that he had been assured that, if Barkans died, there would be no punishment. In return, he was promised cigarettes and food.

• The following morning, the second day of Barkans's second term in the isolation cell, he was denied his ration of bread and water, even though he was faint from hunger. When he tried to complain, he was beaten.

• On the fourth to eighth days, Barkans was tied by the guards to a metal grating and alternately burned with a red-hot knife and doused with ice water. He became infected with scabies and his entire body began to itch. To keep him from scratching, criminals in the punishment cell tore out the fingernails from his right hand. He lost consciousness from the pain and then was doused again with cold water.

• On the tenth day, the boss of the labor camp asked Barkans: "Now do you respect Soviet power?"

Barkans shook his head no.

"All right, you'll die like a dog."

• At the end of his fifteen days, Barkans was told that for bad behavior his term in the isolation cell had been extended another ten days. He tried to crawl out of the cell and was kicked by a guard, who slammed the door on two of his fingers, severing them.

Barkans finally declared a hunger strike. His scab-covered body turned yellow. A doctor entered the isolator and Barkans begged her to put him in a hospital. She said she was forbidden to give him medical aid.

Feeling that the end was near, Barkans tried to hang himself, but the attempt was foiled by the guards. Shortly afterward, he was again savagely beaten by fellow inmates. The beating continued until he lost consciousness and lay without any sign of life. His cellmates decided that he was dead and summoned a duty officer. Barkans was then taken to a warehouse and his body was laid out on some wooden boards. The next morning, as a hearse arrived to remove his body for dissection, he regained consciousness.

A guard, seeing Barkans begin to stir, panicked and bolted out the door. The camp authorities, when they realized Barkans was alive, at first wanted to put him back in the isolation cell but finally sent him to the prison hospital. He weighed eighty-six pounds. He was found to be suffering from tuberculosis of the bones and lungs, was spitting up blood, and could not stand on his feet.

At one time, Barkans was an outstanding athlete, and his superb physical condition may have made it possible for him to survive. On May 21, 1981, Barkans was still recovering in the camp hospital when he finished his eighteen-month sentence and was free to leave the camp.

MARK MOROZOV, a Moscow mathematics teacher, arrived at the Perm 35 Labor Camp in the fall of 1980, after being convicted of circulating banned literature. He had already been sentenced to exile for circulating leaflets defending dissidents, but this time the sentence was eight years at hard labor and five years in exile.

In addition to being deaf, Morozov had a weak heart and circulation problems in his legs, which made them swell, giving him great pain. In the camp, these problems became particularly acute. Perm 35 is located at the water divide between Europe and Asia, and there is a strong magnetic pole. Watches run either too fast or too slow. The wind changes direction, constantly causing strong headaches and heart problems.

Shortly after arriving in the camp, Morozov was called in to see a representative of the KGB.

The KGB officer told him that if he would renounce his previous dissident activities and write a denunciation of other dissidents, including Yuri Orlov, the chairman of the Moscow Helsinki group, he would try to arrange his early release.

"You yourself know the true nature of your friends," the KGB officer said. "What motivates them is vanity. All we ask of you is the truth. Think of yourself and your family."

At first, Morozov hesitated. He then began to meet with the KGB and discuss the terms of his possible release, rationalizing his decision to talk to the KGB by convincing himself that he could do more for the democratic movement on the outside.

In time, however, he changed his mind and came to the conclusion that his original agreement to enter into discussions had been a mistake.

The KGB, however, was not prepared to let Morozov go. They decided that if enough pressure was put on him, he would recant.

Morozov was put in the isolation cell repeatedly, sometimes for as long as four months. In the isolator, he suffered from hunger and cold and from the lack of human contact. Nonetheless, each time, after his release, he refused to write a denunciation of other dissidents.

In 1984, Morozov was transferred to the Chistopol prison. By this time, his condition had worsened to the point where subjecting him to hunger and cold in an isolation cell could easily have led to a need to amputate his legs, which would have left the KGB with no means to pressure him. Accordingly, the KGB decided to change its approach.

To Morozov's surprise, he was suddenly given permission to wear civilian clothing and was even allowed to avoid being shaved bald. When he asked for a reconsideration of his case, the KGB said that his request was being reviewed at a higher level. For the first time, he allowed himself the luxury of hope.

Morozov knew he was ill and wanted to spend time with his family before he died. He hoped that the KGB would give him an early release in light of his failing health.

Finally, in May 1985, a group of KGB officers from Moscow came to Chistopol to see Morozov. They told him that an early release could be arranged, but he would have to "meet them halfway" and write a "truthful" statement about his dissident colleagues. Despite his failing health, Morozov found the strength to refuse. He now realized that he would never be released and he decided to resolve his fate on his own.

In June 1985, he tried to hang himself and was pulled out of the noose at the last minute. He then killed himself with a massive dose of tablets he had been collecting for years.

The Psychiatric Hospitals

The other pole of the unseen world was the psychiatric hospitals where political prisoners were destroyed with the help of drugs. The most commonly employed drugs were haloperidol, which turned off part of the brain; aminazine, which reduced the victim to a half-stupor; majeptil, which led to acute psychological distress; and sulfazine, which, injected intramuscularly, usually in the buttocks, caused a sharp rise in body temperature and excruciating pain.

The prisoners were usually workers who had committed some act that, in the eyes of the regime, was incompatible with sanity, such as trying to flee the country. Unlike the dissidents, such persons often did not intend to make a political statement, but like the dissidents, they threatened to ruin the regime's mirage of unanimity. The goal of the treatment was therefore to force them to agree that they were mentally ill. In the end, most prisoners did so because the alternative was to have their minds destroyed with drugs once and for all.

ALEXANDER SHATRAVKA and his brother, Mikhail, got out of the prison truck in a narrow, floodlit passageway between stone buildings and stood before the metal gates of the Dnepropetrovsk special psychiatric hospital.

After about five minutes, an orderly and a woman doctor emerged and the soldier who had escorted the brothers handed over a file to the woman.

The doctor glanced at the two new arrivals and then opened the file and studied its contents.

"You wanted to see the world," she said finally, "so you ended up coming to us. All right, they're going to have to be shaved bald."

Shatravka and his brother were escorted into the internal yard of the hospital. They crossed the yard and entered a semi-basement that served as a barber shop. After their heads were shaved, the brothers were separated, apparently to be taken to separate departments.

Shatravka was turned over to a new orderly. He entered the hospital building and was led up a staircase that was enclosed with a metal fence, apparently to prevent suicides. The orderly unlocked a massive door and they entered a corridor lined on both sides by locked rooms. Through the windows, Shatravka saw tight rows of beds and bald men twisted up under white linen as if they had expired there.

Shatravka strained to get a better look. Suddenly, the corridor erupted with idiotic laughter. In a corner, a nurse was laughing with two orderlies. On noticing Shatravka, she broke off her conversation and approached him.

"Tell me what you did," she said in a demanding tone.

"He crossed the border into Finland with his brother," said the orderly who escorted him.

"Crossed the border?" said the nurse. "So what would you have done there? You would have croaked from hunger, you would have dug around in garbage cans. Or did you have gold with you? Well, it doesn't matter. After we're done treating you, you won't need any foreign travel."

Shatravka was taken to a ward, where he lay down on a narrow bed. Exhausted from the journey, he fell asleep.

The next morning, he was jarred awake.

"All right, cattle, get out of the ward. Let's clean up!"

"To the table, to the table, the first shift. You cattle, you didn't wash your hands."

Shatravka tried to leave the ward to go to the toilet.

"Where are you going?" asked an orderly.

"To the toilet."

"Turn around. Everyone goes together. And then you have to ask."

"I didn't know."

"Now you know."

Breakfast was a piece of black bread and a bowl of transparent soup with a dab of butter floating on the surface and several pieces of badly cleaned potatoes and barley on the bottom.

After breakfast, a long row formed in front of a table with various medicines, which the patients drank in handfuls while an orderly stood by to open their mouths to make sure that every tablet had been swallowed.

The patients were then returned to the ward, where Shatravka got his first piece of advice on how to conduct himself.

"Whatever you do," said one of the patients, "don't argue with the doctors and don't insist that you are sane. That will be treated as a flare-up of your illness."

Another patient asked Shatravka what he was in for. He responded that he was a border crosser.

"Don't worry," said the patient, "they won't keep you long. Five years and you'll be out."

"Five years?" Shatravka said in desperation.

"What are you getting excited about? Zabolotny is in his ninth year. Volodka over here is in his seventh."

"And how many years have you been here?" Shatravka asked of his new acquaintance.

"Ten."

A short time later, Shatravka was summoned to see the treating doctor for his department. He decided to agree that he was ill and attribute his every act of protest to the effects of his illness.

"Sit down," said the doctor, pointing to a chair opposite her table. She began reading the papers in Shatravka's file.

"Tell me," she said finally, "were there any mentally ill people among your relatives?"

"No," he said, "my brother and I are the first mentally ill persons of all our relations."

"What made you flee from the Soviet Union?"

"What do you mean? We did not want to flee from the Soviet Union—this is our motherland. Our parents live here. It never even occurred to us to remain in the West. In the first place, we didn't know the language, and where were we supposed to get the money? It would have been impossible to earn anything. After all, they've got unemployed of their own. Our neighbor, a former border guard, promised to take us across the border and then back again."

"Why did you curse and insult the officers when you were handed back at the border?" the doctor asked.

"Don't think that I didn't want to return to the Soviet Union," he said. "It was just that I was stunned to be put in handcuffs and to have the soldiers insult me as a 'traitor.' I wanted to avenge myself."

"In terms of your development," the doctor said, "you resemble a fourteen-year-old boy. Grow up and we'll write you out."

When Shatravka returned to the ward, patients shuffled back and forth in the narrow corridor between the rows of beds. Others slept. Shatravka thought about his performance in the doctor's office and came to the conclusion that he had put her on the wrong track, but he wondered how long he could keep up this farce.

"LUNCHTIME! Wash your hands. Where are you going, cattle?"

The hospital lunch consisted of 100 grams of black bread and 150 grams of gray-tinted "white bread," year-old sour cabbage with a third of a cup of compote to drink. After lunch, the patients were ordered to line up for their medicine. A nurse came running up to the line, looking for Shatravka. "You've also been assigned your medicine," she said.

Shatravka got in line and watched as those in front of him were given entire handfuls of pills.

Finally, he came to the front of the line and felt a flood of relief. They had assigned him two tablets of tisercin, a drug that, although powerful, was not debilitating and did not cause the recipient to lose control of his movements as other drugs did.

THE DAYS BEGAN to pass and, to a certain degree, Shatravka's body adapted to the medicines. He saw how fortunate he was by comparison with patients who received massive "horse's doses" of neuroleptics and who were also forced to work. They stood in a daze, shifting their weight from one foot to the other, holding out their hands and forearms from the elbow like bewildered kangaroos.

For Shatravka, each day began with a lineup, then breakfast, then another lineup, then the exercise period, another lineup, lunch, a lineup, cleanup work, dinner. He was assigned to washing the stairwell, but this was relatively easy because there was little dirt on the stairs.

Once he was out of quarantine, Shatravka was able to participate in the exercise periods in the hospital courtyard, where he socialized with other patients. For several months, he continued to wash the stairwells, but he was then unexpectedly assigned to dishwashing.

This proved to be fortunate because he exercised an hour later, and in the courtyard he spotted his brother.

Shatravka walked up to Mikhail and asked him how things were going.

Mikhail shook his head sadly.

"Don't worry, Misha," Shatravka said, "we'll survive this. No matter what, they'll write us out at some point."

"Write us out? . . . We can go out of our minds here," he said.

"What are they giving you?" Shatravka asked.

"They give me a whole pile of pills three times a day: triftazin, trisedil. I'm so dizzy from them that I have to ask for a corrector, and then it gets a little easier."

"They're giving them to you, but don't swallow them. Teach yourself to hide the medicine in your throat."

"That's easy to say, hide it. The orderlies check your entire mouth with a spatula, and if they notice something, they start giving you injections immediately."

The two brothers walked together in the dense crowd of patients. The courtyard resembled an open latrine. In the center was a large pile of coal covered with spittle and defecation, and each new group of patients augmented a nearby broad, yellow stream of urine. In the middle of the yard was an observation booth surrounded by dusty lilac bushes.

Shatravka saw that admitting to mental illness was not helping his brother. As they walked, he got an idea. He suggested to Mikhail that they try to explain to the doctors that they were not really ill but had only been pretending. He hoped that this would persuade the doctors to reduce the doses they were prescribing for Mikhail.

The next day, Shatravka went to see his treating doctor.

"Anna Vladimirovna," he said quietly, trying to control his nerves. "In prison and in the Serbsky Institute, I pretended to be ill."

"You know that simulation is also an illness," she said, interrupting him sharply.

"When we landed in prison," Shatravka said, "everyone insisted to us that we would be tried for treason. Our crossing of the border was done through such stupidity that it is shameful now even to think about it. We would have never decided on such a step ourselves if it hadn't been for our neighbor, the border guard. He promised to take us there and then back again."

"You are like little children," she said. "They persuaded you. . . . Didn't you have minds of your own?"

"We calculated naively and we didn't realize that we were committing a terrible crime," Shatravka said.

"All right," she said, "you can go. After we've treated you, we'll write you out."

Shatravka realized that he had failed. Not only had he not persuaded her that he had been lying about being ill, but he had given her reason to believe that he secretly considered himself to be sane and so was not being critical toward his illness.

The next day Shatravka went out into the exercise yard and met his brother, who was anxious to know what had happened during his talk with the doctor.

"Her answer was that lying is also an illness," Shatravka said. "Do you see where we've landed? Among genuine idiots. If we tell them the truth, they consider it a sign of illness. If we start to lie, they take it as a reliable remission."

Shatravka said there was no way out but to continue to agree with the doctors that they were ill.

"I don't think I can do it," Mikhail said. "I simply can't think. It's as if my brain has stopped as a result of all this medicine."

"Listen to me, Misha," Shatravka replied, "there is no other way. If you don't pretend to be sick, the doctors will decide that you are completely deranged."

ONE EVENING, a new nurse checked out Shatravka's ward and, apparently in no hurry to get out, began talking to Adam, one of the debilitated patients. When she grew tired of him, she turned to Shatravka and said, "What made you cross the border?"

"I did it out of foolishness," Shatravka said. "I wanted to travel."

"In order to travel?" she replied. "They've got plenty of their own unemployed. You would have been climbing in the garbage. That's why the Finns handed you back."

"A typical Soviet idiot," Shatravka thought to himself, but to argue with her would have been dangerous.

"It's a good thing you didn't murder anyone on the road," she said. "That's probably because you didn't meet anyone."

"What do you mean?" Shatravka objected. "We were the type of people who couldn't cut off the head of a chicken and you talk about killing a man."

"They would have killed you. That's for sure. In films, spies are always killed on the border."

"That's how it is in films," Shatravka said, "but in life it is entirely different. In the first place, we weren't spies. And in films they intentionally create sharp situations so it will be more entertaining."

"There it is, there is your illness!" she said. "You are an absolutely genuine sick person. You don't believe in anything. You need to be treated. Well, that's all right. You will be treated."

Shatravka began to curse himself for contradicting the nurse. He was sure she would report on the conversation to the doctors the following day.

The nurse left Shatravka alone and turned to the others in the ward.

"We'll soon build communism!" she said. "Now, we live well. We have everything and there is plenty of bread. Not like the way it was earlier. And when we build communism, it will be even better!"

Adam, who was feeble-minded, said, "What kind of communism? How long does it have to be built? And maybe we'll, in general, not build it."

"We'll build it, Adam. We'll build communism. We just have to work better. Just hope to God that there will be no war."

The nurse became emotional and her voice began to break. "The imperialists, the Americans, are arming. If it weren't for them, we would have built communism a long time ago. But what is America to us? Now China threatens us. But we'll smash them! Did we smash the Germans? We smashed them!"

As the discussion intensified, Adam jumped from his bed and he and the nurse began to discuss various strategic issues, but Shatravka could no longer bear to listen.

For him, the only relief from the atmosphere of the psychiatric hospital came at night. For all the many months that he was a prisoner, he dreamt dreams that closely resembled one another. He dreamt of crossing the border. There was always a chase and he ran with all his strength, aware that if he were caught, he would be put in a special psychiatric hospital. At the last moment, he found himself on the other side of the border and was seized by a feeling of the sweetest bliss. And then, the dreams were interrupted and he would toss and turn in bed trying to resurrect them.

VIKTOR DAVYDOV, a student from Kuibyshev, was arrested for circulating banned literature and sent to the Serbsky Institute in Moscow, where he was held for several weeks and examined by Dr. Svetlana Gerasimova.

"How is your mood?" she asked.

"I don't know," he said. "I see everything in black colors."

"This blackness—is it even or with shadows?"

Davydov suddenly realized she was trying to get him to say that he was having hallucinations and explained that the reference to "black colors" was only a metaphor.

During his stay in the Serbsky Institute, Davydov insisted on his sanity but was nonetheless diagnosed as suffering from "sluggish schizophrenia." He was then sent to the Butyrki prison, where he shared a cell with a thief who, as it happened, had been incarcerated in the Smolensk special psychiatric hospital and told him what to do if he was committed.

"You have to admit that you are ill," he said. "That is the only way to get out, and the earlier you do it the better."

From the Butyrki prison, Davydov was sent to a prison in Kazan prior to being admitted to the Kazan special psychiatric hospital. The guards told Davydov he had to have his head shaved. He refused and was immediately taken to a room and given shots of aminazine and haloperidol. The shots left him in a daze, burning with thirst but too weak even to rise from the mattress in his cell.

When it came time for Davydov to be transferred, he had to be carried down the steps.

The doctor at the special psychiatric hospital who admitted Davydov took pity on him. "Okay," he said, "three days relax."

IN THE SPECIAL psychiatric hospital, the treatment continued. Davydov was given majeptil, and he slipped again into a drug-induced daze. Davydov found that what passed through his mind resembled an unwinding film. The ability to think critically disappeared. His mind focused only on what was in front of him—the wall, a window, the door, another wall. He tried to stop the film and direct his thoughts, but it was impossible. His memory melted away and impressions created by his immediate surroundings bore in on him relentlessly. With a sense of horror, he became convinced that he was losing his mind.

AFTER TWO MONTHS at the Kazan special psychiatric hospital, Davydov was taken to the Sverdlovsk railroad station.

"Where are they taking me?" he asked a guard.

"Blagoveshchensk," the guard replied.

After a torturous forty-five-day train journey, Davydov arrived in Blagoveshchensk, on the Chinese border. He and four others were then taken to the hospital.

The walls of the hospital were wet and the windows in the wards frosted over. Davydov entered a long corridor, where, at regular intervals, patients gathered behind horizontal and vertical metal bars to look at the new arrivals.

The patients had been shaved bald and were dressed in tattered pajamas. They stared blankly, their faces transformed into odd masks by the medication. Davydov became convinced that they were more heavily medicated than the patients at Kazan.

Through the bars, they asked questions, "Where from?" "Why?" but their voices had a toneless quality.

Looking at their yellowed faces and frozen eyes, it seemed to Davydov that he had landed on another planet.

There were four other patients in his cell. One heard voices. Another claimed to converse with birds. The third was hyperactive. The last was withdrawn. Watching them, Davydov sank into the deepest despair.

As he waited to be examined by a psychiatrist, he decided to agree that he was mentally ill.

He was examined by Vyacheslav Belanovsky, the chief doctor in the receiving department.

"Do you consider yourself ill?" Belanovsky asked.

"Yes, of course," he said.

"Why do you consider yourself ill?"

"Because the doctors at the Serbsky Institute pronounced me ill," he said.

Other doctors also examined Davydov.

They asked him if he considered himself to be ill. He said yes, and they asked, "Why?"

"Because I am in a hospital," he replied, as if stating something obvious.

After several weeks, Davydov began to see that his strategy was a success.

At first, he was not given any medication. Finally, he was assigned a light dose of aminazine, which he was able to tolerate. Eventually, the doses of aminazine were discontinued and he was given only Valium.

Davydov was assigned to cleanup work in the kitchen and then to the textile shop, where he worked at a sewing machine making aprons. At the same time, however, he had contact with other political prisoners who, because they refused to agree that they were mentally ill, were medicated savagely.

Yegor Volkov, a worker from Nakhodka, was first committed in 1968 for leading a workers' protest against a violation of an agreement over pay. When the doctors asked Volkov, "Do you understand that you are ill?" he replied, "No, I am not sick, I am a political prisoner."

In response, Volkov was treated nearly without interruption. He received tisercin, haloperidol, aminazine, triftazin. He developed stomach ulcers and high blood pressure, but nothing would make him say he was mentally ill. After a time, it seemed he no longer thought of freedom but only of not giving in.

IN DECEMBER 1981, after a year in the hospital, Davydov was interviewed by Valentina Timofeeva, the chief doctor. "Tell me," she said, "do you understand that your past activities were the result of being ill?"

"I can't judge, I'm not a psychiatrist."

"But you must have some idea."

"No, I don't. At the Serbsky Institute, I was diagnosed as suffering from 'sluggish schizophrenia.'* In sluggish schizophrenia, the symptoms are very lightly expressed. The sick person has no idea

---

*A diagnosis frequently used to justify the psychiatric confinement of dissidents, but never accepted as medically valid in the West.

whether he is sick or not. This can be determined only by a qualified psychiatrist."

"All right, forget the question of illness. Tell me, when you engaged in your past activities, were you morally correct?"

"If I was ill, then what I did was right in that my activities were normal for a sick person."

"Do you plan to return to your former activities?"

"No, I don't plan to do any sick things."

Davydov spent one more year at Blagoveshchensk, receiving only Valium, and then he was freed. His two years at Blagoveshchensk was an unusually short time for a political prisoner.

ON DECEMBER 12, 1980, Iosif Terelya, a Ukranian nationalist, was called to the office of Colonel Babenko, the head of the Dnepropetrovsk special psychiatric hospital.

Waiting for him were Babenko; Dr. Nelya Butkevich, the head of the department where he was held; and Lieutenant Colonel Kapustin of the Dnepropetrovsk KGB. Terelya had spent three years in solitary confinement in the hospital and had only recently been moved to a general ward. Now the question was whether he should be released.

"Do you recognize that you are ill?" Butkevich asked.

"I was pronounced mentally ill by the leading psychiatrists in the Soviet Union," Terelya said.

"We know that," Babenko said, "but what do you think?"

"I think the same thing as the leading psychiatrists of the Soviet Union."

"That's not an answer," said Butkevich. "Obviously, we did not treat you enough."

"Nelya Mikhailovna, you are forgetting the condition I was in when I arrived here in 1977. It's only thanks to you that today I can answer questions so intelligently."

"All the patients," Butkevich said, "say they are healthy; you say that you're ill."

"I say that I *was* ill, but now, thanks to you, my health is better."

"Tell me, Terelya," said Butkevich, "did you do the right thing when you wrote a protest against the arrest of Rudenko?"

"I don't remember," Terelya said, "because I was ill."

"What do you think about the grain embargo that was imposed by Carter?"

"I don't know any Carter."

"Carter is the president of the United States."

"That's all the more reason for me not to know him. I've only seen Brezhnev in photographs, so how could I know Carter?"

"But you and your wife sent a protest to Carter about emigration for political, economic, and religious reasons. Well, did he help you?"

"I don't remember about the period when I was ill."

"Terelya," Kapustin said, "there is a decision to free you. How do you view this?"

"I think it's quite normal," Terelya said. "I've been cured. This is a hospital, after all, not a prison."

"But Korchak says that we are hangmen and he is in a prison," said Babenko.

"Korchak and I are not necessarily in agreement," Terelya said. "But if he has such an opinion, perhaps he has a clearer view of things."

"Iosif Mikhailovich," Babenko said, "you have said that you are a Christian, not a political man. What did you mean by that?"

"Just that politics never interested me and I always aspired to God and to love."

"But belief in God," Babenko continued, "is politics. The capitalists build their aggressive foreign policy on this."

"Belief in God is absurd," added Butkevich, "in the scientific medical literature, this is called mass psychosis."

"I didn't know about that," Terelya said, "or I guess I just never read about it."

"This is because you don't read specialized literature," Butkevich said. "Did you know," he said, changing the subject, "that Plyushch is in a Canadian clinic and that he is being treated there?"

"I'm not acquainted with Plyushch and don't know anything about his illness."

"What about your friend Plakhotnyuk, is he ill or not?"

"Plakhotnyuk is a doctor, he knows better. I haven't seen him since 1972, at which time he was normal."

"In fact," said Butkevich, "he's sicker than you are."

"Do you know," Kapustin said, "that your wife gave information to the West that we hold mentally healthy people in special psychiatric hospitals?"

"My wife is also a Soviet doctor," Terelya said, "she has her own opinion."

"Well, you should tell her that you are ill," said Butkevich.

"She doesn't believe me."

"What do you have to say about Sakharov?" she asked.

"I'm not acquainted with him."

"Do you know that Sakharov receives money from the CIA and subverts the strength of our government?"

"I don't know about this."

"Do you believe the Soviet press?"

"Of course I do, I'm not ill."

"Don't be sarcastic. Sakharov is an enemy. Don't think that we're afraid to send him here, too; it's just that the authorities wait for the moment when he will change his views."

"Terelya," Babenko said, "you announced that you would work to legalize the Uniate Church. How do you feel about that now?"

"I didn't know that there was an underground church."

"You wrote about this yourself in the Western press," Kapustin said.

"Obviously, I was very sick at that time."

"All right," said Kapustin, "but you also want a separate Ukraine."

"I thought it was separate."

"In general, yes," Kapustin said, "but you want it to separate from Russia."

"Excuse me," Terelya said, "but all of the republics, as independent entities, enter into the framework of the Soviet Union."

"All right," said Kapustin, "but how do you feel about the withdrawal of the Ukraine from the federation of Soviet republics?"

"The Ukraine is not ready for this."

"Why?" Kapustin asked. "Is it the wrong time or just the wrong situation?"

"Things are all right as they are. Now you don't need a visa for a trip to Moscow."

"If there hadn't been so much commotion about you," said Babenko, "you would have been home a long time ago."

"Who made the commotion?"

"Your false friends," said Kapustin. "Sakharov and those around him used your illness to subvert Soviet power."

"How can a man's illness subvert such a powerful regime?"

"It's true," said Kapustin. "And you were used by Zionist circles in their goals."

"I don't know any Zionists."

"They act through hidden networks."

"This is something I don't understand."

"This is not for an ordinary person to understand," said Kapustin.

"We must be certain," said Butkevich, "that you won't end up here again. You have a wife, a daughter. Live for them. Don't get involved in any more nasty affairs. Understand that we are closer to you than any of your so-called friends. We really don't want to do you any harm."

"Then how am I to understand the fact that you forbid me to write or to paint?"

"When you begin to write poems," said Butkevich, "your illness returns. In the future, there is no need for you to write any poetry, even poems about flowers."

"Who is going to give me work once I'm free?" asked Terelya.

"Don't worry about that," said Kapustin, "we'll speak to the comrades in Uzhgorod and everything will be taken care of."

"Just rest," said Babenko. "Work won't disappear. The most important thing that you must do is to understand our Soviet reality."

10

Glasnost

In the beginning was the Word.
—John 1:1

As DAWN BROKE on a June day in 1991 in the forest outside Moscow, a car bearing Sergei Rybin, a reporter for Russian television, and his cameraman drove unnoticed through the gates of Nazarievo, a vacation community for the Soviet elite. The two men parked the car and then, walking along a dirt road, approached a security guard outside a food store. Rybin nodded at the guard, and the cameraman began filming the two-story wooden dachas in the village with their spreading verandas. He then started filming the soaring birch trees and the abundant goods in the store. "They live well here," said Rybin to the guard, who did nothing to interfere with their filming.

"No one lives better," the guard said, a sad smile breaking his wrinkled face.

"How do they live in comparison with you?" Rybin asked.

"They get caviar and take it by the kilogram," said the guard, who was wearing a blue uniform with green epaulettes, "but I can't even have a hundred grams. They are given fifteen kilograms of sugar but in my village the quota is one and a half kilograms per person."

"There's no justice," said Rybin.

"No," said the guard, "of course not."

Eight days later, the segment was shown on "Vesti," the nightly news program of independent Russian television, in a report on the privileged lives of high party officials. The following day, shoppers queueing in Moscow's barren food stores were outraged. "Did you see the program last night?" they asked. "Those scoundrels."

For five years, glasnost was used as a weapon in the political struggle between Gorbachev and his opponents. As a result, the heroes and villains in Soviet citizens' political pantheon changed, as did the understanding of hostile and friendly countries and the ideological conflict that gave birth to the cold war. Having started as an intraparty ploy, however, glasnost ended by destroying the faith in communism that had been the regime's greatest source of strength. The change, in turn, doomed the system because it was faith in communism that had helped to justify the sacrifices of an entire people.

MARCH 1982

The snow outside was coming down in streams, illuminated by the light of the streetlamps, as Leonid Borodin, a writer and Russian nationalist, tried to explain the mentality fostered in the Soviet Union with the help of the regime's control over information.

"What separates us is not just a different political system," he said, "but two different states of consciousness. In the West, people organize life around things which are tangible—a big house, clothes, a new car. But people here have no access to those things. What matters to us is the victory of our ideals. Soviet people are very sincere. They sincerely want for Negroes in the United States to have full freedom. They want for the day to come when the peasants in Salvador will see justice triumph. There is no selfishness here. We want good for everyone."

Borodin took a final drag on the end of a cigarette and rubbed it out in a metal ashtray. "When they built the Bratsk hydroelectric station," he said, "I was a Komsomol volunteer. We lived in tents in the middle of the wilderness. There was no fresh food and no running water. We were tortured by mosquitoes. There was a prison camp nearby with about a hundred prisoners. We ate worse than the prisoners and we worked harder. After work, we were so tired that we fell into our beds. That was in 1957. There was a lot of romanticism then. We suffered more than the prisoners, yet, to this day, I remember those days fondly."

Borodin left the room, paced for a few minutes in the corridor, and, when he returned, sat down, lit another cigarette, and fell into a long, racking cough.

The KGB had conducted a search of Borodin's apartment a month earlier, and he knew his days of freedom were numbered. With a respiratory ailment, his life would be in danger in a labor camp.

"People live badly in this country," he said, "but we are sure that we are stronger. If it becomes necessary, we will eat the leather off our shoes. Americans won't eat the leather off their shoes. If Reagan asked them to, he wouldn't be reelected. But we will. Capitalism is the exploitation of man by man and that is evil. We have to fight against that evil. If America builds one hundred tanks, we'll tighten our belts and build one hundred and two.

"People here feel colossal righteousness in their behavior. Did you ever watch Gromyko at the United Nations when he speaks? His expressions? There is not a trace of self-doubt. He shows absolute confidence in his correctness.

"This regime doesn't want territorial supremacy or economic supremacy. It wants ideological supremacy, the ideological supremacy of socialism over the whole world. This is why, when the West stands on the sidelines and shouts you are slaves, bound together, following like animals, why don't you free yourselves, the only answer from us is an ironic laugh. We are ascending Everest. Before us is the radiant goal and nothing will stop us."

The mentality described by Borodin ruled in the Soviet Union for years, mobilizing the population to sacrifice in the name of an earthly paradise that was forever receding in the distance.

The late writer Vladimir Kormer said, during a conversation in the early 1980s, that, in fact, there was moral political unity in the Soviet Union but not behind Marxism-Leninism. The unity existed behind the desire to live according to an idea and to force all others to do likewise. It was the drive toward unanimity that explained some of the negative characteristics of the dissident milieu, which was permeated with rumor-mongering and intrigues and divided by intolerance and sectarianism.

Kormer thought that, with a few outstanding exceptions, the ideological mentality, the sharp rejection of anything alien, was common to all Soviet people. "If Solzhenitsyn had come to power," he said, "he would have hung Sakharov or at least exiled him. If Sakharov had come to power in the Soviet Union, he would have been more liberal, but if Sakharov's wife had come to power, she would gladly have hung Solzhenitsyn."

In addition to sectarianism and a basic lack of respect for the opinion of others, there was a leadership complex that ran particularly deep in the intelligentsia. In 1968, before the invasion of Czechoslovakia, Pavel Litvinov and Viktor Krasin tried unsuccessfully to agree on who was the leader of the dissidents. During an argument, Krasin said to Litvinov, "How dare you speak to me that way, I'm the ideologue of the Russian democratic movement." This did not impress Litvinov, who insisted that he was more important than Krasin.

The ideological atmosphere of Soviet society was reflected in relations between people who concerned themselves in any way with politics. Among such people—and this category included the majority of the unofficial intelligentsia—friendship almost always had connotations of comradeship with its demand for uncritical idealization. The intensity of these friendships was evident among dissidents who formed an extended family on political grounds, virtually living at each other's houses, exhibiting photographs of each other, and interesting themselves deeply in each other's personal affairs. It went without saying that this type of friendship became insupportable if there was the slightest change in the political outlook of the parties. Under those circumstances, a disagreement between friends was understood as a betrayal, and the closest friendship could turn into the most unforgiving enmity, with people suddenly waking up to and expatiating at length about the repulsive and despicable personality traits they had overlooked for years when the object of such an attack was a close and valued friend.

The importance of control over the information media in this situation could not be overestimated. With every significant event in the world, the Soviet media was transformed into a vast echo chamber that broadcast a weird but completely consistent version of current reality. This false reality was interposed by the media between the average citizen and empirical reality, nullifying the role of individual judgment. For the Soviet citizen, encased in a seamless shroud of false information, it was reality as understood by the regime, and not reality itself, that shaped his basic political convictions.

The onset of glasnost created an opening in this claustral system. As a result, its effect proved both devastating and impossible to control. The crisis of consciousness led immediately to pressure to limit glasnost as a destabilizing element. Party liberals, however, now had a stake in glasnost. At the same time, journalists began to assert their independence. Many had spent their professional lives writing propaganda and, given the chance to reclaim their integrity, were not ready to be silenced again. They took risks, and, defending their right to express themselves freely, they played an important role in the mental liberation of the Soviet people as well.

ON AN AUTUMN DAY in 1989, Vladimir Vigiliansky, a journalist with the magazine *Ogonyek*, got off a bus in an outlying area of Yessentuki, a city in the Krasnodar region, and walked past a row of ramshackle wooden houses to a quiet lane. A light wind rustled a sea of fallen leaves.

Vigiliansky came to a small house and knocked on the door. After a few minutes, the door opened and he recognized the daughter of a Moscow friend, who invited him into a tiny room. Coal glowed in the iron stove and the walls of the room were covered with books and drawings, mostly landscapes in colored pencils, charcoal, and watercolors. The daughter of Vigiliansky's Moscow friend took his coat and led him to Yerofiniya Kersnovskaya, who lay, half-paralyzed, in a narrow metal bed.

Several months earlier, Vigiliansky had read Kersnovskaya's memoirs of her years in the Stalin-era labor camps, which included hundreds of drawings of camp life, and he had decided to try to find her. He had read camp literature before, but what struck him about Kersnovsksaya's book was its insistence that the experience of the camps actually brought the prisoners closer to God. The text, at 1,500 typewritten pages, was too long to be published in *Ogonyek*, but Vigiliansky wanted, at least, to publish the drawings. There had been no revealing photographs or films of Stalinist labor camps and so the drawings were a priceless historical document.

Kersnovskaya, who was eighty-three years old, looked up at Vigiliansky with a curious expression. Her last official visit had been on the occasion of her arrest. Now, after years in the labor camps and almost two decades of work as a miner, she was completely bedridden. She could not even walk to get water from the pump on the street.

Vigiliansky began by trying to tell her about *Ogonyek*. He told her that *Ogonyek* would not rest until all the crimes of the Stalin period had been exposed. "There is nothing to be afraid of now," he said. "Thanks to Gorbachev, it's possible to say and do anything. Who could have predicted this?"

To Vigiliansky's surprise, Kersnovskaya seemed to be little impressed. "I don't trust this Gorbachev," she said. "He is a liar, and if he lies in one thing, he'll lie in all others."

"Your drawings are powerful anti-Stalinist propaganda," Vigiliansky said. "They need to be published."

"I want to publish my book as a whole. To publish only the drawings would give a false impression."

"But if the drawings are published in *Ogonyek*, you'll become famous. It will be easier to find a publisher for your book."

Kersnovskaya fell silent. Vigiliansky knew from her friends in Moscow that seeing her book published was all Kersnovskaya had to live for. For the next several hours, he argued that she had an obligation to share her drawings with the people. Finally, as darkness fell and the lights went on in the surrounding houses, Kersnovskaya agreed to permit publication of the drawings in *Ogonyek*.

RAISA BOBKOVA, who taught the history of the Communist Party at the Institute of Trade in Moscow, reacted with shock to new information that was appearing in the press. There were articles about the suppression of genetics in the Soviet Union. Also, more material about the Bolshevik revolutionaries was being published, much of which showed them to be ruthless and power-hungry. For years, Raisa had taught her students that the first and second Soviet five-year plans were overfulfilled; now she learned that they had not been fulfilled and, in fact, had not even come close to being fulfilled. She had taught for years that the focus of the Fourteenth Communist Party Congress was industrialization, but new information showed that the real point of the congress had been the destruction of Lev Kamenev and Grigory Zinoviev,* and that Stalin, besides changing the speech he had given at the congress for publication, had also penciled in applause.

Raisa was so ashamed that she wanted to hide, although some of

---

*Two of the original Bolshevik leaders who were purged and eventually executed by Stalin.

the questions raised in the newspapers had occurred to her before. Every week, attention at the institute turned to the letters column of *Ogonyek*, in which survivors described their experience during the Stalin era. One day after the magazine published a series of letters describing the fate of farmers in the Ukraine during collectivization, including mass starvation and cannibalism, a colleague approached Raisa in tears.

"Did you see *Ogonyek* this morning?" she asked.

"Yes," Raisa said.

"Well," she said, "it seems to me that all the years that we spent teaching, we can just cross out."

At first, Raisa continued to defend the party. In an argument with her friend Yelena Sukhorukikh she said, "We started with nothing and the party is responsible for our welfare." She also continued to work on an article about the role of propaganda, arguing that it inspired the political activism of youth.

As the months went by, however, and the stream of revelations turned into a flood, Raisa began to reevaluate her view of reality. She thought about the nature of man and the sources of evil. She wondered what it was that allowed some men to manipulate others and turn them into raw material for the furtherance of their ambitions.

ONE MORNING in August 1990, Vigiliansky was surprised in his office at *Ogonyek* by a young girl dragging an enormous bag of letters and telegrams along the floor behind her. As the leader of the public fight to free *Ogonyek* from party control, Vigiliansky had called on the magazine's readers to send letters of support, but he had not expected such a response. He hoisted the brown paper sack onto his desk and began reading.

"We demand freedom for *Ogonyek*!" read one letter.

"Tell the apparatchiks to keep their dirty hands off *Ogonyek*," said another.

"We are with you! If the evildoers win, I cancel my subscription," said another.

Vigiliansky called other members of the editorial staff to his office. Almost a thousand letters had arrived in one day and all of them supported *Ogonyek*'s fight for independence. "Take these letters," Vigiliansky said to his secretary, "put them in bundles, and send them to the Communist Party Central Committee."

Vigiliansky then took the party to court, challenging its right to retain assets that it had defined as its "property." This was more controversy than the party wanted. With its power crumbling, party officials did not seek a public confrontation over the way they appropriated hundreds of newspapers, magazines, and printing plants in the 1960s. They dropped their claim to *Ogonyek* and the state committee registered it as a magazine under its staff's control.

ON A NIGHT in September 1989, Vladislav Starkov, the editor of *Arguments and Facts*, the largest newspaper in the Soviet Union, went to the front of a room crowded with members of the staff and said, "Gorbachev is not satisfied with our work. He says that we are organizing the masses against the party and has suggested that I resign." Starkov looked pale and nervous. "Boys," he said, "nothing works. They have too much strength." A wave of indignation went through the hall. The reporters knew that if Starkov was fired, a new editor would fire them and it would be the end of *Arguments and Facts* as an independent newspaper.

After Starkov finished speaking, Nikolai Vzyatkov, his deputy, suggested that the staff elect Starkov the newspaper's editor. He passed out paper ballots and the staff voted unanimously to name Starkov to the post. From that point on, he was not only an appointed leader but also an elected one. He told the meeting that he would refuse to leave his post.

For years, *Arguments and Facts* was a bulletin for Communist Party lecturers. Its task was "counterpropaganda" and it carried articles on unemployment, drug abuse, and crime in the West as well as statistics, many of them inaccurate. In 1987, however, in keeping with the new policy of glasnost, a decision was made in the party Central Committee to provide more information to party lecturers, and the principal vehicle became *Arguments and Facts*.

The newspaper began to print answers to readers' questions. It published items on the price of products in the collective farmers' market, demonstrating, for the first time, the existence of serious inflation in the Soviet Union. It also published information on auto accidents, alcoholism, and thefts. In 1988, it started to print birth and death rates, which had always been strictly classified.

Almost immediately, the newspaper gained a reputation as a

place where citizens' inquiries could be answered honestly. Its circulation increased and it was inundated with new letters. In an article comparing meat consumption in the United States and the Soviet Union, *Arguments and Facts* said that consumption in the Soviet Union was 62 kilograms a year (in reality, it was only 40). But it also stated that the annual figure for the United States was 120 kilograms. In November 1988, *Arguments and Facts* stunned readers by saying that the norm in America was 57.3 square meters of living space per person compared to only 9 square meters per person in the Soviet Union.

The newspaper, however, could not continue indefinitely publishing truthful information under the tutelage of the party.

In May 1989, Soviet citizens were transfixed by the first session of the Congress of People's Deputies, and in keeping with the new spirit of democracy, *Arguments and Facts* asked its readers to rate the deputies they thought had performed best at the Congress. To the surprise of the staff, Sakharov received the highest rating followed by Yeltsin and Gavriil Popov, an economist. Gorbachev finished seventeenth.

Starkov was on vacation when the survey results were published. When he returned, he was called to appear before the Central Committee and ordered "to put his party card on the table." A few days later, Gorbachev called a meeting of the editors of the central newspapers. Picking up the issue of *Arguments and Facts* with the survey, he accused the press of "irresponsible leftist lurches." He then said, referring to the survey, "Such things disorient the population," and told Starkov that if he were in his place he would resign.

GENNADY MARCHENKO, a journalism instructor at Moscow State University, began to give lectures on the ideological struggle in the early 1980s. The themes were well prepared. There were several worlds, the world of capitalism and the world of socialism and an undefined third world for which there was a continuous battle. Capitalism was organized to destroy socialism and to force the socialist countries to adopt its ideology.

Information was supplied to Marchenko in the Moscow Party Committee and by *Arguments and Facts*. If there was a summit meeting, he described how the U.S. president looked, how often the leaders met, what they agreed on and where they disagreed. He told the audience that the American president sometimes asked about dissidents and the leaders often discussed exchanges.

Gennady tried to stiffen the ideological resolve of his listeners. He explained that capitalists tried to use psychological methods against the Soviet Union, including the distribution of music, T-shirts, and videos of films like *Rocky* and *Rambo*, which he had never seen but which he described as hostile to the socialist world and designed to destroy the spirit of youth. He also frequently talked about Vsevolod Novgorodtsev, a disc jockey for the BBC Russian service, whom he had never met. He described Novgorodtsev's habits, how he related to people, joked with them, and tried to put them at their ease. But, he explained, the purpose of his program was to insult the Soviet Union.

When glasnost began, Gennady assumed that it would be temporary. He remembered the Hundred Flowers Campaign in China, when intellectuals were encouraged to express themselves and then were repressed, and he assumed the same thing would happen in the Soviet Union.

Nonetheless, as more and more factual information became available, particularly in the previously orthodox *Arguments and Facts*, he began to have doubts. There began to be a change in the political atmosphere. Audience members at lectures began to ask questions. They inquired about the power struggle in the leadership and about Gorbachev's wife, Raisa. Many expressed outrage over the fact that Raisa accompanied Gorbachev on his travels abroad and began to ask, "Who elected her?"

IN 1987, Soviet authorities began to stop jamming Western radio stations and the newspapers started to criticize low Soviet living standards. All of this took Gennady by surprise. One morning, however, he had an even bigger shock. The Soviet press published a shortened version of a speech by Ronald Reagan, the chief imperialist himself. Reagan spoke about the need to establish cultural relations and, as it transpired, only a few paragraphs about the situation of human rights in the Soviet Union were censored.

Marchenko had long had doubts about some of the arguments he made in his lectures. For example, he suspected that state property removed the stimulus to economic initiative, but he never spoke about this. As perestroika gathered force, however, he began to be braver. He moved from exposing the ideological enemy to self-exposure. He said, for example, that there were no important ideological influences in American music, and the fact that a Russian put a pair of American jeans on his Russian behind did not mean that he was a victim of ideological aggression.

In fact, Gennady realized that the lecturers had themselves been brainwashed. On a fall afternoon in 1987, he spoke on the ideological struggle to instructors in the railroad institute and, for the first time, expressed views that had been ripening in his mind over the previous two years. He said the balance of forces in the world was changing and there was a need for contacts instead of armed confrontation. The ideological struggle would not disappear but would instead become a civilized argument between people who had things in common.

Marchenko's speech evoked livid objections, but it was an act of self-liberation. In a lecture to a group of students, he questioned the notion, which is central to Marxism, that it is society that forms the individual personality. He said that the Marxist conception was too narrow and that it made personality the hostage of society. In a lecture on religion, he said it was necessary to consider the positive aspects of religion, including the cleansing of the soul in communication with God. There had been a powerful religious impulse throughout history.

As liberalization progressed in the Soviet Union and relations with the West steadily improved, lectures on the ideological struggle, which had always been well attended because of their aggressivity, began to lose popularity. At the same time, Marchenko noticed that other lecturers were expressing themselves freely. In factory meeting halls and the auditorium of the Knowledge Society near Dzerzhinsky Square, lecturers, who had spent decades answering "Western propaganda" that their audience had never been given the opportunity to hear, were now arguing that it was time for reconciliation with the West, asserting that a great deal of what had been written in the West about the aggressive behavior of the Soviet Union had been accurate.

In late 1988, as Soviet newspapers filled with articles of a pro-Western nature, lectures on the irreconcilable struggle between two ways of life began to be increasingly rare. Finally, the Knowledge Society, which provided lecturers in response to requests from party organizations, canceled all further lectures on the ideological struggle. Lecturers were no longer ready to speak on the topic and the audience for it had disappeared.

AFTER THE MEETING in the office of *Arguments and Facts*, Starkov suffered a minor stroke and stopped coming to work. This, however, proved fortuitous. When the Central Committee began calling the newspaper to ask when Starkov was going to submit his resignation, they were told he was ill and the matter would be discussed when he got well.

In the meantime, members of the editorial staff organized a campaign in Starkov's defense. The first step was to approach the foreign press, which started to write about the confrontation. Reporters from *Arguments and Facts* then approached Soviet publications. At first, the Soviet press was afraid to take Starkov's part. Finally, however, Vladimir Molchanov, the host of the popular television program "Up to and After Midnight," invited Starkov to appear on his program and describe his conflict with the authorities. With that, the press also began to rally to Starkov's defense.

The party authorities, aware of *Arguments and Facts*'s popularity, had hoped to remove Starkov quietly, even offering him positions with other newspapers or magazines. Pickets in support of Starkov, however, appeared outside the paper's offices on Malaya Bronnaya Street, and meetings in its defense were held in large factories. The employees of the Moscow subway threatened to strike if action was taken against *Arguments and Facts*.

The staff lobbied high officials and particularly the board of directors of the Knowledge Society, which officially had to vote to fire Starkov. Finally, on the night the vote was to be taken, busloads of workers arrived in front of the Knowledge Society headquarters with signs reading, HANDS OFF *ARGUMENTS AND FACTS!* Inside the building, Starkov's assistant editors paced nervously in the corridor outside the meeting hall where the vote was taking place.

Shortly before 6 p.m., the doors of the meeting room opened and a smiling Starkov informed his supporters that the battle had been won. Behind him, the board members of the Knowledge Society filed out, and they were also smiling. The society had voted not to demand Starkov's resignation. A body that had previously been totally subordinated to the party had chosen to heed the voice of public opinion instead.

ON A PEACEFUL AFTERNOON in May 1989, Natasha Serova, a Leningrad television journalist, and a cameraman left their car in the village of Levashevo and began to follow a rutted road in the direction of a nearby pine forest. As they walked, they passed dachas with wooden fences and piles of chopped wood in the yards. Finally, the forest closed in around them. After about fifteen minutes, they came to a clearing. It was here, according to a KGB officer who had spoken to Serova ten days earlier, that the bodies of thousands of Stalin-era purge victims were buried.

The cameraman began filming and Natasha stood in the tall grass, now filled with wildflowers. The light filtering through the branches of the towering pine trees gave the clearing the atmosphere of a cathedral. She tried to imagine how it had been—the exhaust of the trucks, the echo of constant shots in the woods, the fresh corpses, each with a bullet in the back of the neck.

Finally, the cameraman said he had filmed enough and they returned to Leningrad, where the footage was used in a broadcast of the program "The Fifth Wheel" about the Stalin era.

The next morning the telephone rang in Serova's office. She could tell from the caller's voice what she was about to say. "Are you telling me that our life was in vain?" said the caller. After each broadcast on the Stalin era, there were waves of such calls, many from people on the edge of despair.

"If the ideology of the government was false," Natasha said, "this does not mean that life was in vain. The ideology was not right, but life was not in vain."

IN 1988, Bella Kurkova, a journalist in the youth division of Leningrad television, and four other colleagues, Vyacheslav Kanavalov, Viktor Pravdyuk, Clara Fatova, and Serova, met at the Kavkaz Restaurant to discuss the possibility of organizing a new program that would combine reporting and a review of the arts. For years, the journalists had suffered under stringent ideological censorship. The release of political prisoners, however, had given them hope that they were witnessing the start of a new era. They agreed to try to create a new program and to call it "The Fifth Wheel."

Serova and Fatova began filming, using spare equipment as it became available. By March 1988, two broadcasts had been recorded. The first program was a portrait of the artist Pavel Filonov, a member of the Russian avant-garde who refused to adapt to the requirements of socialist realism. The second was a three-hour satirical sketch by the comedian Arkady Raikin. Against the background of completely orthodox programming, both caused a sensation. The station was swamped with congratulatory letters and telegrams and the career of "The Fifth Wheel" was launched.

"The Fifth Wheel" began to discuss other artists of the avant-garde, including Malevich and Kandinsky; banned poets such as Mandelstam, Pasternak, Akhmatova, and Brodsky; and the bards Alexander Galich, Yuli Kim, and Alexander Gorodintsky. Soon, nearly all of Leningrad and much of Moscow was staying up late to watch "The Fifth Wheel."

In May 1988, with the anti-Stalin campaign having begun in earnest, the staff of "The Fifth Wheel" invited victims of Stalin-era repression and their relatives to come to the headquarters of Leningrad Television on Chapigina Street to tell their stories. The meeting took place on Sunday, May 14. By 10 a.m., the street was filled with thousands of persons bearing documents and photographs. Inside the building, Serova saw that every floor was crowded with people trying to learn the fate of parents and grandparents, or at least the time and place of their death. The crush of people continued until late at night. Everyone was weeping. As Serova and a cameraman went through the crowd, asking one person after another to describe the circumstances of a loved one's arrest, what was most painful was to see that many of them, fifty years after a relative was taken in the night, still nourished the hope that somewhere, in the vast Soviet Union, he or she might still be alive.

IN 1987, Marina Filatova, a teacher of scientific communism, was on leave from the Institute of Oil and Gas, working on a graduate degree at Moscow State University, when the press began to publish letters from readers and, for the first time, the results of public opinion polls that showed the disaffection of workers. Filatova had always taught her students that the Soviet Union was the homeland of workers, but with the publication of these polls, she began to question how much she really knew about workers. Not long after the articles started appearing, she was invited to participate in a polling project organized by the department of sociology at the university and, curious, she agreed to go.

On a summer afternoon in 1987, Filatova appeared before a group of workers in Ivanovo in the wagon where they normally ate lunch and passed out questionnaires. The workers, who perspired freely in the wagon as the sun refracted through the grimy windows, and whose faces were dirty and bruised, studied Filatova with a mixture of annoyance and curiosity. She explained that the Ministry of Construction wanted to know what had changed during the first two years of perestroika. "Take as much time as you like," she said, "and if there is something you would like to add, use the space at the end." Outside, other workers were returning to the construction site after their forty-five-minute lunch break and cranes had begun working again on the skeleton of what was to be a metal processing factory. Inside the airless wagon, however, the men sat at their places without moving.

"I'm not writing anything," one of them said.

"Why not?" asked Filatova.

"Do you really think your questionnaires will change anything?"

Filatova said that change was coming. The fact that the ministry had sent her to conduct a survey showed that there was a new attitude toward the feelings of workers. The workers, however, did not react and no one made a move to fill out the questionnaires.

Finally, the chief engineer intervened. He accused the workers of trying to intimidate Filatova and told them that no one was leaving the wagon until they had filled out the forms. The workers then answered the questionnaires and left the wagon to return to work.

The scene was the same everywhere. In Orel, Filatova told workers at the site of a future sugar factory that by answering the questionnaires they would help the ministry to improve their conditions; still they refused to do so until forced by their superiors. In Kursk, at the site of another factory under construction, the workers, at first, also would not answer the questions.

For years Filatova lectured students that, in the Soviet Union, the means of production belonged to all. But the workers she interviewed obviously did not think that the means of production belonged to them. Her doubts deepened when the testimony of survivors of

Stalin-era atrocities began to be shown on "The Fifth Wheel." Filatova was moved by the stories of people who could be living next door.

In 1987–88, Filatova's life assumed a strange pattern. Consigned to continue writing a thesis on an orthodox theme during the day, she began at night to visit the special collections of the Institute for Scientific Information, which contained books that had been banned in the Soviet Union but were freely available in the West. Access to the special collections was restricted to teachers of ideological subjects who were considered politically reliable, and Filatova started to read books about democratic society and the works of Weber and Machiavelli.

Filatova had been raised on the notion that, in politics, the ends justify the means, but she was beginning to think that the problem was not that simple. If the ultimate goal of a system was the welfare of the individual, the means the system employed could not be immoral. If, however, the goal of a system was to advance the interests of a specific class, the means the system employed were almost automatically immoral because it made sense to repress all other classes. This, in turn, raised another question. If communism was not scientific, what was it? Nonscientific communism?

At Moscow State University, where she also gave lectures in scientific communism while working on her thesis, the students began to stamp their feet when lectures commenced. Some sat and read the newspapers. Many wrote letters to the dean asking him to cancel the subject because it did not conform to reality.

In December, Filatova completed her dissertation on economic relations between the Soviet Union and the countries of COMECON (Council for Mutual Economic Assistance).* In January 1989, she returned to the Institute of Oil and Gas, where the students were no less rebellious than those at the university. She went to a faculty meeting and, in the presence of fifteen teachers, announced she was refusing to teach scientific communism any longer. From now on, she said, she would teach political science. The head of the faculty, unwilling to risk a confrontation before a group of teachers, many of whose faith in the ideology had also been sorely tested by the events of recent years, reluctantly agreed.

---

*A body founded in 1949 by the Soviet Union to promote the economic integration of the Eastern bloc.

. . .

THE SELF-EMANCIPATION of "The Fifth Wheel" created near-panic in the Leningrad party organization, which found that they could not even impose minor restrictions on the program for fear of the public's response. In September 1988, "The Fifth Wheel" showed a film of police breaking up a demonstration at the Kurapaty burial ground in Belorussia, where the bodies of thousands of victims of Stalin-era terror were exhumed. The segment was banned by the station management but, in response, the staff of "The Fifth Wheel" refused to do the program. The next day, three thousand people demonstrated in protest outside the Leningrad telecenter; in the end, the film was shown.

In December 1988, at the time of the Armenian earthquake, Kurkova prepared a commentary blaming the deaths of fifty thousand people on shoddy construction in a known seismic zone. The director of Leningrad television ordered Kurkova to drop the commentary. She responded by denouncing the censorship on the air. It was the first time that a broadcaster had openly challenged censorship on live television, but no action was taken against her.

As the press became freer, the mood of the people started to change. The journalists of "The Fifth Wheel" became celebrities, easily recognizable on the street, and passersby who once avoided television cameramen now spoke willingly on camera in the belief that their opinions mattered and something might change.

At the end of 1988, in an attempt to influence journalists through persuasion, Galina Barinova, the head of the department of ideology in the Leningrad Party Committee, came to a meeting of the staff of Leningrad television. "We know the people," she said, "and what you are doing leads to an unhealthy atmosphere. We are afraid of explosions and bloodshed. Don't forget, the party started perestroika." Her appeal, however, had little force without the threat of firings, and, in fact, was ignored.

By the beginning of 1989, as the Soviet Union prepared for its first semi-free elections, Leningrad was a different city from what it had been only a year earlier, in no small measure because of "The Fifth Wheel."

The broadcasts that had the most important political effect were three programs on the privileges of the party elite. The first focused on leaders' dachas on Stone Island near Leningrad. Zoya Belyayeva, a reporter for "The Fifth Wheel," climbed the walls with a camera-man to film the lavish mansions, some of which had servants' quarters. The last segment was aired on March 17. Nine days later, every important party leader in the Leningrad area was defeated in his bid for election to the All-Union Supreme Soviet, including the oblast and city party first secretaries.

THE RESULTS LEFT the local party in a state of shock, and the first reaction was to send an investigative commission to Leningrad television. At a joint plenary meeting of the city and oblast party committees, "The Fifth Wheel" was denounced. Speakers said it was little wonder that the population had voted against the candidates of the party after months of brainwashing by the program.

For Kurkova, the pressure meant that "The Fifth Wheel" itself was threatened, and she was inspired to enter the second round of elections. During the campaign, she participated in a televised debate and denounced Yuri Soloviev, the still powerful head of the Leningrad party organization, for his monopolization of television time and facilities.

Two days after the elections, in which Kurkova finished well but did not gain a seat in the Congress, she received a summons from the Leningrad party organization to explain her remarks during the election debate. The session of the Congress of People's Deputies had opened, however, and it was no longer possible for the Leningrad party to give orders to one of the most popular television personalities in the country. Kurkova refused to go. Instead, several weeks later, Soloviev himself was fired. Kurkova returned to planning new programs.

Leningrad television remained a part of Soviet central television, but the relationship was uneasy. In January 1991, the killings in Lithuania were followed by the imposition of strict censorship on central television. "The Fifth Wheel" responded by showing a film of the massacre of unarmed demonstrators in Vilnius and, in introducing the film, Kurkova warned that the program could be interrupted at any moment.

In the end, the film was shown, but the tension over the independence of the staff of "The Fifth Wheel" did not disappear. On April 9, 1991, Leonid Kravchenko, the head of the State Committee on Radio and Television, read from a pile of letters during a televised phone-in in which viewers supposedly complained that "The Fifth Wheel" was anti-Soviet and called for action against Kurkova. In June, however, Gorbachev authorized the creation of independent Russian television. Kurkova and "The Fifth Wheel" announced that their conflicts with Kravchenko were over because they were taking "The Fifth Wheel," one of the Soviet Union's most popular and authoritative programs, to the new channel.

11

Homo
Sovieticus

Could it be that I was the only coward on earth, I wondered. The thought was terrifying. Lost in the midst of two million madmen, all of them heroes, at large, and armed to the teeth!
—*Louis Ferdinand Céline,* Journey to the End of the Night

THE TRAIN FROM THE URALS arrived at the Yaroslavl station at 6 a.m. on a freezing morning in December 1988, and Mikhail Kukobaka, having gathered his prison belongings in a single sack, stepped down onto the already crowded platform. Ten years had passed since he had last seen Moscow, and he glanced around at the crowds before walking to the station building and then out onto the street.

The area of the three stations was already busy. Long lines waited for taxis, buses trailed exhaust, and the red "M" of the metro station burned in the morning frost. Kukobaka had the address of Vyacheslav Bakhmin, an ex-prisoner and former dissident, and he decided he would contact Bakhmin for help in finding a place to stay.

Passersby glanced at Kukobaka, who was still wearing his gray camp uniform, black threads visible where his name tag had been, but he was barely aware of them.

Kukobaka approached a policeman and asked how he could get to Novosibirsk Street. The policeman gave him directions and then asked to see his documents. Kukobaka pulled out his certificate of release from the Perm 35 Labor Camp. The officer studied it and told him he had seventy-two hours to leave Moscow.

"I'll stay for as long as I consider necessary," Kukobaka replied.

He began to walk away and then turned and said to the policeman, "Do you know who you are talking to? I am the last political prisoner to leave the camps."

At that moment, a man in a beret who was standing nearby came up to Kukobaka and began shaking his hand warmly.

Kukobaka had spent sixteen years in confinement for the crime of trying to have political discussions with Soviet citizens. Now, passersby were offering him their congratulations. He realized that times were changing and that people were changing.

KUKOBAKA FELT a change in the atmosphere while he was still a prisoner. In the autumn of 1986, the harassment and torture of prisoners in the political camps reached unprecedented levels, yet at the same time, the prisoners were astounded to read the first critical articles in the Soviet press. Most of them thought glasnost was a trick to fool the West, but Kukobaka was not so sure.

In early 1987, the authorities began to liberate political prisoners. The only condition was that the prisoners had to ask to be pardoned. Most of them accepted this condition, but Kukobaka refused, on the grounds that he had not committed any crime. This unwillingness was to cost him another two years in confinement. Kukobaka was finally released on the eve of Gorbachev's trip to the United Nations in December 1988. One day, the camp authorities summoned him to headquarters and told him he was being transferred. Instead, he was released and his certificate said he had been pardoned.

During his first days in Moscow, Kukobaka did not work, living on the money he had earned in the camps over many years. Eventually, however, he began selling independent newspapers, and as he talked to people in Pushkin Square, on Gogolevsky Boulevard, and on the Arbat, he saw evidence of a sea change in Soviet attitudes.

Early 1989 was the height of the anti-Stalin campaign, and as material about mass executions and the destruction of the peasantry under Stalin appeared daily in the press, arguments erupted everywhere about whether "Stalinism" was the natural outgrowth of socialist ideas or whether it represented an aberration. No one, however, doubted the veracity of the exposure of Stalin itself.

One day in March, after a demonstration on Gorky Street,

Kukobaka got into an argument with an older man in a karakul cap who was cursing the democrats. The older man said that Stalin did the right thing by shooting people.

The remark enraged Kukobaka. "You're not a typical pensioner. A typical pensioner does not wear a karakul cap. You must have performed some special service to the state."

To Kukobaka's surprise, he was immediately supported by the crowd. The people around him began to abuse the Stalinist. "Surviving Beriaist," they shouted. "You yourself are a hangman, that's why you defend hangmen." "You are a former NKVD agent, you took part in the crimes." The older man argued with the crowd. "Under Stalin, prices were lowered, there was order, there was enough of everything," he said.

THE CHANGE in attitudes that swept the Soviet Union was evident in official encounters.

Kukobaka was from Bobrusk in Belorussia, and when he was freed from the Perm 35 Labor Camp, the authorities listed Bobrusk as his future residence, although he said he wanted to live in Moscow. During his first few weeks in Moscow, Kukobaka went to the local police and tried to get a passport, but when they looked at his certificate of liberation, they told him to go to Bobrusk. In response, he stopped trying to get a passport for the next nine months.

In the spring of 1990, however, Kukobaka decided to make another attempt. He went to Alexandrov in the Vladimir oblast, where he was arrested for the first time in 1970, and asked for a passport at the town's only police station. When an official saw that Kukobaka had been without documents for nine months, he told him to come back and speak with the boss of the militia.

Kukobaka returned to Moscow and went back to Alexandrov a few days later. This time, however, he arrived with a pile of newspaper clippings about his case. Kukobaka went into the office of the militia boss, a man in his thirties, who studied Kukobaka's certificate of release and said that he would have to start an investigation because Kukobaka had spent nine months without a passport.

At that point, however, Kukobaka began to tell the officer about his life. He described his years as a political prisoner, how he had gone to the Czech consulate in Kiev to express his sympathy with the Czechs after the invasion of their country in 1968, how he was arrested and confined in labor camps and mental hospitals, how he was beaten. He talked about people he met along the way. He showed the militiaman clippings from the *Chicago Tribune, Baltimore Sun, New York Times*, and, in Russian, from *Russkaya Mysl*. He also showed him letters he had written about prison conditions, which had been published abroad.

To Kukobaka's surprise, the man began to show an interest. He asked about life in the camps and what he thought about the situation in the country. As the hours passed, other officers joined the conversation and asked Kukobaka about his future.

Finally, after three hours, the police boss said, "Give him a passport. Maybe one day he'll say a kind word about us."

Kukobaka broke into a broad smile and the policeman said, "Yes, the times are changing."

ON FEBRUARY 23, 1991, Kukobaka and twenty other demonstrators from the Democratic Union* decided to picket the celebration in Manezh Square on the Day of the Soviet Army.

They carried placards and Russian and Lithuanian flags, but it was Kukobaka's signs that were the most provocative. They read: SOVIET ARMY—SCHOOL OF MURDERERS, and GENERALS—TRAITORS TO THE RUSSIAN PEOPLE.

The crowd in the square, which was pro-army, objected to the presence of the demonstrators. One man shouted, "The Soviet army is a school of murderers and what is the American army, not a school of murderers? What is the army supposed to do, build houses? An army is supposed to kill and destroy."

Not everyone tried to reason with Kukobaka. People began to throw things at the demonstrators. To prevent a pitched battle, the police formed a cordon between the crowd and the demonstrators.

The crowd was irritated by the placards and tried to reach past the police in order to punch the demonstrators. Kukobaka took a blow to the face. There were anti-Semitic cries: "Kikes!" "Zionists!" But despite a lot of jostling, the police maintained a steady separation between the two groups. What was most astonishing to Kukobaka was that they seemed to sympathize with the demonstrators. A

---

*The Soviet Union's first self-proclaimed independent political party, founded by former political prisoners in 1988.

woman in the crowd shouted at the police, "Why don't you stop this disgrace?"

A policeman answered, "You have your opinion. They have their opinion. They express their opinion. This is democracy."

DURING THE YEARS of stagnation, I had no idea of the world," said Sergei Osintsev, a drama student in Tyumen, one night as we talked in the Tyumen theater. "Besides the Soviet Union, nothing else existed.

"As far as America was concerned, the great mystery was why they didn't want to live in peace. Reagan was so bloodthirsty that it seemed as if he only wanted war. We waited for America to attack us. We assumed that someone in the United States would push the button and that would be all, since we, of course, would then push the button against them.

"In school, they taught us how to defend ourselves against a poison gas attack. They had us try on gas masks. They taught us how to assemble a Kalashnikov and counted the number of minutes.

"Everyone assumed that these measures were taken in our defense, and that we had no choice because we had a neighbor like America which thought of nothing but piling up arms.

"It was difficult to imagine people living in America. It was like the dark side of the moon except that it was full of murderers, drug addicts, and prostitutes and, in general, was a place where a person could be killed at any moment. They showed unemployed people dying on the streets, although now they say that the unemployed don't live so badly, if you believe our newspapers today.

"When glasnost began, they started to show films about the United States. The program 'Vzglyad' ran a series entitled 'Letters from America.' In one of these programs, they showed a film about the American police. In America, the police stand in defense of the individual. If you ask an American policeman for help, he'll give it to you at any moment.

"We also began to see pictures of American stores and I began to wonder why don't we have that here, why should I stand in line for hours for bread. Americans don't have the humiliation of standing in lines. In America, you can call and they deliver.

"In America, there live people. Here, there live guinea pigs on whom first they tested socialism and now they're testing perestroika.

"Earlier, people thought we would reach communism and everything will be free and we'll all begin to live well. Now we've come to the conclusion that nothing will be and all there is is a struggle for power. There was the program of five hundred days. It is not clear whether we accepted it or not. This is the third day of the transfer to the market economy, but I haven't seen a single change.

"Now I have a positive attitude toward America. I am in favor of private property. I think that if there is private property, they can do surveys and determine what type of theater people want. As it is now, when there is a new play, there is a full house on the first night and then fewer and fewer people come. The theater seats 670, yet in the audience there can be only 30 or 50 people. There can be as few as two.

"People don't go to the theater because they don't know what money they're going to have to live on. The stores are virtually empty and the only thing you can buy is sea cabbage.

"I have only lived for twenty years and I already don't believe in anything. When I was a Pioneer, I believed in a radiant future. Now I think we're standing in the entryway to a black hole.

"We don't have the ability to think freely. They taught us to think within a certain framework.

"I wouldn't emigrate to America. I would go there simply to look around. To live there would be frightening. I don't think I'm capable of freedom, and there, everything would depend on me. Maybe if I went there, I would become accustomed to it. You have to adopt a new way of thinking and change yourself entirely.

"I feel some kind of attachment to this land. I was born here. Russian is my native tongue. In America, I'm afraid that I wouldn't be necessary to anyone."

"GLASNOST OPENED OUR EYES because we knew absolutely nothing," said Marina Baranova, a librarian in a factory in Tyumen, as we talked in an office of the sociology faculty of Tyumen University.

"I believed in socialism as a young girl, but then how could I not believe in socialism if everywhere I turned, on the radio, television, and newspapers, all I heard was that this was the happiest, richest, best country in the world.

"I lived in a rural area on the territory of a state farm, and I saw that the harvest was never gathered to the end and that the grain was left in the fields, but I assumed that our state farm was the exception and that everywhere else the harvest was being gathered.

"When Gorbachev came to power, I began to follow what was happening in the country. In 1986, I took an exam on the history of the Communist Party and one of the questions concerned the unmasking of the Trotsky-Zinoviev bloc. On the basis of the textbooks, I argued that Trotsky and Zinoviev were enemies and it was necessary to condemn them. A year later, they were rehabilitated. It turned out that they were not enemies after all.

"The teachers were in complete disarray and they did not know what to teach. As for us, we lost all interest in the history of the party and, in general, in the history of the country.

"During this time, there was a sharp change in the attitudes of students. Lenin to me was a kind of God. I thought the revolution was good, but later came to the conclusion that it was taken over by a gang of criminals and ruined. Now, I see that it was the revolution itself which was at fault.

"The October Revolution was a tragedy for Russia. With time, this will become clearer and clearer."

"EVEN A HALF YEAR AGO, I believed that Lenin was in general a great man, but now I don't think that anymore," said Vadim Pracht, a student at Moscow State University, as we talked one night in November 1990 in the dormitory room he shared with two classmates.

"I used to find it unpleasant to hear jokes about Lenin. I believed that he was a saint. Maybe in a year I'll think it's necessary to remove all monuments and remove him from the mausoleum.

"Several years ago, I would have been amazed to hear about the different republics. They were like the states in the United States. We all believed in socialism. Our credo was friendship between peoples.

"I assumed that the United States was a country of enormous contrasts and that there was a small group which lived well and as far as simple people were concerned, I was convinced that they lived worse than we did. I thought, thank God I was born in the Soviet Union, where everyone is guaranteed a decent living—not luxurious but decent. In the United States, I assumed that everyone lived in fear for the following day.

"When I heard about the struggle for human rights in the Soviet Union, I thought that the person speaking was simply a scoundrel. When the U.S. said that we violate human rights, I thought that it is the U.S. which violates human rights and the colored population were not only second-class citizens but outcasts. This was the impression that we got from television.

"I thought that there was a small clique at the top which lived well and thought only of keeping power in the hands of the bourgeoisie, and the people who lived around me in Khmelnitsky all thought the same way.

"I went into the army and was isolated from glasnost and what was happening in the country, but when I came out in 1989, I began to read and was shocked by what I learned. I read *The Gulag Archipelago* in *Novy Mir* and was surprised by the sheer scale of the repression. I did not realize that for any innocent word, it was possible to land in a labor camp and I didn't understand that this network was so developed that people landed there who until the very last second believed in Stalin.

"In the spring, there was a film about the Netherlands on the television program 'Up to and After Midnight.' They showed a festival with flowers, streets where people did not have to spend all their time in queues, a country where a person did not have to worry constantly about where he would obtain a piece of meat or take a vacation with his family. There was a friendly atmosphere between people, people smiled at each other. Here, if you smile at someone, you get an insult in return."

ON A SUNNY AFTERNOON in the late spring of 1990, Dolores Akhmetova, a university student who worked as a guide in the Lenin museum in Ufa, noticed that a tour leader was entering the museum accompanied by only fifteen tourists.

Akhmetova was puzzled that the group was so small. She was accustomed to large tour groups. Before, no group ever contained fewer than forty people.

She took the guide aside and asked why she was bringing so few people. "I announced that we had arrived at the Lenin museum," the tour leader said, "and half of the tourists refused to get off the bus."

For years, the attitude toward Lenin in Ufa was semi-religious, and the atmosphere in the Lenin museum, a log house where Lenin spent three weeks in 1900 while visiting his wife, Krupskaya, resembled that of a church. Visitors listened quietly as Akhmetova and the other guides showed them exhibits depicting Lenin's life, and young children were brought through the museum as part of their history lessons. When Akhmetova took visitors to the spartan second-floor room where Lenin stayed with Krupskaya, the visitors were as respectful as if filing past a bier.

Akhmetova's attitude did not differ from that of the people who visited the museum. She regarded Lenin as an outstanding political leader and thinker, and saw her work as a fitting way to acquaint people with his greatness.

For this reason, the tour leader's remark made a strong impression. Akhmetova understood that if people were not only no longer interested in the Lenin museum but unwilling even to enter the building, something fundamental had changed in Ufa and in the Soviet Union as a whole.

Akhmetova had gone to work in the Lenin museum in April 1988 as Gorbachev was entering his fourth year in power. The press had become much freer and Gorbachev had announced a series of reforms, the purpose of which was to bring about a return to "Leninism."

Then, around the time she started working in the museum, glasnost, which had been restricted to the exposure of corruption under Brezhnev, expanded and began to publicize the crimes committed under Stalin.

The revelations changed the atmosphere in the country. Like most young people in Ufa, Akhmetova had little idea of the scale of the repression under Stalin, but as the testimony of survivors appeared in the press and mass burial grounds were shown on television, she was overwhelmed by the extent of the crimes. She had always regarded collectivization as necessary. Now, after reading the accounts in the press, she realized that collectivization had been carried out at gunpoint, and that adults had lied to her about Soviet history for years while she was growing up.

Nonetheless, several months after it began, the anti-Stalinist campaign was already passé. At first, students at the university clipped articles about the crimes of the Stalin period and brought them to class, but in time, interest fell and they ceased to talk about it.

The exposure of Stalin filled every newspaper and was the constant theme of television programming. It seemed that every Soviet official, including KGB officers, now considered it his duty to make some contribution to the unmasking of Stalin. At the same time, every fault in society, from the shortages of goods to the absence of law, was attributed to Stalin's legacy.

But at the height of the anti-Stalin campaign, Akhmetova's psychology professor told the class that "the founder of the Red Terror in our country was Lenin." Akhmetova was appalled by the remark but found it impossible to forget.

The revelations about Stalin at first did not turn most people against Lenin. People continued to visit the Lenin museum in large numbers, but there was a gradual lessening of the traditional reverence. Visitors, particularly those from cities like Moscow and Leningrad, asked questions about Lenin's private life, which would have been unthinkable before. Was it true that Lenin and Krupskaya had never married, or, on the other hand, had Lenin married Krupskaya simply because he found it convenient to work with her?

Akhmetova answered that the museum had documents which showed that Lenin and Krupskaya were married in a church ceremony, and there were letters in which Lenin professed his love for Krupskaya. Other questions concerned whether Krupskaya was Lenin's second wife and whether he had a mistress.

The anti-Stalin campaign declined in intensity, but this did not mark the end of the unraveling of the official version of history. Instead, there began to be articles in the press that implicated Lenin. Lenin was not mentioned by name, but there were references to famines in 1921, when he was in power. There were articles about the Kronshtadt uprising, which the Bolsheviks suppressed. The uprising had always been depicted as a counterrevolutionary mutiny. But now it was connected with the reduction to starvation levels of the food supply for workers in Petrograd.

The appearance of these articles planted seeds of doubt about Lenin in the minds of many, and the effect was heightened when his monument in the center of Ufa was partially disassembled for repairs and it was discovered that the base had been built with gravestones from the local cemetery, including those of children. The markings had been concealed by turning the headstones inward.

Akhmetova nonetheless retained her faith in Lenin. She told herself that even if Lenin was in some way involved in brutal acts, they occurred at the very end of his life, when he was too ill to have played a major role.

Others drew different conclusions. One October day, just before closing, a woman who seemed in despair came into the museum. She said she taught history at a local institute and now believed that her life's work had been wasted.

FOR MOST OF 1989, the press only hinted that Lenin was involved in acts of cruelty. In February 1990, however, article six was removed from the constitution and a watershed was crossed in the treatment of Lenin. For the first time, it was stated that Lenin was aware of the acts of terror committed in the early days of Bolshevik rule.

One night in March, a student from the oil institute in Ufa approached Akhmetova in the museum and asked if she still maintained her faith in Lenin.

Akhmetova did not know how to reply.

The student mentioned the shooting of hostages in the immediate postrevolutionary years, about which there had been stories in the press. "Do you think he deserves the attention we give him?" he asked.

"He still deserves attention," Akhmetova said, "but we give him attention in an improper form. Instead of reading his work, we write him poems and put up monuments to him. We do not do what is necessary."

"Why have you not changed your opinion?" he asked. "There is confirmation that he was really a cruel person."

"I think it's too early to reach any conclusions," she said. "We have to become acquainted with all the information before judging."

As the months went by, the press published details about Lenin's acts of cruelty. In a broadcast that stunned the guides at the museum, "Vzglyad" implicated Lenin in the attempted murder of an Orthodox priest who offered to donate food for famine victims if the Bolsheviks would stop taking consecrated objects from the churches. The guides were so taken aback that they denied to visitors having seen the broadcast in order to avoid having to respond to it.

In April, the effect of these revelations began to be noticeable in the museum. The number of visitors fell from seven hundred or eight hundred a day to two hundred. On some days, only a hundred people visited the museum, and it was on one such day that a group of workers from Chelyabinsk refused to get out of the bus.

Soon, the reaction of the Chelyabinsk workers became common.

Akhmetova thought it was unnecessary for individuals to advertise their attitude so aggressively, but she noticed hostility even on the part of those who entered the museum. They stood silently and seemed angry. They showed no interest in her explanations. After the visitors left, she found notes in the visitors' book such as, "For what was all this built?"

KUKOBAKA, the students, and Akhmetova were only a few of the millions who were affected by the new policy toward information during the years of perestroika.

With the help of ideological censorship, the regime had presented the world to the Soviet public in such a distorted manner that nearly every aspect of given reality, from the successes of the Soviet space program to unemployment in the United States, was taken directly or indirectly to confirm the superiority of the Soviet system.

When Soviet citizens began to throw off these imposed illusions, the Communist regime was doomed because, despite the hopes of Communist liberals, the Soviet population could not be endlessly manipulated. Once the regime had lost the mandate of heaven as a result of glasnost, the pendulum of public opinion did not stop in the middle of its trajectory but had an irresistible tendency to move to the opposite extreme.

The collapse of a fictitious universe, however, did not change the underlying psychological traits of a people who, for seventy years, had been subordinated to a false idea and, in the process, had lost all appreciation of transcendence. These traits include a drive to live in a world of illusions, a tendency to see individuals as interchangeable, and a proclivity for reducing everyone to the same level.

Despite the changes that swept the Soviet Union, they remained integral to the national personality and have been visible for decades through the changing kaleidoscope of political and nonpolitical events.

THE MOST IMPORTANT TRAIT of Soviet citizens was the drive to escape the real world and live in a world of illusions.

In June 1980, six months after the invasion of Afghanistan, I decided to make a trip to Shadrinsk, a city of eighty thousand located a hundred miles east of the Ural Mountains.

The people I knew in Moscow did not believe the government's claim that the intervention in Afghanistan was in response to a "call for help," but I thought the attitude might be different in the "deaf places" scattered over the Eurasian landmass, where most Soviet citizens live.

I had pored over a map in my office looking for a destination and finally settled on Shadrinsk, which was near the geographical center of the Soviet Union. Bill Schmidt of *Newsweek* agreed to go with me and we booked two tickets in a second-class compartment of the trans-Siberian express.

The rays of the late afternoon sun filtered through the windows of our compartment as the train rolled through the forests and thickets around Moscow, past weathered wooden villages and the crowds of provincials waiting on the platforms of suburban stations.

One fellow passenger was a retired schoolteacher who said he had taken part in the meeting on the Elbe between Russian and American troops in 1945. He reminisced about the friendly relations which existed between the two countries at that time.

"We'd be friendly to this day," he said, "if it hadn't been for Churchill. In 1946, I was waiting to be demobilized when Churchill made his speech in Fulton about the 'Iron Curtain.' They canceled my demobilization order and I had to serve a whole extra year.

"You see," he added, "it was all the fault of Churchill."

We began to talk about the Olympics, which were on the minds of nearly everyone at the time, and I asked the schoolteacher how he felt about the American boycott, which had been announced by President Carter.

"It's a shame the American team isn't coming," he said. "I understand that it's connected with Afghanistan, but this is politics. Politics shouldn't interfere with sports. These things are separate."

"So you disapprove of the boycott?" I asked.

"I feel sorry for the sportsmen, to lose out after all that training."

We stepped into the corridor and continued our conversation as the birch trees and open fields of the Moscow oblast rolled past outside the window. I had hesitated to mention Afghanistan, but when the schoolteacher himself mentioned it, I asked him how he felt about the war there.

"We just gave Afghanistan help," he said, apparently perplexed by the whole controversy, "just as the Americans gave us help during the Second World War."

"So you don't see the war in Afghanistan as an invasion?"

"Not at all, this is Soviet help. It's all official, the appeal for help was printed in our newspapers."

The schoolteacher returned to our compartment, but Schmidt and I remained in the corridor for the next several hours watching the panorama of forests and fields. We talked to many others during the thirty-nine-hour train ride to Shadrinsk, but the schoolteachers' sentiments seemed to be shared by nearly everyone. No one doubted—or appeared to doubt—that the Soviet invasion was "fraternal aid" offered in response to the Karmal government's "call for help," although the Karmal government did not exist at the time the aid was requested, a fact that should have been obvious to everyone.

As darkness fell, a stillness fell over the train. The wagon attendant brought glasses of tea to the passengers and the music that was broadcast over the public address system was turned off. The only sound was the rhythmic clicking of the wheels.

Word had spread that there were two Americans on the train, and various passengers, anxious to talk to us, joined us in our compartment with bottles of vodka. They included a worker from Arkhangelsk, a young soldier, a worker from Leningrad, and an official from Minsk. The gathering provided another opportunity for a discussion of the Olympic boycott and the invasion of Afghanistan.

The Leningrader said that, in his opinion, President Carter was trying to intimidate the Soviet Union, but no matter what Carter did, the Soviet people were fully behind the decision to assist the Karmal government in Afghanistan.

"Not all Soviet citizens are in favor," I said. "What about Sakharov? He condemned the invasion and then was exiled."

The atmosphere in the compartment was friendly and our fellow passengers poured out glasses of vodka for us, but the reference to Sakharov touched a raw nerve.

"Sakharov was not punished for anything he said," the schoolteacher said. "The Soviet Union is a democracy. Here, people are punished only for concrete actions. What Sakharov wanted was to create a government of scientists so that he could be the head of that government."

"That's right," said the Leningrader. "Sakharov lives here but works against the interests of the state. He should have been locked up a long time ago."

"Do you think it's right to lock people up just because you disagree with them?" Schmidt asked.

"You have the same thing in your country," said the official from Minsk. "You criticize us over Sakharov but look what happened to Muhammad Ali when he stood up against the war in Vietnam. They were ready to put him in prison."

"In *Literaturnaya Gazeta*," the schoolteacher said, "they wrote that Sakharov received money from abroad to write anti-Soviet propaganda. It was written right there in *Literaturnaya Gazeta*."

I asked the schoolteacher if it ever occurred to him that what was written in the Soviet newspapers might not be true.

"How could it not be true?" he said. "They don't distort the news. The news is instantaneous. They show correspondents in New York, Washington, London. These are facts. You can't distort facts."

"Do you ever listen to the foreign radio stations?" I asked.

"Five or six years ago," he said, "people listened to the Voice of America or the BBC because they broadcast news immediately while our radio gave the information only after two or three days. But now our radio broadcasts information faster than the Voice of America, so interest in the foreign stations has disappeared."

At this point, the worker from Arkhangelsk, who had been silent while the other argued, broke in.

"They write what they want you to read," he said. "They give their side, but you don't see them giving Sakharov a chance to express himself."

I was taken aback by this comment, which showed that some common sense still survived in the Soviet provinces, but no one reacted to the worker's observation and he again fell silent.

"But what about the foreign stations?" I said. "They say there was no appeal for help."

"At first," the schoolteacher said, after some hesitation, "there was some talk that the fighting in Afghanistan was a civil war. This idea may have come from the foreign radio stations. But when people saw there were no victims and no injured people and when no one knew about any funerals, we decided that it could not be a civil war. A civil war would have produced more victims."

The conversation continued, but it became obvious that what was taking place in our compartment was a meeting between two different worlds. We shifted to other subjects but, in each case, the attempt at communication foundered on the readiness of our interlocutors to treat the "truth" of official statements as inarguable. There was some communication when we discussed factual questions—for example, about the price of Western goods or Western salaries—but none at all when we turned to more sensitive issues, for example, history.

"Why do people in the West dislike Stalin so much?" asked the Leningrader.

"He killed millions of people," I said.

"You say that people were killed," the Leningrader said, "but maybe it was necessary to do it."

"Stalin feared the internal bourgeoisie," said the schoolteacher.

The reference to Stalin inspired the young soldier, who was en route to Khabarovsk, to ask another question. "Why does the West attribute the killings in the Katyn forest during the last war to us?"

"The judgment of experts in the West," I said, "was that those killings were carried out by the NKVD while the area was in Soviet hands."

"But it was established by Soviet experts that Katyn was the responsibility of the Germans," the schoolteacher said.

"I guess it depends on who you want to believe," I said. "Stalin had every reason to want to destroy the Polish officer corps, and no one in the West doubts that he did it."

The visitors went back to their compartments and Schmidt, the schoolteacher, and I undressed and went to sleep in our respective berths as the train raced east under a starlit summer sky. By the next morning, we had left Moscow far behind us and were deep in central Russia.

On the afternoon of the second day of our journey, I was standing in the corridor with a young, uniformed soldier who, like me, was looking out at the passing countryside. After a time, we fell into conversation and he said he had served near Alma-Ata but had been demobilized and was on his way home to Krasnoyarsk.

I asked him if he knew anyone who had fought in Afghanistan. He said that no one from his unit had been sent there.

We stood looking out at the ramshackle villages and vast, plowed-up fields, which spread out for miles under a pale blue sky, and, at length, I asked how he felt about the war.

"I support the presence of our troops in Afghanistan," he said. "We want to put Afghanistan on the right path with a socialist government and modern industry so it can be independent of its neighbors, like China and Pakistan."

The soldier was about twenty years old and had broad cheek-bones and slightly slanted eyes.

"But what if they don't want to be put on the right path," I said. "Or maybe they have their own opinion about what is the right path?"

"In that case, we should try to persuade them with examples," he said.

"But what if they can't be persuaded?"

The young soldier shook his head and smiled skeptically. "I think they do want progress," he said. "They invited us in."

THE TRAIN CROSSED the Ural Mountains and the border be-tween Europe and Asia during the night.

By the time we woke, we were traveling across a grassy plain where the only towns were a string of wooden villages set at regular intervals along the horizon. The landscape was nearly unchanging until, after several hours, we approached the outskirts of Shadrinsk.

Shadrinsk was a nineteenth-century merchants' town that had become a small industrial and agricultural center. As the train neared the city, we passed log cabins with bluebells in the yards and concrete apartment blocks with rusting iron balconies. Unused railway sidings were dotted with marigolds, and tall grain elevators rusted in the sun.

As we entered the city, we passed several factories. The train came to a stop at a one-story station.

SCHMIDT AND I were met on the platform by a woman from the city council who drove us to the Hotel Ural, where we checked in.

We then quickly unpacked and left the hotel. We knew no one in Shadrinsk, but as we stopped to talk to people on the street, we learned that our impending arrival had been announced in every fac-tory and school in the city. We decided to try to take advantage of this to make the acquaintance of as many people as possible.

It was a cloudless day and the afternoon sun beat down on the treeless central square. Young girls with nothing to do sat on benches around the war memorial. At the Motherland Cinema, just across the main road, a new film was being advertised, entitled *From Your Loved One, Don't Be Parted*. On the side streets, old women looked out curiously from the windows of leaning log houses warped from centuries of rain and snow.

We walked down side streets, finally emerging on the bank of a river. The grass along the river was a brilliant green in the afternoon sun. Under feathered clouds in a blue sky, wizened old women sat on the stoops of wooden houses. Two policemen warned a young boy not to cut the branch off a bush. Not far away, a woman in a print dress did her laundry in a barrel, and the chirping of birds mixed with the sound of splashing as young girls swam to a grassy island from an improvised base on the muddy shore.

What impressed me most about Shadrinsk was the otherworldly quality of the place and its lack of relation to events in Afghanistan. From the riverbank, we walked back in the direction of our hotel. The friendly residents nodded or waved to us, but they seemed to have little idea what to make of our presence there. We stopped in a souvenir store, and two salesgirls began to blush when they saw us, one hiding her head behind the other. For the people of Shadrinsk it seemed that our presence had as much relation to their daily lives as a visit from outer space.

By the time we returned to the central square, it had gotten cooler. The benches around the war memorial were nearly empty. At our hotel, we entered the restaurant and sat down at a table. The band, which had been warming up, began playing. The patrons started to dance, and what appeared before us was a gallery of provincial types.

A squat Red Army officer with thick eyebrows and beady black eyes danced with a fat girl in a black-and-white polka-dot dress. Another officer, with thinning hair and a weak chin, danced with a raven-haired woman with a spreading bottom who was six feet tall in her heels. A Georgian with black sideburns and angular features danced with a blotchy peroxide blonde in a jeans suit, and a ruddy-faced man with matted, greasy blond hair and a blue sports shirt that outlined his enormous belly danced with a big redheaded girl with bright lipstick and a gold tooth.

As the music picked up, the dancers improvised. One was bobbing, one was swaying, one seemed to be jogging in place, one had his hands on his partner's bottom, and another was trying to get close to his partner but was continually being pushed away. Two young men danced with each other. Fat women shook their hips.

Drunks kept time. The dancers responded frantically to the deafening electronic music that drowned out any conversation and rever-
berated off the walls.

For most of the evening, Bill and I were kept in isolation. The
waitresses, aware of who we were, shooed away anyone who tried to
sit down next to us. Eventually, however, we were invited to a table
occupied by several workers from the Shadrinsk auto parts factory,
and we began to talk about politics.

One of the workers, whose name was Volodya, asked us why the
Americans were not coming to the Moscow Olympics. I mentioned
the invasion of Afghanistan.

"You talk about an invasion of Afghanistan," he said, "but there
was no invasion. We only offered our help. The fact is that we Russians are ready to help any country. We helped Cambodia, where the
Maoists committed genocide. How many people died there? Three
million? It makes your hair stand on end. We helped Vietnam. We
are ready to help anyone."

"I think sports and politics should be separate," said a second
worker, also named Volodya. "We know all about Afghanistan. Afghanistan is our southern neighbor. They appealed to us for help, not
to the United States. But that's beside the point. This is politics. I put
a fence around this question. Sports is one thing, politics is something
else. We should be able to say, 'All right, we have our differences, but
at least we can compete. . . .' "

"If I had my last loaf of bread and you needed it," said the first
Volodya, "I'd cut it in half. I don't care if you are English, American,
Vietnamese, Israeli. I don't care what you are. We're all people. I'm
sure that we went into Afghanistan for purely humanitarian reasons,
to help others."

This meeting was to set the tone for our visit to Shadrinsk. During our stay in the city, Schmidt and I found almost no one who dis-
approved of the invasion. The local newspaper, *Shadrinsk Rabochy*, and
the regional newspaper, *Zauralskaya Pravda*, dedicated most of their
news coverage to the grain harvest or truancy at the factories, and
the national newspapers and television depicted the invasion as "fraternal help." The result was that in isolated Shadrinsk, propaganda
was reality.

On the morning of our second day, we met with Leonid
Dmitriev, the head of the Komsomol, who spent several hours pro-

viding us with facts. He said that Shadrinsk had six hospitals, seventy-five retail stores, forty-five cafeterias, four thousand private cars, eight hundred weddings. . . .

When I asked him how people in Shadrinsk had reacted to the invasion of Afghanistan, he said he could not comment on areas that were outside his responsibility.

"But you must have heard something," I said.

"Yes," he said, finally, "the attitude of the people is no secret. We support the policies of the Central Committee."

At lunchtime, we were joined at our table in the hotel's restaurant by a muscular, crew-cut construction worker. "You Americans are clever people," he said. "My God, you are clever. You came here to ask about Afghanistan. And in how many countries do you have your forces? How many bases surround the entire Soviet Union? Afghanistan is our southern neighbor. Just remember that. We gave aid to Afghanistan just the way we sent aid to Spain in the Spanish civil war, to keep the war from spreading. In case you're interested, everyone here supports the government."

In fact, the impression of unanimity in Shadrinsk would have been all but overwhelming had it not been for one discordant incident.

That afternoon, Bill and I went for a walk and came upon a derelict church that was covered with broken, weathered scaffolding except for the red bell tower and golden cupola and cross. Crows nestled in the empty windowpanes and a group of boys played amid the scaffolding, running in and out of the church's hollow interior. In the churchyard, an old man was filling some pails with sand. Trying to make conversation, I asked him if restoration work was continuing. He laughed and said, "The state has more important objectives than restoring churches.

"First they destroyed the churches, now they're restoring them," he said. "I remember how they destroyed this one. They blasted holes in the walls and burned the icons. Then they took the silver and gold. They said they needed the metal for industry."

I tried to continue the conversation but the man put aside the shovel, lifted the pails, and, ignoring our presence, walked through the tall weeds into a neighboring lot.

The encounter was the only one in which I heard a comment from a resident of Shadrinsk that suggested an unfettered view of reality. Everywhere else it was as if I had entered a backwater of peaceful delusion where all information reached the inhabitants only after being filtered through a veil of lies.

That night, in our room, I tuned in the BBC Russian service on my short-wave radio and picked up a very clear signal. Listening to the reports, I wondered why foreign radio broadcasts seemed to have so little effect. I came to the conclusion that truthful information was not persuasive, in part, because people had little opportunity to act on it. On an issue like Afghanistan, what was broadcast by the BBC directly contradicted the version of events offered by Soviet sources of information. It therefore may have actually reinforced the official line by forcing the residents of cities like Shadrinsk to affirm their faith in the system simply to assure themselves that the world they lived in was not absurd.

The next morning I went for an early walk. A light fog lay over the city and the buildings and benches were covered with dew. It occurred to me that I had found the beating heart of the Soviet Union, a place far from the world of Moscow and Leningrad, where, in sublime isolation, a system of total control over information produced its intended result.

I finally entered the only bookstore in Shadrinsk, which was on the central square. The manager, a small, birdlike woman, began asking me about life in the United States and, to my surprise, she became increasingly ecstatic over my routine answers, apparently overwhelmed by the possibilities for friendship between the United States and Soviet Union represented by the appearance of an American journalist in Shadrinsk.

That afternoon was spent in random wanderings, and at night, Bill and I went to an outdoor dance floor on the edge of town to talk to the teenagers who gathered there.

The area was lit by floodlights and framed by weeping willow trees. Not far away was a stagnant pond. The band was loud and out of tune. We both had offers to dance and, afterward, Bill asked my partner, a pretty nineteen-year-old shopgirl, if the fact that she liked Western jeans and music meant she did not like the Soviet Union.

"No," she said, emphatically, "I love the Soviet Union."

The vast Eurasian sky was full of stars and I had the sense that a *dieu trompeux* presided over this forgotten town where, in defiance of all rational logic, people were suffused with the sense of participating in the march of historical progress, and gave the impression of silently marching in step.

On our last day, Schmidt and I walked in the city gardens. We spoke casually with several people before striking up a conversation with Oleg, a worker at the local telephone equipment factory.

It was a sunny, humid day and we sat down with Oleg on a bench in an old, unpainted gazebo. He said he had come to Shadrinsk in 1968, and this led me to ask him how people in Shadrinsk had reacted to the invasion of Czechoslovakia.

"Everyone was for it," he said. "We've always been friends of the Czechs and this was a request for help from the Czech government."

Bill asked Oleg if he knew what the attitude had been in 1956 toward the invasion of Hungary.

"I think there was confusion about why there was a revolt, but people believed that this was an attempt to seize power by rightists and we were right to suppress it."

We left Oleg, after agreeing to meet later that evening at the hotel, and continued to walk through the city gardens.

The thick foliage seemed to absorb the heat and the air was full of flies. Parents pushed baby strollers and women walked arm in arm. The intense sunlight filtering through the trees threw deep shadows on the sidewalks, and the branches and leaves formed thick canopies over the winding dirt paths. There were men in uniform, and it was easy to imagine the potential of an army composed of people like those in Shadrinsk, going into battle convinced of the rightness of their cause but with no real idea what they were fighting for.

That evening at the hotel's restaurant we saw Oleg and joined him at his table, where he was sitting with several of his friends.

After toasts to "peace" and "friendship," Oleg became emotional.

"Tell Carter," he said, "that the Russians don't want to fight. Tell him we know how to fight, but we don't want to fight."

He drained a glass of vodka and then recited the poem by Yevtushenko "Do the Russians Want War?" As he came to the end of the poem, Oleg repeated the last lines at the top of his voice: "RUSSIANS DON'T WANT WAR, RUSSIANS DON'T WANT WAR, RUSSIANS DON'T WANT WAR."

Oleg's friend Vitya interrupted the conversation and said that events in Afghanistan were proof that the Soviet Union never abandoned a friend.

I asked Vitya whether he was troubled by the fact that the Soviet Union claimed to be helping the government of Afghanistan but the Afghan president, Hafizullah Amin, was killed by the Soviet forces as soon as they arrived. Vitya paused and I got the impression that this problem had occurred to him.

"There could have been two governments," he said thoughtfully, "one popular and the other antipopular. We supported the popular government of Babrak Karmal. We don't have all the information. We can't see the peaks of policy. We see only what is known to us, but we know enough to take a view."

THE DRIVE OF CITIZENS to live in a world of illusions was also witnessed by my Soviet friends. One such friend was Adolph Muhlberg, whose exposure to irreality lasted thirty-three years.

Muhlberg was born in Latvia in 1931; in 1939, he and his mother emigrated to Germany, joining the exodus of Volksdeutsch back to the Reich. After the war, he lived in the Ruhr district but ran away from home repeatedly, trying to find work on a ship. He was finally put in a reform school, but he ran away again and began traveling all over Europe. On a sunny afternoon in 1948, Muhlberg found himself on the platform of a railroad station in the Black Forest, where he met a Soviet citizen who was also waiting for a train.

Thirty years later, Muhlberg could not remember anything about the stranger, not his name or what he looked like, only that he was a Russian or a Belorussian and about forty years old. The meeting, however, changed the course of Muhlberg's life. Muhlberg told the stranger that he wanted to become a sailor and the stranger suggested that he go to the Soviet Union. He said the Soviet Union was a paradise and that he could work on any ship he liked. After three decades of Soviet experience, Muhlberg realized that the stranger had not been lying. He had merely idealized Soviet conditions to the point that he believed what he was saying was the truth. He directed Muhlberg to the Soviet military mission in Baden-Baden and, seven weeks later, knowing next to nothing about his country of destination, Muhlberg boarded a train with other repatriates bound for the Soviet Union.

Muhlberg longed to escape from dreary postwar Germany, but despite his wanderlust, he was not prepared for a land where the population lived in a world of myths.

He was processed in a repatriation camp near Grodno and then boarded a train for Riga, where he got his first exposure to an alien mental universe.

As the train rolled through the countryside, Muhlberg overheard two collective farmers. One of them said, "On our kolkhoz everything depends on the chairman. If there is a good chairman, there are leather boots and people can buy them." Muhlberg was puzzled by this remark. In Germany, people were poor, but they regarded their poverty as temporary, the result of a devastating war. The idea that people dreamed of a kolkhoz run efficiently enough so that there would be money for boots struck him as strange. The other collective farmer said, "In our kolkhoz, the situation is good. This year I salted a barrel of cucumbers and cabbage." This remark astonished Muhlberg even more. If being able to salt a barrel of cabbages and cucumbers was "good," then what was the norm?

He arrived in Riga and went immediately to Liepája, where he had spent his childhood before the war. He had pleasant memories of Liepája and so was stunned by what the city had become. The port was sealed off behind concrete walls topped with barbed wire and secured by border guards. The Latvian newspapers warned against "saboteurs" and the bridges were protected. Bridges had not been guarded in Germany, even during the war.

In Liepája, the local officials sent Muhlberg back to Riga, where he was given another example of the Soviet mentality. He was told that he could not be a Soviet citizen because he gave up Latvian citizenship in 1939. When he said that he did not care about citizenship, he only wanted to be a sailor, the officials said he could not become a sailor because he was a stateless person. They informed him that he also could not leave the country and suggested he settle in Daugavpils, 150 miles from the coast.

Muhlberg was only seventeen, but he began to understand that coming to the Soviet Union had been a mistake. He went first to Daugavpils and then to Kurtspils, where he found work tending a windmill. The pay, however, was not enough to live on, and, in desperation, he left Kurtspils for Moscow, hopping rides on trains.

In 1949, there was no German embassy in Moscow and so Muhlberg asked for directions to the Austrian embassy. Since he spoke Russian poorly, he was sent to the Australian embassy. He rang the bell there and a policeman stepped between him and the door.

He was arrested and taken to the Lubyanka,* where he was interrogated before being sent back to Latvia. Six weeks later, he was arrested again and sentenced to eighteen months for violation of the passport laws. Less than a year after arriving in the Soviet Union, he was already in prison.

Muhlberg was released from prison in the early 1950s. Once free, he traveled to the Odessa oblast, where he went to work on a collective farm and saw how people could live in a world of illusions.

In the 1950s, a collective farmer was not permitted to leave his kolkhoz except by a unanimous vote of the members. When Muhlberg told the farmers that this meant they were slaves, they replied that this was "kolkhoz democracy" and they were "the freest people in the world."

BY THE TIME I met Adolph Muhlberg in the early 1980s, he was living with his Russian wife and their children in the village of Berendeevo in the Yaroslavl oblast. A short time later, he suffered a heart attack and moved with his family, for an extended stay, to an apartment in Moscow on Zubovsky Boulevard.

It was at about this time that Muhlberg's return to Germany began to look like a realistic possibility. The West German embassy agreed to defend his claim to West German citizenship, and with this in mind, he began to seek out dissidents and foreigners in Moscow. At the same time, he continued to have encounters with ordinary citizens, and I asked him to try to record these experiences as if he were already on the outside.

Muhlberg's experiences during this period were typical of the Soviet phase of his life.

ON VICTORY DAY (May 9), 1981, Adolph Muhlberg found himself in Clinical Hospital No. 51 after a second heart attack. With him in the general ward were eight other patients, who, noticing the name "Adolph," took an interest in his background.

One of his fellow patients, inspired by the holiday, decided to engage Muhlberg in conversation.

"Tell me," he said, "do you love Hitler?"

*Headquarters of the secret police.

Muhlberg felt an almost cosmic tiredness. It was more than he could bear to respond to such a question. But in light of the interest the question had aroused, he saw no way out.

"Hitler was a dictator," Muhlberg said. "What is more, a totalitarian dictator, so, of course, I can't feel anything but hatred for him."

"And what about our Stalin?" asked a Georgian in the adjacent bed. "Do you love Stalin?"

"That's right," said one of the Russians, "do you love Stalin?"

"In the March plenum of 1956," Muhlberg said, "and, I should add, at the Twenty-first Party Congress and at the Twenty-second Party Congress, everything that needed to be said about Stalin was said. You are party people. I'm a simple man. You should know yourselves what's been said about Stalin."

This provoked excitement in the ward as the patients became irritated at being lectured to by someone with a name like "Adolph."

"What do you know about the congress? Were you there?"

Several began cursing "that idiot Khrushchev."

"The trouble is," Muhlberg said, trying to explain his position, "that to find real progress in this country you have to go back twenty years."

"That's rubbish," one of the Russians said. "There was nothing wrong with Stalin. In fact, his only mistake was that he didn't give Zhukov permission to go further. Zhukov would have gone to the Atlantic. Then all of Europe would have been Soviet."

"That's right," said another, "that was a mistake of Stalin. All Germany would be Soviet and West Germany wouldn't be threatening us."

Muhlberg, lying on a bed between the others, saw there was no easy way to extricate himself from this conversation.

"You know," he said, leaning on an elbow, "butter doesn't come here from the GDR but only from West Germany. If you had taken over West Germany that butter would have never gotten here. I also saw chickens from West Germany in the stores. You wouldn't have had those either. In fact, the truth is that you didn't win the war, West Germany won the war."

To Muhlberg's surprise, no one objected to what he had said. The other patients fell silent and appeared to be listening with interest. "After the war," he said, "West Germany was almost entirely in ruins. Today there are almost seventy million people in West Germany and they have twenty-five million cars. That means over one car for every three persons. Seventy-five percent of the population takes holidays abroad. Sixty percent of the people are overweight. If they had built collective farms, that would not have been the case."

He went on to share other information about the West German standard of living, and later, when one of the patients in his ward was called to the telephone, Muhlberg heard him say: "You congratulate me on Victory Day, but you should congratulate the West Germans."

A short time later, however, one of Muhlberg's visitors was told by his doctor that some of the patients were complaining that Muhlberg was carrying out anti-Soviet agitation. The doctor said it might be necessary to see if Muhlberg was mentally ill. That was all Muhlberg needed to hear. Although still in his hospital gown and recovering from a heart attack, he fled the hospital in a taxi, not returning until days later to pick up his clothes.

ON A QUIET Sunday morning, Adolph Muhlberg and his son went to buy bread in a store on Zubovsky Boulevard. As they stood waiting in line to pay for the bread, Muhlberg noticed that a clean-shaven man of about sixty appeared to be studying him.

They left the store and walked out into the bright sunlight on the street. As he stood waiting at a red light in front of the Nikolai v Khamovnikakh church, he saw that the man from the store was now standing next to him.

"I can't understand it," the older man said. "Everything is done for young people. Everyone wants to be young, and yet you grow a beard and try to be old."

"Look at the golden cupolas of this church," said Muhlberg, turning to the man. "This is ancient Russia becoming young again. Young people are starting to learn about what was here before."

"Tell me, are you a believer?" the older man asked.

"I'm not a religious person," Muhlberg said. "But I hate it when they persecute religious people."

"Where did you get the idea that religion is persecuted?" the older man asked. "Here everything is open."

"I got the idea that religion is persecuted because it happens."

"There was such a terrible war, so many people were destroyed," the older man said. "Here we stand for peace, for happiness, and you say we persecute."

"The fact that there was a war, that was horrible. And that there was fascism. I understand that there could be nothing worse. But consider the facts. You say that fascism destroyed millions of people, but the Bolsheviks destroyed sixty million."

The two men and Muhlberg's son crossed on the white strips that marked the pedestrian walkway on Komsomolsky Prospekt.

"I am a senior teacher in the higher military academy," the older man said. "Where do you get your figures?"

"If you are a senior teacher, then you are probably interested in demography. If you study demography and other sources, you will see that the figure is exact."

"But when were these people destroyed? People don't just disappear," the older man said.

"They were destroyed all during your lifetime. They shot the White Guards, the bourgeoisie, the intelligentsia; they starved the peasants during and after collectivization. There was 1937, the Stalinist terror."

The older man began to get angry. "Look at what they do in America," he said, shaking his finger. "They murder each other."

"America is the freest country in the world," Muhlberg said, "and every country should take it as an example."

"You are a bourgeois element," said the older man, rapidly becoming unnerved. "People like you, we destroyed fifty million."

"Thank you," Muhlberg said. "Thank you for confirming my figures. I said sixty million and you said fifty million. But thank you anyway for speaking the truth."

Muhlberg turned and kept walking. The older man continued to shout something, but Muhlberg could not any longer distinguish the words.

ONE NIGHT, Muhlberg, Mikhail Berdnikov, a friend of Serebrov's, and I walked into the quiet courtyard of the Nikolai v Khamovnikakh church, where we began to talk to the night watchman, a small, friendly man in a beige uniform. Noticing my accent, he asked where we were from. I said I was an American and Muhlberg said he was a German.

As we were about to leave, the watchman said to Muhlberg, "Guard peace. Peace is like the air we breathe." He then added, "Now this new American president is threatening us."

Muhlberg put his hand on the watchman's shoulder and said, "We're not military specialists, are we? In fact, we can't be sure who threatens whom."

The watchman scratched his face and looked at Muhlberg with interest.

"Take the border between east and west," Muhlberg continued. "That border runs between the Federal Republic of Germany and the GDR, does it not?"

The watchman nodded.

"Now, on this border, there are Soviet troops and tanks and rockets, aren't there?"

The night watchman agreed again.

"But that puts those Soviet tanks only 300 miles from Paris and only 120 miles from Bonn. The troops of NATO are 1,200 miles from Moscow. . . ."

"I know what you are going to say," the watchman interrupted heatedly, "but answer me this: When has Russia ever attacked anyone? When?"

"What about the campaign against the Chechen-Ingushi in the nineteenth century or the attack on Finland before the last war?" asked Muhlberg. "The attack on Finland was an undeclared war. Finland was at peace with the Soviet Union."

"All right," said the watchman, "did Hitler declare war? Was that war declared?"

Muhlberg hesitated for a moment to collect his thoughts.

"There was a treaty and we were fulfilling the treaty," the watchman said. "We didn't attack Germany."

"Yes," Muhlberg said. "Hitler attacked the Soviet Union, but after the treaty with Hitler was signed, the Soviet Union attacked Poland. The Soviet Union and Germany divided it in half. Wasn't that an attack?"

The night watchman began to smile. "Oh, I see you know history," he said a little admiringly.

The watchman hesitated for a moment and then a fierce gleam came into his eye.

"Well, what about Israel?" he said.

"What about Israel?"

"They should take that bomb and drop it on Israel," he said.

"How can you say that?" Muhlberg asked. "Such an ancient nation, which, after two thousand years, was reestablished."

The night watchman began to tremble and grabbed Muhlberg by the arm. "I don't care," he said, "they're kikes and they'll die kikes." He pulled Muhlberg to a nearby bench and forced him to sit down. "Tell me this. Who betrayed Jesus Christ? Judas, right? For thirty pieces of silver. A Jew betrayed his own people."

"Yes," Muhlberg said, "but this was an internal affair of the Jewish people. Jesus was a Jew. All the apostles were Jews."

The raised voices seemed out of place in the quiet courtyard of the church. Berdnikov and I had other things to discuss so we walked away, but from a distance we heard that the conversation had turned to the Baptists, whom the night watchman described as schismatics and whom Muhlberg praised for their honesty and devotion. The watchman said there were only two real faiths in Russia, Russian Orthodoxy and the Old Believers.

Further discussion took up the question of who were Marx and Engels. Muhlberg said that they were a Dutch Jew and a German Englishman. At various points, the night watchman expressed his amazement at the extent of Muhlberg's knowledge, but at no point did Muhlberg succeed in convincing him of anything.

Finally, we parted. The night watchman wished us well and said, "Remember, the most important thing is peace."

MUHLBERG WOULD have been ready to stay on in Moscow indefinitely, but his contacts with dissidents and foreigners had been noticed by the KGB, and the militia started to drop by the apartment on Zubovsky Boulevard to ask whether he was registered.

At the same time, despite the active assistance of the West German embassy, he made no progress in his efforts to get an exit visa, and he feared that his presence in Moscow would inspire the authorities to arrest him either for passport violations or on vagrancy charges. In the end, he decided that he could not afford to take that risk. He left the capital with his family and returned to Berendeevo.

In Berendeevo, Muhlberg spent his time writing petitions to Soviet organizations, arguing with the residents, and working on his memoirs. He was less visible in Berendeevo than in Moscow, but he remained vulnerable. In this tenuous situation, he invited Andrew

Nagorski and me to visit him, the better to emphasize that he was known to foreigners and not completely without defense.

Andy and I left the capital on a freezing Sunday morning and drove north over potholed roads past tiny villages before reaching the town of Pereslavl-Zalessky, whose derelict cathedrals and peeling facades gave it the appearance of an inhabited ghost town.

From Pereslavl-Zalessky we turned onto a country road, where we found that our way was blocked by a three-foot-high mound of gravel and sand. After several attempts, we managed to drive around the mound, extricate ourselves from the mud, and continue on our way.

As it happened, our decision to visit Berendeevo had a decisive influence on Muhlberg's fate. We notified the foreign ministry forty-eight hours in advance and, in that period, the authorities apparently decided not to waste any more energy keeping Muhlberg in the Soviet Union. Muhlberg was notified that, after thirty-three years, he had permission to leave.

Nagorski and I left Moscow unaware of this, however, and so we were unprepared for the scene that greeted us on arrival in Berendeevo.

We arrived at 11 a.m. The air was full of blowing snow. The wooden houses of the village were outlined starkly against an oppressive gray sky. Muhlberg's home was located near the end of a street of wooden houses and bare trees. It leaned to one side and had windows that slanted downward.

We knocked on the door and, when we entered, were surprised to see, seated in front of the coal stove, a stolid man in his forties with a red, simple face and an older, bearded man with horn-rimmed spectacles.

The man with a beard pulled out some documents and said, "I am a journalist and this is a representative of Soviet power, the mayor of Berendeevo."

Muhlberg was obviously agitated and, pointing to us, he said to the red-faced mayor, "These are my friends."

The journalist seemed to find it distasteful to be meeting us under these conditions, but he said he worked for *Rabochy Sever*, the oblast newspaper, and had come because "this person," motioning toward Muhlberg, had just received permission to emigrate.

The journalist and the mayor then showed their identification to us. "This is to show you we are not from the KGB," the journalist said. The documents did nothing to reassure us. We waved them away and sat down on the bed alongside the coal stove as Muhlberg offered the journalist and mayor some chairs. Laundry hung overhead and there was a samovar on the battered windowsill. Nina, Muhlberg's wife, busied herself in the adjoining kitchen.

"So you see how a Soviet citizen lives," the journalist said, as if to acknowledge that we had found what we were looking for.

"Tell me," he said, with a grave expression, "it's interesting for us professionally, why have you come to see this kind of a shack?"

I told him Muhlberg was our friend.

The journalist smiled bitterly. He glanced at Muhlberg and then, turning to us, said, "Your friend, what do you see in him? There are so many interesting people I could introduce you to. They could tell you things that would make you stand with your mouth open."

"That's excellent," I said, "why don't we meet them?"

"I know someone," he said, "who has been working in the restoration of churches or monuments of architecture. He could tell you more about this area than you ever wanted to know."

"We're ready to meet him at any time."

"But tell me why, it's intriguing for me. Why do you come to see this man, why is he interesting for you?"

"Well, if you must know," I said, "it's a personal matter. These are our personal relations. We knew each other in Moscow, and, frankly, I don't think that the reason for our visit is any of your business. Who invited you here? Did Adolph invite you?"

"They came to give me the news about the granting of my visa," Muhlberg said.

The reality of the situation began to sink in.

"The visa?" I said. "Does this mean you can leave the country?"

The journalist and the mayor nodded glumly.

"After thirty-three years," I said, "they are finally going to let you go." I hesitated a moment, taken aback myself by the news.

Finally, I turned to the mayor and the journalist and said, "Let's drink a toast."

Muhlberg poured out some vodka for the five of us and I lifted my glass and proposed that we drink to "Adolph's new life."

The two Soviets sat silently holding their glasses.

"You're not going to insult me by refusing to drink?" I asked them, enjoying their discomfort. It was too laborious and too painful to recall the many times I had been pressured into drinking toasts to "peace," "friendship," and other dubious concepts as defined by the Soviets.

They looked on forlornly and said they would drink, and at last each of them downed his vodka.

I returned to the subject of why we were interested in Muhlberg. "Since you've brought such good news," I said. "I suppose I should explain to you why we've come. Adolph, for us, is a very interesting person. He was born in the West and grew up in the West. He has a Western mentality. Yet he lived for thirty-three years in the Soviet Union. Try to imagine the situation. It would be the same thing as if a Soviet citizen lived for thirty-three years against his will in the heart of China. Wouldn't his experiences be of interest to you?"

"We have good things here and we have bad things," said the journalist. "I admit it. So why do you listen to someone who tells you only bad things?"

"This man is an invalid," the mayor said, referring to Muhlberg. "Who will take care of him in the West?"

"How do you imagine the West?" the journalist asked Muhlberg. "Do you think it is all milk and honey?"

Muhlberg said that West Germany was a welfare state where the ill and handicapped were taken care of and he knew what to expect.

The mayor then changed the subject. He said to Muhlberg, "What don't you like about our country?"

"There is no democracy here," he replied.

"What do you mean by 'democracy'?" the journalist asked.

"The right to emigrate," Muhlberg said. "They don't keep people by force in countries in the West. There are other things. You can buy rolls in the morning. You can read in the newspapers that they criticize their own leaders. There are cartoons of Reagan. Here, if you say something against the leaders, they lock you up."

"Your notion of democracy is infantile," the journalist said. "When someone mentions democracy to you, you think of rolls. I want you to know that I speak my mind, I speak out frankly, and for fifty years, no one has put me in prison."

"I've been imprisoned twice," Muhlberg said.

"There must have been a reason," the journalist said firmly. He then glanced at Nagorski and me.

"What do you tell them about Soviet life?" he asked Muhlberg.

"About how people drink."

"You see! He just tells you this type of thing. Let's talk honestly. I'm no anti-Semite, no anti-German, although I am antifascist. But we were destroyed in the war."

"So was all of Europe," Muhlberg said.

"Why don't we switch to a more neutral subject?" I suggested. "Tell me," I said to the mayor, "how many people live in the town."

To my surprise, a sly look came into his eyes. "Why are you asking?" he said.

The journalist interrupted him and said, slightly embarrassed, "You can tell him. It's not a military secret. There are about three thousand people in the town."

At this moment, the door opened and a uniformed policeman came in.

"Is that your car on the road?" he asked, referring to Nagorski's car, undoubtedly the only Volvo in Berendeevo.

Nagorski said it was.

"I noticed that one of the tires is flat. Can I see your documents?"

Andy gave him his documents and the man began to examine them. I had not brought my passport along and, in general, did not carry it, since I disliked having to present it to any policeman who took an interest. I gave him my American Express card, the only piece of identification I had in my wallet.

The policeman studied the card attentively and asked what it was, at which point the journalist said that it was a document which guaranteed payment for bills.

"As a colleague, I can vouch for them," he said and then winked at us.

The policeman asked if we had had any trouble on the road from Pereslavl-Zalessky. His "question" confirmed for Nagorski and me that the authorities had been responsible for the gravel heaped up in piles on the only road that linked Pereslavl-Zalessky with Berendeevo.

The policeman then suggested we leave before it got dark, as we might have trouble going back. He added there was nothing for us to see in Berendeevo, no historical monuments.

We walked out to the car and inspected the tire, which we later learned had been punctured with a knife. The policeman made himself as intrusive as possible while we changed the tire. He then offered some last comments on Muhlberg. "You could have done better in picking a friend," he said. "I know him. He's not a good type. Drinks a lot."

The policeman's odd remark underscored Muhlberg's vulnerability. As we got into Andy's car, I was struck by the eeriness of a country which could swallow a man for thirty-three years and then suddenly cough him back up.

12

The Roots
of Fanaticism

Alone in the world, we gave the world nothing and have taken nothing, we have in no way contributed to the progress of human reason and everything that came to us as a result of this progress, we distorted.

—*Pyotr Chaadaev,* First Philosophical Letter

ONE NIGHT, while working late in the office of the *Financial Times*, I received a call from Mikhail Berdnikov, who asked me to meet him in the home of a woman he had been treating in the center of Moscow. I left my office and, slightly after 11 p.m., arrived at an old building where a broken chandelier hung in the darkened, stone lobby. A long row of blue metal mailboxes at the base of a marble staircase indicated that the building had been converted into a warren of communal flats.

In the entryway of apartment 16, a young man in an undershirt sat smoking in a threadbare armchair. Not far away, a woman in a bathrobe stood talking on the telephone.

I was met by Misha and Pyotr Reznichenko, who led me down a long corridor and opened the door to a narrow room. Inside the room, on a bed against the wall, framed between a small night table and a cupboard, was a head of white hair lying on a dirty pillow. An old woman tried to lift herself up and I saw a gaping mouth with a few yellowed teeth and then smooth cheeks and soft gray eyes.

I approached the bed and Anna Izraelovna, Berdnikov's friend, extended a firm right hand to shake mine. She asked Berdnikov to help her sit up and Reznichenko put her left arm in a sling.

"Excuse me," she said, "this is not familiarity but the excitement of the presence of a new person." Anna Izraelovna sat up with Misha's help and I realized that she had urinated on the bed.

I turned away and looked around the small room, which had a certain coziness about it. The cupboards were crammed full of Anna Izraelovna's personal belongings and on top of them were piles of books. There were bottles of medicine on some of the tables and the teapot was boiling on the hotplate. I sat down next to Anna Izraelovna on a chair beside her bed.

"I deeply respect England," she began, ". . . for the involuntary decency of the English people."

I interrupted her to explain that I was an American.

She hesitated and added that she also respected America.

"But," she said with more emphasis, "you cannot understand what we understand in Russia. You can know that 5 or 10 million people died in collectivization, that yet another 20 million died in the war and that yet another 20 million were people we killed ourselves, but understand me correctly, you can only look on in amazement, you cannot understand what this means because the West does not have the spirituality to understand what happened here."

She began to tremble involuntarily and her chin shook.

"You in the West devote yourselves so completely to material enrichment that you only guarantee your spiritual impoverishment. People here have suffered and we have very little, but in our suffering has come understanding, and this is something that you Western people will never understand because you haven't lived as we've had to live.

"Misha," she called softly, and Berdnikov came over. "Forgive me," she said, "I get very tired." Berdnikov helped her to lie down again in bed.

She sighed and I could see that her frailty was bringing the conversation to an early close. As I got up to leave, she said, "I hope I haven't offended you with what I've said. . . . Please, as a favor, allow me to kiss you." I bent down and she kissed me on the cheek. "Bless you," she said, "come back again."

THE DESIRE TO LIVE for an ideal was not just a matter of isolated individuals in the Soviet Union. The hunger for higher meaning characterized people from all walks of life. It was this which made Soviet citizens credulous and self-sacrificing and cut them off psychologically from the pragmatism of the commercial West.

During my first years in the Soviet Union, I often wondered why atheistic communism triumphed in Russia, which was once regarded as perhaps the most religious country in Europe. But the longer I lived there, the more I became convinced that it was not an irony but a historical inevitability that a people who had long ceased to value the moral judgment of the individual, would one day throw off its mental bondage to a messianic religion in favor of a messianic ideology.

Russian life, with its intensity of likes and dislikes, its lack of a sense of individual responsibility, but also the capacity for commitment and self-sacrifice, is set at a higher pitch of emotional intensity than life in the West, where respect for freedom, based on a traditional appreciation of ethical transcendence, is able to bring a moderating influence to bear on worldly conflicts.

Soviet citizens were involved in a constant search for spirituality with which to endow their brief and often miserable lives. But this search had nothing to do with transcendence. They looked instead for a single source of absolute truth and expected it to be clear, inarguable, and revealed to them here on earth.

Secular God Seekers

People with a secular outlook searched for an intellectual system.

One night, I went to see Gennady Shimanov, an anti-Semitic and anti-democratic Russian nationalist. At my request, he described his evolution.

Shimanov said that it all began in the early 1960s. The Twentieth Party Congress had exposed the crimes of Stalin and after years of being assaulted by the regime's materialist ideology, people were groping for an ideal that could point the way to a better life. One expression of this was the poetry readings in Mayakovsky Square, in which many who would later become well-known dissidents participated.

At the same time, in the Historical Library on Starosadsky Lane, it was possible to read the émigré Russian philosophers whom the authorities had not bothered to remove from the shelves, assuming they were of interest only to narrow specialists.

In this atmosphere, Shimanov decided he would search for truth and, once he found it, organize his entire life accordingly. He had been raised an atheist and a materialist, but, like others, he discovered the Historical Library, where he began to read Kropotkin, Berdyaev, Berishkovsky, Dostoevsky, Shakespeare, and Bulgakov. He read even when he had almost nothing to eat, and gradually, under the influence of Dostoevsky and the Russian religious philosophers, he came to the opinion that, if there was any sense in life, it did not come from Marxism-Leninism.

Shimanov lived in a shed in a courtyard on Potapovsky Lane that had been built by his grandfather, and he began to invite some of the other readers from the Historical Library to come home with him. In time, the house filled up with a wide assortment of characters: philosophers, black-market operators, adventurers, homosexuals, bandits.

The people who stayed with Shimanov formed a floating community. As a rule, their days began in the Moscow cafeterias, where bread was provided free with a meal. Typically, one person ordered a meal and six others split it. The group would then repair to the library, spend the day reading, and return to Shimanov's, where they would stay up talking until 3 a.m. They slept on whatever was available, beds, folding beds, sofas.

One of those who found his way to the house was Yuri Samoilov, who said that he had spent ten years in Kolyma for participating in an anti-Soviet organization. Samoilov was erudite, had no money, and proved quite charming. He told everyone that after ten years in Kolyma he did not believe in anything, and he argued that the most important thing in life was to make money.

Samoilov tried to put his principles into practice. He persuaded a group of Moscow writers and philosophers that he could get morphine from Tashkent and transport it north to Kolyma, where there were many drug addicts, and sell it at a huge profit. All he needed was money to buy the morphine. The writers, charmed by Samoilov and greedy for a share of the profits, gave him money. He collected thirty thousand rubles and then disappeared and was never heard from again.

With the easing of repression, a number of communal apartments emerged in Moscow where people gathered who were not in agreement with the official ideology. One such flat was the home of Yuri Mamleyev, a mathematics teacher. Another was the apartment of Yelena Stroyeva, who received foreigners at a time when foreigners almost never met with ordinary Soviet citizens. It was possible to find Catholics, fascists, homosexuals, poets, artists, and surrealists at these places. Alexander Yesenin-Volpin, who at the time was an anarchist, visited, as did many of the poets who read their verse at Mayakovsky Square.

Shimanov became acquainted with Mamleyev in the Historical Library at a time when he had still not formulated his own views. Mamleyev told him he was an idealist and follower of Kant. When Shimanov said he was a materialist but not a Marxist, it seemed to him that Mamleyev looked at him with black hatred.

Mamleyev wrote stories about the struggle between good and evil in which good always triumphed, but a change came over him as a result of his acquaintance with Samoilov, who had taken a large sum of Mamleyev's money. Mamleyev began writing stories mocking the good in the world. He said that God was his personal enemy and he tried to found his own religion, which he called Yainost, from the Russian *ya* for I. The main tenet of this faith was that he was the only real thing in the world and all others were his impressions. Shimanov asked if this meant that when Mamleyev spoke to him he was really speaking to himself, but Mamleyev avoided an answer.

Shimanov tried to learn something from everyone he met. One of the habitués of the Historical Library was Lev Barashkov, a disciple of Nietzsche and Chaadaev, who spoke in favor of absolute individualism and renounced all morality. Another member of this circle was Ilya Barashkov, who came to people's homes in a Nazi uniform. He spoke fluent German and knew Hitler's speeches by heart. Later, he became an Old Believer and grew a beard. There were also a group of mystics who were interested in Eastern philosophy and persuaded a young artist to share their interest.

In a country slowly trying to recover from all the years of Stalinism and materialism, the mystics were able to persuade the artist that Chandra, the tiger in the Moscow zoo, was one of the materializations of Buddha, and that it was possible to receive higher knowledge from him if you looked at him persistently in the eye. Exploiting his sincerity and susceptibility, the mystics sent the artist to the zoo, where he spent hours standing in the cold looking at Chandra, while they had sex with his wife.

* * *

SHIMANOV MADE the acquaintance of Konstantin Puchkov. Puchkov was a language student who had a dream in which he felt he saw truth (*istina*), but when he woke up, he could not remember what it was. He had the dream again, but he could not remember it. On the third night, he once again had the sensation of being alone with *istina*. Through an act of will, he woke himself up and, using a burned match, wrote something on the back of a box of cigarettes and fell asleep again. The next morning he read on the cigarette box, "the smell of kerosene." That was what *istina* was.

Puchkov had large, thoughtful brown eyes, a pensive expression, and an angular face. He had gracious manners and spoke English beautifully. After learning the content of his dream, he decided that the only way to discover truth was to dedicate himself to it completely and renounce ordinary life. He quit his institute, left home, and became a vagabond, sleeping on staircases when he could not stay with friends. He stopped eating but preserved his gracious manners, which presented a striking contrast to his way of life and cadaverous appearance. He worked from time to time and even managed to hold down occasional jobs as a translator, but he was in the grip of something not of this world. In the late 1960s, he got a job as a watchman on the riverbank in the Vladimir oblast. One morning, he was not found at his station, and a few days later his body was fished out of the river, cause of death unknown.

MOSCOW IN THE 1970S and 1980s was a city awash in healers, yogists, Krishnaites, parapsychologists, and the followers of various gurus and nature worshippers.

Among the gurus one of the most famous was Porfiry Ivanov, who was also known as "The Teacher." Ivanov was six feet six inches tall, with enormous broad shoulders and a long white beard, which had not been cut for many years. When he was a young man, Ivanov found force in his hands and learned that he could use this force to cure people. It was at this time that he also began to take off his clothes. He had a vision while sitting on the top of a hill. He saw an enormous long snake that began coiling, and he understood that the snake was universal evil, and that all the evil in the world came from the fact that man offended nature.

He traveled all over Russia in the 1930s, wearing only shorts, even in bitter cold. A sect of Evangelicals who were flagellants found him in a village in the North Caucasus. They had wandered for years looking for a "naked God." The flagellants took him back to their village of Bogi in the Rostov oblast, which was renamed Novo-Kondruchy after the war.

No one is certain who from the outside world discovered Ivanov first. But he began to be visited regularly and, in time, he worked out a system of teachings. He preaches the unity of man and nature and warmth between people. He advises his pupils, who include students from Rostov as well as intellectuals from Moscow and Leningrad, to stand barefoot on the earth not less than twenty minutes a day, to wash themselves twice a day with cold water, and to fast for four hours on Wednesdays and for seventy-two hours from Friday through Sunday. He never uses the word *God*. He always says he consults with nature, and he always speaks about various miracles involving people who were affected by nature.

For many years, people from surrounding villages came to him to be cured, and his abilities as a healer caused his reputation to spread. In 1970, he was put in a mental hospital and was only freed in 1974, after his pupils collected enough money to buy a color television for the chief doctor.

Every year, on the Soviet Day of the Teacher, hundreds of people from the surrounding villages and his pupils from all over the country gather on a hill near the village to listen to Ivanov's stories and seek his advice.

In 1978, Ivanov came to Moscow to speak to the director of the Moscow oncological center on Kashirskoe Highway. He brought letters from thirty individuals who said he had cured them of cancer. The temperature was 30 degrees below zero centigrade and he walked barefoot through the snowy streets, dressed only in shorts. The doctors at the center refused to speak to him, but finally the director of the center told him, "Get dressed and I'll speak to you."

"How can I dress?" said Ivanov, offended by the doctor's manner. "I am a naked fact."

In 1979, when several hundred gathered in Novo-Kondruchy to pay tribute to Ivanov on the Day of the Teacher, the authorities in Rostov, who had tolerated Ivanov for a time on the assumption that he was a harmless rural crank, decided that the situation had gone too far and a new sect was being created. The village was surrounded by soldiers and the crowd was dispersed.

IN THEIR FINAL YEARS, the Old Bolsheviks saw a lot of each other in the Lenin Sanatorium near Kratova Station and in Hospital 60 on the Boulevard of Enthusiasts. One of them whose experience became familiar to me was the mother of A.I., a shy, soft-spoken woman who was totally dedicated to Marxism-Leninism.

A.I. believed that his mother was probably fanatical by nature. When her brother died of tuberculosis in Belorussia, she was so grief-stricken that she ate out of her brother's plate in order to contract the disease. (She did infect herself and was only saved because, as a member of the Komsomol, she could be treated in a special hospital in the Crimea.) As a young woman, she participated in the "class war in the countryside."

In the 1930s, A.I.'s mother became a teacher of social science in a Moscow institute. She was so devoted to Marxism-Leninism, and so oblivious to what was going on around her, that, at times, she ignored her own well-being, which could have been better served by taking the doctrine less seriously. On one occasion, when one of Stalin's theoretical contributions was being discussed at a party *sobraniye*, she rose to say that what Stalin had said was not new but only a reformulation of a known position. She was not ready to allow anyone, even Stalin, to misrepresent Marxism. It was only because her colleagues chose not to denounce her that she avoided arrest.

A.I.'s mother did not reject Stalin during his lifetime, but the exposure of his crimes at the Twentieth Party Congress allowed her to make sense of doubts she had, until then, managed to repress. In the end, she fully approved of the exposure, by Khrushchev, of the "cult of personality." This, however, did not affect her faith in Communist doctrine.

Periodically, a young party official from the raion committee, who obviously knew next to nothing about Marxism, would appear at her institute with a checklist in order to evaluate her teaching of a subject to which she had devoted her life. She would demonstrate before others his utter ignorance.

A.I.'s mother had a tendency to fantasize. No amount of mere experience, for example, could alter her faith in the sacred qualities of the Soviet worker. When A.I. mentioned that Solzhenitsyn had called the Soviet Union "a lie elaborated into a way of life," she said, "He can only make such a statement because he doesn't believe in the working class." When a drunken maintenance man showed up at the door, seeking a bribe to perform his required work, she did not see him for what he was but only as a shining example of the international proletariat.

GRIGORY SERGEIEVICH N———, another Old Bolshevik, was a member of the party since April 1917 and a participant in the revolutionary events in the Urals. He read *Pravda* every day and also received the Sverdlovsk newspaper. In order to be fully informed, he listened to the Voice of America, the BBC, and other foreign radio broadcasts and also tuned in every night to "Vremya," the nightly news program on Soviet television. All of this information helped him to reach his conclusions about the world situation, and he wrote continually to the Central Committee with advice on Soviet foreign policy.

In 1985, he made the following suggestions:

The Polish government should not pay any interest on its Western loans. It was difficult to refuse to pay back the principal, but Poland should definitely not pay the interest. The answer to the problem of Afghanistan was to organize a Komsomol brigade to combat the aggression from Pakistan—"volunteers," as they were called in the Spanish civil war.

In the Western Hemisphere, the Soviet Union should put its missiles in Cuba and in Central America. It should also try to agree with Canada. After all, the United States was friendly with Turkey and put its missiles not far from the Soviet border.

Grigory Sergeievich was proud of any sign of his status and showed a visitor a note of thanks that he received from the Central Committee for the first of two letters that he sent them, but he was concerned because they had never answered his second letter.

SOPHIA MAGARIC was born in Riga and studied medicine in Petrograd. In 1917–18, she did underground work for the Bolshevik Party in Latvia and then returned to Russia in 1918, where she worked as a medical volunteer during the civil war. In 1934, she was excluded from the party for her work in the Latvian Communist underground and this probably saved her life. When the purges began, they were directed against current members of the Communist Party.

After Stalin's death, Magaric rejoined the party. Her son, Vladimir, tried to ask her about the purges but she refused to answer. He asked her how she could join a party that had inflicted so much suffering, but she refused to respond to this too. Despite her reticence, Magaric took her party obligations seriously. She attended *sobraniyes* regularly, and after an exhausting two-year battle, she was granted uninterrupted seniority in the party. She continued to read Marx and Lenin and the reminiscences of Old Bolsheviks, and she expressed respect for Lenin.

One event in particular seemed to awake in Magaric a sense of party feeling. This was the fiftieth anniversary of the revolution in 1967, when it was well known that there were going to be awards given to persons who had contributed to the founding of the Soviet state.

Magaric rarely spoke about anything connected with the party, but, unusually for her, she mentioned several times to Vladimir that the granting of awards would be coming up soon. She felt that on the basis of her prerevolutionary work in the underground, participation as a medical volunteer in the civil war, and fifty years of irreproachable service as a doctor saving hundreds of children from death, she qualified for the Order of Lenin, the highest award.

She was called to the raion party committee shortly before the anniversary and given the "sign of distinction," the lowest award. The sign of distinction was given routinely to all Old Bolsheviks, even those who joined the party much later, and a pattern had developed according to which Jewish Old Bolsheviks tended to get the sign of distinction whereas the higher orders went to Russians.

When Magaric came home, she said nothing but it was obvious to her son from her expression that she was deeply distressed. A friend of hers called and asked, "Well, what did you get? A Jewish order?"

Magaric was despondent for a long time. She said nothing, but her unhappiness was reflected in her voice and expression. She knew that she deserved the Order of Lenin. She had remained loyal and steadfast, despite all the years of hardship. She had silenced her own doubts and continued to participate in meetings of the party, and now, at the age of seventy-one, she wanted some sign of recognition that never came.

. . .

THE SITUATION OF the Old Bolsheviks was very familiar to a silver-haired man in Moscow who, in the 1930s, had been a high official in the Soviet government. Through a lucky draw in the "lottery," as he put it, he was not shot during the purges. He was arrested in 1939 and spent many years in the labor camps, emerging from the Gulag after Stalin's death. The former official sometimes talked about the attachment of the Old Bolsheviks to Marxism-Leninism.

"If a man loses faith in his past," he said, "he sometimes looks for a rescuing thread. For many of the Old Bolsheviks, this thread is the party. They have a desire to, as they put it, 'go back to Lenin.' They try to analyze the current situation on the basis of what Lenin would have done and they usually come to the conclusion that, despite everything, they must serve this government that Lenin created.

The former official said that many of the Old Bolsheviks tried to reexamine their beliefs, but they almost always stopped short of criticizing Lenin and the October Revolution. "One person rejects Stalin," he said. "Another rejects Stalin and some acts of Lenin. In the first instance, they blame Stalin for the fact that he wiped out the Old Bolsheviks."

Having subordinated their lives entirely to the demands of the movement, the Old Bolsheviks could not reject Marxism-Leninism without admitting that their entire previous life was a mistake, a dilemma which, to a certain extent, they imposed on the entire country. There were very few among the Old Bolsheviks with the inner strength to make such an admission.

"It's impossible to talk to these people," the former official said. "They are like unstoppable phonograph records, repeating schizophrenic observations that have no relation to reality.

"Now, some people dwell more in their minds on colleagues, family members, or friends who were arrested or killed. They recall their faces, the arguments they had, they try to prove to themselves that, while the purges were going on, they did the only thing they could have done. They say that the work of the revolution is unfinished, while others, on the border of senility, ramble on about 'judicial errors.' "

Believers

Believers search for miracles. . . .

At 5 a.m. on a cold autumn morning in November 1981, I got off the train from Moscow in Velikiye Luki, walked through an empty waiting room, and emerged on a large square. I had come to try to find out about a miracle that had supposedly taken place there more than twenty years earlier.

As the surrounding forest became a silhouette in the dawn's blue light, I walked through the sleeping city and crossed the wooden bridge over the Lovat River, arriving at length in an area of log houses divided by a dirt road that led to the base of a knoll. Halfway up the knoll was an Orthodox church.

In Moscow, Father Sergei Zheludkov told me the following story: In 1959, during Khrushchev's campaign against religion, a young girl in Velikiye Luki who was believed to be crippled for life began to walk again after praying at the Shrine of Xenia the Blessed in the Smolensk cemetery in Leningrad. The girl was named Nina Novikova. She was about eighteen and had been paralyzed and unable to walk without the help of crutches for many years.

Novikova was often in pain and sometimes had to lie motionless for days. She might have given up hope of ever walking again had not a group of believers urged her to travel to Leningrad and pray for relief at the shrine.

Nina went to Leningrad that autumn and prayed at the shrine, and a miracle occurred. After a lifetime of paralysis, she was suddenly able to walk. When she returned to Velikiye Luki, she was walking unaided and her recovery brought joy to the believers.

The sight of Novikova walking without crutches in the middle of Khrushchev's campaign against religion, however, created panic among the local party officials. She was summoned to the KGB, where they demanded that she state that she had been cured by doctors. She was interrogated by a KGB agent who told her to take off her crucifix. When she refused, he struck her in the face. A priest in Velikiye Luki wrote to Khrushchev to complain that Novikova was being persecuted, which, in turn, led to the priest being accused of slander.

There was a penetrating dampness in the air, and the church and adjoining graveyard were thick with greenery and trees. The gloomy silence was broken only by the cooing of the pigeons in the bell tower and on the church's slanted roof.

The first rays of daylight revealed an overcast day, and there was no sign of life around the church. Just before 8 a.m., however, old women in black coats and shawls, some of them hunchbacked and a few walking with canes, began to arrive from all directions, stopping to bow low and cross themselves, and then turning and hobbling up the weathered brick walkway to the church.

By 8 a.m., the churchyard was again empty and I entered the church. In the dim, filtering light, the believers began to buy candles and soon the lights of hundreds of burning candles were reflected in the protective glass of a dozen icons. Gentle old women kissed the glass covering the icons, bowed low, and kissed the floor of the church before gathering in the area in front of the altar to wait for the service to begin.

The service lasted for two hours and, when it concluded, many of the worshippers dropped to their knees and bowed with their foreheads to the floor before filing out into the churchyard.

Although it began to rain, a number of the believers lingered, and I approached some of them to ask whether they knew anything about a young crippled girl who had been cured after praying at the shrine of Xenia the Blessed in Leningrad.

One woman said she did not know anything about any miraculous cure. The priest also said he had never heard about it. One of the few men who had attended the services said that nothing of the kind had ever happened. The crowd began to disperse.

I noticed a tiny, hunchbacked woman with a wrinkled face and slightly crossed eyes. I asked her if she knew about a crippled girl who once lived in Velikiye Luki and had miraculously begun to walk.

"You mean Nina," she asked, holding the ends of her gray shawl under her chin, "the girl who walked on crutches?"

"Yes," I said, "that's the girl I'm thinking of."

"Oh, yes," she said, "that's Nina Novikova. She hasn't been seen for years."

The old woman hesitated for a moment, as if trying to recall something. "Nina was a nice girl," she said, "but they wouldn't leave her in peace. She walked to this church."

"When?" I asked. "After she was cured?"

"Yes, afterward. She had never walked before, no one had ever seen her."

I asked the tiny woman to sit with me on one of the wooden benches, and as we sat down, a woman with round, rosy cheeks and a gray mustache sat down on the bench on my other side. I tried to continue the conversation with the tiny woman but the new arrival pulled my arm sharply and, having gained my attention, started telling me about a miraculous cure that had been performed by a witch in Odessa.

Not sure why she was repeating this, I asked her if she knew anything about a girl named Nina Novikova.

"No," she said, "I never heard anything about her," and then she looked at me fixedly.

"Why are you interested in this case?" she asked.

"I'm just curious," I said.

"Oh, no," she said, grimacing and shaking the hairs on the end of her chin, "that kind of questioning isn't the result of just curiosity."

There were informers in every Soviet church, and there was something unmistakable about the calculating look in this woman's eyes. I turned my back to her and began to listen to the frail older woman.

"How did you react," I said, "when you saw Nina walking?"

"We were very happy," she said softly with a gentle expression in her watery eyes. "We took it as a sign from God."

While we spoke, other women came over to join us. They spoke freely and I realized that earlier they had been silent out of fear. The story they told in the churchyard differed in some respects from what I had heard from Father Sergei in Moscow. They said that Novikova broke her back while skiing, and when she lay in the hospital, the slightest vibrations caused her such pain that she screamed in agony. The doctors tried various treatments, but nothing helped. Finally, she was sent home and the doctors arranged for her to receive an invalid's pension, an admission that nothing further could be done for her.

One of the women said she was a nurse and had treated Nina. She said that she saw a spinal X-ray and that Novikova's spine was so grossly bent and misshapen that it would have been impossible for her to walk in that condition.

When Nina returned from Leningrad, however, she was walking normally. As news spread of her cure, the local authorities accused her of making religious propaganda. When she refused to say she had been cured by doctors, an article appeared in the local newspaper accusing her of pretending to have been cured by God.

At first, Novikova hid in her mother's house and seldom went out. She then went to live with one of the believers. Finally, she left Velikiye Luki to live in a women's monastery.

The churchyard had become very quiet. After the story of what happened to Nina Novikova had been told, I saw that besides the swaddled old women clustered around me, the only other person in the vicinity was a young man in a black jacket standing at the lower end of the brick walkway.

When our group broke up, the mustached woman who stood firmly at my elbow asked me to come with her to meet an exorcist, but I ignored her and walked with the nurse on the brick walkway and then down the dirt road, which led into the city. The man in the black jacket followed us, ducking behind bushes in an effort not to be seen.

After I had been back in Moscow for several months, I again met Father Sergei and told him about the trip to Velikiye Luki. He then admitted that he had been the priest who had complained to Khrushchev about the persecution of Novikova. When I told him what I had learned in Velikiye Luki, he said it conformed in general to what happened there.

"I didn't hear that there was a skiing accident," he said, "but that could have happened. As for the X-ray, I don't believe that. At the time, people said that Nina was paralyzed, not that her back was broken. The paralysis was of unknown origin."

Father Sergei said he was only saved from a slander charge when a believer told the procurator that something out of the ordinary had happened to Novikova, and the case was closed for lack of evidence.

He indicated it was true that Novikova left Velikiye Luki, but he could not say if she went to live in a monastery. He was never able to find out what happened to her because, in the wake of the problems he had because of the miracle, he left the town as well.

AT 8 a.m., on April 26, 1987, in the tiny village of Grushevo in the Western Ukraine, nine-year-old Maria Kizyn left home and, closing a wooden gate behind her, began walking down a dirt road in the direction of the church. It was a gray, overcast day with patches of snow still on the ground. Suddenly, Maria felt waves of warmth coming from the direction of the church. She looked up and noticed a woman in black hovering about three feet above the ground in front of the church.

Maria ran back to her house.

"Mama," she shouted, "the Virgin Mary has appeared."

Yaroslava Fyodorovna, Maria's mother, immediately ran out with Maria to the church. She also saw the shadowy image.

Maria and her mother told the neighbors. Within fifteen minutes, the news had spread throughout the entire village.

As the days passed, the shadow did not disappear. It remained visible, like an immaterial statue, and word of the appearance of the Virgin spread throughout the Drohobicz *raion*. Within two weeks, the entire Lvov oblast was discussing it and, in Lvov itself, there was a rumor that the Virgin was dressed in blue and yellow, the national colors of Ukraine.

People began going to Grushevo. As the crowds grew, foreign radio stations reported on this apparent appearance of the Virgin Mary. By June, pilgrims were arriving by the thousands. On any given day, the village was crowded with anywhere from 40,000 to 100,000 persons. It became impossible to get a train to Dorozhev, the nearest railroad station. In the center of Grushevo, around the church, a continuous crowd of thousands kept vigil, many of them holding white candles.

The local authorities were taken aback. They stopped buses and cars from Lvov and Drohobicz, and said there was a quarantine because of the illness of cattle. When their cars were stopped, however, people proceeded on foot, and the dirt roads leading to Grushevo began to be littered with abandoned vehicles. By the time the KGB tried to close off the roads leading to Grushevo entirely, it was too late. The river of people could no longer be turned back.

Ivan Gell, a historian and recently released political prisoner, was living with his mother in the village of Klitzko near Lvov, where he worked as a shepherd on the Bolshevik collective farm, helping to care for 183 cows. He heard about the appearance of the Virgin almost immediately but could not leave the cows. By the time he arrived in Grushevo, it was already the end of May. When Gell approached the village, the cupolas of the Ukrainian church were illumined with a halolike glow. He pushed to the front of the crowd and saw a floating shadow, the image of a woman and a child about

five feet from the walls of the church. It had very clear delineation
and people were praying in ecstasy.

As Gell looked at the image, he was overwhelmed with the feeling that the time he spent in prison was not in vain. He felt the solidarity of thousands who wanted religion and wanted a Ukrainian
nation.

In May, Gennady Sitenko, a night watchman at the Puppet
Theater in Moscow, heard from a friend about the appearance of the
Virgin Mary in Grushevo. For several months, Sitenko had thought
that the Virgin would soon be appearing, so when he heard about
the events in Grushevo, he was not surprised and decided to visit
monasteries in Ukraine. He went to a monastery in Kiev and then to
a monastery in the village of Alexandrovka, 120 miles from Belgorod,
where the Virgin Mary appeared in the 1920s. Standing on that
ground, he felt he was on sacred soil. He then went to a monastery
in Mukachevo and, finally, to the Uspensky Pochaev Monastery in
Pochaev. In Pochaev, he was told how to travel to Grushevo.

On June 14, Sitenko took a bus to Grushevo; the bus stopped five
miles from the village, and from there a local resident gave him a
ride the rest of the way. When he arrived at the church, he saw that
there were thousands of people, many of them on their knees.

It was a rainy day and, at first, Sitenko did not see anything. But
then, after a minute, he saw the Virgin hovering next to the balcony
and bowing to believers.

This is how Gennady described what he saw:

"Energy came from the balcony and made the greens more vivid
and brighter. It rained and the flow of energy began to change the
surroundings, which began to glow in gold. In gold, the world became ten times richer and brighter.

"A light came from the Virgin and the whole area began to resemble a living golden icon. The heavens became gold, the rain
disappeared and the light from the Virgin pulsed.

"I felt a flow of light on myself that went to my heart and exceeded a mother's love by ten times, as if a light wind covered me.
The greatest symphony in the world sounded in me. When the militiaman looked at me suspiciously, I realized that I loved the
militiaman."

In the evening, there were thousands of people with candles in
their hands. A few people cried because they did not see the Virgin,
but then gasped when they spotted the movement of her hand.

The KGB and plainclothes police tried to pull people out of the crowd. When they heard organized praying, they shouted over loudspeakers, "Stop it! Don't interfere with order!"

A priest said, "We pray for our Ukrainian people, for our children, and for the sinners and atheists who persecute us."

As it began to get dark, two enormous aviation searchlights were rolled into the area and shined on the church, but the image was still visible. The next day, the local newspapers claimed that the searchlights had demonstrated that the shadowy figure was an optical illusion, but pilgrims continued to come to Grushevo to see the Virgin Mary for weeks thereafter.

13

Ukraine

"Ukraine Has Not Yet Died"
—Ukrainian national anthem

KIEV, AUGUST 24, 1991

A FAINT LIGHT FILTERED through the opaque-glass ceiling of
the hall of the Ukrainian Supreme Soviet as Leonid Kravchuk took
his place at the table in the elevated speaker's box and the deputies,
still shocked by the events of the last six days, filled the benches in
even rows. Three days earlier, the coup to preserve the Soviet Union
had come to an end, and now the question of independence for
Ukraine hung in the air. No one believed that the Communists, who
held the parliamentary majority, would vote for independence. But
workers in Kiev's biggest factories were being organized to seize the
parliament if they refused.

At 10 a.m., Kravchuk declared the meeting open and two opposition deputies, Ihor Yukhnovsky and Dmitro Pavlichko, demanded
that he give an explanation of his failure to call the people into the
streets during the coup.

Kravchuk appeared calm and self-confident. He said that his goal
had been to prevent the imposition of emergency rule in Ukraine,
that he had deliberately not called for demonstrations to avoid giving
the authorities a pretext for repression. "I had no troops under my
command and there was no Ukrainian KGB," he said. "Sovereignty

351

has to be backed up. But if the coup plotters had put tanks on the streets of Kiev, my reaction would have been different."

When Kravchuk finished speaking, democratic deputies said he displayed cowardice during the coup and he should be deprived of the right to rule. Kravchuk, however, was unmoved. "I was forced to maneuver," he said, "to preserve peace."

The next person to speak was Stanislaw Gurenko, the first secretary of the Ukrainian Communist Party. Opposition leaders in Lvov had raided party headquarters and found copies of instructions from Gurenko to local Communist organizations telling them to follow the orders of the coup committee. Gurenko, however, was arrogant and matter-of-fact. He said that the party did not participate in the coup and would continue to be society's ruling force.

Gurenko's remarks evoked expressions of outrage in the hall. Deputies began shouting "Shame!" and dozens of them ran up to the podium shouting, "You should be arrested." Gurenko tried to continue speaking but he was drowned out; as the chaos heightened, Communist and opposition deputies shouted at each other until it looked as if fights would break out at any moment.

Finally, Larysa Skoryk, a deputy from Kiev, regarded by Ukrainian Americans and Canadians as "the pit bull of the opposition," elbowed her way through the deputies surrounding the podium, entered the speaker's box, and pushed Gurenko out of the way physically, shouting, "He has no right to speak. He should be arrested." Seeing that there was no way he could finish his speech, Gurenko stepped down and left the hall. Kravchuk then called a break and the hall was cleared.

By now there were nearly ten thousand demonstrators in the square outside the parliament building carrying hundreds of blue and yellow Ukrainian flags and signs reading WE ARE NOT SHEEP and BYE, BYE, U.S.S.R. Vyacheslav Chornovil, a deputy and former political prisoner, left the building to speak to the crowd. "We'll stand our ground there," he said. "You stand yours here."

After the break, the nationalists began making speeches. There were calls for the creation of a Ukrainian army and accusations that the party was responsible for the killer famines in the 1930s and the nuclear accident at Chernobyl. Volodymyr Yavorivsky, a deputy from Kiev, said that the history of Ukraine was one long struggle for independence. "Our grandchildren won't forgive us," he said, "if we miss this chance." Many of the Communists sat holding their heads and staring at the floor. Finally, Yukhnovsky called for a vote on independence and Kravchuk called for another break.

The Communists left the hall and met in the cinema in the basement. They were completely disoriented. The Russian parliament had suspended the Russian Communist Party the previous day, and most of the Communists felt they had no choice but to distance themselves not only from the coup but also from events in Russia. The idea of Communists taking the initiative to dissolve the Soviet Union, however, seemed to most of them incredible. One of the deputies said, "I don't see why we should be independent. We've done nothing wrong."

The discussion, however, soon began to focus on the critical question of whether the Communists could continue to hold power in an independent Ukraine. Some of the Communist deputies began to argue that, with Yeltsin in charge in Moscow, independence was a way to save Communist domination in Ukraine, perhaps under a different name. At the same time, everyone realized that the Communists risked losing everything if they resisted and the parliament was dispersed by force. Gurenko summed up the situation: "If we don't vote for independence, woe to us."

At 4 p.m., the Communist deputies began to negotiate. Olexander Moroz, their leader, contacted the opposition caucus with the message that he would find it difficult to vote for independence without a referendum. A short time later, Pavlichko, Yukhnovsky, and Yavorivsky gave Moroz the text of a declaration with a clause providing for a referendum.

At 5 p.m., debate on the declaration began in the caucus. Many of the Communist deputies were unable to remain in their seats. They stood up, tried to calm themselves, and began pacing. Finally, a vote was taken on the declaration and, by a show of hands, the Communists decided to give it their support. Afterward, they filed out of the basement meeting room, still shaken by what they had done but arguing among themselves that this was the only way for them to hold on to power in Ukraine.

At 5:55 p.m., a tense silence filled the hall of the Supreme Soviet as the deputies took their places and prepared to vote on the declaration of independence. Kravchuk announced he was giving the floor to Levko Lukyanenko, another former political prisoner, who had spent twenty-three years in Soviet labor camps.

Lukyanenko replaced Kravchuk at the chairman's platform and

called for a vote on whether Ukraine should be declared an "independent, democratic state."

As the deputies inserted cards into the voting machines on their desks, all eyes turned to the electronic monitor on the wall. There was a pinging sound as the apparatus registered the votes and the deputies waited for the verdict of history. Suddenly, the results flashed: 392 in favor of independence, 4 opposed. The hall erupted in a storm of applause.

The nationalists believed they had achieved their goal of an independent Ukraine, and the Communists believed they had avoided catastrophe and would be able to save their positions in a new Ukraine.

At 9 p.m., Kravchuk agreed, at Chornovil's request, to allow the crowd into the hall. The doors were opened and the people poured in, carrying an enormous yellow and blue Ukrainian flag. As the flag was spread out over the table for members of the presidium, nationalists began singing "Hey u Luzi Chervona Kalyna," the unofficial hymn of Ukraine, and also the national hymn, "Ukraine Has Not Yet Died." Lukyanenko called for order without success. Finally, after about ten minutes, the hall calmed and Lukyanenko said, "The cause for which many generations fought and suffered has been realized. What other nations have long taken for granted—their own state— we at last have achieved."

The scene in the Ukrainian parliament marked the end of a process that had taken more than five years. When Gorbachev and his colleagues initiated the policy of glasnost, they had little notion that it would lead eventually to the separation of Ukraine. With the advent of glasnost, however, the direction of Ukrainian history changed. Glasnost broke the magnetic hold of the Marxist "internationalist" ideology, and by acquainting Ukrainians with the details of Russification and the artificial famines in Ukraine in the 1930s, it also helped cast Russian-Ukrainian relations in a different light. For the first time, many Ukrainians began to see their country not as a "fraternal republic" but as an oppressed country, and nationalism began to reappear.

Ukraine's drive for independence was the product of this reappraisal. In Western Ukraine, the part annexed by the Soviet Union after the Second World War and immediately subjected to mass terror, the determination to throw off Soviet domination always existed. In the rest of Ukraine, however, it developed gradually, as increasing numbers of people—disoriented by the collapse, under the impact of freer information, of the universal theory that once defined their lives—experienced a crisis of consciousness and began to change their view of a once familiar world.

THE FIRST IMPORTANT event in Ukraine's drive for independence was the inaugural Congress of the Ukrainian Popular Movement for Restructuring (Rukh), Ukraine's first political opposition, in Kiev in September 1989.

In 1987, independent clubs started to be organized in Ukraine, including environmental groups such as the "Greens" and the Shevchenko Society of the Ukrainian Language, whose purpose was to defend the Ukrainian language. Nonetheless, the atmosphere in Ukraine continued to be repressive, particularly in comparison with that in the Baltics. Dissenters were arrested and fired from their jobs, and samizdat newspapers were seized. In September 1988, police in Lvov attacked a crowd of demonstrators with dogs.

In March 1989, however, a group of writers in Kiev, under the influence of the growing national movement in the Baltics, announced the formation of Rukh. The group, at first, took pains to stress its loyalty to communism. Its program, which was published in the newspaper *Literaturnaya Ukraina*, called for democratization and cultural autonomy, but it also spoke of the "leading role" of the party and the "perfection of socialism." Nonetheless, members of the Shevchenko language society began circulating petitions in factories, demanding that the organization be allowed to exist. In a matter of weeks, they had collected hundreds of thousands of signatures in support of Rukh, principally in the Western Ukraine.

The idea of Rukh also gained support in Kiev, and the need for such an organization was debated on Ukrainian television. By the time the founding congress opened on September 8, 1989, the new organization was the center of attention throughout Ukraine.

At the Rukh Congress, which was attended by 1,500 and watched on television throughout the republic, speakers described the artificial famine of 1933, Russification, the injustices of the social system, and the effect of the explosion at Chernobyl on Ukraine's ecology with a frankness that was unprecedented in an officially sanctioned public forum. Although many speakers tried to give the impression that they were proponents of reform and therefore interested in preserving the Communist system, there was an undercurrent of revolt. At the end of the first day, a representative of the Latvian popular front stood up and said, "We are all going in one direction, the liquidation of the Communist dictatorship and the creation of a multiparty system."

The hall exploded with applause.

AS HE LOOKED out at the crowd that had gathered for the Rukh Congress in the Kiev Polytechnical Institute, Miroslav Popovich, chairman of the Kiev division, had the sensation that he was witnessing a national gathering of all Ukraine. Never before had he been in a meeting where so many different types of people— Cossacks, Orthodox clergymen, coal miners, Crimean Tatars, party officials—were expressing themselves so freely.

After a day spent discussing Ukraine's ecology, elections to the Ukrainian Supreme Soviet, the state languages in Ukraine, national symbols, and ethnic issues, including anti-Semitism (which was condemned), the speeches turned to the issue of political control in the republic. Lukyanenko said, "Our history is a history of occupation, but we have suffered most under the Russians. This is why our goal must be to leave the Soviet Union." Sergei Konyev, another delegate, called for an "end to the reign of political dinosaurs." He said that Vladimir Shcherbitsky, the party leader, should be brought to trial for his handling of the Chernobyl nuclear disaster. "There can be no talk of reform in Ukraine when the criminals responsible for Chernobyl are still in power."

As Popovich watched from his place on the stage at the table for members of the Rukh leadership, he became convinced that a national renaissance was under way.

For years, Popovich worked in the Institute of Philosophy in Kiev and wrote works on the philosophy of science and mathematical logic. One of his books was *Logic and Scientific Knowledge*, a discussion of scientific reasoning for general readers. The manuscript did not have any quotes from Marx or Lenin; when the first proofs were ready, Popovich was threatened with dismissal for "political nearsightedness" and forced to add the citations. Some time later, he organized a scientific conference and was accused by a representative of the Central Committee of "crude methodological mistakes." It turned out he had not opened a brochure summarizing the conference papers with a quotation from Brezhnev. Even after Gorbachev first began to speak of the need for change and to use the terms *glasnost* and *perestroika*, it seemed to Popovich that Shcherbitsky resisted reform in Ukraine. The central Soviet newspapers had become freer, but there was no liberalization of the press in Ukraine and there was no change in the leaders at the top.

The situation began to change, however, as a result of the accident at the Chernobyl power station, April 26, 1986.

On the night of April 27, Popovich met a teaching assistant in the vestibule of the institute who seemed frightened and out of breath. "Did you hear the news?" she asked. "There's been an accident at the Chernobyl power station."

"Do you know what happened?" Popovich asked.

"I don't know," she said, "but I've heard it was serious."

Popovich went home and tried to listen to a broadcast on one of the foreign radio stations over the jamming. He knew that if there had been an accident, it would not be reported on Soviet radio. But even on Deutsche Welle, he heard nothing.

By the following day, however, Kiev was swept with rumors, and on April 29 the BBC carried the first detailed reports of the explosion and radioactive gas leak and told residents of Kiev to close windows, wash floors, and stay indoors.

Confusion began to reign. There was no indication from any Soviet source that the citizens of Kiev had anything to fear, but there were rumors of mass evacuations from the site of the reactor. Foreign radio stations, audible despite the jamming, were saying that the explosion had involved the largest release of radioactivity in nuclear history. On May 1, a beautiful, sunny day, the Ukrainian Communist leadership organized the traditional May Day parade and the Kreshchatik, Kiev's main street, was filled with workers with red banners, Ukrainian folk dancers twirling and jumping, and children with paper flowers, all of whom were unaware that they were being exposed to doses of radiation in the air nearly two thousand times higher than normal.

On May 2, however, Kiev was swept with panic. The reason was that the foreign radio had broadcast that the Communist leaders were evacuating their children. By the end of the day, nearly everyone was trying to send children and women of childbearing age out of the city. On May 3, with the official media still silent about the accident, Popovich led a discussion on local television about the economy. He knew there had been a major catastrophe but he did not dare mention it on television. After the program, Popovich escorted a Moscow official, who had been one of his guests, to the railroad station, where hundreds of people besieged every train, trying to get relatives into packed passenger cars. The official became frightened, and he and Popovich went from platform to platform trying to find a way to get him on any train leaving Kiev. With Popovich's help, the official finally squeezed onto a train for Moscow late that night.

On May 4, Popovich took his daughter and granddaughter to the station, where there was now complete chaos. Tickets had become meaningless. Fights broke out on the platforms as people tried to squeeze women and children into the passenger cars. The compartments soon became so crowded that it was impossible to close the doors, and each train left the station as packed as a metro train at the height of rush hour. Finally, Popovich got his daughter onto a train for Leningrad and handed his granddaughter to her through the window.

IN THE MONTHS following the accident, there was a gradual expansion of glasnost, but Popovich did not take the changes seriously. It was only in 1989 that he became involved in an event which was to radicalize consciousness in Ukraine, the formation of Rukh.

One afternoon in February, Popovich was invited to the House of Writers by Vyacheslav Brukhovetsky, a literary critic, and Boris Oleinik, the party secretary of the union of writers, and asked to help organize a Ukrainian popular front, like the ones that already existed in the Baltics. A friend of Popovich's was already writing the economic program for the organization and he agreed to join.

On March 20, Rukh held an organizational meeting in a small theater on Tchkalova Street that was attended by sixty people, most of them party members and well-known official writers. The participants did not request permission for the meeting, so it was illegal under the laws then in effect.

The mood at the meeting was tinged by nationalism, which was particularly strong among Kiev's writers. All of the discussion was in Ukrainian and one of the demands was for a law forbidding parents to choose the language of instruction of their children. In their speeches, the delegates also charged that party officials were inhibiting perestroika and said that "Ukraine is the Vendee of perestroika." At the end of the meeting, Ivan Drach, a poet who had been the acting chairman, turned to Popovich and unexpectedly suggested he become the chairman. Rukh was oriented, at least officially, toward support for Gorbachev, and Popovich's attitude toward Gorbachev had changed in the three years since Chernobyl. If he previously distrusted him as much as any Communist leader, he now believed that Gorbachev represented progress, and that if the population did not defend him, he would be removed. He decided to accept the position.

Three days after the first meeting, Rukh's program was published in *Literaturnaya Ukraina* and soon groups of support were organized in factories and scientific institutes, and ordinary citizens began to contact the leading members of Rukh and ask for their protection in dealings with the Soviet bureaucracy. In only a few weeks, Popovich thought he saw the growth of an embryonic opposition.

In April, members of the Kiev organization raised the question of a founding congress for Rukh. On April 2, Kravchuk, the party chief for ideology, came to the headquarters of the writers union and met with Popovich and other leaders of Rukh, but no agreement was reached. Kravchuk said that Rukh should commit itself to helping the party improve the lot of the people, and the Rukh representatives, in turn, accused party leaders of caring only about their privileges.

After this initial meeting, Popovich began to meet with Kravchuk separately. He tried to persuade him that it was advantageous to allow the congress to be held in Kiev because, with the present Rukh leadership, it would be possible to have a dialogue. If Rukh was persecuted, the present leadership would be succeeded by different people and they would be more difficult.

Kravchuk finally suggested a televised discussion on the question of whether Rukh was really necessary in a situation in which it was the party that was carrying out perestroika. Popovich agreed. The broadcast was announced and Popovich was soon inundated with offers of anecdotes to illustrate the absurdity of the party's attempt to hold onto exclusive power. Popovich used several of them and Kravchuk did not know how to respond.

In the second discussion, Kravchuk simply threw up his hands and said he did not understand why Rukh was necessary.

Having failed in the attempt to persuade the public that Rukh was redundant, the party tried to sabotage the founding congress with endless procrastination. The Rukh leaders wanted permission to use a large hall in Kiev for the congress, but party officials said that the Rukh program was poorly written and they could not tell what kind of organization they were dealing with. Articles in the Communist-controlled press said that Rukh wanted to inspire hatred against Jews and Russians and to force them to send their children to Ukrainian schools.

While this was going on, Rukh branches were forming rapidly in all parts of the republic, and it became clear that continued resistance to it would provoke a confrontation that the party, under conditions of perestroika, would find difficult to sustain. The Communist leaders decided instead to try to co-opt Rukh and permission was given for the founding congress in Kiev on September 8.

AS THE CONGRESS continued, Popovich felt uneasy about the militant tone of some of the speeches. Rukh had been divided between those who wanted to support perestroika and those who desired independence. It seemed to Popovich, however, that without having constituted itself into a true organization, Rukh was already emotionally committed to independence. Blue-and-yellow flags were scattered throughout the hall and nearly a hundred resolutions were passed, many of them about historical events beginning with the seventeenth century. Former political prisoners, grouped in the Ukrainian Helsinki Union, recalled past oppression, which added to the atmosphere of suppressed radicalism. In addition, the delegates were aware that they were being watched on Ukrainian television, which encouraged emotional speeches.

Finally, Ivan Saly, chairman of a raion party committee in Kiev, stunned the audience by calling for greater autonomy for Ukraine and demanding the resignation of Shcherbitsky. His appearance demonstrated that Rukh had potential support even among some leaders of the party. When asked whether the party would be able to work with Rukh, Saly responded, "We have to."

The establishment of Rukh gave a focus to activism in Ukraine. In the months after the founding congress, the frequency of mass demonstrations increased, culminating, on January 21, 1990, in the next important event in Ukraine's drive for independence: the "Ukrainian Wave." In this show of support, more than 300,000 demonstrators formed a human chain linking Lvov and Kiev.

.   .   .

THE CENTER OF grass-roots activism quickly became Lvov. Most of Western Ukraine had never been part of the Russian empire, and after it was annexed by the Soviet Union, 10 percent of the region's population was exiled to Siberia. As a result, national feeling there was as strong as in the Baltics, and people began to organize against the Communist regime the moment there was a reduction in police terror.

On September 17, 1989, Lvov witnessed the largest demonstration in its history to mark the fiftieth anniversary of the entry of Soviet troops into the city under the Molotov-Ribbentrop Pact. Fifteen priests of the banned Greek Catholic (Uniate) Church led an open-air service at noon for nearly 250,000 persons in the square in front of the Porokhov Tower. The participants said prayers and then marched with candles and icons through the city in a broad stream to the gates of the St. Yuri Cathedral, which was closed to Uniate believers, and held a service. At 7 p.m., the demonstrators gathered again in the city center for a silent vigil in memory of the victims of the Soviet occupation. At 9 p.m., they returned home and turned off their lights and put candles in the windows, transforming the entire city into a flickering memorial.

When the first demonstrations began, parents in Western Ukraine begged their children not to take part, saying, "You'll be shot just as our brothers and sisters were." But seeing the mass support for Ukrainian nationalism, people lost their fear.

On October 1, 1989, thousands of demonstrators marking the "Day of Lvov," marched through the city center behind a young girl in national dress who was tied up with only her legs free. A rumor spread that some students had been arrested. Part of the crowd left the march and went to the central police station, where they were told to disperse. Many, however, caught in a cul de sac, did not leave. The police then attacked the demonstrators, beating some of them savagely. Nearly forty people had to be hospitalized. In response, the local Rukh leaders called for a general strike, and on October 3, all work in the city, with the exception of emergency services, stopped. It was Rukh's first demonstration of political power. The police were never again to attack a group of demonstrators in Lvov.

By the end of October, Rukh activists, confident of support for Ukrainian nationalism in Western Ukraine, developed a plan to communicate the activism of Western Ukraine to the rest of the republic by organizing a human chain between Lvov and Kiev.

• / •

A STEADY RAIN washed the spires and facades of central Lvov on January 21, 1990, as Mikhailo Boichyshyn, a worker in a conveyor factory who had become a Rukh leader, started his car and began slowly navigating through the crowded cobblestone streets. Everywhere he looked, he saw crowds of people carrying the Ukrainian flag.

As he left the old city, Boichyshyn turned into a new district, where he passed long columns of demonstrators, some led by Uniate priests. Finally, Boichyshyn emerged on the highway to Kiev, where he saw a sight that convinced him that Ukraine's drive for independence was unstoppable. The highway cut through open, straw-colored fields that reached out to the horizon under the gray, wet sky, and on both sides of the road and for as far as the eye could see, demonstrators stood, like an unending picket fence, with linked arms and waving flags, in a show of support for a free Ukraine.

Boichyshyn came from a family that, like most in Western Ukraine, was touched by repression. His mother was exiled to Siberia and an uncle died in the Vorkuta mines. During the Brezhnev years, Boichyshyn was not politically active. But when liberalization began in the Soviet Union, he organized a branch of the Shevchenko Language Society in his factory. The group's first official act was to address statements to the factory management in Ukrainian. In March 1989, after the announcement of the formation of Rukh, Boichyshyn set to work in his factory to organize a branch.

The idea of Rukh attracted great interest among the workers because, unlike the Shevchenko Society, which focused on language, it meant potential political opposition. There had not been any legal political opposition in Western Ukraine since the area was annexed by the Soviet Union in 1944, and in the wake of postwar terror and Russification, the area smoldered with suppressed Ukrainian nationalism. As the Rukh branch met in the conveyor factory, other branches were organized spontaneously in other factories. In a matter of months, Rukh had become a mass organization in Western Ukraine.

Boichyshyn's life started to change. Soon, he was staying out every night, meeting with other activists in apartments and factory halls, discussing ways of expanding Rukh's dense network of local organizations.

He also took part in demonstrations. On May 1, Boichyshyn joined the vanguard of the five thousand to six thousand demonstrators about a hundred yards from the city hall where local Communist leaders prepared to review the May Day parade. Suddenly, the crowd surged and broke through the police cordon. Boichyshyn fell and was kicked by police, but other demonstrators flooded into the parade area and marched past the official reviewing stand carrying placards with nationalist slogans and Ukrainian flags.

By September, when the Rukh founding congress was held, the Ukrainian flag was being displayed everywhere on the streets of Western Ukraine, and there were demonstrations to commemorate the anniversaries of important events in the life of the short-lived independent Ukrainian republic or the commemoration of major deportations. The demonstrations grew larger until they attracted as many as 100,000 persons.

Despite this outpouring of nationalism in Western Ukraine, however, Boichyshyn and other Rukh activists in the region were disturbed by the obvious absence of nationalist fervor in heavily Russified Eastern Ukraine. Boichyshyn traveled regularly to cities in Eastern Ukraine in hopes of helping to reproduce the success in mass organization that Rukh had had in Lvov. He also wanted to try, by preaching ethnic harmony, to soften the image of Ukrainian nationalists as intolerant of other nationalities. But everywhere he went he encountered puzzlement or hostility.

In Ternopol, Boichyshyn took part in the ceremonial reburial of the victims of a Stalin-era execution squad, and after the reinterment, he spoke about the history of political terror in Ukraine. During most of the speech, the audience listened respectfully, but when he said that it was Lenin who gave the first orders for shooting priests, there were shouts of protest and people in the crowd began to say that it was all lies.

In Poltava, the bus in which Boichyshyn was riding was stopped by the police and forced to pull over to the side of the road. Rukh sympathizers met the buses and said that activists were being taken off trains and police were stopping cars with Lvov license plates. They also reported that people in Poltava had been warned for days that extremists from Western Ukraine were planning acts of terror. Seeing that there was no chance of holding a planned rally in the city center, Boichyshyn led the demonstrators to a nearby park, where he argued that Ukraine would be able to control its own fate only under conditions of independence. Many of the onlookers, however, identified the demonstrators with the followers of Stepan Bandera.

"You're Banderites," they said.

"That's right," many of the demonstrators answered, "we're Banderites. Bandera worked hard for Ukraine to become a European state."

"But he committed atrocities."

"It was during a time of war and no one's hands were clean."

Finally, a woman in the crowd shouted, "I agree that Ukraine should be independent, but you can't come out this way against Lenin, against the red flag and all we fought for in the Second World War."

In Donetsk, Rukh activists, including Boichyshyn, went from mine to mine handing out leaflets and literature. Almost nowhere were they well received. Sometimes they were turned away at the mine entrances. But even when permission to talk to the miners was granted, they made little progress in changing people's minds. "It's all the same to us what language we speak," one miner told Boichyshyn, "as long as there is sausage."

Boichyshyn referred to the people who expressed these views as "sausage people."

"The historical situation is such," another miner said, "that we always lived with Russia."

"The fact is," Boichyshyn told him, "we were forced to live with Russia."

"But Russia means timber, gas, and oil."

"Actually, all these things are taken from Ukraine," Boichyshyn said.

As they repeatedly experienced hostility and skepticism in Eastern Ukraine, Rukh activists, including Boichyshyn, became convinced of the need for actions that would link both parts of the republic. This led to plans for the Ukrainian Wave.

Driving down the highway, Boichyshyn saw that the turnout for the Ukrainian Wave had exceeded even his most optimistic expectations. The original plan had been for the demonstrators to be separated by ten meters and to hold a ribbon between them, but in many parts of the route, instead of a ten-meter separation between demonstrators, people stood with linked arms three and four rows deep.

Boichyshyn traveled up and down part of the route, addressing problems as they arose. In Novgorod-Volinsk near Zhitomir, a gap appeared in the line. The local authorities had told the inhabitants that cutthroats were coming and had frightened them into staying away. Boichyshyn and other activists succeeded in busing in replacements from Western Ukraine. When some factories refused to release buses or said there was no gas, Boichyshyn and his colleagues appeared to demand the buses and paid rent for them. He had had his doubts as to whether the demonstration would be supported in the eastern part of its route, but it drew an enthusiastic response throughout the republic. The human chain was not only complete, it was extended in a loop from Lvov to Ivano-Frankovsk.

In Kiev, there was a huge rally attended by an estimated sixty thousand persons. There were also meetings in Kharkov, Zaporozhe, Odessa, and Donetsk. By the end of the day, Boichyshyn, who had worked tirelessly to organize the Ukrainian Wave, felt convinced that the rift in the country was beginning to be bridged.

AFTER THE UKRAINIAN WAVE, the national movement turned its attention to the artificial famines of the 1930s, and the next important event in Ukraine's drive toward independence was the commemoration of the genocide in September 1990 in Targan, a village near Kiev.

By early 1990, the full psychological impact of glasnost was being felt. Mine shafts filled with the bodies of Stalin's victims were being excavated all over the country. It seemed that every day, new skeletons were being exhumed and candles were being lit. Most disturbing for Ukrainians, however, was the testimony that was published in the newspapers about the artificial famines directed against the peasantry during the 1930s, particularly the famine of 1933.

For years, it had been common to regard the boundaries between Soviet republics as unimportant, but Ukrainians now learned that during the 1930s, the boundary between Russia and Ukraine had been the demarcation between life and death because the Soviet authorities did not inflict an artificial famine on Russia.

People in all parts of the republic were forced to think about the difference between Soviet and Ukrainian identity. The Ukrainian language, long confined to Western Ukraine and the countryside, began to be more widely spoken and Ukrainian scholars, for decades prevented from writing about their history honestly, started to describe Ukrainian history as a litany of Soviet and Russian crimes.

The country remained divided. In March 1990, the first semi-free elections in the history of Soviet Ukraine gave Rukh a striking victory in Western Ukraine, but the Communists, taking advantage of their widespread control of the workplace, prevailed in the rest of the country. As a result, Kravchuk was elected chairman of the new parliament and only about a fourth of the deputies were democrats. By this time, however, there had been a change in the attitude even of Communists. On July 16, the Ukrainian parliament, under the influence of the sovereignty declaration in Russia, asserted Ukrainian control over the republic's resources as well as the right of Ukraine to have its own army and establish Ukrainian citizenship.

IN VIEW OF THIS rising national consciousness, the desire to know the past became, for many people, an obsession, and it led thousands of Ukrainians to converge on Targan.

On September 7, 1990, as the setting sun bathed the Targan cemetery in its slanting light, Olexandra Ovdijuk held the hand of her friend Olisa Maslo and cried freely. She could hardly believe that, after so many years, the world was remembering what had happened in this remote place.

Volodymyr Manyak, a Ukrainian historian, ascended the stairs of a wooden platform that had been erected over three elevated burial mounds beneath which were the bones of 360 people who died of starvation in 1933. Nearby was a statue of a little girl bearing a cross. On the statue was written: "Through starvation and brutal work, they were deprived of life."

Ovdijuk waited for Manyak to begin. How, she wondered, could mere words describe what had happened here?

On a gray November morning in 1987, Ovdijuk walked out to the mailbox for her copy of *Selsky Visti*, the Ukrainian agricultural paper. She took the paper back to her small wooden house, sat down next to the coal stove, unfolded it, and received a shock. In a front-page article, the newspaper gave a detailed description of the 1933 famine.

Ever since the beginning of the new policy of glasnost, the newspapers had been getting freer, but Ovdijuk had not expected anything like this. She ran out of the house to the home of her friend Olisa Maslo, who had also survived the famine.

"Have you seen the newspaper?" Ovdijuk asked.

"I saw it."

For more than fifty years, the two women had talked about the famine only among themselves. Ovdijuk had taught history in the village school, praising the "achievements" of socialism. She had not breathed a word to her students about the famine. But she and Maslo had long ago vowed that they would one day collect the names of the residents of Targan who died of starvation.

"Well, are you ready?" Ovdijuk asked.

"I'm ready."

"What if they arrest us?"

"I'm not afraid."

It had been a lifetime ago, yet to Ovdijuk it seemed only yesterday.

First, the Soviet authorities arrested the best farmers, including Ovdijuk's father. They then herded the rest into collective farms. When production fell, they blamed the result on "sabotage." Squads of "activists" were sent into the villages in the fall of 1932 to confiscate "hidden" grain. The raiders entered homes, tore up the floors, and stabbed the earth with iron rods. They took everything, the entire harvest, all the reserves, and the entire seed fund.

The peasants begged the raiders to leave something of the grain behind, but they were ignored.

In December 1932, with hunger already spreading over the Ukrainian countryside, Ovdijuk's mother took her by wagon from the Poltava region to Targan, where she had been born, and left her with her uncle, Grigory Ovdijuk. She then went to work in the Sumi oblast, where conditions were rumored to be better.

By the end of 1932, the remnants of the grain fund were exhausted. The peasants subsisted on potato peels and waited for relief from the cities. But relief never came. Emaciated horses died and the people cut up their meat and ate it.

At first, the villagers thought there had been some terrible mistake, but as the days passed, they started to realize they were the objects of a diabolical plot. First, medical and government representatives stopped coming, then roadblocks were set up along the highways to keep the peasants from leaving. Military guards surrounded the railroad stations, even the most insignificant. The villagers saw, to their horror, that the authorities had decided to imprison them in the countryside and that there was no food.

There began to be a desperate fight to find something to eat.

People dug up acorns and ate mice, rats, sparrows, ants, and earthworms. They ate tree bark, blades of grass, and autumn leaves. First the children died, then the old people.

As the famine deepened, one student after another in Ovdijuk's school stopped coming to class. One day, shortly before the school was closed, the teacher asked Ovdijuk and two other children to find out why Timosh Babenko had not come to class. When the children went to Babenko's home, they learned that his mother, driven mad by hunger, had chopped him up with an ax.

By late February, the sounds of normal life in the village had given way to an impenetrable silence. The villagers' only hope was the winter wheat, but the winter wheat was buried under layers of snow. In a frantic effort to cheat death, the villagers ground up bone and ate shoe leather, they ate sorrel, lichen, and nettles.

On a blustery day, a man with wild hair and burning eyes entered the house where Ovdijuk lived with her two cousins, a boy of five and a girl of nine. The man had a knife and he took the girl Alina and pulled her arm to him and began trying to cut off a piece of flesh. She was so emaciated, however, that there was nothing to cut. "You're only bones," he screamed. He was ready to murder the girl when he noticed some beets lying just outside the door and ran out of the house to get them. The terrified children quickly closed the door behind him.

The specter of death was everywhere. The arms of the villagers turned to sticks and their stomachs ballooned hideously. They could not stop urinating. As the wind howled over the snow-covered fields, bodies piled up in yards and on the huts' earthen floors. A driver with a horse and wagon rode slowly through the village and collected the bodies and then rode to the cemetery and threw them one by one into an open pit.

Ovdijuk managed to avoid death because her uncle had a job on a nearby collective farm and was given a regular portion of flour. In late March, however, she and her cousins' legs began to swell. Ovdijuk wrote to her mother, "Come and get your daughter because we are dying." Finally, in late April, Olexandra's mother arrived in Targan with a sack of corn flour. When Ovdijuk's five-year-old cousin saw his aunt, he said, "We are saved!"

After feeding her family, Olexandra's mother took her daughter for a walk through the silent village. Leaves were appearing on the trees but there was no sign of life in the huts. Finally, they came to the home of a cousin, Adam Kaplun. When they opened the door they saw three dead children laid out on the kitchen table side by side. On a nearby bench were two more dead children. Kaplun was not there. Olexandra learned that he had died earlier. The mother, who had arranged the bodies, sat in a chair. When she saw Olexandra's mother with a sack of corn flour, she said, "Now, I'll die, too." She stood up and expired before their eyes.

By 1987, much had changed in Targan.

The clay houses with thatched roofs that lined the muddy roads at the time of the famine had been replaced by brick houses. There were television antennas and telegraph lines. The earth had become bountiful and the collective farmers raised grain, potatoes, sugar beets, vegetables, corn, and buckwheat in the fertile fields.

Where a deadly silence once reigned, the sounds of geese and roosters added to the noise of tractors and motorcycles. The eight months of famine in 1933, when 360 of the village's 900 people starved to death, however, lived on in the memory of those who survived it. Officially, there was no famine. It was impossible to read about the famine. If the famine was mentioned in a novel, the novel was censored. If a collective farmer dared to call attention to the famine, he risked arrest. But the older villagers spoke about the famine among themselves.

Ovdijuk and Maslo were already on pension, but with the first published accounts of the famine, they visited every house in Targan where there were people old enough to remember what had happened. At first, the people were afraid to talk. The slightest noise outside the door led them to freeze in fear of the KGB. Some survivors began to cry and could not go on as they remembered their friends and family members who died a slow and gruesome death from starvation. But others spoke clearly and in great detail. Ovdijuk asked them to write down the names of every person they knew who had died in the famine, including the small children.

As she gathered names, Ovdijuk became a haunted person. She saw the victims as they had been before death overtook them, and each of them seemed to be saying to her, "What about me? . . . and me . . . don't forget my name."

Soon, other residents of Targan began compiling their own lists, and Ovdijuk compared theirs with hers to confirm the names of the victims in each ill-fated clay house.

While Ovdijuk and Maslo were compiling their lists, the newspaper *Literaturnaya Ukraina* began to discuss the famine. The paper published excerpts from a book by Volodymyr Manyak and Lidia Kovalenko, in which they said that the famine was an act of genocide against the Ukrainian people. The paper also published an appeal to those who remembered the famine to write to Manyak and Kovalenko. Ovdijuk wrote to Manyak and he traveled to Targan and recorded her testimony and published her list of the starvation victims of Targan.

Ovdijuk's meeting with Manyak proved to be fateful. He invited her to Kiev to testify at a symposium on the famine, and then, when it became necessary to choose a spot to commemorate the victims of the famine, he selected Targan.

"What happened in 1933," said Manyak, "exceeded all the dark dreams of all the hangmen of the world. The perpetrators had high positions in the Communist system and turned their punishing sword on their own people. In the earth lie 9 million of our people. A similar act of bestiality does not exist in history."

As he spoke, thousands of yellow candles cast aureoles around the faces in the crowd. "There is no analog to such a crime of a government toward its own people. The famine was directed against Ukraine and specifically against the village. The village was the guardian of the national spirit and the national language and customs."

The crowd began to sing "Ukraine Has Not Yet Died." Johann, the episcop of the Zhitomir eparchy, called for the preservation of the "undying memory of the innocents murdered by famine." The people in the crowd crossed themselves and prayed. A folk ensemble entertained the crowd with a song entitled "Red Kalina," after the Ukrainian national tree.

Finally, there was a memorial dinner at midnight and then the crowd dispersed.

As they walked back into the village in the moonlight, Ovdijuk and Maslo passed a few remaining thatched huts and the row of weeping willow trees that the wagon of emaciated corpses had passed on the way to the burial pit in the cemetery.

Ovdijuk remembered a little girl who refused to leave her dying mother, who had tried to abandon her at a nearby railroad crossing in the hope that she would be picked up by the police and adopted. "Oh, little girl," she thought, her heart aching, "do you still live on this Ukrainian land where your mother died?"

In the weeks after the memorial service for the Targan famine victims, Ovdijuk recalled the years of silence about the famine and realized that something fundamental in the country had changed. Year after year, she had taught that Soviet history was the story of "great achievements," including collectivization. Now, the famine was being discussed openly. In the church in nearby Parkhomovko, regular services were being held for the victims of the famine.

The greatest change, however, was political. With keener awareness of the horrors of the famine, people saw the Kremlin as their victimizer. For years, the Ukrainian village preserved its customs and language but made no show of dissent. Now, the attitudes long harbored in the villagers' silent hearts began to be shared throughout the republic.

The city had come to them.

AFTER THE TARGAN ceremony, nationalism swept over Ukrainian society, eventually affecting even the armed forces. The culmination of Ukraine's drive toward independence was a meeting, on July 27, 1991, of Ukrainian officers in Kiev to prepare for the creation of an independent army.

BY THE FALL OF 1990, the power of the Communist establishment in Ukraine appeared to be crumbling under the twin blows of glasnost and a worsening economic crisis. On September 14, Lvov became the sixteenth city in Western Ukraine to take down a monument of Lenin, and throughout the republic, food disappeared from the stores and the lines for gas were half a mile long.

On September 30, more than 100,000 people rallied in front of the Council of Ministers building to demand implementation of the declaration of sovereignty and then marched down the Khreshchatik, where they were joined by others until their number reached 200,000, making it the largest anti-Soviet demonstration in Kiev's history. Students set up tents in Revolution Square with the same demands and announced that they were going on a hunger strike. The number of hunger strikers in the square steadily increased, and the crisis was resolved only with the resignation of the prime minister, Vitaly Masol.

On March 17, in the Soviet Union's nationwide referendum, 70 percent of the Ukraine voted in favor of preserving the Soviet Union, but 83 percent had voted yes to a question of whether Ukraine should be part of the Soviet Union on the basis of the declaration of sovereignty. There were sharp variations according to region. In Western Ukraine, only 15 percent of the voters were in favor of preserving the Soviet Union. In the Russian-speaking Eastern Ukraine, however, up to 80 percent supported preserving the Soviet Union.

By the beginning of 1991, a split had developed among Communists in the Supreme Soviet. The "imperial" Communists supported a Union Treaty proposed by Moscow that called for central control of finances, customs, the KGB, the army, and all union factories. At the same time, the national or "sovereign" Communists wanted Kiev to control Ukrainian industry. Under the influence of growing nationalist sentiment in the republic, the sovereign Communists began to be the clear majority.

In the meantime, draft evasion in Western Ukraine became nearly universal, and as the press published numerous reports about the deaths of Soviet army recruits accidentally or during hazing, there were demands throughout Ukraine that soldiers from Ukraine serve only on the territory of the republic.

On February 2, despite warnings from higher Soviet army officers and intensive shadowing by the KGB, a group of two hundred Ukrainian officers met in Kiev and passed a resolution demanding the creation of separate Ukrainian armed forces, which they said was the logical result of the declaration of sovereignty.

In April and May 1991, agitation continued among Ukrainian officers. Despite harassment and threats of retaliation from the army high command, the officers who had met in Kiev in February prepared for a founding congress of an independent Ukrainian Union of Officers in the capital to be held in July.

Colonel Vilen Martirosyan looked out at the four hundred officers who filled the meeting hall in the Kiev House of Teachers that July 27 and prepared to speak. The atmosphere in the hall was so tense that many of the officers did not dare wear their uniforms. Martirosyan, however, was in uniform. "It is simply not acceptable," he said, "that a mother has to fear that her son will be murdered in the army. In a Ukrainian army, this will not happen."

The building was surrounded by army patrols that had orders to arrest officers in uniform, and Sharikov, head of the political directorate of the Kiev military district, had threatened to drown the delegates in the Dnieper River. Police from Western Ukraine, with blue-and-yellow ribbons marked "security" around their arms, patrolled the halls and checked the identification of journalists. But there were whispers about future court-martials and rumors that the meeting would be broken up by force.

Martirosyan introduced women from the Soldiers' Mothers of Ukraine group. Holding photographs of soldiers in uniform with black ribbons across the upper-left-hand corner and, in one case, a photograph of a soldier in his coffin, the women choked back tears as they described the fate of their sons in the Soviet army. One woman described how her son was beaten to death by older, Central Asian soldiers when he refused to clean the floor with a toothbrush during a hazing exercise. Another told of a son who died of sunstroke after being exercised for six hours in 104-degree heat without the benefit of an adaptation period. Another mother related how her son and scores of others were mowed down "accidentally" by machine-gun fire during a murderous training exercise.

When the mothers' group had finished making its statements, Martirosyan, who was sitting at a long table against the backdrop of a large Ukrainian flag, said, "Our sons are being killed in the service of an imperial army. Empty declarations of sovereignty are not enough. If Ukraine is moving toward not just 'paper' independence but the kind of independence that every other state has, we need an independent Ukrainian army."

Martirosyan arrived in Rovno in 1985 from Siberia, taking command of the First Ukrainian Regiment. Conditions in Rovno were typical of those in the Soviet army at the time. Commanders received apartments out of order and helped themselves to scarce consumer goods from the city warehouse. Soldiers were abused with profanity and there was widespread drunkenness.

Martirosyan, however, had developed ideas for democratizing the armed forces while he served in Siberia, and by 1986, amid the talk of perestroika, he decided to try them out.

Martirosyan's first goal was to put a stop to *dedovshchina*, the beating of young recruits by soldiers a year or two older. He did this by calling in the parents of the aggressors and asking them to use their influence to get their sons to stop the attacks. He asked the soldiers which officers commanded the most respect and used their recommendations as a basis for promotions. He discouraged abuse in the ranks, and instead of assigning punishment duty to violators of discipline, he tried to shame them by taking photographs of those who fell asleep while on guard duty and hanging them in the corridor.

The soldiers responded to Martirosyan's methods, and the First Regiment soon had the best indicators for discipline and military readiness in the Thirteenth Army. Martirosyan's success, however, alienated his military superiors. Commissions began showing up at the First Regiment nearly every week, ostensibly to check on the theft of gas or food and misuse of equipment but actually to look for an excuse to transfer him to another regiment. By the fall of 1988, as Soviet organizations, including army units, nominated candidates for the elections to the national Supreme Soviet, Martirosyan was beginning to feel the pressure, and to protect himself from further harassment, he took the novel step of running for office.

Although an Armenian, Martirosyan soon became an ardent Ukrainian nationalist. In fact, by the end of 1988, nationalists were the only true independent political force in Rovno, and Martirosyan knew that he could not win without their support. Although he spoke in Russian, Martirosyan promised to support Ukrainian as the state language and to study the language himself. This satisfied local nationalists, who gave him their support. When the results were counted, Martirosyan, running against five other candidates, took 87 percent of the vote.

In the months that followed, Martirosyan became an active democratic leader and this, in turn, led to the politicization of the soldiers in the First Regiment.

At first, there was resistance to Ukrainian nationalism in the Regiment, even on the part of those who were loyal to Martirosyan. The Russian soldiers feared they would be excluded from a Ukrainian army or forced to leave Ukraine. Almost all of them were skeptical of the Ukrainian nationalists and pointed out that the blue and yellow Ukrainian flag had been used by partisans who committed atrocities during the war.

Martirosyan's nationalist allies, however, began to meet with the soldiers. They spoke about the 1933 famine and Communist Party corruption and argued that the only future for Ukraine was as an independent state.

Gradually, the regiment was won over. Many were affected by the details of Stalin-era genocide, particularly the famine, but the most important consideration was the notion that only by breaking up the Soviet army into national units would it be possible to do away with the degradation that was the lot of the average Soviet soldier.

On June 29, Martirosyan addressed the Ukrainian Supreme Soviet on the question of sovereignty. He said there was a danger of violence from the right and warned that there were forces in the army that were capable of overthrowing this parliament and any like it.

On July 16, the Ukrainian parliament approved the declaration of sovereignty and, amid general support in the republic for requiring that Ukrainian soldiers serve only on the territory of Ukraine, sentiment in the First Regiment swung more in the direction of support for a separate Ukrainian army. Soon, officers favoring a separate Ukrainian army, inspired in part by the example of the First Regiment, appeared in other military units.

On November 26, General Mikhail Moiseyev, the head of the Soviet army general staff, addressed the Supreme Soviet and said he would not consider the possibility of having Ukrainian citizens serve exclusively on Ukrainian territory because this would amount to dismembering the army, 17 percent of which was made up of recruits from Ukraine.

Despite this warning, however, in Zaporozhe, an entire air-defense regiment refused to carry out the order to transfer its base to Semipalatinsk, where nuclear tests were conducted. The wives of the officers went on a hunger strike in the town's central square and officers asked Kravchuk for political asylum.

Finally, against a background of rising tension within Soviet army units based in Ukraine, officers from all over the republic, including the First Regiment, met on February 3 in Kiev to discuss the establishment of a Ukrainian Union of Officers, an obvious precursor to a separate armed forces. Martirosyan did not attend the original meeting, but after intense discussions in the corridors, the organizers decided to offer him the chairmanship even though he was not a Ukrainian. Delegates had been impressed by his speeches in the Congress and, since he was a people's deputy, they knew he would be protected from arrest. Following the meeting, many officers who attended were immediately fired for "discrediting the name of a Soviet officer," but plans for a founding congress of the organization continued in military units throughout the republic until, finally, the date for the opening of the founding conference was set.

After Martirosyan finished his remarks, there were a number of speeches from the floor. A colonel from a unit near Uzhgorod said, "I think we can all agree on the need for a Ukrainian army, but the army should be created by an act of the Supreme Soviet. If the people begin to arm themselves, repression is inevitable." Another delegate called for an end to Communist political activity in the army and said that if the party had political officers in the army, Rukh should have them as well.

There was discussion of regional "hot spots," like Baku, where the Soviet army had intervened in January 1990. The delegates said that these were foreign wars and that Ukrainians should not have any role in them. One delegate claimed that a higher percentage of Ukrainian soldiers were sent to hot spots than soldiers of other nationalities.

"We have seen in Tbilisi, Baku, and Vilnius," Martirosyan said, "the use to which an imperial army can be put. The Ukrainian army must be different. It must be used only to defend the people, not to attack them."

The delegates, many of them retired and reserve officers, burst into applause.

BY AUGUST 1991, five years of glasnost had completely destabilized the totalitarian system in Ukraine, giving the republic a sharp sense of its separate identity. Yet only the residents of Western Ukraine overwhelmingly supported the idea of an independent state. The event that pushed people in all parts of the republic toward support for full independence was the August 19–21 coup.

The coup reminded all Ukrainians of their powerlessness in the Soviet system. For three days, the fate of Ukraine depended entirely on events in Moscow. Ukraine was about to sign a new Union Treaty that would provide for greater autonomy than had existed before, but the coup raised the possibility, if the plotters were victorious, that the republic would face not autonomy but mass arrests. When the coup failed, the threat to Ukrainian self-determination was lifted— though not because of any actions taken in Ukraine.

In the face of this reality, Ukraine was swept by a nationalist reaction. Reporters for Kiev radio and TV threw off Communist control and began calling for a ban of the Communist Party. Nationalist deputies worked out a plan to put Ukrainian independence to a vote of parliament and to seize the parliament building with the help of militant Kiev workers if it was not approved.

On the twenty-fourth, the proposal to declare independence was put to a vote and, by a big majority, which included almost all of the votes of the demoralized Communists, the motion carried and independence was declared.

LVOV, DECEMBER 5, 1991

The sky was iron gray and it was freezing cold as the bells of the St. Yuri Cathedral announced the victory of independence in the December 1 referendum. The Ukrainian population had voted everywhere for an independent state, officially confirming the decision of the parliament. In Lvov, the vote in favor was 92 percent. In some parts of the Lvov oblast, the vote for independence reached 99.5 percent.

Thousands of people were packed together in the interior of the church holding candles or kneeling on the stone floor. In the courtyard, thousands more stood in furs and greatcoats in the slowly falling snow.

In the crowd were former human rights campaigners as well as the resisters of an earlier generation, partisans who had fought in the woods after the Second World War and, after years in Soviet labor camps, were only now beginning to speak in public about their previous role.

The vote in the Supreme Soviet for independence in August further tipped the balance in Ukrainian opinion in favor of independence. In the autumn months, even attitudes in the heavily Russified Eastern Ukraine began to change. The failure of the August coup and the willingness of Communist deputies to vote for independence, and their failure to defend the Soviet system, helped to convince Russian speakers that the wheel of history had turned and that Ukrainian independence was inevitable. They therefore allowed themselves to be persuaded that there would be greater prosperity in an independent Ukraine and voted for independence.

.   .   .

MIROSLAV-IVAN LUBACHIVSKY, the cardinal of the once banned Greek Catholic Church, walked to the altar and stood surrounded by icons in ornate silver frames.

"The independence that we have now," he said, "is not our triumph alone but that of previous generations.

"Earlier, many fought for independence and were killed, but we achieved our goal peacefully. We must now do everything to save this achievement.

"There is still a long road ahead."*

*At about 9:45 p.m., on the night of January 15, 1994, Mikhailo Boichyshyn, by that time chairman of the secretariat of Rukh, left the headquarters of the organization to go home. At about 11 p.m., two armed men pushed their way into the building past the guards and said they had a "package for Boichyshyn." Boichyshyn never reached his apartment and no clues were ever discovered as to his fate.

Boichyshyn had had sole responsibility for Rukh's financial affairs and as a result of his disappearance Rukh candidates were deprived of vital material and organizational support two months before the first parliamentary elections in independent Ukraine, March 27, 1994. Rukh leaders believe that this led to a loss of five to ten seats for Rukh in the elections, in which the Communists received the largest share of the vote.

14

Religion

When everything people had has been taken from them ... they seek salvation in some transcendent force.
— *Mikhail Bulgakov,* The Master and Margarita

DECEMBER 1991, 9 p.m.

THE FALLING SNOW cast a veil over the city, turning Moscow's skyscrapers into looming gray shadows and the roofs of buildings into horizontal layers of white. A bus stopped on Verkhny Novospassky Lane and a young man in a worker's cap got out and headed for the Novospassky Monastery.

Sergei Osipov, a construction worker and ex-convict, had been raised an atheist but recently had begun to attend church services.

Osipov walked in under the entry arch and crossed the courtyard of the monastery over cobblestones wreathed with powdery snow. He stopped to look at the panorama of the city with its streetlamps and apartment lights, and he then climbed the steps of the monastery church to join hundreds of others for the evening services.

The service lasted three hours. Some of the believers, particularly women with children, sat on benches along the stone walls, but most preferred to stand. After the service was concluded, the interior of the church emptied out while about a hundred persons, including Sergei, stayed to confess.

Three monks moved lecterns into place in front of a wall of ancient icons in ornate gold frames, and believers formed long lines. Sergei joined the second of the three lines. The interior of the church was silent except for the faint crackling of candles burning in the golden icon holders.

The line moved slowly forward and Sergei watched as Soviet citizens shared the concerns of their battered and luckless lives. At a little before 2 a.m., it was Sergei's turn to confess. He spoke to the priest for almost twenty minutes. The priest listened carefully, occasionally stroking his beard. Finally, Sergei bowed and the priest covered him with his vestments and said a prayer. Sergei kissed the Bible and cross and then walked back out into the cold and through the monastery arch to the street, where he flagged down a cab for the ride home.

THE SCENE AT the Novospassky monastery was a reflection of the fact that, by 1991, religion was experiencing a rebirth in the Soviet Union.

For decades religion had been severely persecuted. When the Communist regime reversed the hierarchy between man and God, the suppression of religion became its most important philosophical priority. The regime did not ban religion, but it created the conditions for it to die on its own. Children were taught atheism in the schools and formal religious instruction was forbidden. At the same time, it was impossible for an adult believer to pursue a career.

"No, there is no religious renaissance, as it's sometimes said," remarked Father Sergei Zheludkov on a Moscow night in 1982. "In Pskov, there are only a few people who go to church. No journalist or teacher goes, because that would cost them their jobs. Children don't wear crosses. They don't want to be harassed at school. But even if the persecution didn't exist, it's hard to say how many people would come.

"Most of those who attend church services are old women. It seems there is something in the emotional nature of women that makes them more receptive to religion than men. The women form a kind of club. They may gossip during the services, but their presence reflects the failure of the Soviet government to destroy religion completely. Those who worship in the churches are former Komsomols. They were born in 1910 or a little earlier. They were children of the revolution who threw off their atheistic indoctrination in the pain of a lonely old age."

IN 1988, there began to be a change in religious policy.

In April, Gorbachev met with Patriarch Pimen in the Kremlin. It was the first time that a church leader had been received there since Stalin had met with church leaders during the Second World War. The official press, which had always depicted believers as evil and superstitious, began to portray them more sympathetically. Petitions to open churches that had lain untouched for ten to twenty years were satisfied and local officials ceased harassing priests.

Gorbachev's strategy of reform brought about a change in the atmosphere of society.

When belief ceased to be persecuted, it assumed an aboveground existence, and the first tendrils of a religious revival in the Soviet Union began to emerge.

The change was reflected in individual fates.

RECHNOI, WESTERN SIBERIA, JULY 1987

As a hot sun beat down, Alexander Gorbunov, a local Communist Party secretary, stood at the end of a group of wooden houses watching as a giant excavator bit into the earth, digging a trench for water pipes for the Rechnoi state farm.

In the distance, a horse-drawn wagon pulled bales of hay and a car sped by sending up large clouds of dust.

Suddenly, however, there was a cracking sound and Gorbunov felt his hands begin to shake. The excavator, which had been digging up black earth, was now scooping up human bones. As the digging continued, the excavator's scoop filled repeatedly with bones and skulls, which were lifted high into the air and dumped on the side of the road.

Gorbunov began shouting to the driver to stop and, at last, the operator turned off his machine. But the driver protested that he had a plan to fill, and Gorbunov, who represented the party, could not give him a reason why the work should not continue.

He knew that there had been a Stalin-era labor camp in the vicinity. In fact, in the Siberian farmland, the setting sun often revealed strange mounds covered with luxurious grass and dotted with mushrooms. Older people had long said that they contained human remains. But until this incident, Gorbunov had never actually seen any bones. Shaken and upset, he left the site and returned home.

Gorbunov, a party member since 1974, worked in the village of Achair as a mechanic in the tractor repair station of the Pervomaisky state farm. In early 1987, he was already losing faith in communism, but he was elected party secretary of the state farm and he involved himself in all aspects of its functioning.

He hoped that, as a party secretary, he would be able to help individuals, but his experience as a leader in the Communist system convinced him that he was part of an unreformable structure. He saw how the state farm director, Vladimir Nozdrichev, gave apartments to his cronies and how alcoholism reached the point where the bosses of the collective farm had to milk the cows themselves because everyone else was dead drunk.

In 1987, the authorities began to encourage the creation of "informal organizations" to aid perestroika, and the director of the house of culture in Achair, a descendant of Siberian Cossacks, organized a Cossack choir. Gorbunov, who was also of Cossack descent, joined the choir. At the same time, churches opened in Omsk and the surrounding villages and Feodosy, the archepiscop of the Omsk-Tarsk eparchy, appeared on local radio and television.

Affected by the apparent change in the official attitude toward religion, a choir member suggested that the choir travel to Omsk to receive the blessing of Feodosy. Gorbunov had never been in a church but, troubled by the incident in Rechnoi, he agreed to go. When Feodosy learned that the members of a Cossack choir had arrived, he dedicated the service to the resurrection of the Siberian Cossacks who, he said, organized their lives on the basis of religion, discipline, and respect for elders.

The service in the Omsk Cathedral lasted for more than two hours and Gorbunov was moved by it. Afterward, when Feodosy walked through the church with a silver cross, Gorbunov joined others from the choir and kissed the cross.

Later, Feodosy spoke to members of the Cossack choir and urged them to open a church in Achair to honor their ancestors.

When Gorbunov returned to Achair, he decided that, even though he was a party secretary, he would try to organize the opening of a church. There was an empty building in the village that had earlier housed a medical clinic, and Gorbunov began gathering signatures in the village asking that it be turned over to the eparchy so that it could be used as a church. He soon gathered three hundred names and, on this basis, the village council voted to satisfy his request.

The donation of the building inaugurated a voluntary collective effort unheard of in Achair. The idea of a church was new and, for that reason, it inspired enthusiasm. Workers throughout the village began appropriating state materials for the reconstruction of the future church. Timber was taken from the collective farm warehouse, linoleum and paint from the repair shop, and metal and wire from the electrical shop. At the same time, volunteers whitewashed the building, repaired the floor, and repainted it.

By Easter Sunday, April 7, 1991, the church was finally ready and the first service was held. Archepiscop Feodosy attended and, afterward, met with the residents of the village who gathered outside.

"Who organized all this?" he asked.

"Alexander Gorbunov, the party leader," said people in the crowd.

"Glory to God," said Feodosy. He then turned to Gorbunov and said, "Alexander Vladimirovich, how about becoming a priest?"

"I'm the party secretary," said Gorbunov, "if I become a priest, people won't understand me. Besides, you need knowledge."

"You'll study in our Omsk spiritual academy," Feodosy said. "We don't need great sermons. We need priests who can perform rites."

Gorbunov was completely taken aback by the suggestion, and he asked for time to consider it. A short while later, he quit the Communist Party, resigned his job at the tractor station, and went to Omsk to study for the priesthood. While studying, he worked for Feodosy as a driver and returned to Achair in August wearing a cassock and cross.

Father Alexander began to officiate in the newly restored church. On Sundays, ten to fifteen people attended the services, but on holidays there were as many as two hundred.

At first, Father Alexander was the object of skepticism, as many in the village said they would never be able to trust a priest who had once been a party secretary. In time, however, he won over many of the skeptics.

THE REBIRTH OF RELIGION in Achair set in motion a chain reaction. Longtime residents of the village remembered that there had been a monastery, which was disbanded in 1924 when the three monks who founded it were arrested and shot. At the same time, Vitaly Meshcherikov, the director of the Rechnoi state farm, impressed by the success of the Achair church, offered 100,000 rubles toward the construction of a church on the territory of his state farm. Father Alexander suggested instead marking the site of the mass burial ground on the Rechnoi state farm with a monastery. Feodosy gave his blessing to the idea and Meshcherikov agreed.

Father Alexander, however, was still plagued by a lack of knowledge about the killing grounds. In late 1991, he went to Omsk, where he met Ferenz Nadh, a survivor of the Leningrad blockade and a former criminal investigator in Omsk, who had made a study of the area's labor camps.

Nadh said the camp near Achair was a prison farm where the prisoners raised food for eighteen other labor camps in the Omsk region whose inmates built factories, oil processing plants, apartments, and hydroelectric stations. The inmates were, for the most part, members of the intelligentsia—lawyers, doctors, and teachers. They raised vegetables by hand, without boots or warm clothing in rain and subzero cold. There was no medical care and the prisoners died of pneumonia, dystrophy, and dysentery at the rate of about ten a day. This did not bother the camp authorities, however, because trainloads of prisoners arrived in Omsk every week, so the camp population was being constantly replenished.

The camp operated for more than twenty years before being dismantled after Stalin's death, and Nadh estimated that the bones of as many as sixty thousand were now interred in the burial pits of the Rechnoi region.

When the state farm was organized, the collective farmers often found bones when they dug foundations or sank wells, and no one was surprised when children were found playing with bones or even with a human skull. Sometimes women gathered bones and buried them in the village cemetery. But the farmers made no effort to locate the burial pits or to commemorate them.

After Father Alexander returned from Omsk, he regularly visited the site of the mass grave that he had seen cut open four years earlier by an excavator. On one occasion, he came upon a woman who had fenced off land on the site for a garden. "You can't plant there," Father Alexander said. "People are buried there."

"They won't give me land in another place," she said. "If I can't plant here, I'll hang myself."

Convinced that the monastery was an urgent spiritual necessity, Father Alexander tried to raise money for the project. He asked his parishioners to contribute, and he described the plans for a future monastery in a radio broadcast from Omsk. "A person can be moral only when he thinks of those who came before him, his ancestors," he said. "In the monastery, priests will read psalms constantly and pray for those buried on the site as well as for all the other Orthodox Christians who died in the labor camps of Siberia. The monastery will also collect information about the region's Stalin-era labor camps and make it available to relatives of the victims."

The response to Father Alexander's appeal was immediate. People brought money to the eparchy in envelopes. One woman wrote, "I'm donating money that I owed to my grandmother. She died and so I'm giving it to the church." Others explained that they were donating to honor a relative or to mark a marriage or birth.

One morning a woman appeared at Father Alexander's home in Achair with a cow.

"Why did you bring a cow?" he asked

"My father died in the camp," she said, bursting into tears. "His bones are buried there. We got permission from the collective farm and then gathered the dairy maids and chose the best cow."

On October 30, 1991, a group of about forty, including Father Alexander and Archepiscop Feodosy, gathered at the site of the mass grave. The sky was overcast and an icy wind blew across the fields.

As the crowd watched, Father Alexander and four other priests raised a tall wooden cross over the burial ground. Archepiscop Feodosy read psalms and asked the Lord to calm the souls of the victims whose remains were buried there. "We pray for the dead in another world and they pray for us in this world," he said.

Suddenly, the gray clouds parted and people began shouting, "Look, a light in the sky."

Father Alexander turned to those around him. "This is a sign from God," he said. "On this spot there will be a monastery."

INYAKINO, CENTRAL RUSSIA, JULY 7, 1989

As the sound of thunder echoed in the hollow interior of the Uspensky church, wizened old Maria Apalina crossed herself and a young, bearded priest sang the evening prayers. Yellow candles burned in silver candleholders and Apalina looked around her as the other old women followed the service, some with tears in their eyes. Until a month earlier the church had been closed; this was the first service in twenty-one years. Suddenly, lightning lit up the fields and rain poured in through the church's open roof. A gust of wind blew out many of the candles. For Apalina, this was nonetheless one of the happiest days of her life.

Her thoughts went back to a scene fifty-two years before. It was June 1937, a hot summer day, and Apalina, a fifteen-year-old girl at the time, was working in the fields of the Dobrovolets collective farm along with other children from the village. Suddenly, she heard the ringing of the church bells. She began to run and she saw that the other children were leaving their work in the fields and also running toward the church. When they arrived, there was a large crowd and, in front of the church, a group of military vehicles.

Men in uniform were in the bell tower breaking the wooden supports of the bells with sledgehammers and then throwing the bells to the ground. Most of the village men remained in the fields, but the women in the crowd were screaming, "What are they doing with the bells?" Children were crying.

A soldier in the crowd said that the bells would be used to make weapons. Suddenly, Andrei Semyonov, the chairman of the collective farm, appeared and climbed to the top of the bell tower. In a frenzy, he grabbed a sledgehammer and began to break a wooden support. In his rage, however, he swung wildly and, as the crowd watched, lost his balance, stumbled crazily, then slipped and fell sixty feet to the ground, dying instantly.

Hours later, the church was padlocked for good.

The closing of the church inaugurated a period of religious persecution that continued in Inyakino for more than fifty years. With no functioning church in the village, Apalina and her parents traveled for services to the church in Baravoye, seven miles away, one of two left open in the Shilovo raion, which had a population of 52,000.

The bosses of the collective farm, where Apalina's family worked, forced the collective farmers to "volunteer" for a day of unpaid labor on Sundays. The teacher in the village school, on the eve of religious holidays, issued warnings to children not to go to church, and in Baravoye, teachers and young Communists harassed students who tried to attend church.

Meanwhile, the Uspensky church slowly succumbed to the ravages of time. First the icons were removed, then the lock was broken and the insides were gutted. Finally, the roof gave way and the floor buckled. The wooden cupola, which had slowly rotted, came loose during a violent storm and collapsed into the church's interior.

By the 1980s, the village of Inyakino had all but lost its religious faith. If a child was noticed in church in Baravoye, he was ridiculed before the class for obscurantism and expelled from the Pioneers.

Apalina's six children had long since refused to go to the Baravoye church or any other, and only Apalina and a few elderly women preserved Orthodox traditions, meeting in each other's homes and reading prayers without a priest on Easter and the holidays of Trinity and the Feast of the Assumption.

In 1988, however, Apalina was startled to see religious figures, including Patriarch Pimen, appearing on television. She conferred with other believers in the village, who told her that they had read in the newspapers that churches were being opened. Emboldened by the apparent shift in the atmosphere, Apalina and several other religious women approached Viktor Romanov, the chairman of the collective farm, to ask him to help them get permission to reopen the Uspensky church. To Apalina's astonishment, Romanov agreed.

A YEAR LATER, permission was finally received to reopen the church and a change came over the village. The church, which had been built in 1793, was a ruin. There were logs hanging from the ceiling, the floor was buckled, and much of the stairway had rotted away. The interior was filled with rotting wood, straw, hills of seed, and miscellaneous garbage. But Romanov allocated collective farm funds for the renovation and dozens of people volunteered to help. The job proved to be immense. The believers worked for a solid month removing garbage. The floor was replaced and the stairway rebuilt. The hanging logs were taken down.

By July 1989, enough space had been cleared to hold a service, and several elderly women brought icons they had hidden in their homes for decades and set them up in the rafters. A priest, Father Ivan Marten, was assigned to the congregation and, as a storm lashed the countryside, the first service was held.

As the months passed, the collective farmers became accustomed to the presence of a functioning church, and Father Ivan began to celebrate marriages and funerals, while Apalina sang in the choir. At first, some of the collective farmers were angry about having collective farm money used to restore a church, but Romanov, whose mother had been a devout believer, dismissed the complaints. "My purpose is to build, not to destroy," he said.

Even teachers began to attend services, and in September, before the beginning of the school year, almost fifty children took communion. "People became kinder to each other," said Apalina. "They began to fear God and worry about their sins. Earlier, people were like dogs. They had no pity, no kindness. Even the party bosses became different. They became more polite. Earlier, they were not so polite."

OCTOBER 1992

A fire burned in an iron stove in the newly restored church. The floors were freshly painted and icons were hung on the white stone walls.

As the light of an overcast day filtered in through the tall, arched windows, Apalina and the rest of the choir sang the prayers for the dead, and the villagers crowded around the open coffin of a thirty-nine-year-old mother who had died of cancer. Father Ivan walked back and forth, spreading incense from a golden holder. The mourners lit candles to symbolize the lighting of the deceased's path to God.

The dead woman's father burst into tears. Finally, a group of young men with white armbands lifted the coffin onto their shoulders and carried it out through the arch in the bell tower and led a procession of villagers around the church.

The mourners then gathered on the road. Among them were hobbled old women like Apalina and young children. A brass band began to play a funeral march and Apalina and the others accompanied the young woman's body on its final journey to the village cemetery, about a mile and a half away.

Afterward, Apalina recalled that for years she did not even have her own Bible. "We now teach the children God's law," she said, "and they will be different. He who reads the Bible knows what will be. I read the Bible and so am not surprised or horrified by anything."

She then mused on the events of the last few years.

"Who would have expected such a change?" she said. "But then again, even an angel cannot see God, so why do we expect to?"

CORRECTIVE LABOR COLONY 5, OUTSIDE LENINGRAD

On a biting cold day in March 1990, Vladimir Khotko, a convicted murderer, stepped to the center of the football field to address his fellow convicts. Gathered around him were 1,500 inmates serving time in the maximum security labor camp. "We have just been told that we have permission to build a church on the grounds of the camp," said Khotko. "No one will help us, but if we find the money, we can build."

Silence fell over the crowd. Khotko studied the faces of the prisoners—murderers, rapists, hooligans, and thieves. Most had never heard of the Ten Commandments, much less observed them in their own lives. Finally, a group of prisoners began circulating with open rucksacks through the crowd and an unexpected thing happened. First a few prisoners and then nearly all of them reached into the pockets of their prison jackets and pulled out wrinkled bills. Some gave five rubles, some twenty-five.

Within half an hour, Khotko had collected eighteen thousand rubles. This was more than enough to get started.

The plan to build a church was part of Khotko's effort to redeem himself through religious faith. After finishing school in Leningrad, Khotko went to work at the Kirov Tractor Factory in Tikhvin and became Komsomol leader, and then, at the age of twenty-five, chairman of the trade union. He seemed destined for further promotions, but in 1985, he divorced his wife. At first, there were no repercussions, but the couple became involved in an increasingly angry dispute over possession of their one-room apartment. They tried several times to settle the issue without success. Finally, they met in the apartment of a friend, where, according to the court record of the case, they began to argue. The argument grew heated and Khotko started to hit and kick his ex-wife savagely. By the time he stopped beating her, she was dead.

The blows that killed his ex-wife also shattered Khotko's world. He was arrested and taken to the Leningrad investigative prison, where, a few days later, he tried to hang himself. When he recovered from the attempt, he learned that two thousand workers at his former factory had signed a petition demanding he be given the death penalty. The trial took place in December 1986, and Khotko was sentenced to thirteen years at hard labor.

For a former Komsomol activist, the transfer to Labor Camp Number 5 was a passage to another world. Khotko had never before been in trouble with the law and had no record of violence. On the other hand, he had technical experience as a result of his work at the Kirov factory, and this meant he could make an economic contribution. He was put to work as foreman of the construction shop. He worked up to seven days a week and twelve hours a day repairing the camp's workshops and barracks.

In the first years of perestroika, the camp regime was little changed. The prisoners could not address members of the administration except as "Citizen boss," and the only conversations that were tolerated were those clarifying the regulations. Any prisoner wearing a cross had it ripped off. In the spring of 1988, however, there were signs of liberalization. Prisoners, for the first time, were given permission to address the guards by name and foreigners visited the camp. At the same time, the labor camp was opened to priests.

At first, a prisoner who tried to talk to a priest was ridiculed. In time, however, the attitude changed. The prisoners saw that the priests, alone among visitors to the camp, were ready to meet with them and discuss their problems. Many appreciated the fact that they could trust a priest not to repeat what he was told.

As the months passed, Khotko began to feel remorse for the killing of his wife. He worried about his young daughter and hoped that there was a guardian angel who would protect her.

The priests brought copies of the Bible to the camp and Khotko began to read it. He saw that it taught kindness. The criminal code did not give him the sense of right and wrong that the Bible did and, at the same time, the Bible said that sin could be redeemed and the sinner could be forgiven.

Father Vladimir Sorokin arrived in the camp from the Leningrad spiritual academy and started to hold services in the camp club. Slowly, a group of about forty prisoners, including Khotko, formed around Father Vladimir and began attending services regularly.

The experience of going to services changed Khotko. He realized he was not an atheist in his soul. He recalled bitterly how he had believed in Marxism-Leninism and taught the ideology to others. Other prisoners had also lost their faith in the ideology, including former officials who had been arrested, unfairly in their view, on corruption charges.

Khotko discussed his feelings with them and, finally, he and five other prisoners asked Sergei Matyukin, the head of the camp, for permission to build a church.

Matyukhin was surprised by the request and at first he refused. The six prisoners, however, wrote petitions to the Leningrad Ministry of Internal Affairs, and in February 1990, Matyukin changed his mind and said they could try. He insisted, however, that the church have no crosses, bell towers, or bells.

Even in giving limited permission, Matyukin took a risk. The country was ruled by Communists and the camp was policed by its "operative department," which was linked to the KGB. The department was a threat not only to prisoners but also to liberal members of the prison administration. Formal permission, however, was all that was necessary for Khotko. He did not think the KGB would long tolerate the construction of a church on the grounds of a prison, and so he immediately began a race against time.

In March 1990, he and the five other prisoners, with Matyukin's permission, organized the meeting of the prisoners at which they collected the eighteen thousand rubles. They then recruited Timur

Khuriev, a prisoner who had been an architect, to develop a design for the church and arranged with Matyukin for builders from the construction section to use camp equipment, including a tractor, excavator, and crane, in their off-hours.

Finally, in June 1990, as the prisoners were about to begin to build, Metropolitan Alexei II of Leningrad arrived at the camp to bless the church's first stone. For many prisoners, it was the first time they had ever attended a service.

On the night of the dedication, Khotko, determined not to waste time, gathered the builders and, using pile drivers, worked until dawn to sink reinforced concrete pillars for the framework of the church. Friends of the prisoners brought bricks to the camp in their cars and trucks. During the summer months, the construction crew worked almost until dawn. Slowly, the foundations rose.

The progress of the prisoners in building the church aroused the anger of the operative department. Khotko was called to the department and ordered, as foreman of the construction shop, not to release men and materials for the church project. When he refused, he was warned that he and the other initiators of the church undertaking would be transferred to labor camps in Siberia and the Urals.

Khotko knew that the slightest change in the political climate would make it possible for the operative department to carry out its threat. Nonetheless, work on the church continued.

The operative department repeatedly refused to allow trucks with bricks into the camp, forcing Khotko to appeal to Matyukin. Finally, members of the operative department went to the local brick factory and commandeered thirteen thousand bricks that were intended for the church and had already been paid for by the prisoners. It was only when Leningrad television reporters, alerted by Father Vladimir, reported the incident that the bricks were released.

A definitive break in the conflict finally came when, with the death of Patriarch Pimen, Alexei II was named Patriarch and he began to discuss the construction of the church in interviews with the local and national press. The widespread, favorable publicity for the project stayed the hand of the operative department. Freed of intimidation, the prisoners sped up their work on the church and made plans to add crosses, bell towers, and bells.

In April 1991, the prisoners finished the base and icon painters from the Leningrad spiritual academy arrived with an iconostasis they had painted for the altar.

With work about to begin on the roof, however, prices in the Soviet Union were tripled by Prime Minister Pavlov and the prisoners ran out of money. The project was saved when two former prisoners who had gone into business contributed 100,000 rubles and 500,000 rubles, respectively, to the project. Shortly thereafter, Alexei II arranged for the donation of four bells for the church and two tons of copper to cover the metal frame of the church's cupolas.

In April 1992, two gold-covered crosses, donated by the spiritual academy, were placed on top of the cupolas, and on September 11, the church opened its doors.

The church, with its cupolas, bell tower, and cross rose above the sheds, barracks, and factories of the camp. Services were held three times a day and attended by as many as two hundred prisoners.

In October 1992, Alexei II appealed to Yeltsin to pardon Khotko. "Those who performed the miracle of building this church," he said in a letter to Yeltsin, "deserve to be freed."

Epilogue

There is something in our blood which rejects all true progress.
—Pyotr Chaadaev, First Philosophical Letter

NOVEMBER 1993

ON THE STAGE of an assembly hall in a Moscow factory, a perspiring, thickset man with close-cropped hair and a loosened tie shouted at two of his supporters to raise a banner with the words "We Need a Great Russia" as high as possible over their heads.

The men lifted the banner, but the poles supporting it began to bend and the banner drooped toward the floor. "Do you see the condition of Russians," said Vladimir Zhirinovsky, the leader of the Liberal Democratic Party, to the crowd of about three hundred in the hall. "We cannot even hold up a slogan about our own greatness."

Zhirinovsky had campaigned tirelessly since the beginning of the election campaign for the new state Duma. "Only reliable state borders can save us," he said. "As a minimum, we have to return to the borders of the Soviet Union, but it would be better to return to our 1913 borders when the Russian empire included Poland and Finland.

"We can frighten foreigners and I tell you frankly that I will blackmail them. I will tell them that if you interfere in the affairs of Russia, we will take appropriate measures. We will do this because we are hungry, degraded, and insulted, and this was done to us by you. The Americans will not fight. They do not know how. In space,

394

there are weapons aimed at the United States. If Yeltsin said that part of our rockets will be aimed away from America, I say that we will aim all rockets at America. Our submarines will patrol off the shores of America. The last historical role of Russia is to save the world from American expansionism."

With the conclusion of his speech, Zhirinovsky was surrounded by the crowd. Would he agree to talk to a group of students? "Students, please, without a doubt . . ." Would he accept a letter from the sister of a woman who had been unfairly fired in Podolsk? Zhirinovsky took the letter and stuffed it into a breast pocket.

As Zhirinovsky and his party emerged into the cold night air, there was an unmistakable sense that he was gaining strength with the confused and resentful voters of Russia.

ZHIRINOVSKY'S RISE WAS made possible by the failure in Russia to establish a state based on law.

The last months of 1991 witnessed the death rattle of the Soviet Union. Gorbachev and his supporters struggled to preserve some type of union structure, but the centrifugal pressures were becoming overwhelming.

By late November, although the Soviet Union continued to exist, almost all decision-making had passed to the republics. The only republic capable of singlehandedly destroying the union, however, was Russia, and Yeltsin hesitated. He wanted to preserve the union but he wanted to eliminate Gorbachev as head of state, which he could not do legally as long as the Soviet Union survived. Finally, he decided to break with the Soviet structure. He ordered the Russian government to stop paying taxes into the federal budget, and its example was soon followed by the other republics.

In November 1991, the Congress of People's Deputies of the Russian parliament held its fifth meeting and by a large majority granted special powers to Yeltsin, including the right to rule by decree. The Congress also gave him the right to name the heads of administration in the oblasts and passed resolutions approving the general outlines of economic reform, including price liberalization.

On December 1, Ukrainians voted overwhelmingly for independence in a referendum and, on December 8, Yeltsin, Kravchuk, and Stanislav Shushkevich, the leader of Belarus, met secretly in the Belovezhsky woods near Brest and agreed to replace the Soviet

Union with a Commonwealth of Independent States. Yeltsin informed President George Bush of the agreement and only afterward asked Shushkevich to relay the news to Gorbachev.

At first, Gorbachev tried to fight the Belovezhsky agreement, calling for a special session of the Soviet Congress of People's Deputies, but this idea was abandoned when Central Asian leaders adhered to the pact and it was ratified by the Russian parliament. Yeltsin, meanwhile, began to liquidate the institutions of the Soviet Union, closing the Soviet Foreign Ministry and taking over the Internal Ministry and Ministry of Security.

Gorbachev finally acquiesced and, on December 25, resigned in a televised address. The flag was lowered over the Kremlin and, almost sixty-nine years to the day after it was founded on December 30, 1922, the Soviet Union ceased to exist.

IN THE MEANTIME, most of the power of the Soviet Union passed to Russia and, in Russia, to Yeltsin.

For the first time in centuries, Russia was without an empire and it now had an elected president. But Yeltsin quickly showed that he had no respect for the separation of powers. The Supreme Soviet started to meet but Yeltsin demonstratively ignored it. Under the law that granted him special powers, he had the right to issue decrees that took effect within two weeks if the Supreme Soviet did not object to them. Yeltsin, however, often issued fifteen decrees at once, leaving the Supreme Soviet no time to evaluate them.

Yeltsin appointed Yegor Gaidar, a former department head at *Pravda*, as vice premier and minister of economy. Gaidar's plans included freeing prices and limiting growth in the money supply in order to force bankruptcies and the beginning of economic restructuring. His speeches were filled with economic terms many deputies did not understand. It eventually became clear, however, that he wanted to eliminate at a stroke nearly the entire planned economy.

Ruslan Khasbulatov, at first, was Yeltsin's ally. He helped to organize the vote that gave Yeltsin special powers as well as ratification of the Belovezhsky Pact. But in consideration of his help, he expected an important role in the government. Instead, he was ignored, as was Rutskoi.

On January 2, Gaidar put his economic program into effect. In freeing prices, he predicted they would rise three to five times and then begin to fall. In fact, they jumped five to seven times in the first month, wiping out the savings of the entire population. Elderly persons who had put money aside were suddenly penniless. Food consumption fell sharply (it later stabilized), and the men and women of the Second World War generation appeared on the street to sell their belongings.

The accelerating inflation led to a shortage of turnover capital, which forced halts in production and, in a heavily monopolized economy, when one factory stopped producing, all the factories that depended on it stopped producing, too. To survive, factories ran up huge debts to each other, waiting to be bailed out by the state.

The first protests came from the Front for National Salvation, which was formed in October 1992 and included those who opposed the breakup of the USSR. Soon, however, Khasbulatov, angered at being ignored by Yeltsin, also joined the opposition. At the same time, he tightened his control over the Supreme Soviet by rewarding those loyal to him with foreign trips, the best apartments, and official cars.

In April, amid rising popular discontent, Aman Tuleev, chairman of the oblast soviet in Kemerovo, said the reforms were impoverishing the people and called for a prime minister with genuine industrial experience. Khasbulatov added his view that the reformers were "inexperienced boys."

In the meantime, it became clear that the Central Bank would have to loosen credit policy to liquidate the interenterprise debt, which soon stood at 3 trillion rubles, or half the value of industrial production. In mid-1992, the credits were issued and inflation shot up from 10 percent to 25 to 30 percent per month. Production in the first half of 1992 dropped more than 20 percent against the same period of 1991.

In this situation, both Khasbulatov and Rutskoi intensified their attacks on the government. They were joined by the directors of military factories who formed a group called the Civic Union, under the leadership of Arkady Volsky, a former member of the Communist Party Central Committee. By the end of June, Yeltsin, who had been supported by two-thirds of the parliament in November, faced a situation in which two-thirds of the parliament now opposed him.

The government turned its attention to privatization, but this did nothing to lower the tension between the executive branch and the legislative.

What was contemplated was the largest peaceful transfer of property in history. In light of this, the question became not whether to carry out privatization but who would carry it out and have the opportunity to distribute buildings, factories, and land. At first, both the government and the parliament appeared to be involved in the process. As the months passed, however, it became clear that privatization would be enacted by decree and the process would be controlled by the government.

Yeltsin made no effort to start a dialogue with his critics in parliament. In September, the government, as part of its privatization program, issued vouchers with a face value of ten thousand rubles to every Russian citizen. Each was to be used to buy a share in privatized Russian industry. It was hoped that this would help create a class of owners. In practice, however, citizens did not know what to do with the vouchers, many of which were sold for money or bottles of vodka.

In the meantime, the broader privatization effort was yielding a mother lode of corruption. Commercial firms were formed to sell oil and gas, the export of which had previously been a government monopoly, and these firms received export licenses from government officials in return for bribes. The participants in this trade, in this way, became millionaires by decree, and they and others with access to state assets deposited huge sums of money abroad and engaged in conspicuous consumption in Russia, where more luxury model Mercedes cars began to be sold than in all of Western Europe combined.

Seeing all this, members of parliament became outraged at being denied a share of the spoils.

AS THE COLD WEATHER approached, about half the population was living below the poverty line. Instead of seeking compromise, however, both sides adopted positions of "all or nothing." Khasbulatov described Yeltsin in private as a "drunkard" and "mentally ill," and proposals circulated in the government for abolishing parliament. Yeltsin tried to concentrate all decision-making in the executive branch and, by the end of November, the Russian government had as many bureaucracies and bureaucrats as had existed under the old USSR.

Yet despite the catastrophic decline in living standards, public sympathy was largely on the side of Yeltsin. Khasbulatov was a Chechen and ethnic prejudice worked against him. Perhaps more important, the majority of Russians continued to believe that, with the fall of communism, radical reform was still the only hope for a better future.

On December 1, the Seventh Congress met and Yeltsin's special powers expired. The deputies' first move was to introduce a constitutional amendment giving the Congress the permanent right to approve the prime minister and other key ministers. The motion fell short of the necessary two-thirds majority, but there was little hope of saving Gaidar, whose permanent appointment could be rejected by a simple majority. In a gesture to the Congress, Yeltsin agreed that parliament could have a veto over the ministers of defense, foreign affairs, security, and internal affairs. The Congress, however, accepted the concessions and rejected Gaidar. Viktor Chernomyrdin, an industrial manager backed by the Civic Union, became the first permanent prime minister.

Finally, the Congress agreed to hold a referendum on April 11, on the principles of a new constitution. Yeltsin, however, announced on March 20, in a televised address, that he was signing a decree banning any activities by the parliament limiting the powers of the president. This led to a motion for impeachment on the grounds that, with his decree, Yeltsin had violated the existing constitution.

Finally, an impeachment vote was taken in the Great Kremlin Palace and, although the measure was supported by a majority, it failed for lack of a two-thirds vote. A short time later, a new referendum was set for April 25 on the subjects of trust in the president and his economic policies.

The result of the referendum was a strong victory for Yeltsin. The show of public support stunned the deputies, who believed that Yeltsin's economic policies were unpopular.

Buoyed by the referendum results, Yeltsin continued to rule by decree, although his November 1991 grant of special powers had run out. In response, the parliament began sending Yeltsin's decrees to the Constitutional Court, in this way freezing their implementation. The result was that laws and decrees were soon in conflict all over the country and Russians did not know who wielded rightful authority.

In the meantime, the social crisis in the country deepened.

CHILDREN'S DEPARTMENT, BAKULEV
INSTITUTE, MAY 6, 1993

As swaddled children were rolled past on gurneys and anxious mothers tried to get the attention of the medical personnel, Dr. Valentina Shvedunova talked urgently in a quiet room off the corridor with Yuri and Irina Zhuravlev, the parents of twelve-year-old Sergei. "Your son is dying," she said. "The infection is spreading and we don't have the antibiotics to fight it. Our only hope is a radical operation."

Yuri and Irina both began to cry.

In a ward two doors away, Sergei was throwing up and gasping for air. "If this is the only hope of saving our son," said Yuri, "there is nothing to argue about. But please operate as soon as you can."

Sergei entered the Bakulev Institute in March 1993 for balloon angioplasty to correct a narrowed arterial heart valve.

The procedure involves the insertion of a catheter through an artery of the leg or arm into the heart and the inflation of a balloon inside the heart to correct the narrowing of an artery or heart valve. Sergei needed the procedure because the "leafs" of his arterial heart valve were joined at the edges, allowing only a small opening for the flow of blood and pushing the pressure in Sergei's left ventricle up to 260. An operation was recommended when the ventricular pressure exceeded 150.

Sergei lived in Tver, a small city sixty miles from Moscow. His father was a local journalist and his mother taught kindergarten. He went to school and studied hard. His heart defect was well compensated and, aside from an occasional lack of energy, he had no complaints. Sergei's ventricle, however, could not compensate for the defect indefinitely. In time, it was certain to begin to fail, after which the damage to Sergei's heart would be permanent.

Sergei entered the hospital on March 19 and the procedure was performed the next day with apparent success. The blood pressure in his left ventricle fell to 140, still too high but much better than what it had been. In the days immediately after the procedure, Sergei, a quiet, studious child, spent most of his time reading.

Dr. Keto Mchedlishvili, the pediatric cardiologist who was at-

tending Sergei, assumed that he would soon be going home. On the
third day, however, he ran a fever. This made the doctor uneasy.
Under the Soviet regime, the Bakulev Institute had twelve to fifteen
antibiotics in its arsenal, including the most modern antibiotics in the
world, such as monospur, longastef, and fortum.

By the spring of 1993, however, the available antibiotics had been
reduced to five—chloforan, brulamicin, gentamicin, ampicillin, and
oxacillin—and even some of these were in short supply.

Dr. Mchedvishvili knew it was not uncommon for children to run
a temperature after balloon angioplasty, but Sergei's fever appeared
three days after the procedure. This meant that he might have con-
tracted an infection.

Mchedvishvili tried to put ominous thoughts out of her mind.
She knew that if the infection was serious, the institute might not
have the antibiotics to fight it.

The critical shortage was one of the most serious problems at the
institute and because of it, doctors invariably used the most common
antibiotics first, even if they were those to which the bacterial agent
was most likely to be immune. This was the case in the treatment of
Sergei. He was given injections of ampicillin and his temperature
dropped. His hemoglobin, however, which should have been above
ten, fell below nine.

Sergei was then sent to the institute's rehabilitative center, a
former Communist Party rest house in the forest outside Moscow. He
spent his time there playing Ping-Pong and chess with other patients,
reading and walking with his mother in the surrounding woods.

Five days later, he again began to run a temperature and was immediately brought back to the institute. This time he was given blood
transfusions and an antibacterial agent, metradzhil. His antibiotic
was changed to chloforan. The doctors—Dr. Shvedunova; Lyudmilla
Plotnikova, the deputy head of the department of children's surgery;
Bagrat Alekian, Sergei's surgeon; and Dr. Mchedlishvili—were now
seriously concerned.

The fact that Sergei had been running temperatures on and off
for nine days meant that he almost certainly had an infection. At the
same time, his arterial blood pressure was falling, indicating involvement of the arterial heart valve. Echocardiagraphs, however, did not
show anything and Sergei's blood cultures all came back negative.

Under the Soviet regime, highly sensitive cultures were developed
in military laboratories, but those at the institute were all produced

by the civilian Russian pharmaceuticals industry. They were notoriously insensitive and slow to produce results.

The chloforan had some effect and, again for a few days, Sergei's temperature returned to normal, but it soon rose and reached 101.3 degrees. The doctors gave Sergei gentamicin and oxacillin. Once more, his temperature dropped for a few days and then rose.

On April 21, a culture finally identified the infection as staphylococcus but did not indicate the strain. At the same time, the doctors continued to take echograms; on April 23, more than a month after the ballon angiography was performed, the ultrasound picked up the first signs around Sergei's heart valve of vegetative growth.

It was now clear to the doctors that something had gone terribly wrong and an operation was inevitable if they were to save the boy's life. As she watched the situation unfolding, Dr. Shvedunova recalled another patient and another era.

In 1986, a six-year-old girl had developed bacterial endocarditis after an operation to correct a defect in the intraventricular barrier. To fight the infection, the doctors at the institute used a whole battery of antibiotics, only two of which—chloforan and gentamicin— were available to them today.

Dr. Vladimir Podzolkov, the chief of the congenital heart disease department, arranged, through the State Committee on Pharmaceuticals, to buy monospor with hard currency specifically to prolong the life of this one child.

Forty-two days after the original operation, the girl was operated on again. The doctors gave her only one chance in a hundred to survive, but she did. The antibiotics had held the infection at bay long enough for the surgery to save her life.

The doctors gave Sergei brulamicin but it had little effect on his temperature, which fell only briefly. The infection was progressing and ten-year-old antibiotics were doing little good.

Sergei and his mother now were the object of the worried apprehension of the whole ward. On April 23, Dr. Mchedvishvili asked to talk to Irina. "The situation with Sergei is becoming serious," she said, "his heart valve is infected and he is not responding to therapeutic treatment. We are now considering a second operation."

Shaken by the news, Irina left to call Sergei's father in Tver. Dr. Mchedvishvili, in the meantime, went to see Vladimir Kovalenko, the head of the institute's medical department. She explained the situation to him and Kovalenko gave her a set of vials of a new Swiss antibiotic, teopan, which the institute had been sent as a sample.

"You can use this," he said grimly, "but there is only enough for four days."

By April 25, Sergei showed indications of serious illness. He sat quietly in his room reading *Robinson Crusoe*, but he began to experience shortness of breath and to throw up.

The teopan produced a temporary improvement, but all efforts to find additional vials either in warehouses or through the State Committee on Pharmaceuticals failed.

Sergei's father arrived at the institute, and doctors and nurses entered Sergei's room constantly. For the first time, Sergei showed signs of being afraid.

On April 29, plans were made to operate. Dr. Skopin, a surgeon who had had considerable success in transplanting aortas and heart valves to adults using techniques that he and Dr. Anatoly Malashenkov helped develop, examined Sergei and decided he could operate.

Sergei, however, was now showing signs of severe cardiac insufficiency. He was breathing in gasps, his abdomen filled with fluid, and he threw up constantly. The ultrasound showed large abscesses had formed in his arterial heart valve and the walls of the aorta.

The diameter of Sergei's arteries was too small for an artificial heart valve. Skopin decided instead that he would have to replace Sergei's arterial heart valve and aorta with parts taken from an accident victim.

The prognosis, however, was not good. The institute did not have a hemosorption device—a machine that, with the help of antimicrobe and antitoxin filters, was capable of filtering blood and reducing the impact of infection. As a result, the operation would have to proceed in the face of a raging infection, and the heart muscle might not be able to stand the shock of this new intrusion.

After Yuri and Irina agreed to surgery, preparations to operate began to be made in earnest. Irina tried to feed Sergei, but he said that it was difficult for him to eat and he would rather read instead. He watched with growing apprehension as his parents cried in his presence, but he remained calm and uncomplaining, reading *Robinson Crusoe* until moments before he was wheeled out of his room on a stretcher into the operating room, which was just down the hall.

The operation lasted for four hours and, technically, it went well. Sergei's aorta and heart valve were replaced and the abscess, which by now had enveloped his entire heart, was drained. At the conclusion, however, when Sergei was taken off the heart-lung machine, the doctors could not restart his heart. After twenty minutes, Dr. Skopin left the operating room and told Yuri and Irina that their son was dead.

SERGEI'S DEATH stunned the staff at the Bakulev Institute. Many had grown to like the quiet, studious boy who endured the ordeal of his last few days stoically and without complaining. They could not forget that Sergei had been in outwardly good health when he entered the institute six weeks before, and could have been expected to live well into his twenties if the angioplasty had not been performed.

"The feeling of fear that we have very few antibiotics and nothing with which to treat patients is always with us," said Dr. Shvedunova.

MEANWHILE, OUTSIDE the hospital walls, the power struggle between Yeltsin and the parliament continued.

In May, the crisis of authority began to affect the process of drafting a new constitution. Yeltsin, dissatisfied with the draft of the Supreme Soviet commission, convened an assembly dominated by representatives of the executive branch to work on an alternative draft. As a result, there were soon two centers of constitution-writing, neither of which recognized the existence of the other.

At the same time, there were bitter conflicts around the question of privatization. Vouchers had been distributed to the population, but they were regarded as inflationary and ineffective, and deputies feared that mafia money would soon use them to buy up the industrial base of the country. They favored a form of privatization in which the workers would hold shares in their own factories, outsiders would be barred, and the factories, in practice, would continue to be controlled by their directors.

In mid-May, the government privatization program was presented for ratification to the Supreme Soviet, which rejected it.

The refusal infuriated the government, which decided not to

present a new version to parliament. Instead, the government continued to carry out privatization by decree.

It now became evident that neither the executive branch nor the parliament was interested in resolving the differences between them.

It finally came time to approve the budget for 1993. The executive branch had projected a monthly inflation rate of 8 percent a month, but by summer, the rate was 20 to 25 percent. In response, the Supreme Soviet recalculated the budget, raising pensions and increasing salaries to teachers, doctors, and others paid out of state funds. The result was a deficit of 28 trillion rubles, or 25 percent of the total national product.

The government said that the parliament's revised budget would destroy all efforts to contain inflation and wreck the reform process. Yeltsin vowed to ignore it.

The tension escalated sharply.

In August, Yeltsin promised a "hot autumn," and began visiting the bases of critical army units in the Moscow oblast to shore up support. He also raised the salaries of officers two to three times. Yeltsin and Khasbulatov exchanged invitations to resign. Finally, on September 18, Khasbulatov, speaking before a meeting of deputies, attacked Yeltsin personally, raising the subject of Yeltsin's alcoholism.

"It is unacceptable," he said, "when officials give the impression that there is nothing wrong with [drinking]. . . . After all, he drinks, that means he is one of us. But if he is 'one of us' "—and with this, Khasbulatov gestured in the direction of the Kremlin and pulled back his third finger with his thumb and then snapped it against his throat—"let him occupy himself with peasant work and not government."

The gesture and Khasbulatov's remarks were promptly reported to Yeltsin, who decided it was time to finish with the parliament once and for all.

On September 21, Yeltsin issued Decree No. 1400 abolishing the Congress of People's Deputies and the Supreme Soviet. He announced that elections for a new, smaller body, the State Duma, would be held on December 11–12.

The deputies reacted by refusing to leave the White House, and the government turned off the heat, water, and electricity and surrounded the building with barbed wire and then with police and internal troops.

By September 1993 the population was indifferent to both sides in the conflict, but members of nationalist and fascist fringe groups arrived at the White House to defend the parliament. They were given weapons by deputies who feared that the building would be stormed and, on the street, demonstrators, mostly Communists, gathered to protest the dissolution of the parliament and were beaten by the police.

With the army leaning toward Yeltsin and regional soviets all over the country supporting the parliament, talks began in the Danilovsky Monastery to try to resolve the crisis, but both sides remained unyielding.

On October 2, in an atmosphere of steadily rising tension, there was a battle between police and demonstrators in Smolensk Square. On October 3, thousands of Communist demonstrators gathered in front of police lines at the Krimsky Bridge. The demonstrators stood a hundred yards from a cordon of OMON (Special Assignment) police armed with truncheons and shields in the middle of the span.

For nearly a week, demonstrators had been beaten by the police, and many of the victims, now armed with bricks and clubs, were in the front line.

"All right," said Vitaly Urazhtsev, a people's deputy, "let's go." Suddenly, there was a hail of rocks and the marchers threw themselves on the police lines. As more and more demonstrators pushed up from the rear, the line broke and the police were stripped of their truncheons and shields and then beaten with their own clubs. To the surprise of the crowd, the police fled.

The demonstrators began moving toward the White House. At Smolenskaya Square, they attacked a barricade of fire engines and trucks and once again the police and internal troops withdrew. The crowd took over nearly twenty trucks, many of them with the keys still in the ignition.

The march toward the White House resumed. The trucks seized on Smolenskaya Square smashed through the barbed wire around the White House, with the marchers close behind. The crowd then entered the Square of Free Russia on the building's north side. Once again, the police did nothing to resist.

Nikolai Troitsky talked to the demonstrators as they entered the square.

"How did this happen?" he asked.

"I don't know," a demonstrator said. "First, they did not allow us to pass, and then they let us go."

Another demonstrator said, "Yerin has gone over to the side of the people. The police are on our side!"

Rutskoi, Khasbulatov, and the rest of the parliamentary leadership emerged on the balcony of the White House facing the square. There was a sea of red flags and constant, deafening shouts of "Hurrah!" and "Revolution!"

Faced with this spectacle, many of the deputies lost their grip on reality. After a thirteen-day siege cut off from the outside world without electricity and water, it seemed to many of them that they were looking not at a Communist mob but at a spontaneous and successful popular uprising.

Protected by two guards who held shields in front of him, Rutskoi said, "We have won. Now we have to form columns and take the mayoralty and then Ostankino."

He called on men of military age to form detachments and went downstairs to inspect them. By this time, however, a large contingent of the fascist Russian National Unity group of Alexander Barkashov was heading for the mayoralty.

The crowd attacked the mayoralty from two directions. The largest group massed in front of the main entrance. There, two trucks seized by the demonstrators plowed into the windows. A smaller band, led by the Barkashovists, went to the rear of the building, smashed the plate-glass windows, and entered through the tangled venetian blinds. By this time, the police had fled, leaving behind buses and trucks, some of which also had the keys left in the ignition. The fighters started the vehicles and left for Ostankino.

In the space of two hours, Moscow had been transformed. The police had disappeared and buses and trucks with automatic weapons and the Soviet red flag sticking out of the windows left for the Ostankino television center, meeting no resistance of any kind. At the same time, thousands of unarmed people headed for Ostankino shouting, "Down with the Traitor Yeltsin!" and "Beat the Jews!"

The first trucks with demonstrators arrived at Ostankino at 5:30 p.m. The demonstrators saw that, despite the seizure of the mayoralty, the telecenter was virtually unguarded. There were no roadblocks and traffic rode up and back on Korolyeva Street, between the two telecenter buildings, as if nothing were happening.

The marchers who had gone to Ostankino on foot began to arrive and, by 7 p.m., there were nearly four thousand in the square,
including about fifty armed with automatic weapons. Some demonstrators built barricades with boards and construction materials, and
the crowd was organized into columns. Young men asked for empty
bottles and Molotov cocktails.

The demonstrators assumed they were about to repeat their success in storming the mayoralty.

Suddenly there was a loud crash as military trucks smashed the
plate-glass windows of the first floor of the television center. A young
man came forward with a grenade launcher on his shoulder, which
he seemed to be carrying for the first time.

There was a five-minute pause, the grenade launcher was fired,
and a grenade blew off the door.

The demonstrators now prepared to seize the telecenter and begin broadcasting to the entire nation.

At that moment, however, dozens of machine guns opened fire
on the demonstrators from inside the building. The square was rent
with screams and the firing continued with violent intensity until the
orangish-yellow tracer bullets melted into a single fiery squall. Most
of the armed demonstrators, including some Barkashov fascists,
were shielded by a roof over the entryway, but nearly everyone else
was exposed and the ground was quickly littered with the wounded
and dead.

As the wounded lay in pools of blood, calling out "Don't
shoot," "Please, help us," their bodies were repeatedly raked with
bullets. The soldiers, stationed behind concrete walls in a darkened
building, fired at anyone who lifted his head. They shot a bicyclist
who unwittingly rode into the battle area and riddled a street
washing machine, causing streams of water to pour out of the
cistern.

Everywhere there were shattered bodies and separated limbs.

Trucks began driving into the battle zone to evacuate the
wounded. Andrei Babitsky, a correspondent for Radio Liberty, left
his shelter in an underpass to carry on his back a fifty-year-old man
who could not walk.

"Where are you injured?"

"Somewhere on the shoulder and buttocks."

Suddenly, Andrei felt two dull thuds in the man's back. The man
stopped talking. Moments later, as he lifted him into the cabin of a

truck, Babitsky saw that the shirt on his back was soaked with blood and he realized that the man had been shot dead.

One of the deputies, Igor Muraviev, crawled to a truck about fifty feet away. As he lifted his body, bullets hit the asphalt sending up red sparks under his chest.

The crowd spread out over Korolyeva Street looking for shelter in the park. Armored personnel carriers moved up and down the street firing at random and then aiming lower and lower in an attempt once and for all to rout the demonstrators. Yet many of them refused to flee, taking shelter behind trees and rocks, hoping for help from military units they believed would rally to their side.

There were calls to go to the White House to get more arms, but by 9 p.m., with tracer bullets still lighting up the sky and screams still audible in the night air, it was clear that the battle for Ostankino was lost.

In the meantime, four television channels were disconnected. Only Russian Television, broadcasting from a reserve studio, was still on the air. It announced that Ostankino had been seized by an armed mob. At 8:45 p.m., Gaidar appeared on Russian television and called on Muscovites to take to the streets to show support for Yeltsin. Within a few hours, more than ten thousand had gathered in front of the Moscow City Council building.

Yeltsin released a statement in which he said that the street battles were a "calculated action, planned in advance by the former leaders of the parliament." He declared a state of emergency and, at a meeting in the Ministry of Defense, the commanders of the military *okrugs* announced their support for Yeltsin.

By 9 p.m., meanwhile, joy in the White House had given way to shock as deputies began returning from Ostankino. Ilya Konstantinov told the other deputies, "It's bloody kasha." Oleg Plotnikov, a deputy from the moderate Smena faction, said, "I've never seen so many corpses in my life."

In the third-floor buffet, there was a gloomy silence as the deputies began to realize that it had been a mistake to send a mob to storm the mayoralty and try to take Ostankino. Some of the deputies began to speculate on what side the army would join, with most agreeing that the military would be on the side of the stronger.

At midnight, amid growing fear that a storming of the building by pro-Yeltsin army units was imminent, all movement inside the White House was banned. At 3 a.m., a rumor spread that tanks and armored personnel carriers were on their way to blockade the White House. The rumor proved false, but, a short time later, correspondents of state news agencies were instructed to leave.

In the meantime, at approximately 4 a.m., Yeltsin went to the Ministry of Defense and, citing the bloodshed at Ostankino, persuaded Pavel Grachev, the defense minister, to order the storming of the parliament.

At 6:55 a.m., journalists in the sixth-floor buffet were jolted awake by the sound of intense machine-gun fire and saw that the White House was under attack.

For the next eleven hours, army units attacked the White House with tanks and automatic weapons, finally resolving the power struggle in favor of Yeltsin, at a cost of about 150 lives.

IN THE WAKE of the October events, a profound change in mood came over Russia. Although early public opinion polls showed support for the storming of the Russian parliament, as footage of the attack was constantly replayed on Russian television, many began to wonder why seven years of democratic reform had culminated in a power struggle between former allies and a massacre in the center of Moscow.

Within weeks of the attack, the soldiers who had taken part were transferred out of their units in the Taman and Kantemirov divisions outside Moscow for their own protection. At the same time, there were expressions of public support for formerly marginal political figures. In late October, Gennady Zuganov, the head of the Russian Communist Party, appeared on the television program "Public Opinion," along with other political figures, including Gaidar. After the discussion, viewers were asked to call in and rate the performance of the participants. On this occasion Zuganov, who had never been preferred by more than 4 or 5 percent of the viewers, was chosen as the most impressive by 36 percent of the callers, finishing second only to Gaidar.

The government refused to release figures for the number of persons killed in the attack, which led to reports that as many as 1,500 had died. On November 4, the newspaper *Komsomolskaya Pravda* said, "A month after the Moscow tragedy, we don't know the number of dead or their names. Without this truth, it is ... possible to live but it's hard to feel like a human being."

Meanwhile, other papers began to develop the theory of a deliberate provocation. How, they asked, was it possible for the Communist demonstrators to break through police lines and take over the mayoralty and then march unhindered through the city for two hours to the Ostankino television center without being stopped by soldiers or police? And if the police abandoned their posts in panic instead of according to plan, why was Viktor Yerin, the internal affairs minister, given a Hero of Russia award after the events for his part in putting down the uprising?

Graffiti began appearing all over Moscow denouncing Yeltsin as a "murderer" amid signs that, by fighting communism with Communist methods, he had lost his moral authority.

DECEMBER 12, 1993

At 44 Herzen Street, the campaign headquarters of Russia's Choice, the pro-Yeltsin political bloc headed by Gaidar, young men monitored computers and collected the reams of paper spat out by high-speed printers. In the basement, tables were being set up for a celebratory banquet.

Vladimir Boxer, the Moscow campaign director, was aware of reports that Zhirinovsky was gaining strength in many areas. But as he began taking calls from campaign workers and poll watchers, he remained confident that Russia's Choice would emerge with a significant victory.

The first calls were from poll watchers. As expected, there were a few complaints of voting irregularities. At 6 p.m., Boxer received the first results from the closed polling places—hospitals, merchant ships, geological expeditions, and military units. There the voters balloted early and all at one time, so their results were known before any others.

As Boxer wrote down the results, he saw a confusing picture. In many places, particularly military units, Zhirinovsky was doing better than expected. He was relieved to see, however, that the pro-Yeltsin bloc had scored a solid victory in the voting in Moscow hospitals. Traditionally, the hospital vote was nearly the same as in the city as a whole.

At 8 p.m., the headquarters was filled with Russian and foreign journalists and many political and artistic celebrities. Red wine was served and some of the better-known visitors were interviewed by camera crews.

At the same time, a group of people gathered around a television set as Tamara Maksimova, a television announcer in a white dress, opened the gala party in the Kremlin Palace of Congresses, which was described in advance as a "festival of democracy" to accompany the announcement of the results of Russia's first multiparty elections in seventy-six years.

At 8:30 p.m., the Russia's Choice campaign workers received the first significant results from the Far East. To their dismay, the voting in Kamchatka and on Sakhalin Island showed a series of decisive victories for Zhirinovsky. For the next hour, the calls from the Far East continued and the victory margins for Zhirinovsky actually increased, until it was clear that his Liberal Democratic Party was outpolling Russia's Choice by nearly two to one.

Many of the guests had by now retired to the basement for the banquet, but Boxer remained at the telephones hoping that the Siberian returns would bring better news. But by 11 p.m., it was clear that Zhirinovsky's party was also leading in Siberia.

At midnight, the campaign workers received a result from Alexandrov in the Vladimir oblast, the first from a region near Moscow. The vote was 40 percent for Zhirinovsky's party and only 16 percent for Russia's Choice. This news touched off a wave of panic. It was now obvious that the early returns had not been a fluke. Zhirinovsky was running well all over the country.

The workers were still waiting for the results from the Volga River region and the Urals in the hope that the vote there would offset Zhirinovsky's strength in Siberia.

Campaign workers watching the party in the Kremlin noticed that Zhirinovsky and his entourage were now upbeat, circulating through the hall and slapping people on the back. To Boxer's surprise, many members of the liberal intelligentsia lined up to shake hands with him. Maximova, who was having difficulty continuing to smile, told the audience, "Let's not think only about politics. We should enjoy ourselves." At that moment, however, Yuri Karyakin, a literary critic and Yeltsin supporter, who was being interviewed on camera, shouted, "Russia, have you gone out of your mind?"

Finally, Boxer left his place at the telephones and joined the others in the basement, where people were drinking heavily. At a little after 1 p.m., Gaidar arrived and Boxer saw that he was pale and obviously depressed. "Well, Volodya," he said, "do you think we've lost everything?"

"I don't know," Boxer said. "In Moscow, we've won decisively. If we can pick up enough votes in the rest of the country, perhaps we can avoid a disaster."

The campaign workers stood around in tight knots talking in subdued tones about what now appeared certain to be a Zhirinovsky victory. No one was sure what it would mean, but many began to compare the results with Hitler's 1932 victory in the elections to the Reichstag.

As the gloom deepened, the banquet crowd gradually dispersed until, at 3 a.m., there were only about twenty-five people left in the room. A small group, which included Golovkov, sang revolutionary songs, which, as they quickly realized, were the only ones all of them knew.

They sang a Civil War song that ended with the refrain, "I died honestly for the workers." They sang a song from the film *Chapayev*, in which Chapayev, a dying Red Army commander, looks up at circling crows and says:

> *Black crows, black crows*
> *Don't circle over me*
> *You won't get your booty*
> *Black crows, I am free*

Finally, the stunned reformers sang the words of another Civil War song:

> *White army, black baron*
> *Prepare us a Tsarist throne*
> *But from the taiga to the British seas*
> *The Red Army is the strongest of all*

Afterword

IN THE LIGHTLY falling snow, Moscow seemed lost in whiteness, the whiteness of a blank, undelineated sky, of the mist that obscured the apartment buildings and of the snow drifts that covered the roofs and piled up on the street. In the blizzardlike wilderness, people struggled with string bags and bundles, stamping along unshoveled paths. The tree branches were heavy with snow and the exteriors of glass-walled cafés were covered with medallions of intricate frost. Buses lurched and shuddered on the streets and dozens of windows in a gothic skyscraper mirrored the orange sphere of the northern sun.

I had no pressing business in central Moscow on this particular morning, but with my passport about to expire, I decided to go to the American Embassy to renew it. I took the metro from Kolomenskaya to the Mayakovskaya station and, emerging on the street, walked along the Sadovoye Ring Road to the old building on Tchaikovsky Street.

Times had changed, of course. No longer did Russians hurry past the American Embassy staring straight ahead for fear of attracting the attention of the guards. Now, there was a long line of visa seekers outside. I took out my passport and showed it to a gray-coated guard.

There was a moment's hesitation. There was something familiar about the massive, mustached guard. Could I know him from somewhere?

"Mr. Satter," he said, not bothering to look at the passport, "how many summers, how many winters? You know we all enjoyed your coverage."

I suddenly remembered where I had seen him before. It was in the early 1980s. A crowd of foreigners watched as my interlocutor and two other guards dragged a Soviet citizen down the street to the warming house on the corner. The man had tried to run into the embassy. He was shouting, "I want freedom," but it wasn't freedom he would be given but a beating and then "treatment" in a psychiatric hospital.

"You enjoyed my reporting?" I asked.

"Of course," the guard said, still smiling, as if experience with dissidents had forged a bond between us. "I remember that you were the first to report on the germ-warfare incident in Sverdlovsk.* By the way, where have you been?"

I explained that I had been in America and France but now was in Moscow for an indefinite period.

"There are a lot of Americans here now," he said.

"Yes, it's a new era."

"Well," he said, smiling broadly, "good to have you back."

THE HUMAN MIND is a marvelous thing. How difficult it is to enslave it completely and yet how ready we are to cripple ourselves when this is what society requires. The guard was hardly the only former Soviet citizen who, for years, had lived on two levels, sharing in the mentality of the regime with part of his consciousness while perceiving reality normally with the rest. It was only under the impact of free information made possible by the policy of glasnost that he and other citizens began to cast off their ideological roles, and it was this process, more than any other, that led to the Soviet Union's collapse.

During the years when the Soviet Union threatened the whole

---

*In April 1979, an explosion at a secret germ warfare plant in Sverdlovsk released deadly anthrax bacteria into the atmosphere, leading to a large number of deaths. In March 1980, I wrote an article in the *Financial Times* on the incident based on information from unofficial sources, which was later shown to have been highly accurate.

world, it was often overlooked that the country's strength depended neither on tradition, consensus, nor a workable system of law but rather on the plausibility of an idea capable of splitting the consciousness of Soviet citizens and making political loyalty a matter of quasi-religious faith.

In the Soviet context it mattered little that many people were skeptical of the ideology or accepted it only in part. What was important was that the ideology defined the basic intellectual categories for the majority of the population and, in that way, led a vast nation to seek moral absolutes in the requirements of the state.

The ideology was powerful because it provided an alternative to the agnosticism of twentieth-century modernity.

In a situation in which science undermined the credibility of revealed religion, Marxism-Leninism offered an image of reality that was simpler and more consistent than reality itself, and once a citizen learned its basic principles, he never had to be in doubt about anything again. At the same time, to refute the ideology was very difficult. Facts were useless because, with the help of dialectical reasoning, any phenomenon that appeared to contradict it could be interpreted as in the process of becoming its opposite.

Perhaps more important, the ideology imparted a sense of purpose. Soviet citizens were understood as taking part in a great historical enterprise, the building of communism, and the effect of this delusion was to give meaning to what often were bleak and directionless lives.

THE POLITICAL STABILITY of the Soviet Union depended on three factors: an absence of serious national conflict, a quiescent working class, and the solidarity of the ruling elite. All of these conditions were guaranteed by the ideology, and all of them were undermined by glasnost.

For years a principal tenet of the ideology was that socialism was the logical culmination of the national history and traditions of each of the peoples who lived on the territory of the Soviet Union. With the beginning of glasnost, however, this became impossible to sustain. The notion that the Baltic republics joined the Soviet Union voluntarily was not compatible with the details of the secret protocols of the Molotov-Ribbentrop Pact, and the idea of the Soviet Union as a commonwealth of equal nations made no sense against the background of the artificial famines in Ukraine that had claimed millions of lives.

The new information inspired the organization of national movements. The local authorities reacted by creating popular fronts to support perestroika, but the implosion of the ideology left a psychological vacuum that only nationalism could fill, and the original organizers were replaced with people who defended national interests, not Soviet ones.

Soviet ideology also inculcated the notion that Soviet workers had more security and, in general, lived better than their counterparts in the West. The often eerie contrast between workers' confidence in the justice of their social system and their actual conditions, however, did not survive the onset of glasnost. Workers watched films of U.S. supermarkets and realized that this was the abundance that was supposed to have been provided by communism in the Soviet Union.

After coal miners went on strike on July 10, 1989, in Mezhdurechensk in Western Siberia, the action spread to every coal mining area in the country, and the spontaneity and unanimity of the walkout testified to the fact that the ideology had lost its force.

The strength of the ideology before 1985 also guaranteed the unity of the party. Gorbachev's efforts to use glasnost to mobilize the population against his conservative opponents, however, made it possible for party reformers, who earlier could not defend an independent position, to look for help in the higher ranks. The result was a split between conservatives and reformers at every level, which began to be constantly exacerbated. As a result, the ideology that had been intended to guide every aspect of life soon no longer guided even the Communist Party.

WHEN GORBACHEV set out to reform the Soviet Union, he did so against the background of years of experience in the party apparatus that had conditioned him to view the ideology as a technique of manipulation. He therefore failed to realize that for most Soviet citizens, the ideology was an object of faith. It was this that led him to tamper with Soviet citizens' fundamental beliefs.

A theocratic system, however, does not easily lend itself to doctrinal reconstruction. By trying to preserve the structure of an ideological state without an ideology, Gorbachev started a process that could only end either with the end of reform or the fall of the Soviet Union, because once people cease to believe in a totalitarian ideology, they inevitably no longer want to live under totalitarian institutions.

Marx believed that existence determines consciousness, but nowhere was it more obvious than in the Soviet Union, the first Marxist state, that it is consciousness which determines existence. In the Soviet Union, human beings were inculcated with a false consciousness and enslaved by that consciousness.

In this context, glasnost could not but destroy the Soviet system. It was not that any one revelation proved critical for the regime. It was rather that the very idea of truthful information could only shatter the system of collective delusion that treated the regime as the ultimate arbiter of truth and the Soviet system as the realization of mankind's historical destiny, in which each citizen was privileged to take part.

In creating the Soviet Union, the Bolsheviks accepted all three temptations rejected by Christ in the wilderness. But they gained the loyalty of the Soviet people by hiding the fact that they did so in the interests of Satan. The Soviet Union fell because when the long-deceived Soviet people realized, as a result of glasnost, who they had been serving in reality, they threw off their mental bondage to an evil system and began seeking other gods.

A FEW WEEKS AFTER the incident outside the American embassy, I watched as a small crowd gathered around Father Dmitri Dudko in the courtyard of the St. Nikolai Church in Cherkizova, sixty miles from Moscow.

In 1980, Father Dudko was arrested on charges of anti-Soviet agitation for his frank sermons, and a short time later, he stunned the Moscow intelligentsia by appearing on television to renounce his "anti-Soviet activities." After his release from the Lefortovo Prison, he went into seclusion and avoided contact with his "spiritual children." He was eventually assigned to a remote church and now, like many of his parishioners, was trying to find a new path.

"Tell me, Batushka," said a bent old woman, "how should we react to witches and faith healers?"

"Black magic and satanism," said Father Dudko, "are worse than any Bolshevism. They may help the body, but the result is the death of the soul." Another woman asked him why there was so much alcoholism.

"Drunkenness is a sign of our lack of faith in God. Drinking distracts us from cruel reality, but the only way to deal with tragedy is through God. For what we don't get in this life, there is eternal life."

To the question of what is death, he said, "Death is not the end of human existence but only our passage from this world, which is full of grief, to another world, in which there will not be grief, hardship, and worry."

Father Dudko appeared tired. It had been a long time since people came to him for guidance.

A believer said she cured people with magic spells.

"How do you do that?" asked Father Dudko.

"First, I recite the words of an Orthodox prayer and then I add my own magical incantation."

"You should drop the incantation."

"But that destroys the spell."

"In that case," Father Dudko said, "you should stop being a healer."

"What should be our attitude toward Communists who accept religion?" asked another believer.

"Among the Communists, there are many decent people," said Father Dudko. "Communism did not sit deeply in the soul. People said they believed in Marxism-Leninism, but materialism did not satisfy them."

The group followed Father Dudko to his room in a small house next to the church. The question-and-answer session continued late into the night. Outside, a half moon lit the snow. The flames in a woodburning stove licked the logs and this handful of survivors of the Soviet Union looked to an uncertain future with puzzlement and with hope.

Acknowledgments

Russia does not willingly sit for her portrait, and this was never better demonstrated than during the years that I worked on this book.

I began collecting information in 1979, while working in Moscow for the *Financial Times* of London under conditions of police state terror. I tried to expand the book as the Soviet Union underwent revolutionary change and I only finished it after the Soviet Union ceased to exist. Given this set of circumstances, this book could not have been written without the help of many individuals and organizations.

The first person who needs to be thanked is J. D. F. Jones, the former managing editor of the *Financial Times*, who hired me off the night police beat in Chicago, to be the *F.T.*'s Moscow correspondent. I am indebted to him not only for this but also for fostering an atmosphere of intelligence and civility at the paper, and for rallying it and the British Foreign Office to my defense when the Soviet authorities attempted to expel me in 1979. In this encounter, I was also strongly defended by the U.S. State Department.

In Moscow, in the period 1979 to 1982, I was aided in collecting information and protecting my Soviet informants by a group of assistants, many of whom are now colleagues. Marie Broxup, a British Soviet specialist, and my assistant in 1978–79, encouraged me to write a book that would portray the surrealism of life in the Soviet Union. Deborah Seward, now with the Associated Press, was my assistant in 1980–82 and provided indispensable help in recording testimony, classifying our materials, and coordinating my movements, always with an eye to minimizing our exposure to the secret police.

Debbie was aided by Marie Iovanovitch, Lucia Perez-Moreno, and Jane Tempest.

I also was helped in protecting the materials of this project by a group of loyal friends, including Sigridur Snaevarr and Petrina Bachmann of the Icelandic Embassy, Geneviève Meillasoux of the French Embassy, Morris "Bud" Jacobs of the U.S. Embassy, and Strobe Talbott in the U.S.

I also received help from many Soviet friends. Felix Serebrov, Vyacheslav Luchkov, Irina McClellan, and Arkady Shapiro all made efforts to locate persons with interesting experiences for me. In the months before his arrest in January 1981, Serebrov, a member of the Working Commission on the Abuse of Psychiatry, introduced me to Alexei Nikitin, Anatoly Koryagin, Alexander Shatravka, and Adolph Muhlberg, all of whom figure prominently in these pages.

I also want to thank Roy Medvedev, the Marxist historian, who, despite our disagreements, devoted many hours to explaining the Soviet system to me and unselfishly provided me with the fruits of his research, including original and important information.

AFTER LEAVING MOSCOW, I received a number of grants which proved crucial in helping me to meet my expenses. In 1984, I received a John Simon Guggenheim Memorial Foundation fellowship, and subsequently was awarded grants from the Lynde and Harry Bradley Foundation, the Smith Richardson Foundation, the Earhart Foundation, and the U.S. Institute of Peace. This book could not have been completed without this timely and generous assistance.

I also spent the month of November 1986 as a short-term scholar at the Kennan Institute of Advanced Russian Studies in Washington, D.C.

In conducting research outside the Soviet Union, I benefited from access to the resources of Radio Liberty in Munich, particularly the samizdat archive, a rich source of firsthand descriptions of conditions in the Soviet Union. I am grateful to Peter Dornan, Mario Corti, and Suzanne Frank of the samizdat department for their assistance, and to Ivanka Rebet, the Radio Liberty librarian.

In the years that I worked on this book, I received indispensable help from *Reader's Digest* and the Foreign Policy Research Institute in Philadelphia.

Beginning in 1986, the editors of the *Digest* insisted that the U.S. State Department ban Soviet journalists from entering the United States in retaliation for the then-existing ban on entry to the Soviet Union in force against me. As a direct result of this retaliation, the Soviet authorities issued me entry visas and I traveled to the Soviet Union in 1986 and 1988 despite my still being effectively persona non grata. In 1990, the *Digest* threatened to cancel plans for a Russian-language edition of the magazine unless I was allowed to enter the country and, faced with this ultimatum, which was backed up by strong State Department pressure, I was granted a multiple-entry visa.

Besides defending me, the *Digest* also employed me. I was given a steady steam of assignments on Soviet topics in 1990, 1991, and 1992, and it was these assignments which made it possible for me to expand the book to cover the perestroika and post-perestroika periods. I am particularly grateful to former editor Ken Gilmore, editor Ken Tomlinson, Washington bureau chief Bill Schulz, executive editor Chris Willcox, and former international editor J. D. "Dimi" Panitza for their encouragement and help.

In 1990-91, I was a Thornton D. Hooper fellow at the Foreign Policy Research Institute. I spent that year and the following year living in Washington but working part of the week in Philadelphia. For the cooperation and support of FPRI, I am grateful to Daniel Pipes, the former FPRI director, and Alan Luxenburg, the associate director. I also benefited from the help and friendship of Ross Munro, Adam Garfinkle, and Judith Shapiro, all FPRI colleagues, and was greatly aided by Kristen Cooper, my research assistant at the Institute, who worked long hours typing and systematizing my notes.

In 1992, I left to spend a year in Moscow. It was there that I received the unstinting help of Olga Printseva, a Russian scientist whom I had met the year previously. Olga returned with me to the United States in July 1993, and we were married a year later.

In January 1993, I returned to the United States for a brief visit and was reunited with David Edwards, a friend from my days as a graduate student at Oxford University. My financial resources at this point were nearly exhausted and David found remunerative work for me that allowed me to finish the book. My debt to him is incalculable.

In the final stages of the book, I benefited from the comments and suggestions of friends and colleagues who read all or part of the draft. My thanks to Vladimir Voinovich, John Lloyd, Nancy Lippincott, Mikhailo Mikhailov, Marshall Brement, and Charlotte Ballard.

Most of all, I benefited from the patience, solidarity, and guidance of Ashbel Green, my editor at Alfred A. Knopf, Inc.

I want to thank Alexander Shatravka for permission to use material from his unpublished manuscript "Notes from the Belly of the Cannibal," which has since been rewritten and renamed "On the Road to America."

I also want to thank Marie-Helene Gugenheim for her help in the first years of this project and to thank my elder children, Raphael and Claire, for cheerfully accepting the constraints that work on this book put on all of our lives. I owe a debt of gratitude to Gershon Braun, Michael Seidman, Andrew and Christina Nagorski, and Carol Brickey for their friendship and solidarity and to all others, named and unnamed in these pages, who kept faith with me during the many years it took me to complete this book.

I am indebted to Jonathan Brent, editorial director of Yale University Press, for making this paperback edition of *Age of Delirium* possible and to Claire Gerus, my literary agent, for her role in bringing us together.